# Wings on My Heels

# Wings on My Heels

## A Newspaperwoman's story

*To this seat of distinction and culture.*

by
### Ellen Taussig

*All good wishes!*

*Ellen Taussig*

*May 18th, '87*

### Peter E. Randall
### PUBLISHER

### 1986

© 1986  Ellen Taussig
Printed in the United States of America
ISBN 0914339-184

Cover photograph by William W. Dyviniak, *Buffalo
News*.

Peter E. Randall Publisher
Box 4726, Portsmouth, NH  03801

To Brother, Betty and Letitia

# Contents

## Book I  The Growing Years

Wings on My Heels

Part VI  Survival

# Book II  The Harvest Years

Preamble

Part VII  Crowns and Clowns

Part VIII  Ladies and Lakes

Part IX  Birthing of a City

Part X  Across the Land

# Contents

# Preface

We are newsmen and women, we see things vividly, too vividly to hold, and we want to share them.

Each sees the world in his own way, some as artists, some as craftsmen. Whatever way, we cannot contain it: we must bear witness, we must tell of it. Our way is not the secretive, ours is the communicative.

Our vital, often maligned way is our way of giving, our fulfillment. And that's the best a human being can do.

# Acknowledgments

Heartfelt thanks are extended to Charley Young, former Sports Editor of the *Buffalo Evening News*, who edited this book; to Homer E. Baker, former Feature Editor; Rachel K. Cain, former Society Editor, and Erna E. Eaton, all of the *News*, for their editorial assistance and encouragement, and to Edgar A. Singer, III, former Research Editor, Harper & Row Publishers, Inc., for his interest and advice.

To Mrs. James H. Little, Miss Ann W. Hay, Lester Smith, and the late Dr. Eleanor B. Colton for their long-standing support.

My gratitude goes too, to Sally Schlaerth, *Buffalo News* Librarian, and her staff; Ruth J. Willett, Head of the History and Government Department, and Norma Jean Lamb, Head of the Music Department, Buffalo and Erie County Public Library, and their staffs, and to Emma Elwell, Librarian, Cape May (N.J.) Public Library, and her staff.

To the Buffalo and Erie County Historical Society; the Historical Society of Pennsylvania; the State Library of Pennsylvania; the Free Library of Philadelphia; the Philadelphia Department of Records; the New York Public Library; Cornell University Libraries; the Library of Congress and the National Gallery of Art.

Also to the late Harold L. Olmsted and Olaf William Shelgren; and Olaf William Shelgren, Jr., for their assistance with architectural information.

Especial thanks go to Mrs. Dale E. Currier and Mrs. Eugene J. North for their preparation of the manuscript.

Much of the material in this book has appeared in its present or another form in one or another of these publications:

The *Buffalo Evening News*, now the *Buffalo News*; the *Philadelphia Daily News*; the *Camden (N.J.) Courier-Post*.

Also, the late *Philadelphia Evening Ledger*; the *Philadelphia Record* and the *Philadelphia Evening Bulletin*.

There is Egypt in Your Dreamy Eyes (Fleta Jan Brown, Herbert Spencer) © 1917. Copyright renewed. Used by permission of Warner Bros., Inc. All rights reserved.

If You Talk in Your Sleep Don't Mention My Name (Nat D. Ayer, Seymour Brown) © 1911. Copyright renewed. Used by permission of Warner Bros., Inc. All rights reserved.

# Book I

# The Growing Years

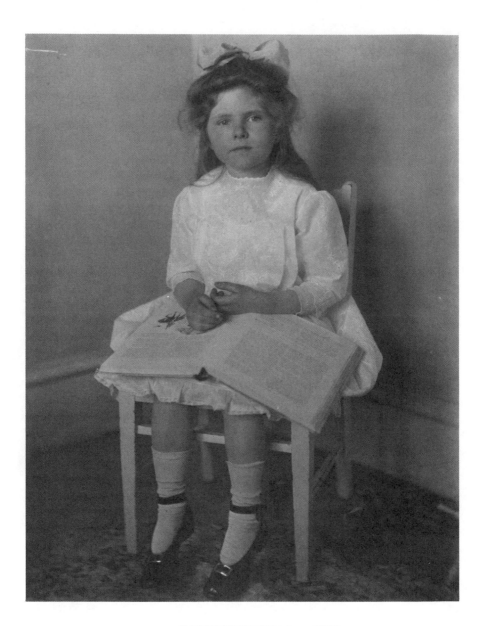

*EARLY EDITION, circa 1911*

# Part I

# Right Side of the Tracks

# 1

## A House With A View

I WAS BORN IN a white pebbledash house with green shutters at the end of a street called East Gravers Lane. Some people thought the name so funereal that they would not have it on their visiting cards.

1906 was a day of visiting cards. People came with them in cases of leather, silver, or even ivory, like the one my grandmother Ellen brought from the Orient, with its carvings of myriad, busy little figures. Big cards for the women and smaller, narrower ones for the men.

The cards were received by the servant on duty --- butler, houseman or maid --- on a small silver tray which stood on the hall table. If the lady of the house was at home, the visitor was seated in the living room and the card borne aloft to her. If she were not in, however, the visitor laid a card of her own and her daughter's for each lady in the house on the tray, and the card of her husband's and son's for each lady and gentleman, and departed. But there was a limit; no matter how large the household, three was the greatest number ever left of any one card. After the visit was completed, the cards were placed in a large bowl, perhaps a Chinese one, where they lingered among others until one day the mistress of the house came along and said: "My, these cards! We must get rid of them!" and they were thrown out to make room for new ones.

The house was about a mile from Gravers Lane Station on the Reading Railroad to Chestnut Hill, a suburb of Philadelphia. A chalet-type building to which one descended by a long flight of steps from the street, it was built in 1872, allegedly from the design of Frank Furness, who later did the Pennsylvania Railroad's terminus, the Broad Street Station, in Philadelphia.

In my girlhood, most of the paths along the street were gravel, shaded by horse chestnut and maple trees. Gray stone, an easily worked limestone, with varying degrees of black or gray mica, is quarried in the Chestnut Hill area, and many of the houses, set on from one to several acres along the street, were built of this stone. Substantial houses, beech and pine joining maples on the lawns. Blight has banished chestnut trees from Chestnut Hill.

The people who lived in the houses were mostly Philadelphians, with an occasional Southern family. They were people of lineage, conservative yet worldly-wise, with that unspoken blend of

religious belief and dislike of ostentation which prevailed throughout
Philadelphia. Several, like the Savages and Pauls, had large
families; others had only two or three children. They rejoiced and
congratulated over birth, grieved and condoled death. Relationships
generally were unaffected and sincere. Years afterward, those who
had lived there and met again, knew a warm glow of intimacy in
remembering Gravers Lane.

Our house stood on about an acre of ground overlooking the
Whitemarsh Valley. On a clear day you could see past the gray-
railed fenced pasture of the Welsh estate across the street and on
over the trees to a stone quarry, embedded in the blue of the valley.
It was an uplifting view. I always have been glad I was brought up
in a house with a view. Daddy and Mother called the house "Green
Arches," for the seven privet arches that rose from the midst of
hedges fronting and dividing the property. They moved into the
house as bride and groom, and no one had ever lived in it before.

Thomas Meehan & Sons, landscape architects, were called in
early, and a planting plan made for the grounds which was carried
out through the years until completed. I have never seen a small
amount of land planted to such esthetic, practical and varied
advantage. One entered the grounds by three wooden steps under a
privet arch and progressed along a gravel path to three more, flanked
by two raspberry-red hawthorn trees. These mounted to a small
terrace and continued on to the front porch. On either side of the
path before one reached the terrace were narrow rectangular beds of
daffodils and narcissus in the spring; fat cabbage roses and
tuberoses in summer. Tuberoses are surely one of the most fragrant
of flowers. On one side of the lawn was a pine tree and on the
other, a white magnolia flowered in the spring. The house was
banded with trellis, from which fell cascades of lavender wisteria in
season, and its great pods in the winter months. Along the fence by
the side porch rambled pink roses and honeysuckle. I doubt if any
street was sweeter in June than East Gravers Lane.

At the back of the house was Mother's garden, separated from
the vegetable garden and the drying yard by privet hedges. To the
left was a pink-flowering, weeping Japanese cherry tree, beneath
which was a circular bed of blue scilla. Steppingstones led from the
backdoor through the flower garden, with its two wide, U-shaped
beds filled with phlox - pink, white and low blue; sweet william,
foxgloves, Canterbury bells, cosmos, coreopsis, larkspur,
columbine, primroses and others. One passed under an arch to the
vegetable garden where a grass path, edged with peonies and currant
bushes, led to a crab apple tree in a circular bed. From there it was

on to Daddy's "orchard," a pear, two or three peach trees and an apple tree or two, the garage and the chicken yard. A cross path at the crab apple tree was lined with gooseberry and raspberry bushes, thus making a four-sectioned planting ground.

In the first section, to the right, were the general low-growing vegetables, and beyond lima beans, corn and grape trellis, hung in the fall with the purple and white grapes which Daddy so delighted in during his Cornell University days. To the left was a strawberry bed, and further on an asparagus one. It was a small Arcady, and in the morning one awoke to the call of mourning doves.

*********

To this house came relatives: My Grandfather, Rear Admiral Edward David Taussig, and Grandmother Ellen; Uncle Joe, later Vice Admiral Joseph K. Taussig, who served as Assistant Chief of Naval Operations, and his statuesque, big brown-eyed wife, Lulie Johnston, of Norfolk, Va.; Uncle Charles A. Taussig, a lawyer, and his wife, dark-haired, blue-eyed Damaris Risner from Nashville, Tenn.; Cousin Fanny Sloan, later Mrs. Ralph Schoolfield Grace, one of the most fascinating people I have ever known; Great-Aunt Fanny Sloan, with flat white curls on her forehead and an hourglass figure; and her sister, Anna Burrows Rowland, a radiant light in her eyes. There were Taussigs from St. Louis: distinguished looking Aunt Clara, Grandfather's sister, and her husband, Benjamin; and plump, affectionate Aunt Emma, a beautiful needlewoman, who during a visit lent me her initialed silver tatting shuttle, which I lost and miraculously retrieved in the grass shortly before her departure. There were Mother's Philadelphia relations -- the Bairds, the Hopkinsons and the Foxes.

My Mother, the former Lillian Meredith Ball, both of whose parents had died before I was born, was descended from William Ball of Devonshire, England, armour makers to the Crown. They emigrated to America in 1712, and in 1728-29, bought the "Hope Farm," a manor created by patents under Colonial Governors Lovelace and Andros from the Duke of York. It was on land settled in 1663, a number of years before Penn founded Pennsylvania. The manor extended about 800 acres northward along the Delaware River, from a creek called Gunner's Run, an area that later became known as Richmond or Port Richmond. Later, Cramp Shipyard was built on part of the Ball Estate.

The name Richmond, appearing so far from Virginia, is believed to have been in compliment to George Washington, whose mother, the former Mary Ball - "The Rose of Epping Forest" - was a distant relative of the Philadelphia Balls. The relationship never has been genealogically traced, but to me, at least, no research is required. My Mother's forehead was a replica of the President's. And often, as I see his countenance of a 25-cent piece, I think of her. It is a forehead of sublime serenity. Ball roots went deep into the establishment of the city of Philadelphia, indeed of Pennsylvania.

Men and women from these strains sat in wicker chairs on the green and white striped-awninged porch on Gravers Lane in the summer, as the scent of the roses and honeysuckle wafted over them. A little piece I wrote years later gives the general aura on the Fourth of July:

### 4th OF JULY FIREWORKS - A FAMILY AFFAIR

Fourth of July used to begin at daylight. Dew was on the grass when an 8-year-old child began preparations in the garden.

Upstairs, parents, grandparents and visiting maiden aunts slept, after praying the night before that the noise would start late.

The child had brought a straight-backed wooden chair out, and three thin paper festoons.

With delight, she opened them out, and suspended them--pink, green and yellow--between the ash and two maple trees. Father would have to hang the Japanese lanterns.

\* \* \*

About 7, Cook --- well aware of the rigors of the day ahead --- "The house full of company and no two of 'em wanting the same breakfast"---made her way down the backstairs to her inalienable domain.

But secretly, Bridget -- burning with memories of the Irish potato famine -- liked the Fourth of July. Wasn't it the day the Redcoats got their deserts?

Bacon scent drifted outdoors, and soon Father came down. He had wanted to sleep, but knew he was expected to hang those lanterns.

The American Flag was then raised. Every house on the street bore a flag.

The "snakes," sparklers and string firecrackers came first. Father dispensed the latter with their smell of gunpowder --- six red packages for each child.

As the first salute of the day to the Declaration of Independence resounded, Mother appeared at the garden door.

* * *

She spoke of the extreme caution required to celebrate successfully the birth of freedom. She warned of danger to eyes and fingers.

By this time, the neighborhood was a staccato chorus of crackling crackers. Children shouted, dogs barked.

Steppingstones were a wonderful place to burn "snakes." A snake, incidently, was a 3/4-inch-high pyramid which when lit --- erupted in a series of pale-toned curlicues, strongly resembling the common earthworm.

The sparklers livened things up. Their tiny stars occasionally pricked, and it was fun to wave them in zig-zag patterns (bewaring of eyes), and to see the shafts grow vermillion as they burned out (careful of fingers, too, of course).

When the supply of little firecrackers was exhausted (sometimes a child saved a pack or two, just to have an edge on the other children) Father brought out the big single ones --- 3 inches long.

They declared in no uncertain terms that "all men are created equal..."

Fourth of July was deadly dull from noon until 4. People took naps or sat around the porch talking of the remote war in Europe and the merits of President Wilson.

As the day cooled, the child was allowed to spread a crepe paper cloth on a large table that had been placed under the ash tree. It was red, white and blue, with paper napkins (a novelty) to match.

* * *

A picnic supper was served at 6. Baked ham, spiked with cloves, potato salad, homemade strawberry ice cream and chocolate layer cake.

As dusk fell, the child squirmed with impatience.

"Isn't it dark enough yet? Father, isn't it?"

Porch chairs were turned toward the front terrace on which stood a mound of fireworks.

"Not quite," Father kept saying. "They'll look prettier in the dark." The wait seemed interminable.

Cook came out and settled herself in a chair at the rear to watch the British re-trounced.

When the fireflies glowed bright, it was time.

Pinwheels came first, swirling rainbow discs on sticks planted in the grass. The fountains bore to ecstatic heights three generations who had never seen a neon light. And finally, the rockets were sent zinging toward the valley, where they cascaded a shower of stars.

* * *

Inevitably the pile thinned and gave out.

How pale and insignificant the real stars looked, as Cook led a weary child to bed.

"Those British got it, but good, didn't they, Sweetheart?" she said.

All this was made possible by domestic help -- a nurse for the children, a cook in the kitchen and a waitress/chambermaid in the front of the house. In later years, a good Negro couple divided the work of house and garden.

The table was abundant, with Sunday breakfasts of creamed dried beef and waffles, stewed kidneys, kippered herring or English bloaters, accompanied by hot bread. On weekdays there was cereal, oatmeal, supposedly good for one's teeth, Cream of Wheat, and fried cornmeal mush or hominy grits with maple syrup.

There was black bean soup with chopped hard-boiled egg floating in it and larded with sherry, and split pea soup made right from peas. Roasts, chops and turkey at holiday time, except goose at New Year's and ham at Easter; shad with the roe in the spring, and squabs at dinner parties. Vegetables came from the garden in summer, and there were lots of spinach and carrots -- which allegedly made one's hair curl. Everyday desserts included prune whip, rice pudding, tapioca pudding with apples, Brown Betty, Spanish Cream, custards, blancmange and blackberry mush, made by pressing blackberries through a sieve and adding cornstarch. For occasions, there were special desserts brought in from the outside, like Dexter's white mountain cake, a cloud of rice flour and powdery icing, and egg-shaped meringues filled with strawberry, bisque or burnt almond ice cream, which arrived wrapped in wax paper and embedded in a wooden tub of ice -- not to mention larger, peaked meringues like Staffordshire castles -- from a place called McNaughton's. At Thanksgiving there was Sautter's pumpkin pie, and come Christmas, plum pudding made in a melon-shaped mold at home, a sprig of holly in it and flaming scarlet and blue with brandy.

The iceman cometh bearing great dripping blocks by tongs; the butter and egg man arrived with butter in oblong pound-blocks and fresh eggs; and the groceries were procured by periodic visits by a Mr. Hendrick from Mitchell and Fletcher in town. Mr. Hendrick sat on a chair in the kitchen and took the order from the cook. Later, he and a Mr. Johnson established a grocery store in Chestnut Hill, with a woman at the telephone who had a voice and manner that could sell anyone who hated, say pickles, a case of them.

The house was heated by coal; 12 tons arrived each fall through a chute put down the side cellar door, a rumbling cascade that prescienced winter. Coal, too, pea coal it was called, was used in the big kitchen range, with kindling wood to start the fire going. Logs were burned in the living-room fireplace.

Laundry was a ritual executed in large gray tubs in the laundry room and pressed with flat irons, heated on the range. There were no detergents but there were stalwart Fels Naptha and Pearl Borax soaps, and lye. Dishes were washed in the copper-sinked pantry in sudsy water made by shaking a mesh soap holder in hot water.

In the early days, the house was lit mainly by gas. As dusk approached, a maid in a black uniform with white collar, cuffs and apron toured the house with a lamplighter, an approximately 4-foot pole with a lighted wick which illumined the glass-shaded jets; and later, Weisbach burners, a gauze fretting that gave more diffused light than open flame. Simultaneously, a similar task was being undertaken by the town lamplighter in the street. Beds were turned down at night, a neat triangle being folded back on the side in which the occupant was to enter. On the second floor of the house at one end were four bedrooms, a study and bath, and at the other, two maids' rooms, a single and a double, and a trunk room. Trunks were a vital part of travel in those days, upright wardrobe trunks for long trips and "steamer" or flat trunks of all sizes for shorter ones.

Reached by a small ladder from the trunk room was an attic, an intriguing place with mysteries such as my Grandfather Robert Hodgson Ball's medicine chest that he took on a Grand Tour of Europe, and unwanted wedding presents. A backstairs led to the kitchen and pantry, the swinging door of which divided the front from the back of the house. Telephones were upright ones. There was a Steinway grand piano in the living-room and a fine Cheney record player in the hall, with selections of Caruso, Schumann-Heink, Galli-Curci, Louise Homer and John McCormack, among others. A big grandfather clock stood in the front hall, a wedding present from Uncle Joe. A large steel engraving of George Washington in a mahogany frame hung nearby, over a dark green Hitchcock bench. There was a generous brass knocker on the front door, and an oblong case in the pantry registered the ring of several bells throughout the house.

Those were the days of "family" doctors, who came - even in blizzards - to deliver babies at home; of a husband tenderly carrying his wife downstairs after two weeks of upstairs post-birthing confinement. Doctors whom one felt were surrogate fathers and friends - even beyond one's family.

Those were the days of mustard plasters and footbaths and cold cloths on one's forehead for fever; argyrol for sore throat; of calomel and quinine; of bread poultices for splinters and iodine for cuts; of a tonic called Panopeptin and beef juice served over rice to build one up after sickness; of something called Eskay's Neurophosphates for shock.

The days of halls hung with sheets soaked in carbolic acid to contain contagious diseases, and oblong yellow signs pasted on front doors even for measles, chickenpox and whooping cough.

And at the last, a spray of flowers by the doorknob.

# 2

# Kith and Kin

THE ARRIVAL OF GRANDFATHER, Rear Admiral Edward David Taussig, and Grandmother Ellen at Gravers Lane was eventful both in enjoyment and tonnage. They traveled extensively in Europe after his retirement in 1909, accompanied by huge individual wardrobe trunks, repositories for the impedimentae of living, collected across the world. It took Ben, the railroad trunkman, and an assistant to get each of these trunks to the spare room.

The Taussigs, one of St. Louis, Missouri's oldest families, came there from Vienna and Prague. They were wool merchants who made cloth for the uniforms of the Austrian army. Labor difficulties developed, and the family legend goes that Adam and Eva Taussig, Grandfather's great-grandparents, sent them hither, subsidized by Eva's 17 strands of pearls that she wears in the portrait they brought with them, a copy of which and another of Adam that now hang in my dining room.

Grandfather, one of ten children of Charles and Anna Abeles Taussig, was one of the joys of my young life. An erect man, about 5-feet-10-inches in height, with a keen gray-blue eye, drooping dark mustache and beautiful hands, he had an air of innate dignity and authority. Above all, he had a zest for life, an enthusiasm, an enjoyment of and positive approach to living. Life was something that flowed through you for a purpose, whether it was pleasure or enjoyment of duty. This verve penetrated the very fiber of his being, and was handed down, in part, to me. As I look back on it, I was more genetically attuned to him than any relative I have known.

Grandmother Taussig was a beautiful woman, about five-feet-two, with lovely naturally wavy white hair, an aquiline profile and deep-set brown eyes. She was the daughter of Joseph Knefler, a native of Arad, Hungary, who entered the Polytechnic School in Vienna at age 14, and was graduated with honors as a chemist. He was also a talented musician. He came to America in 1848, having studied under a pupil of Beethoven. As a girl, Grandmother Taussig was made to practice piano five hours a day. She became an accomplished amateur musician. Great-Grandfather Knefler for many years taught music and French at a private girls' school in Shelbyville, Ky. Grandmother wanted to be told regularly that she was lovely, and when Grandfather died she put on a widow's bonnet with a long veil, which she wore until her own death.

They had five sons: Paul, who died as a midshipman at the Naval Academy; John Hawley, my father, named after Grandfather's friend, Admiral John Mitchell Hawley; Joseph Knefler, who became Assistant Chief of Naval Operations, and later, a Vice Admiral; Charles August, a lawyer; and George, who died as a child.

On their visits to us, they used the spare room. It had a large, mahogany, four-post, valanced bed; a Chippendale bureau with beautiful "beehive" handles; an 18th century mahogany chest called the Kris Kringle Chest because our Christmas presents were stored there; also, a comfortable chintz-covered fireside chair; two Hitchcock chairs; a large, oval pier glass and a bed table on which stood a metal thermos bottle and glasses, and over which hung three mahogany-framed verses which Mother, in later years, thought rather sentimental.

One read, as best I can remember:

Sleep sweetly in this quiet room, oh thou who'ere thou art,
And let no mournful yesterdays disturb thy peaceful heart;
Nor let tomorrow spoil thy rest with thoughts of coming ill,
Thy Maker is thy changeless friend, his love surrounds thee
    still.
Forget thyself and all the world, put out each foolish light,
The stars are watching overhead, sleep sweetly then-
    Goodnight.

After they were settled, Grandfather and Grandmother would come down to the living room where Grandfather, with his long-tailed coat and stiff collar, would "walk the deck" often during his stay. He would pace back and forth from habit acquired aboard ships, ranging from those of sail during the Civil War to modern battleships.

Grandfather was a planner. From my observation, there are people who plan and others to whom planning is an extracurricular activity. Of course one can over plan; one can plan and plan and not act; one can debilitate oneself with planning. But to a certain temperament, it certainly makes a framework for life. The delicate balance between faith and planning is probably one of the arts of life.

"The first Saturday we are here," Grandfather would say, as Grandmother and Mother sat nearby, and yours truly stood at excited attention, "Grandmother and Mother and I will go to John Wanamaker's Tearoom to lunch and a matinee." There was a pause, as his eyes lit up in anticipation of my response to his next annoucement. "And the Saturday following, Ellen and I will go on a little spree."

No symphony sounded sweeter.

John Wanamaker's, a block-square department store with its beautiful marble walls and handsome oil paintings, was and is the mercantile fortress of Philadelphia. In beautifying his store, however, Mr. Wanamaker, whom I think coined the phrase "The customer is always right," raised it above the usual commercial level by its stunning interior and works of art. An enormous central court, surrounded by balconies, has a magnificent organ high on its tiers, on which regular concerts are given throughout the day. In the center of the court is a huge brass eagle which has been the downtown meeting place for thousands for more than 100 years. "Meet me at the Eagle" is a Philadelphia byword.

In due course, Grandfather and I took the train to town, went to John Wanamaker's Tearoom, ate a "Tomato Surprise," a tomato stuffed with chicken salad, and a burnt almond, bisque or strawberry ice cream meringue. Then we walked down Chestnut Street to Keith's Theatre - the apex of the spree. I can still feel the vibrations that theatre sent through me. We sat downstairs in red plush seats that had boxes of chocolate-covered cherries, obtained by inserting a coin in a container on the back of the seat in front of one.

Vaudeville was at its height before World War I. Then and later, I saw many of the great stars of the world, who came to Keith's at the time. There were Sarah Bernhardt -- one of her legs had been amputated -- playing a French soldier on the battlefield; her velvet voice still echoes faintly in my ear; also Gertrude Hoffman, Valeska Sarat, Cissie Loftus, Eva Tanguay, Blanche Ring, Elsie Janis, Bessie McCoy Davis, Houdini, Sir Harry Lauder, et al. After having my appendix out at age 8, I remember regretting that now I would never be able to do the "Snake Dance" Miss Hoffman performed, wearing a stomacher of a filigree of beads.

There were teams of men in brown derbies, dapper suits, carnations in their lapels, spats and canes, who, against backgrounds of formal gardens or street scenes, danced and cracked jokes about marital life. Considered most daring was Eva Tanguay's rendition of "I Don't Care, I Don't Care." People were supposed to care very much about every phase of moral life before the first World War, and Miss Tanguay, throwing care and caution to the winds, was far out, quite far out indeed. I remember sitting entranced by a large woman swathed in gold sequins, probably in those embryo days of the "blues," lamenting some man who had not measured up.  Turning to Grandfather to exclaim on her beauty, I found him gently dozing.

"Isn't she beautiful, Grandfather!" I said.

He opened his eyes and reached for his eyeglasses, which hung from a small, shiny black button in his lapel and whizzed out on a fine chain.  Inspecting the lady in question, he smiled: "Quite, my dear, quite," he said.

After the show we would go to Whitman's Tearoom for refreshment.  I never felt the afternoon complete without it, and I still think refreshment is good after the theatre; it gives one the chance to absorb the emotional and intellectual impact of the performance, to make the transition from theatre to reality.

I remember one occasion when I was treating.  I had my 50 cents weekly allowance, not enough for ice cream or a soda or sundae for both of us.  Nervously, I asked Grandfather what he would like. Leisurely, he inspected the menu.

"I'd like a lemon phosphate, my dear," he said, apparently sensing the situation.  Phosphates were among the least expensive items on the card.

Grandfather and Grandmother were visiting us on the Christmas when we got our first record player - a Victrola, a square golden oak box with a horn that was advertised by a picture of a fox terrier listening attentively.  In the holiday rush, Daddy had just picked up an assortment of records, and as we children stood about, Grandfather's reaction to the opening words of the first one put on linger with me to this day:

They both were having luncheon in a private dining room,
- The meal was great and everything was grand -
When suddenly he saw a wedding ring upon her finger,
As he held her dainty little hand...
                ("He" speaks up as follows)
I can see that you are married,
And you know I'm married too!
And nobody knows that you know me
and nobody knows that I know you
and, if you care to, we'll have luncheon,
Every day here just the same,
But sweetheart - if you talk in your sleep,
Don't mention my name.

"Turn that off, Sir!" Grandfather ordered Daddy from the quarterdeck.

We children played the rest of the record on another occasion, to learn that the lady in question woke up one night to hear *her* sleeping husband uttering the same chorus.

Our grandparents were left in charge of us once when Daddy and Mother were away. One day -- for some inexplicable reason because no one in the family ever swore except Mother, who on rare occasions said "Damn," my brother Hawley, about 8, told a neighboring gardener to "Go to Hell!" The gardener reported it to Grandfather. I can see him now, standing on the front porch, summoning Hawley up the path.

"Come right up here, Sir," he said. (Even in times of crisis, all males, children or adults, addressed each other as "Sir" in those times.) When Hawley arrived, Grandfather took his hand and marched him up to the bathroom where he scrubbed his mouth out with soap. I have never heard Hawley swear since.

Grandfather deplored the somewhat nasal Philadelphia voice, caused, I believe, by the climate which is affected by the location of the city between two rivers. He gave us a book called "The Speaking Voice," and taught us that a pleasant one was one of the most attractive personal attributes. Nor did he approve of our reading the Sunday "funny papers" - not because of their content, which was harmless enough - but because they were "poor art." Yet he had tolerance of human nature. When I would criticize someone, he would place the tips of his fingers together and reprimand me gently with - "Chacun a son gout, my dear, (Each to his taste) chacun a son gout."

Another lift of my life was going into town with Mother. We often walked to the station, and I can see her in a small black hat, slightly turned up at one side, with a square black leather pocketbook in a gold frame and stylish black oxfords. We made a beeline for Sautter's. The Bellevue-Stratford was "the" hotel in Philadelphia in those days, with the Ritz-Carlton running second across the street. But when Philadelphians, particularly with children, went into town just for lunch, Sautter's was the place. It was at 13th and Chestnut Streets, near the Adelphia Hotel, a traveling salesman's house, even at that time.

There was nothing pretentious about Sautter's. It was the epitome of Philadelphia understatement, a two-story restaurant with plain linen tablecloths and bentwood chairs. On the first floor, however, was an enormous marble counter which stretched about two-thirds the length of the room. Behind it were two veteran soda water men; one looked like Punch and the other greatly resembled the man in the Gillette razor blade advertisement of the time. You gave your order for soda water, phosphates or ice cream, and they called it in relays to a woman -- she looked like Carmen -- sitting at a small aperture at the far end of the counter. The woman wrote down the order, which in due time was slung through the aperture and thence, man by man, until it reached you.

The ice cream was served cone-shaped in a small round dish, and could be accompanied by the most exquisite cinnamon bun made with egg dough, light as a feather; or "Queen Cakes," small round yellow cakes with at least a quarter-of-an-inch of swirled white icing. The thing that placed Sautter's among the greats, however, were plunkets, little pillow-shaped cakes liberally sprinkled with powdered sugar, light as a sweetened cloud. They were marvelous with ice cream. Upstairs there was more serious fare, like delicious crab cakes with tartare sauce, or sweetbreads in patty shells. Delicious food served in the simplest possible, understated surroundings by waitresses in black dresses and white aprons.

One paid one's bill at a cashier's cage by the first floor door, presided over by the second-generation Mr. Sautter. A Harvard graduate, handsome, with a tight-lipped, rather retiring air, he sat in an effulgence of gilded iron and accepted your coin.

From Sautter's, one might progress a few doors down the street to Allen's store, which included a millinery shop. At Fall and Easter particularly, this was the custom. Allen's millinery shop had hats on high stands in tall glass cases. In the Fall and Winter the young girls' hats might be of brushed beaver, rather large, with grosgrain ribbon streamers. But in the Spring, they blossomed like a garden. There were Leghorns with colored velvet ribbon and bunches of pink and blue forget-me-nots; or black Milan straws with a wreath of field flowers. Allen's was the harbinger of our Spring and Fall seasons.

Or again, one might go to Steigerwalt, the shoe store, further up the street, where one sat in comfortable chairs and courteous clerks tried on your shoes. Children wore high-buttoned and laced shoes in those days, and I remember a pair of shoes with black patent leather bottoms and white kid or buff suede tops appealed to me. The buttonhook, the shoehorn and shoe trees were standard appurtenances in every house. Patent leather pumps, or course, were de rigeuer for dancing class; one kept them from cracking by applying Vaseline and carried them to and fro in a flannel bag. An intriguing vista to a young girl, too, were the pointed silver or gold evening slippers, or those of satin with large rhinestone or cut steel buckles.  But naturally, they were distant dreams for those under 16.

So - with history always in the air - and with a sort of self-contained satisfaction and peace, we went to town in Philadelphia.

# 3

## Across the Bay

GRANDFATHER AND GRANDMOTHER TAUSSIG had never owned a house until he retired. He had sea duty every three years - Grandmother had waited a similar period after their engagement for his return and marriage. His letter to his Father and Mother, Charles and Anna Abeles Taussig, asking permission to marry her, as was the custom in Europe, seems worthy of inclusion here, in this highly different age. I have no doubt that Grandmother had punctilious leave to gain from her Father, but no written record of it remains. Grandfather, who had just been promoted from Ensign to Master, wrote:

Louisville, Ky.
May 31, 1870

Dear Parents,

There's a young lady in the matter - and that young lady is called Ellen Knefler, a very nice and very quiet girl who says that she fell in love with me not long ago, and not to be contrary I've had the same accident happen to me with regard to her, so that we had nothing else to do but become engaged.

To be sure, I cannot marry her soon, as am young (age 22) and inexperienced, but nevertheless, I hope that this step will meet with your approval, and that you will write to me to that effect before I come home, which will not be this week as my sweetheart says that I cannot go before next Monday, and must come back very soon again. I know, dear parents, that you will both like little Ellen very much, and so have come to the conclusion that you had better congratulate me and wish me good luck. I haven't spoken to Ellen's father nor mother yet, though some people know more about it than they have any business to know. Even after you have kindly given your approval, we do not wish the engagement to be made public, as we do not wish to undergo the usual routine of jokes and congratulations for the unfortunately long time that our engagement must last before we have our own two rooms and a kitchen. So write

soon, call me the worst names you can think of, but send
your love to Ellen and

Your affectionate son,
Eddy

When Grandfather did retire, they bought a big cottage at
Jamestown, R.I., from his cousin, James, a St. Louis banker, who
was an early settler on the Narragansett Bay island. The big, gray
shingle house was the center one of three on Shoreby Hill, an
elevation overlooking open land to the Narragansett Bay harbor and
Newport. A porch, a section of which was glassed in, encircled
three sides. From the day she moved in, Grandmother never
changed anything in the house. The Turkish corner in the living
room, with its copper vase of dried grasses beneath a picture of a
sailor's sweetheart waving good-bye to a ship vanishing over the
horizon; the black walnut upright piano and the Dresden china vases
and ornaments on the mantel remained where they were, as did the
framed sepia pictures of Michelangelo's David, Hannibal's tomb
and similar works of art which punctuated the walls of the otherwise
cheerful bedrooms. The aura was Intelligentsia, 1880. At the back
of the house was a generous amount of lawn, bisected by a path
lined with blue hydrangea bushes, to the left of which was
Grandmother's garden, filled with tall pink phlox and small
sunflowers and dahlias. There was a large wild cherry tree and a
small clump of pines.

To this house came Daddy and Mother and we children; Uncle
Joe and Aunt Lulie with their daughter, Emily, and later, Joe, Jr.,
who as a child, stood up even in the bathtub when the Star-Spangled
Banner was played within his hearing; Uncle Charlie and Aunt
Damaris, as bride and groom; and nurses - the liberators of mothers
during the first years of the century.

I remember the Sunday evening suppers in the white dining-
room with its blue and white Onion Pattern china, and a delicious
walnut-mocha layer cake to top it all off. Aunt Lulie from Virginia
and Aunt Damaris from Tennessee, had a race to see who could eat
the most watermelon, expertly extracting the seeds into a partially
closed fist and rushing along at an amazing pace. I forget who won.

The men, when not on vacation, commuted over week-ends.
We reached Jamestown by the overnight Fall River Boat from New
York, an exciting experience for children, especially, to sleep in a
berth and have dinner in the great dining salon with its large menu of
delightful entrees and numerous accompaniments to the main dish,
served in individual oval dishes, like birdbaths. Then there was

arrival at Fall River in the early morning, with its brackish and fishy smells, and the trip from there to Newport and the ferry across Narragansett Bay to Jamestown.

Grandmother played Chopin and Grieg and Liszt on the dark upright piano, and Aunt Damaris, popular songs. Aunt Damaris had great sapphire blue eyes - I'll never forget the first time I saw her she wore a tocque of pansies - and dark hair arranged in what in those days were called "cootie garages," small puffs coming well down onto the center of the cheek. Her complexion, aided only by cold cream as long as she lived, was like rose petals.

Two songs she sang, as Uncle Charlie stood adoringly at the side of the piano, were:

> For there's Egypt in your dreamy eyes,
> A bit of Cairo in your style,
> The shades of night are in your hair,
> While fragrant incense seems to fill the air.
> All the Orient is in your smile,
> Mysterious as River Nile.
> And you stole my heart, with your cunning art,
> And the Egypt in your dreamy eyes.

Another:

> So, what do you want to make those eyes at me for,
> When they don't mean what they say?
> They make me glad, They make me sad,
> They make me want a lot of things I've never had.
> So what do you want to fool around with me for?
> You lead me on, and then you run away,
> But, never mind, I'll get you alone some night
> and then you'll surely find,
> You're flirting with dynamite,
> So what do you want to make those eyes at me for,
> When they don't mean what they say?

Fascinating listening and watching for a subteen-aged girl.

Occasionally, we would be invited aboard one of the battleships or other ships in the harbor. We were picked up in spunky little launches, their brasses shining and the forepart of their hulls covered with white duck awnings adrip with cotton fringe made by the sailors, whose starched uniforms surpassed even their whiteness. But always in the afternoon, never in the evening. As colored lights festooned the decks of the great ships and music from their bands drifted across the water, how I longed to go to the grown-up dances held aboard them. Saturday night dances at the Jamestown Casino, to which children were allowed early in the evening, seemed confined indeed.

Some afternoons we would take the ferry to Newport, then in its heyday, and go to the Casino, a great nest of lattice and red brick, designed by Stanford White, to sit in the grandstand and see the tennis or horse show. Two images stand out. One is of a Vanderbilt, dark-mustached and wearing a navy blue coat, white trousers and a soft hat, holding a magnificent chestnut horse; another is of Gloria Vanderbilt in a white dress, playing tennis on a grass court, a colorful bandana tied around her head.

I remember I had a broad-brimmed red mohair hat trimmed with currants that made me feel very grown-up indeed.

We were brought up by a rule that if we had any communication with anyone, we must identify ourselves and never conceal or feign our name. Mother and Aunt Lulie broke the rule one summer, however. Mrs. Stuyvesant Fish, whose house on Bellevue Avenue they admired, took the shutters off, leaving it quite bare looking. Mother and Aunt Lulie resolved to do something about it; they sent a postcard to Mrs. Fish, asking if she would please restore the shutters. The card was signed "Punch." Subsequently, Mrs. Fish put the shutters back.

In the midst of children, grandchildren and nurses, Grandfather, in sharply creased white flannels and white buckskin shoes - the continual freshening of white buckskin shoes was a ritual of the time - sat on the cottage porch and looked out at the ships in the harbor. What memories they must have recalled: The earthquake and tidal wave of August, 1868, in the harbor at Arica, Chile, where as a midshipman he was stationed on the *USS Wateree*, and the sea rolled out leaving the ship high and dry, and passengers and crew left the vessel to race to land before the great swell returned; as Commander of the *USS Gunboat Bennington*, his claiming of the atoll now known as Wake Island for the United States, and the planting of our flag there to a 21-gun salute; when the queen of some Pacific Bali Hai asked him to come ashore to dinner, and he replied he would accept with pleasure if she would wear some clothes he would send on in advance.

There were other retired admirals in Jamestown and they formed a congenial group, playing golf and bridge, discussing the affairs of the world and remembering. During World War I, Nicholas Murray Butler, a friend of Grandfather's, called him to Columbia

University to teach English.  He enjoyed the return to some active duty.

Grandfather died in his early seventies in the Naval Hospital at Newport.  We all journeyed to the cemetery at Annapolis, where another 21-gun salute rang out over the bay.  Daddy brought Grandfather's big gold, close-cased watch back to my brother, Hawley, and I was given the gold braid from his uniforms.  He had already given me some of the fiber of his being.  Years later, in World War II, as his oldest grandchild, I would christen a ship named after him.

Uncle Charlie was the most tenderhearted person I have ever known.  A Phi Beta Kappa key from Harvard Law School on his watch chain, a leather-bound copy of Dickens in his coat pocket, he stands as one of the most heart-moving figures of my life.  I used to visit him and Aunt Damaris in later years, at Tuckahoe, N.Y.  One summer morning Uncle Charlie told me: "Ellen, there was a little mosquito in my room last night and it kept buzzing around; but you know, I couldn't swat the little fellow."  On another occasion when I visited them for three months between newspaper jobs, he stood in the front hall as I left, and said: "Come back, anytime!"

All four Taussig boys who survived were athletic.  Uncle Joe succeeded Uncle Paul as an outstanding athlete at Annapolis; Daddy was on the varsity football team at Cornell and was selected on what, at that time, corresponded to an All-American team.  He also was a champion wrestler.  Uncle Charlie followed him on the varsity and All-American teams there.  The brothers stayed close throughout their lives.  Uncle Charlie probably was the most intellectual.  He particularly enjoyed association with his fellow man for worthy causes, among them the Big Brother movement in New York, which he helped organize.  He died in his New York office making out an order for football tickets for the Army-Navy game.  Marvelously well-versed in athletic records of track, shot-putting, discus-throwing and high and long jumping, they were ready in his mind to compare current performance on a gold stopwatch with a second hand.  Names, years and individual achievements also were on mental tap.

The Army-Navy game and the Thanksgiving Day game between Cornell and the University of Pennsylvania, both in Franklin Field, Philadelphia, were highlights of our childhood.  Once Grandfather was attending an Army-Navy game when President Theodore Roosevelt passed him in the grandstand.  "Any more boys for the football field, Captain?" called out the President.  The stirring service academy bands at the games linger in the mind.  Uncle

Charlie always arrived for both these games.    The coaches, strategies, players, field, weather and prospects were vigorously discussed by him and Daddy beforehand.  I was brought up with an unqualified desire to see Navy and Cornell win.

On the occasions when Cornell won, the two brothers would descend to the field and join the crowd that threw fedoras and derbies, in the bands of which were stuck red feathers appliqued with a white "C," high in the air, sometimes never to be retrieved by their rightful owners.

We returned home through the frosty air - it could be very cold in Philadelphia on Thanksgiving Day - to a wonderful dinner dominated by a large turkey - when turkeys, fresh from the farm, were served only a few times a year.  Cranberry jelly was made in a brown, fluted porcelain mold that had belonged to Mother's Grandmother Ball, the result was a large ruby rosette, which culminated in a round, button-like shape we called "the top," vied for voraciously by us children.  There were candied sweet potatoes, creamed onions and peas, and for dessert, Sautter's pumpkin pie with vanilla ice cream.

As we clambered over Uncle Charlie, he told us wonderful stories of animals, imaginative, interesting and continuing.  He took my brother Hawley and my sister Betty fishing for crawfish in a neighboring stream.  He could bring his fine intelligence down to the juvenile level and children were enriched by him.  He also was an avid stamp collector and instructed us in the interest and pleasure of this pursuit.

When Uncle Charlie came to visit, he and Daddy would shave together in the bathroom and sing barbershop duets.  All the favorites of their college days would emanate through the door, and we learned the words of the songs.  There was:

> Old Man Noah knew a thing or two, he made 'em all play
> ball!
> Old Man Noah knew a thing or two, because he knew a
> thing or two, he thought he knew it all!
> Some say he was an Also-ran,
> He was the original circus man!
> Old Man Noah knew a thing or two,
> He was a grand old Man.
> Every night a half-past three
> Noah played poker with the Chimpanzee.
> Noah's got a full-house up his sleeve,

And he's going to hand us a lemon!
Old Man Noah, etc.

There were numerous verses.

"Sweet Adeline" and "Carry Me Back to Old Virginny" rang out and - sung in tones of loyalty and devotion - "Far above Cayuga's waters, with its waves of blue, Stands our noble Alma Mater, glorious to view." There were less delicate numbers.

At the time of the infantile paralysis epidemic in New York, we all went from Philadelphia to Boston by sea, en route to Jamestown. Mother and I were very seasick and confined to our cabins. Daddy had charge of Hawley and Betty. Having left them on deck for some necessity for a few minutes, he returned to find them surrounded by a small crowd. They were rendering one of Cornell's less esthetic numbers:

Skeeta and the Bedbug kept a hotel,
Had 40 boarders and ran it mighty well,
Business got slow, hotel went to crash -
Skeeta and the Bedbug got smothered in the hash.

The crowd was entranced.

# 4

# Classics and Poise

MY EARLIEST SCHOOL DAYS were with four other girls in a second-floor room of the house of William Potter, former Ambassador to both Japan and Italy, and grandfather of my closest friend, Jane Vanuxen Goodman. A teacher named Miss Kent taught Jane and Ethel (Babbie) Laughlin, Josephine Thomas, Helen Hebard and me. It was a big terra cotta stone house, with arched portico and a Victorian aura, set in the midst of several acres of lawn on which grew two magnificent pink magnolias. The trees, and the fact that we got gold stars pasted on a card for good performance, are the highlights of my memories. I was about 6 years old. The following year, three of us entered Springside, a school for girls in Chestnut Hill. Its counterparts were the Agnes Irwin School in the city and the Baldwin and Shipley schools on the Main Line. Springside was then a boarding as well as a day school.

Founded in 1879 by Mrs. Walter D. Comegys and Miss Jane Bell of the South, and inherited by Miss Caroline Susan Jones and Mrs. Lucia Polk Chapman, it offered eight grades of grammar school and four of high school. Springside was housed in a large Chestnut Hill gray stone building. It stood on an elevation below which was a springhouse, thus the name. There were two tennis courts and a basketball court. The three things that Springside dispensed were aspiration, a belief in high ideals and the future; an interest in the arts and history, esthetics and the past; and an intense loyalty to itself.

At the end of the year in June, song night was held around the springhouse, and as alumnae and students gathered to sing folk and classical songs, the grounds were charged with a spirit of devotion. "Laurus Crescit in Arduis" is the motto on Springside's crest. The influence of the school on the character and attitudes of the young women of the area over the past century has been incalculable. Now situated on the former Houston estate in St. Martins, a neighboring suburb, it carries on as a large, generously patronized, successful community institution. It was a more intimate, more classical, less technological Springside in my day. Although the school offered

23

both a college and a general course, less than 25 percent of the graduating class went on to college.[1]

Marriage was the taken-for-granted end of the time, and undergirded the thoughts and activities of a girl's life from her early years, symbolized in some cases, by beautiful "bride" dolls given as Christmas presents. The impact of such a doll is reflected in this bit I wrote years later:

The spare room was always a special room. But at Christmas time it was extra special. Here stood the mahogany Kris Kringle chest, with its 18th century date inlaid in lighter wood below the big brass lock with its huge key. Christmas presents were stored in that chest.

One Christmas, I asked for a bride doll. Mother and Mrs. Gormley, the dressmaker, retired to the spare room behind a closed door for two days.

Two days is a long time to a child of 8; three weeks to Christmas - interminable! Late the second afternoon, a little girl almost burst.

I first saw my bride doll through a keyhole, real wax orange blossoms holding the tulle veil which fell over her white satin gown, a misty illusion of future hopes. I have never seen such a beautiful bride since.

Only a scant handful of young women in the Philadelphia suburban area went on to any sort of professional work. But Daddy was anxious that I go to college, so I took the college course in my last four years at Springside; it included Latin, mathematics, ancient history, French (I had it for all twelve years) and literature, both English and French.

There were no aptitude tests. A child was thrown into scholastic waters and rose or fell on his own innate abilities, which were not analyzed. Interest was the guiding star. A means of livelihood was taken for granted and unplanned for. The world was an oyster, ostensibly opened by knowledge of or acquaintance with the adventurousness of the Phoenicians; the journeys of Aeneas; Ben Johnson, Victor Hugo, Moliere and advanced algebra. Natural selection is stronger than scholarship. Pearls of ability and shells of undevelopment are with us before we open a book; they are our pasture and our fence. Educators today are realizing they cannot

---

[1]In 1985, Springside School was recognized by the United States Department of Education as one of 65 Exemplary Private Schools in the United States.

hold up a mirror of the ideal for students to imitate. The ideal stands, of course, but the student can only reflect on its shining surface that which is innately his. Education can develop and train, it cannot decree the variety of seed planted in the human consciousness. A teacher can only enlighten and water it.

There are different kinds of light in this world. The light of appreciation of literature is a lifelong joy. It inspires, entertains and comforts. I had been brought up in literary surroundings; the candle was lit. Edith Grace Moses, my English teacher, fanned it. Through her, a tall, lanky woman with a sedate mop of pale taupe hair, artist's hands and a tendency toward St. Vitus's dance, this light of appreciation shone. She vibrated to it, and by doing so communicated it to us. She was my most memorable and influential teacher.

Dr. Henry S. Pancoast, a professor of literature at the University of Pennsylvania, also held classes at the school. His "An Introduction to English Literature," 1894, held a message which, had I been old enough to grasp, would have preillumined years of human experience in the difference in characteristics of people with predominantly English, Celtic or Germanic backgrounds. Such earlier insight would have been of great help to me.

A gentle man with a Van Dyke beard, Dr. Pancoast carried his books and papers to class in a cloth bag, fastened by a drawstring. He offered a more scholarly and interpretive viewpoint than the "violin" of Miss Moses' personality, upon which literature was played.

A teacher can say something a student will remember all his life. Another revered instructor, my French teacher, Mademoiselle Adele Audi, once told me: "Elaine, I do know this about you, that whatever you have, you will make the best of it." A remark that has helped me throughout.

Springside emphasized dramatics. It believed that they gave young women poise and grace. If the plays were in French, they increased one's facility with the language, as well as introducing one to the classics, as did English and American plays. It was to dramatics that I turned naturally and joyfully. They occupied a considerable part of my attention during my junior and senior years. It had begun with a Nativity play at Christmas in which, as one of the three kings of the Orient, Balthazar, to be exact, I sang:

"Myrrh is mine; its bitter perfume
Breathes a life of gathering gloom;

Sorrowing, sighing, bleeding, dying,
Sealed in the stone-cold tomb."

Through high school, dramas by Victor Hugo, Rostand and
Molière were interspersed with class plays we both wrote and
performed, plus some vaudeville acts.  I remember an early play I
wrote called "Castanets."  It had a Spanish setting and, of course, I
was the hero.  Patty Denckla, a classmate, somewhat taller than I,
was the heroine, and the climax was when, as I lay wounded on the
floor, she approached, knelt beside me and said, "Julio, speak to
me!"  To which I feebly replied, "I cannot."  Daddy wept with
laughter.

In another skit, wearing a caricature of a false face, with a large
mouth that opened and shut, and dressed in a Red Cross nurse's
uniform, I sang the current wartime hit:

There's a rose that grows in "No Man's Land"
And it's wonderful to see, -
Tho it's sprayed with tears, it will live for years
In my garden of memory; -
It's the one red rose the soldier knows,
It's the work of the master's hand, -
Mid the war's great curse stands the Red Cross Nurse
She's the rose of "No Man's Land."

It brought down the house.

The social accompaniment to school was dancing class.  In our
earliest days, William Kildare, the cheerful, obliging livery stable
owner, who looked very much like Lloyd George, drove us to class
in a hack, a high, square carriage which he backed around to the
pavement so one could enter through a rear door.  It had glass
windows and long side seats facing each other.  We wore carriage
boots quilted inside and edged with fur and carried those patent
leather pumps.

Dancing began at about age 8 with Miss Robbins' class held in
the ballroom of the Philadelphia Cricket Club, a colonial brick
building at St. Martins set in the midst of many grass tennis courts,
a golf course, and - in my extreme youth - a cricket field.  The
ballroom had a stage and a sort of portico at one side where
Mrs. William Joyce Sewell and Mrs. Clark Zantzinger received us.
As we came into the room, the boys bowed and the girls curtsied to
the patronesses.  Curtsies were required of subteen girls in daily
life, whenever greeted by or introduced to an elder.  We then joined

Miss Robbins, our teacher. She was a tall, spare woman with the energy of a large bird, perhaps a rook. Her movements had the elevation of a carriage spring, and yet she was graceful. She was hearty and all encompassing. We were taught the schottish, the polka, the two-step and the waltz. The foxtrot had not yet made its debut. Little girls wore velveteen dresses, black, green or red, with Irish lace collars. Boys wore blue suits, round turndown collars and ties.

The next class was that of Mrs. Charles Stewart Wurts. It was held at the Bellevue-Stratford. By this time, we knew how to dance and had acquired some ballroom manners. Mrs. Wurts' duty was mainly to guide us around the dance floor, to see that the boys danced and the girls had partners, a social rather than a choreographical responsibility. Mrs. Wurts was always cheerful and interested, dressed in sort of draped, flowing things. She wore her hair in a psyche knot, and had a sort of detachment that well suited her activity.

The final dancing class was the Saturday Evening, which was a two-year prelude to a girl's debut in Philadelphia. The class was quite similar to the debut parties which were to follow, with the exception that it was not anywhere nearly as elaborate. The later custom of a girl going about for prolonged periods with one boy was not in vogue. "Cutting in" was the style on the dance floor. A boy simply tapped the shoulder of another boy dancing with a girl and took over as her partner. The old choice which dance cards permitted a girl to accept or decline had gone with the wind. The girl simply received each new partner with good grace. Indeed it was the apex of popularity, greatly to be desired but achieved by only a few, for her to take just a few steps with each partner before another intervened. In the later years of dancing classes, I remember such belles as Elizabeth Machen, Millicent Anne Brengle, and most particularly at future parties, a little girl named Josephine Bromley, who resembled a somewhat more refined looking Mae West; also my future sister-in-law, Letitia Kent.

With great bounce and a genuine interest in having young people enjoy themselves was Mrs. Naudain Duer, the arbiter of the Saturday Evening Class. A tiny woman with a pouf of brown hair, she too had a sort of pleased detachment while keeping a watchful eye on us, corralling here, encouraging there, and generally keeping things moving on the Bellevue-Stratford dance floor.

The stag-line, that dinner jacket-clad group of young men ranging from 16 to perhaps 20, was the real arbiter of the class. On the favor of these men depended a girl's success or failure on the dance floor.  What makes a girl a belle?  It is not necessarily beauty alone; nor does mechanical listening nor witty response fill the bill. Dancing well is unquestionably an asset.  But perhaps a genuine, unfeigned interest in others, for whatever reason, is the best answer. Even then, there is an elusive quality about a belle that is known only to nature herself.

Although there are scores of popular girls in a generation in any city, there are few real belles.  Years later, I met Elsie Mulford, a little woman of Welsh descent.  She had modeled and had the poise and confidence of all Britishers.  Her carriage was erect even in her later years, and her manner outgoing, blithe and encouraging; one felt that beneath it was a genuine interest in one's activities and welfare.  I remember a party when she was about 60, where, without any apparent effort on her part, she held court as the men gathered around her, as she had unquestionably been doing since a young girl.

"The secular mystery that has been hid for ages," which modistes, cosmetologists, beauty parlors and charm schools have never been able to capture.  A widow in her 70s, Elsie Mulford is still "dating."

In June, 1924, I was graduated from Springside School, with 19 other girls in our class.  When it came to mathematics, I just made it.  My father, an engineer of design and inventor with the United Gas Improvement Company, who had received the Edward Longstreth Medal of the Franklin Institute for his inventions in gas apparatus, endeavored to help me with geometry and advanced algebra at home in the evenings.  They were difficult hours for me. Years later, I remember Harold T. Saylor, editor of the *Philadelphia Record*, commenting that no reporter worth his salt was any good at figures.  Perhaps the broad strokes required of newsmen cannot be incorporated with the exactness of mathematics.

In the final mathematics examination, there was the perennial problem about a train crossing a bridge.  In trying to solve it, I wore two holes in the paper copybook in which we wrote our answers. The train refused to cross the span.  Miss Moses, my light and mentor, came to my personal aid.  I was the class poet.  How could I not pass?  Gently she leaned over my shoulder as I perspired before the copybook, and by slight suggestion, nudged the train across the track.  It went right through those holes in the paper across that bridge to my graduation.

And so as the roses and honeysuckle bloomed in Chestnut Hill, wearing simple white dresses and carrying bouquets of flowers, triumphantly - yet with an aura of sadness - we walked slowly to

"Pomp and Circumstance," down the aisle of the Springside gymnasium to the stage for commencement exercises. Surely, idealism is at its height in our lives at our high school graduation ceremonies. The realm of more thoughtful, controversial philosophic and scientific ideas has not challenged our young minds. Literature has opened a vista of the possibilities of human endeavor, and the exuberance of youth believes in the spiritual truth that "with God all things are possible." All is aspiration and faith. The doubts and attempts of the individual to "add one cubit onto his stature" by thought have not yet risen up.

My class poem dealt with ships and it began:

> I gazed out over Life's great broad sea
> And I saw the ships go sailing by,
> Each with its cargo to that haven gate,
> Across the arch of years, across the sky...

The final lines asked  "God grant, as we take to Life's Ocean
Alone o'er us, thy (Springside's) winds
May prevail."

The 1924 Yearbook of Springside School prophesied that I would be a bellboy at the Ritz.

# 5

## Bloom and Sorrow

IN OCTOBER, I was presented to society at a large tea given by my Father and Mother in the Gravers Lane house. There were about 125 girls making their debut in Philadelphia in the Season of 1924-25. Those were peaceful, prosperous years. The first World War was over and the country was glad to rejoice. Although Prohibition was with us, the Depression had not yet reared its shabby head, and World War II was an unimagined nightmare.

The year seldom has been equaled, before or since, in the number of debutante parties in Philadelphia. Luncheons, teas, dances and balls swirled around us and we went to as many as two or three a day. Another popular form of entertainment was the theatre party. Usually someone gave a dinner before it and dancing at the Ritz-Carlton generally followed. The spotlight was upon us - young girls ranging from 17 to 19 - in a way that it never will be again in this country, as the sociological pattern of the Western World has undergone at least a partial revolution. It was heady stuff, bound to increase an exaggerated sense of self-importance in some girls.

The debut originally was designed to introduce a girl to society, specifically the friends of her parents. It also was to provide a marriageable girl with the opportunity to meet suitable young men. The system had value for the individual, too, in that it gave her a sense of worth in the scheme of things and an ease of manner in social situations to last throughout her life. Of course, some of this had been inculcated in her at home, in the family. The debut polished it off. In essence it might be defined as a statement by parents: "Here is my daughter. I have given her a reasonable amount of education. She is now ready for marriage. Isn't she lovely! Come get her."

You had to be suitable. You had to belong to a family of reasonably similar background; you had to be able to support her in a reasonably comfortable manner, and you had to have physical and mental health. Parents were concerned and inquired about these matters in 1924; a mother behind the scenes, a father in the parlor. Yet over it all hung the cerulean sky of the ideal of love as the determining factor in marriage. There were exceptions, of course. Arranged marriages were not admitted to as such, since the old Anglo-Saxon idea of true love, the instinctive response of one human being to another, generally prevailed. At least 90 percent of the debutantes were Episcopalians or Presbyterians. The alternative to marriage was still only a partially formulated plan of attendance at college, with perhaps a career in the uncharted mists of the future. The Roman Catholic concept of celibacy, setting forth the value of lifelong chastity, was not a part of the picture. A girl who did not marry was generally considered unfulfilled. No skylight was offered in the house of the unmarried. Sublimation was the rule, a concept that sought to enfold the illusory and romantic elements of a girl's nature with religious, social and practical ones.

1924-25 was an exuberant and elaborate year. I remember the first tea. Daddy had bought a "Twin Six" Packard touring car from a friend for us children to drive around, and I drove Mother, Mrs. Everett M. Hawley and her daughter, Betty Ogden, to the Main Line to the tea of Eloise Geist, a petite, French-looking girl whose father, Clarence Geist, had been active in developing Florida. The house and the refreshments were elaborate and there were flowers everywhere. Inadvertantly, I sat on a huge bunch of American Beauty roses, resting on the corner of a sofa. Upon the return home in the car, Mrs. Hawley was depressed. "If this is what it's going to be like, Mrs. Taussig," she said to Mother, "I don't think we can undertake it." But Betty Ogden, a tall, statuesque, fair-haired girl, came out with the rest of us and we went to many parties together. Among them was a dance given by Mrs. Goodman, Jane's mother, for her, Eleanor Coleman, Anne Wetherill and myself at the Acorn Club. Jane Goodman, my old friend, did not come out with us. Her mother preferred she take a trip around the world, accompanied by Mademoiselle Audi. They had a wonderful time. Included in their itinerary was a visit to the Crown Prince of Siam, now Thailand, where Mr. Potter, Jane's grandfather, also had served as minister. They were entertained at a large dinner party with elaborate favors and Jane, making her way through one of the dishes, a small custard, found, to her horror, snails, a great delicacy in Siam, at the bottom of the dish. It's one thing to order escargots in a restaurant where one can look them in the face, so to speak, and another to find them hidden under something else.

The number of bouquets and cut flowers and arrangements a girl received at her debut was amazing. It also was the style to send ostrich feather fans on which were fastened corsages of gardenias or even orchids. At my tea, I wore my Great-Grandmother Sarah Hodgson Ball's wedding dress of ivory silk rep, embroidered in bands of daisies, roses and other flowers. It had to be slightly let out in the waist for my 25 inch one, but I made it. With this I wore her two miniatures, both surrounded with pearls; one, set in a brooch, was of her mother, Mary Ann Cook Hodgson, the daughter of Alexander Cook of Philadelphia, and the other, set in a wide gold bracelet, was of her son, Robert Hodgson Ball, my maternal grandfather.

Illustrative of the consciousness of and emphasis on lineage was my correction of one of the guests we received. Admiring the miniature pinned to the front of my dress, she exclaimed, "Your grandmother!" "No," I replied, "my Great, Great-Grandmother." Another guest looked at me and said, "Your Grandmother!" referring to Mother's mother, the former Lillian Burrows, "was a driven beauty!" Just where that left me was indefinite. I carried a large, old-fashioned bouquet, about 12-inches-across, of tightly arranged flowers edged with a wide paper frill. I have the big, round, light wooden box it came in today, although the years have nearly worn my name and address from the lid.

The Winter whirled on toward Lent. Then the parties would stop until after Easter. For me, however, the gaiety came to a halt before then. In mid-February, Daddy entered the hospital for an operation. He did well. Three days before he was expected to come home, we were called there suddenly in the morning. Mr. Kildare drove Mother and me there, now in a Ford taxi, with all possible speed. In two hours, Daddy was dead.

Grandmother came up the path in her long window's veil, Uncle Charlie with a bunch of violets. Uncle Joe was at our side. Men my father had known stood out on the lawn in the March air, as the house was full at his funeral.

The first chapter of my life was over.

# Part II
# The Search

# 6

## Beyond the Periphery

MOTHER STAYED ON IN the big house for several years. She and Daddy had been close. She loved the house and garden and was loathe to give them up. Brother was 13, and my sister Betty, 11, I, 18 and unmarried. It was a lovely place to train and launch children.

Daddy had wanted me to go to college. But success in dramatics at Springside and my encouragement by teachers, added to my own enjoyment of them, made dramatic school my goal. It was almost more than Daddy could understand. The theatre was not as accepted in those days, and to him, college had high value. But I held to my goal, to attend Sargent's School in New York, now the Academy of Dramatic Arts. It was supposed to be the finest of its kind.

Now, however, it was only April, and five months stretched ahead before I could enter. Mrs. Goodman was chairman of the Cooperative Shop, where secondhand things, from china to clothes, were sold for the benefit of the Jefferson Hospital, of which her father, Ambassador Potter, had been board chairman. She asked me to come in and help. It was my first business experience of any kind.

I remember an incident on one lunch hour. I was sent to the bank to deposit the daily cash, and in the lobby I met Jack Ballagh, a great beau about town, who asked me to lunch with him. Any girl in Philadelphia would have been delighted to have lunch with Jack Ballagh. He was tall, slender, with amused brown eyes and a lovely smile. But I had been sent to deliver the cash of the Cooperative Shop for the day. Regretfully, I declined. It was a taxing decision; I wanted to have lunch with him so much. But the bank deposit was in my hands, I had been made responsible for it. I was expected back at the shop, and that was that. Such small decisions reflect on our training and who can estimate how much they influence our future?

In the summer of 1925, I went to work in John Wanamaker's Department Store, where Grandfather and I had gone to lunch on those glorious sprees during his visits to Philadelphia, and had enjoyed Tomato Surprise in the big tearoom on the top floor. This time, I entered by the basement, where I punched a time clock to work on the first floor selling scarves. My objective was to help with tuition for dramatic school. Daddy, who had always been the epitome of health, had held a large amount of accident insurance, but a more moderate indemnification for health.

I remember my Great-Aunt Nance, Mrs. Charles Rowland, coming in to my counter.  Inwardly, it must have been a startling sight for her to see the grandniece - to whom she had given a silver muskrat coat trimmed with red fox as a "coming-out" present the previous fall - so employed.  It just wasn't done in Edward VII's time.

Few women in the area or surrounding ones where I lived worked in 1925.  The two I knew of were Gladys Mueller, several years older than I, who had gone to Springside, and a still older woman, a Miss Drayton.  I think they both sold books.  We had no training for business by which to make our living.  We had been given an appreciation of literature, some mathematics, Latin, ancient history, French and, in some cases, simple bookkeeping, but no shorthand or typing courses.  Selling was the only field open to us. The question of whether we could or could not sell was not considered.

The scarf counter was on one side of the aisles off the Grand Court of John Wanamaker's.  Scarves were worn in those days, the usual neck-length ones, and wide, flowing chiffon models at weddings and evening parties.  Older saleswomen had charge of the latter flowing apparel.  My stock was confined to neck-length scarves.  They were folded in envelope fashion and laid in overlapping lines on the counter.  A customer's examination of them and the consequent disturbances of the line required that they again be put in order.  This was not easy for me.  In fact, if I had realized then that the handling of material things was not my cup of tea, that I lacked any aptitude for it, I would have saved myself years of frustration and difficulty.  But I did not know the self that Polonius told his son to be true to; I knew what I liked, but I didn't know what I was.  And the social circumstances under which I lived and my training offered no other choice.  Small paperback books of the classics and semiclassics were published at 10-cents each in those days, and I had several behind the counter.  They were small enough so that your hand could practically conceal them, and when there were no customers about, or scarves to be tidied, I would read such works as *Swift on Conversation* and simliar high-flown titles.

Chestnut Hill had two types of population:  the people who owned the houses and those who took care of them.  I had never really met anyone outside this periphery or other similar Philadelphia suburbs, or milieu in other cities or resorts, until I went, first to the Cooperative Shop, and then to John Wanamaker's.  An exception, of course, was when I was taken as a small child to stay at the Norfolk Navy Yard where Grandfather was commandant. The picture was very much the same there, only translated into the military, national personages, officers and their wives and children, and scores of military personnel without rank and Negro and Filipino servants. I still can see Fred, the veteran Negro houseman, smoothing embossed spreads on the beds with a yardstick; the softly lit living room with a deep sofa and refectory table, and a screen in the dining room behind which was a small lacquer cabinet filled with trays of bonbons for dinner parties. I was not yet four, because later, at that age, Grandmother Taussig took me from Philadelphia to Norfolk to be flower girl at Uncle Joe and Aunt Lulie's wedding. We went by boat. En route, Grandmother agreed that the straps of my cream-colored, mercerized undershirt could be lowered under my white embroidered muslin, blue-sashed dress. At the end, however, owing to cold weather, and to my irate frustration, she refused to lower them. Eve blooms early in little girls.

I had not seen an example of rank in general civilian life until I went to Wanamaker's. However, five o'clock was the magic hour. From the semicircular entrance on Juniper Street, with its several revolving doors, issued the buyers - big-bosomed women strutting like pouter pigeons and men in expensive lightweight suits and imported panamas. As the grandly uniformed doorman saluted them by name, they walked out into the sultry summer air from the great marble public palace where they reigned to the privacy and quiet of home. Men and women who had reached success up a long ladder, aspired to by many; and their every step and gesture signified they had arrived at the top, at least in their mercantile world. There is a tangible presence about material success. A Nobel prize winner may look like a down-and-outer in baggy trousers and jacket, but a buyer always looks as though he could buy the best and wears it with éclat.

*********

There were floorwalkers and "floor ladies" too, in stores in those days. The floorwalkers were men of presence, sometimes wearing morning coats and cutaways, and the floor women were well turned out and had considerable facade. The floorwalkers handled acute problems and generally "cased" departments to see that all was going well. The floor women were the State Department of a store, combining a sharp eye with a conciliatory manner. I had a wonderful floor lady. Ida Henninger was a big, statuesque woman with a high, white, crinkled pompadour.  She was dressed in black, as were all store employees then.  She wore "lingerie" touches too - immaculate, flattering white collars and cuffs or jabots. She was cheerful and enjoyed her position in life.  In between customers, she would talk.  She had the start of her day timed to a fine point:  the coffee was perking as she took her bath and by the time she had hooked her brassiere, a substantial one, it was done. Other domesticities ensued while she did her hair.  Over it all hung a little bird cage made of lemonade straws, holding a small artificial bird, Miss Henninger's symbol of coziness and home.  I listened, fascinated, to this kindly woman.  Like a crested cockatoo, she swooped down on exchange or credit slips, weighing, signing, soothing and generally controlling demands and complaints of the public.  When these were too much for her, she referred them to the floorwalker, Mr. Campbell.  I don't know whether Mr. Campbell had ever read *Swift on Conversation,* but he certainly heard a lot of it.  I think it was John Wanamaker, himself, who proclaimed the merchandising motto of the future - "The Customer is Always Right."  Be that as it may, Mr. Campbell's charge in life was to keep the customer from robbing the store without losing the customer.  In the 1920's, that was delicate work.  His manner was slightly injured, as if the customer, by even suggesting a credit or return, offended him personally.

Events that defy conventional behavior sink in deeply and make an indelible impression upon the young.  I have never forgotten an occurrence one day in the scarf department of John Wanamaker's. A large, rather blowsy woman came in with two very expensive chiffon scarves that had been sent to her in the suburbs by special delivery; stores sent things out by special messenger on occasion, at the time.  The woman wanted to return them.  Miss Henninger, realizing that she was out of her depth, ushered the lady to Mr. Campbell.  The floorwalker lifted the folds of the expensive top chiffon scarf gingerly, and evidently questioned the propriety of taking the merchandise back.  But the customer stood her ground on the marble floor of John Wanamaker's, with its marble walls that echoed like Kentucky's Mammoth Cave.

"You can ask anyone at the wedding, but I swear to God I never wore it!" said the lady in tones that reverberated down the aisle. Mr. Campbell obliged.  To one who had been brought up never to raise one's voice in public - indeed, that it was preferable never to raise it at all - the episode proved to me that if you raise it high enough you usually can get what you want.

# 7

# Dimmed Footlights

IN THE SUMMER OF 1925, Mother and I went to New York and I was enrolled in Sargent's School. That Fall I entered the school which was situated in the office building connected with Carnegie Hall. Arrangements were made for me to live at the French School, a boarding school for girls at 12 East 95th Street, run by an attractive, white-haired Frenchwoman. I, of course, would not be a pupil in her school, but would have a large second-floor bedroom there, along with several other boarders. Mother was anxious that I continue my French. I would have my meals with the pupils and only French was spoken at table. I would also attend performances of the Metropolitan Opera with them.

There were young men and women from all over the country at Sargent's School. A few of the men had shoulder-length hair, a sign of artistic temperament rather than social revolt in those days.

The two girls I remember were Mary Hogue, a Springside alumna, younger than I, whom I met in the lobby the first day I arrived, and a girl from Texas named Tazia Dock, a golden-haired Mary Pickford type, dressed in black velvet and, on her finger, a carved jade ring extending to the knuckle. Mary Hogue was a sweet girl with fluffy brown hair, deep-set eyes, a retroussé nose and a wistful expression.

We were given a dictionary with the British pronunciation of words to purify our Pennsylvania, Texas or other accents and various expressions of speech, to teach us really to speak the King's English. It is a facet of the theatre not emphasized in dramatic training in the United States today, but which so delights the American public on British broadcasts.

I stood in front of the mirror and did the vowel exercises the school assigned - "A...E...I...O...U" echoed in firm tones throughout my bedroom at the French school and in my one at home, when I went back on vacations. And from a well-equipped makeup box filled with greasepaint, powder, rouge, liners and cold cream, I practiced the art.

The Masons, who had a temple in the Carnegie Hall building, allowed the Academy to use a short flight of red-carpeted steps in the Grand Lodge Room on which to teach us how to fall downstairs without hurting ourselves. Relaxation, of course, was the trick.

Among other courses, we took one called "Vocal Expression," in which we were required to tell the image that came to mind when a certain word was announced. I can remember being struck by the differences in human imagination when the word APPLE was offered. Some students thought of the fruit on a tree, another, fruit arranged in a copper bowl, but Tazia Dock topped us all. Tilting her head in graceful recline, she said in broad Southern tones, "Ah jus' think of the springtime!"

Still another class taught us to make a break mentally before we moved from one action to another on the stage, not to run them all together. In the deepest sense, acting is the creation within the mind of the thoughts, actions and reactions in which the character portrayed is involved. This training, to consciously separate one act from another, has been of help to me in general living throughout my life. One cannot see the full image or significance of an act when it is crowded up against another.

The tragedy of all this was that when I mounted the stage to read the lines, I could not act. The exuberant flow of ability and enjoyment that had borne me along in my Springside years, in which I had been so encouraged by teachers and performance, and that had become a shining goal was stopped at its source. Daddy's death had doused the light.

Gradually, in the Winter I spent at Sargent's School, I recovered from a nervous breakdown. I was not among the "promising" students asked to return for the second year of the two-year curriculum.

But the words of the Rev. Malcolm Peabody, our minister at St. Paul's Episcopal Church in Chestnut Hill, (later Bishop of Central New York), still ring in my ears; he probably had seen many such cases after World War I:

"I can tell you this, Ellen," he said with earnestness, "this will never happen to you again."

And it never did.

# 8

## The Marts of Trade

I WENT BACK TO Philadelphia and began to write monologues which I gave at private parties and club events. I also dabbled in amateur and semiprofessional theatricals. The great Ruth Draper, and Cornelia Otis Skinner who followed her, were performing in those days. I went to see them and wrote some monologues of my own. But to me they were lonely work. I wanted some response from the other side of the fence, and not to be limited or entirely dependent upon my own imagination. The theatricals were desultory and unrewarding.

Again, I turned to selling - the only field that seemed open to me. However, this time I chose a more specialized shop, the Blum Store at the corner of 13th and Chestnut Streets. It was a women's speciality shop run by a Mr. and Mrs. Maurice Spector, fine merchants with a keen eye for style, a rival of Bonwit Teller a few blocks up the street. Blum's was widely patronized.

I told Mr. Spector, who interviewed me, he was fortunate to have me come in to apply for a position in his shop. He immediately engaged me at a salary of $18 a week. It is one of the peculiar psychological facets of this world that unmitigated confidence brings positive results.

I was assigned to the French Salon, which sold high-priced, high-styled women's and misses dresses. It was a long room surrounded by private fitting rooms and a large bridal parlor. It was furnished in comfortable sofas and reflected in many mirrors. At either side were large stock rooms, where the dresses were kept. Two elevators at the front of the room brought customers from the ground floor.

Dressed in black, a staff of about 20 women served the trade under the gentle yet dignified presence of Mrs. Thompson, the floor lady, who resembled the French singer Irene Bordoni, and had the air of a black satin-clad pouter pigeon. As customers got off the elevator, they asked Mrs. Thompson, standing in the middle of the floor, for their favorite saleswoman, or one was procured for them by her. If she were not around, one of the sales staff stepped forward and offered her services. I was in the presence of seasoned saleswomen, fashion conscious, with a native ability to transact the passage of merchandise. Equipped with it, some had come up the ladder from lesser departments and all had earned their following. A few were past masters, like Pearl Stofman, Cecelia Pearlman and a Miss Moser. I also vividly remember a Miss Simpson who sold blouses on the mezzanine.

Miss Stofman and Miss Pearlman were the active, interested, dedicated type of saleswomen, but Miss Simpson and Miss Moser were something else. They had the invaluable quality of being able to transact business through thought. In the blouse department, Miss Simpson, a round, white-faced young woman with pale golden hair parted in the middle, standing behind a counter, would hold up a blouse on a hanger with one hand, and with an absolutely expressionless face pronounce the price - "$12.98." The weight of thought that she put behind the display of that blouse had sales force. She didn't have to ingratiate, she didn't have to smile; she had only to stand, hold and speak. Upstairs, Miss Moser, with short henna hair and personality, and a sort of relaxed coordination of her slim figure, practiced the same technique; in fact at times her manner was one of boredom. She asked nothing and she usually got all she wanted. I believe selling, like acting, is a talent.

I opened my sales years at the Blum Store sartorially well-equipped. Somewhere I had heard that if one stood on one's feet for long periods, one's ovaries fell, as did the arches of one's feet. I arrived in a well-boned corset (waist size 26 now) and an exorbitantly expensive for those days, pair of lizard and black patent leather oxford. "Peaches" Wainright, another girl who also arrived from the suburbs, experienced considerable growth of her feet while working at the Blum Store. A tall, slender girl, she finally required a size 8, unusually large for the time. As the months wore on, I appeared in a pair of more corrective shoes; unfortunately, they were brown. Mr. Wilson, the rotund director of personnel, and Mrs. Thompson were standing together on the salon floor the morning I first appeared in them. Mrs. Thompson called me over.

"Miss Taussig," she said tactfully, "those are very handsome shoes you are wearing." I looked down at my feet, pleased. "But may I suggest that you have them dyed black?"

Mrs. Spector, the joint owner, appeared from time to time on the floor. A woman of lion-like head set on broad shoulders, she had a particularly sweet expression, as if she were enjoying the life she lived and cared for the human race. She was genuinely interested in finding the right clothes for people, and she had an unerring sense of style. She combined both authority and service. I admired her tremendously. I remember one morning we both appeared in the same black wool crepe Schiaparelli dress with a white satin tie.

Hers had probably cost nearly $100, a large amount then, and mine was a copy at about $16. She just smiled as she saw me.

The French Salon was divided into two departments, Misses and Women's, the latter of which sold larger and more mature clothes. Four principal buyers presided over it. On our floor was Betty Weinstein with dark hair parted in the middle and a slim, stylish figure. She was then allegedly 50 but looked 35. She would sit in a chair, looking beautiful, and call "Stock!" to bring one of the several stock girls to do her bidding. Telling the girl what garments she wanted, she would rise upon their arrival and, holding them up one by one, explain their merits to the customer. Her entire sales operation was like one of two women, she and the customer, having tea and discussing their personal wardrobe. She handled dresses as if they were part of a person, an extension of the customer's personality.

Then there was Miss Ida, a short, light-haired woman, also with personality, who was one of the squarest shooters I've ever met. In an atmosphere of heated competition and among a highly demanding clientele, she remained balanced, cheerful and fair. Her assistant, Lizzie Zeldes, a Russian, although also a good sport, was quite different; big and dark-haired, she was more dramatic, wore long pearls and had a striding walk, in contrast to Miss Ida's accelerated trot. You might say that Miss Zeldes had something of the grand manner, but she, too, was genuinely interested in her customers - perhaps more from a sales point of view than Mrs. Spector or Miss Ida. She was a more cultivated woman.

In the Bridal Salon, where regular clothes also were somtimes shown to important customers, I was called in on occasion to assist Miss Zeldes.

The three Dorrance sisters of the Campbell Soup fortune, were waited on there. Their mother, Mrs. John Dorrance, a charming woman, sat gracefully by as the girls tried on dress after dress, bought and special ordered. Special orders were the custom in those days; a woman might like a dress, but want it in another color. The store was glad to oblige. About three weeks was the usual time required.

We worked from 9 to 5 six days a week, and our day began fixing the stock in the long, quiet stockrooms, where each saleswoman was assigned a section of dresses to check whether they were properly hung on hangers, fastened, sized and the belts clasped. The task was a frustrating one to me. I needed people or sound or print, other than price tags, to arouse my interest. It was sheer mental labor for me. I would emerge from the task feeling as if my head was filled with cork.

I had begun to write verse in the evenings at home, and the nullification I felt in this duty brought forth these pained lines, as well as I can remember them:

> Jesus, the sun is rising,
> I'm in the crowds' subway,
> Jesus, I hear your garments blow,
> As I ride to work today.
>
> Jesus, the stock's untidy,
> Slowly your presence unfolds,
> In the beautiful rhythm of silence,
> As I pile fine ladies' clothes.
>
> Jesus, the sun is setting,
> I'm in the crowds' subway,
> Jesus, the night is coming,
> Exquisite peace after the day.

Anne Leithman, a fellow saleswoman who later was married to John Endicott, thrived on all aspects of the floor. We became lifelong friends. She went on to become a very successful buyer in the Blum Store proper, and later in Hartford, Conn. Her mind moved with agility from merchandise to customer to salesmanship; she was an excellent business woman.

One night a month, we stayed late and took stock. That was better. There were vocalized numbers, descriptions, as well as prices of garments. It had more to give it rhythm.

I learned several things in the Blum Store. The first one was that he who sells and he who buys - regardless of position, education or friendship - are on opposite sides of the fence; there is an unbridgeable gulf between the customer and the salesman which must always be observed. It is the natural tension of the operation. It happened thus: A girl with whom I had gone to parties came in to buy some clothes. When she departed, she left a gold cigarette case in the fitting room, which, when discovered, was quickly sent upstairs to the Lost and Found. She was notified and came into the French Salon. The store provided me with a questionnaire to certify that the case was hers. On it there was a question: "Is the customer White, Oriental or Black?" Knowing this girl, having wined, dined and danced in her company, I humorously, along with the other questions, asked her this one. She drew herself up, furious. "What do you mean?" she said. I must have backtracked in some way, but I have never forgotten the incident. It was a valuable lesson.

A second thing I learned at the Blum store was the limit of human tolerance. How much tolerance does service imply? On Saturday afternoon, into the store would come prospective brides with their mothers and sometimes additional relatives, often foreigners, speaking broken English. This was particularly true of the less expensive fifth floor where we sometimes were sent during busy periods. Mother and daughter, and perhaps one or two others, would shop the town and look at costume after costume. The veteran salesgirls knew how to handle them, but I was a victim in their hands. Enthused by the costumes and endeavoring to give service and to make sales, I wore myself ragged. I lost motivation in the mass of offerings - a thing a salewoman can never do. In fact, no one in any line can affort to be suffused by his/her medium.

Again, I learned a lifelong lesson: that there is a type of person who must be controlled, to whom you cannot give all of your heart, and in association with whom you must say - "Thus far - and no farther." This is not an idealistic piece of knowledge, but it is psychologically true.

Another thing which I had been taught as a young girl was reimpressed upon me, the value of condolence. Daisy Huelbreiner, the treasurer of the Blum Company, lost her mother and I, rank-wise, mounted several flights of echelon and actual stairs to her office by sending her a letter of sympathy. Miss Huelbreiner was touched and never forgot my, what should be only natural, thoughtfulness.

I also learned professional discipline and manners. One morning, arriving late, I found my timecard removed from the check-in rack. Going to the Personnel Office, I was informed that it was because I had been tardy and would be docked. I don't know where I had picked up the following expletive, perhaps during those stock-taking nights when a tired sales staff would let down its hair, and the air was charged with a variety of them. Bursting into Mr. Wilson's office, minus my timecard, I demanded, "What the Hell?" this meant. Mr. Wilson gave me a steady eye and said simply: "Miss Taussig, you're fired."

I retreated downstairs and gave thought to the incident, then retracted my steps, apologized and was reinstated. But it, too, was an important lesson.

Finally, I learned not to eat solid food when I was rushed or upset, a habit emphasized later by a veteran fellow reporter in the newspaper business.  On those Saturdays when the future brides came to our door, I ate something that I could digest easily; a particular favorite was vanilla ice cream and stewed apricots.  All my life I have had an excellent digestion.  Miss Stitt, a member of the French Salon sales force who resembled a French print, loved desserts and always had two of them; she was thin as a rail.

Another buyer was Fanny Theodore, a pretty woman with straight blonde hair worn in dips over her cheeks, dark brows and beautiful eyes.  She was very expressive as she talked with the clientele, and used her well-shaped, beautifully manicured hands well, as she showed the dresses.

I did learn to sell clothes at Blum's, if, indeed, selling can be taught.  I learned it was unwise to show too much merchandise; when a customer was debating among two or three dresses, not to bring out a fourth.  I learned to suggest calling a fitter to turn up a hem or a cuff "to see how it looks."  I learned to introduce other articles of clothing - hats, shoes, and bags - to complement the one the customer had come in to buy.  But it took an executive of the store to enunciate what was in my mind.      ·

Nathan Hamburger, a Yale man, was in the sports department where I was selling one day.  He used to drop in on different floors and observe what was going on.

"You don't like to sell, do you, Miss Taussig?" he asked perceptively, yet in a kindly manner.

I do not recall what I replied, but he had hit the nail resoundingly on the head.

In 1934, as the Depression continued to make inroads into the Blum trade, and my sales record failed to measure up, I was laid off.  I didn't realize it at the time, but it was my swan song from the world of trying to get people to buy material goods.  Truthfully, I had never cared - really cared - if they bought or not.  I needed to earn money, loved pretty and stylish things, but the "caring connection" between the right ones of those things on the right people - and of convincing them that they were right - was as alien to me as a groundhog to a trapezist.

# 9

## Samplers and Sweets

WHITMAN'S, THE NATIONAL CANDY concern, had two restaurants in Philadelphia, showplaces for their confections. They were advertising in the Philadelphia Evening Bulletin for a hostess. I applied. By this time, I had come to regard myself as a working person. I had become accustomed to wearing black satin or crepe de chine or, in winter, wool crepe; pearls and sensible, supportive shoes.

Mrs. Ethel Hunt, an Englishwoman, was the manager of Whitman's. She interviewed and engaged me. Later, she told me there had been about 500 applicants for the job. One of the restaurants was on Chestnut Street near 13th and had been there for many years. It was there that Grandfather and I had gone for refreshment after our attendance at Keith's Theatre. The other was in a fascinating new building of French design at 17th and Chestnut.

It was there I was to work. The building had three restaurant floors: a soda counter and restaurant behind the elaborate candy shop at the front; a men's grill done in Early American furnishings on the mezzanine, and on the second floor, two large dining rooms, separated by a hall for the elevator. In the front dining room which looked out on Chestnut Street, and in the hall, Whitman's had hung a remarkable and valuable collection of samplers testifying to their noted Sampler box, along with silkwork pictures, all in handsome frames. The samplers, of course, dealt with moral virtues, from tidiness to chastity, painstakingly done by children and adults from the 17th century on. The silkwork embroideries usually depicted women sitting under weeping willows by tombstones, bemoaning the decreased. The back dining room was done in handsome oil murals of Colonial times. Both rooms were furnished in mahogany tables and chairs. The atmosphere created was a highly ethical and traditional one.

I had twenty waitresses under my supervision. The hours were from 10 to 3, with two hours off before the 5 to 8 dinner hour. Every morning, inspection was held at which the black uniforms, white collars and cuffs, aprons and caps, hairdos and fingernails, shoes and stockings of the waitresses were passed upon. Any untidiness was immediately corrected.

At 11 o'clock the public began to come in to luncheon. My job was to inquire how many wished to be seated, to find a table that suited them, and to present them with menus. The waitresses who had been there the longest had the best "stations" or groups of tables. I assigned others to newcomers. I immediately liked the position. I enjoyed greeting the people, the menu did its own selling, except when they asked what was especially good or for suggestions of what to order. It was not necessary for me to urge them to buy anything, nor did I have to handle any material goods.

All restaurants are divided into two parts. The front part belongs to the maitre d'hôtel or hostess and the back part to the chef. The pantry door is the dividing line; back of it the chef reigns supreme. There were three chefs at Whitman's: Rudolph, the head chef, an Italian who looked somewhat like Mephistopheles, slender, long-faced, with a bristling waxed mustache; the second chef, Arthur, a steady, handsome, smiling German; and the third chef, a sturdy Czechoslovak.

Mrs. Hunt handled the help well. Diplomacy, however, was the secret in dealing with Head Chef Rudolph. One memorable evening stands out: about 40 clergymen were dining on the mezzanine floor, which was sometimes engaged privately in the evening. The first course, fruit cup, was duly served and was to be followed by Chicken á la King and vegetables. Unfortunately, the Chicken á la King got stuck in the dumbwaiter between the main dining room kitchen on the second floor and the mezzanine kitchen below.

I was summoned to the kitchen as the clergymen ate the fruit cup, to find it in a high state of excitement. The curses of Head Chef Rudolph had driven the waitresses, like frightened sheep, into one corner of the room. I was told afterward that his words involved the Madonna and pigs. Arthur, the German, got into the dumbwaiter and tinkered with the supporting cables in an effort to fix it. It was all too much for the Czechoslovak. He went out on the balcony at the rear of the kitchen, overlooking the alley, and beat his soup ladle against the iron rail.

As the dumbwaiter refused to move, the question now arose of who was to tell the clergymen of the delay. The night manager, a young man named John Boehm, who had also come into the kitchen, declined; he simply could not face 40 religious. So I told them of the holdup. They were nice about it, and shortly afterward the Chicken á la King was retrieved and served.

As one looks back on far more serious challenges in life, such a one does not seem momentous. Backed by the pressure of the time, however, such things seem like Rubicons to cross. One wonders if the ability to meet these challenges is indigenous to us, or if each Rubicon bridges our way to the next?

I gained a more intimate knowledge of human nature at Whitman's than at Blum's or John Wanamaker's. The public is more relaxed when it is eating than when it is buying clothes. These incidents, among others, taught me the wide differences between human beings, and the impossibility of judging them by conventional standards, indeed, the futility of doing so.

To the dining room each weekday evening came a once beautiful woman who was a buyer in one of the department stores. For many years, she had been the mistress of one of the owners. As a young girl, she had come to work in his establishment, he had seen her, and that was it. Now, a bit portly, but still lovely in modish black crepe, a smart black hat, with a single emerald on her hand, she enjoyed a quiet dinner alone, or with a fellow woman buyer, in our dining room. As I circled the room, I would often stop by her table for a little chat.

One night she said: "Miss Taussig, this has been a very gratifying day to me. I have just completed a plan for a marble subterranean vault for my brother who died recently." After expressing my sympathy, I returned to the elevator to await further customers. The hallway, like the dining room, was surrounded by samplers which stitched out admonitions against sin and exaltations of virtue. It looked, I mused, as if sometimes one merged with the other.

There was the man who brought his wife in to luncheon and sat at a front table so he could see the models dressing and undressing in an upper store window across the street. And the woman who lost a gold filling in an entree and verbally raised the roof.

Louis P. McIlhenny, a born salesman with an observant eye, was president of Whitman's. One of his detailed concerns was that the corned beef hash in the men's grill be served very crisp and brown. It was an admonition that floated continuously through Mrs. Hunt's consciousness.

Mr. McIlhenny sent Mrs. Hunt to New York to get ideas for menus. She took me along. We visited five restaurants in one day and returned home feeling like capons. There was a wonderful French place, with plain white tablecloths and little gilt chairs, where we enjoyed an exquisite sauced luncheon. We ended up with dinner at Sherry's. As we had gone in early in order to get the train back to Philadelphia, there were only two other people in the dining room - a very tall, thin man accompanied by a little woman. I can see them now, dancing alone on the highly polished floor to the tunes played by the dinner musicians.

The private parties increased at Whitman's and a large room was added to the fourth and top floor to accommodate them. It was a great success. I took reservations, offered suggestions for menus and, with the help of two other hostesses, one a friend, Janet Kendig, who had joined me there, supervised the events. It was delightful, pleasant work.

One afternoon there was a women's club luncheon and, as was often the custom, book reviews were presented. One was on a book by Tobias Wagner, a member of the old spice importing family in Philadelphia, with whom I had gone to dancing class. It was about fox hunting in Chester County. As I listened to the review, I thought to myself: "If Toby Wagner can write a book, I certainly can write something."

I had gone as far as I could with Whitman's. They would raise my salary no further. That book review at that women's club luncheon was a turning point in my life.

# Part III

# Wings at Last

# 10

## "Just Gossip About People"

AGNES CHURCHMAN, A SISTER of my friend Janet Kendig, was a society "stringer," a correspondent paid on a space basis, ($8.00 a column of type), for the *Evening Public Ledger.* A number of women who went about in Philadelphia were engaged in this type of work. She had 200 cards of names the *Ledger* Society Department wished to contract regularly by telephone, to find out what they were doing and weddings and births in their midst. Agnes had been doing this work for some time and was now ready to relinquish it; someone else would be required to take on the cards.

The *Evening Public Ledger* was situated in a block-square building at Sixth and Chestnut Streets, near Independence Hall. Nearby was the Curtis Publishing Co., with its beautiful mosaic mural designed by Maxfield Parrish and executed by Louis Comfort Tiffany in the huge lobby. I made an appointment to see Mrs. Anna May McCabe, the society editor, about the cards. She explained that I would do the work at home and it would take only a few hours a day. After four years in a speciality shop and four in a restaurant, working at least eight hours a day, six days a week, I was geared to something more intensive. Dressed in black from head to foot, stockings excepted, with a decided air of indoor employment about me, I asked Mrs. McCabe if she did not have any eight-hour-a-day positions. She did not.

I took the 200 cards home to my bedroom in Chestnut Hill. It was not the same bedroom I had shared with my sister, Betty, on Gravers Lane. My brother Hawley had married and Mother had sold the Gravers Lane house and moved to a much smaller one, part of a group of twelve surrounding a courtyard, near the Chestnut Hill Pennsylvania Railroad Station. But as usual, she had decorated the little house to perfection. My sister, Betty, after six years of art study at the Pennsylvania Academy of Fine Arts and the Moore Institute of Design, was restoring portraits. Eventually, the Academy was one of her clients. Sullys, Peales and Gilbert Stuarts filled the house. She later took a studio on Germantown Avenue.

After eight years of going out to work in the morning, my new working environment was indeed a change. I sat at my desk in the bedroom and telephoned the 200 people on my cards in turn, two or three hours a day, asking if they were entertaining, having visitors, planning trips or had any news for the society columns of the

49

*Ledger.* Most of the people were cooperative, for it had already become the style to accept, even want publicity, instead of the old way of a woman's name appearing in the paper just when she made her debut, was married, gave birth to a child, and when she died. I had a good voice, which helped. At the end of the month, I would paste in strips all the published items I had collected and take them in to Mrs. McCabe. For five months my earnings averaged about $50.00 a month. Mother and Betty kept me financially afloat.

Anna May McCabe was a rather large-featured woman with a gift for promotion. She had iron gray hair wrapped in braids, a strong, quick brain and a sense of quality. She could take a production like, for instance, the LaScala Opera Company, and put it on the map. With many contacts, she was able to arouse the interest of prominent women in a project, enlist them and get them to serve as sponsors. She had a genuine interest in the social life of Philadelphia and a wholesome respect for prominent families. Her manner was not ingratiating or insincere; she naturally gave them what she considered their deferential due.

Mrs. McCabe's husband, Andrew, was not well and she bore the burden of financially supporting the family. There were two boys and a girl, Andrew, Jr., Aloysius and Elaine. Aloysius was graduated summa cum laude when he studied law at Harvard and married a girl who also did. Mrs. McCabe was very bright. When The *Ledger* folded, she took a test in shorthand, which she had not used for years, and came flying through with 130 words a minute. She was fair and could laugh, and we laughed. I recall she said to me: "Ellen, remember, there is always a tomorrow in the newspaper business." She meant that a gray day today, might turn out to be sunny one tomorrow, but she also meant that what you wrote today you must stand by tomorrow. Another thing she said was: "This, too, will pass." It was a saying that helped her throughout her life.

We became dear friends, and I shall always remember this first editor who steered and helped me through the doors of journalism, an encouraging and salutary influence in my life as long as she lived.

**********

Society reporting was an important phase of the newspaper business in 1938, although not as important as it had been in 1928, for already Mr. Roosevelt had raised his silver head and declared that $25,000 was enough for the rich to live on, and the "common man," the average worker in factory and plant, was coming into the focus of the limelight. A sinister expression, "fellow traveler," had also appeared on the national scene. But society news was still important.

In addition to telephoning the names on my cards, Mrs. McCabe began sending me out to cover events: opera, debutante teas and dances, weddings and receptions, prestigious club or organization meetings, hunt meets and dog shows.

At every important change in our life, every milestone, there probably is a day, even an hour, which consciously or unconsciously marks the passage from one part of it to another. One crosses over a bridge which leads from the shore of our former intent to another land. Time and circumstances, often desire, have landed us on the opposite shore and there is no turning back.

My passage from a searching, groping girl to a reporter occurred on the night I was sent with a photographer to take pictures of people going up the steps of Philadelphia's Academy of Music, on an opening night of the Metropolitan Opera. Heretofore, my jobs had been those of at least attempted service. I had been in no way conspicuous or assertive. Now as I stood in the November cold approaching people whom I had formerly been among, asking them to pose, holding the flashlight for the photographer, being both conspicuous and acquisitive - in short, being everything that my training had precluded - I passed from citizen to reporter. My life was changed; there would be no return and the years would assure that I would never be quite the same again. I was no longer a marcher in the parade but a reporter of it. I have held up the flashlight for forty years, and I have never had a desire to lower it.

Philadelphia and environs are about as English as anything we have in America. So many of its early settlers came from there. English customs, from goose to plum pudding to hunting to cricket, have been carried on. Nathaniel Burt, whose book, *The Perennial Philadelphians: The Anatomy of an American Aristocracy*, appeared in 1963, raises the question if Philadelphia has not produced, perhaps, the only true American aristocracy. Undoubtedly this has been contested, i.e., Boston, Baltimore, Charleston et al.

The important things to remember in a society column in those days were who was there and what they wore. What the spectators did, other than arrive in a tally-ho or lean against a fence, was negligible. The names - there was, as in all cities, a hierarchy of names - came first, and the costumes second. Again, as E. Digby Baltzell points out in his *Philadelphia Gentlemen: The Making of a National Upper Class*, (1958), which is considered the definitive work on the city's social system, some names which were distinguished in the 17th and 18th centuries have vanished from the face of Pennsylvania; and others, unknown even in Colonial times, have taken their place. At any rate, a society reporter was pleased when she could include in her column a Cadwalader or a Biddle, the Philadelphia equivalent of a Boston Cabot or Lowell, i.e., "In Boston, the land of the bean and the cod, where the Lowells speak only to Cabots and the Cabots speak only to God." The Philadelphia counter-axiom to this is: "When a Biddle's drunk, he thinks he's a Cadwalader."

The hunt meets and horse and dog shows were, and still are, a vital facet of life on the Main Line and in surrounding Chester County. Horse and dog shows usually are given for the benefit of some hospital. There was often a grandstand. The hounds in the dog shows usually were tended by Scotch or Irish grooms, ruddy-faced Britishers in sport hats and puttees.

We wrote out our stories in longhand and gave them to veteran telegraphers, who, by Morse code on small tickers, sent them on to the papers, a distance of say 20 to 30 miles. In later years, when out of town on assignment, we took our copy to Western Union offices, wherever we might be; nearly every comparatively small town had one. A great relief came over one, as often late at night, when one delivered one's story at the W.U. office and went back to one's hotel to sleep. Few rests are sweeter than that of a reporter who has finished his copy and is free of it. But this dispatch by veteran telegraphers, sitting in a small tent at horse or dog shows, had a particularly romantic, almost medieval quality about it. The casual but sure, almost magical passage of thought from one place to another smacked just a little of a runner from the jousts of the Round Table, hurrying to bring King Arthur the results. The pride of a young stringer on hearing his story ticked across even so few miles is understandable.

Here is an example of what sped over the wires:

Bryn Mawr Horse Show, Sept. 20 (1938) - It's jolly horse show weather - there is no "neighing" about that. Society, patrician horses and blue ribbon hounds arrived for the forty-third annual Bryn Mawr Horse Show with the chanticleer this morning.

A decidedly Kentucky accent drifted about the hound show ring, as velvet-capped grooms from southern states whispered inspiring words in their charges' floppy ears.

The crisp, privet-edged ring was active with black, brown and gray beauties winnowing enjoyment.

Smart Philadelphians in English tweeds, vivid stocks and classic felt applauded with zest.

Mr. J. Stanley Reeve has donned a pearl gray bowler and tweeds with taupe necktie and vest...

A cerise brocaded stock accents Mrs. A. Biddle Duke's riding habit...

Sidney S. Sharp, in canary yellow wool, is accompanied by her little hound, Scuttle. This is Scuttle's first horse or hound season. She looks terrified, but unquestionably will gain confidence as the afternoon wears on...

Again - May 18, 1939:

The bugle call to horse echoed across the rolling countryside at Rose Tree yesterday, and along the dumbell course, etched in white fencing and sprinkled with buttercups, to the newly-leaved treetops veiled in faint blue haze.

Scarlet jockey caps were pulled a little further down, glossy manes given a final good-luck pat, the air punctuated by a shot - and they were off for the first card of the eighty-year-old Fox Hunting Club's spring race meeting.

Mrs. Gouverneur Cadwalader, watching the flying picture from her box, wore a suit of light tan tweed, fastened with square leather buttons. Her natural straw hat with a high crown was banded by two tiers of grosgrain ribbon.

Stepping into her black coupe with its wide yellow stripe, Mrs. Howe Low wore a taupe gabardine tailleur, one lapel accented by a small wooden duck. With this went a chartreuse felt hat shaped like a jockey cap, and matching quilted pocketbook.

In the spring of 1939, the *Ledger's* managing editor decided he wanted a society column that incorporated bits of harmless gossip about Philadelphians. The daily society column of the *Evening Ledger* had long gone under the title "Just Gossip About People," with the fictitious byline of Nancy Wynne. To augment coverage of general social events, the paper now sought more personal items, and someone to write them. Inez Robb, of the *New York Daily News*, who gained entrance to fashionable houses by a polite manner and the wearing of white gloves (an open sesame to butlers), was setting an example of a more intimate type of society reportage which may have sparked the idea.

The assignment would be the coverage of selected general social events, as I had been doing intermittently for almost a year, and in the course of them to pick up flotsam and jetsam for the column. One person would write it; five, including me, tried out. I sat in that little bedroom overlooking the garden in Chestnut Hill and began composing small bits about people and things I had seen in my social rounds as a correspondent. All the stifled imagination of the previous years came to my aid, like a freshet suddenly released, as I typed out - by then I had learned to type - five trial columns on a rented typewriter.

A few days after submitting the columns, Mrs. McCabe called me into the office and offered me the post, as a regular staffer for The *Evening Public Ledger* at $25.00 a week. Much later, she told me that the managing editor, upon reading the columns, had said: "Get that girl - at any price."

Many years have passed since that spring afternoon when I came out of the *Ledger* building onto the street, but I can still feel the wings that lifted my mind and spirit. At last, at last - I had found my way!

# 11

## Two Pointed Foxes

### Just Gossip About
### PEOPLE

### by Nancy Wynne

*Fancy Fields*
*A Castle Overseas*
*In the Victorian Manner*

---

I could tell fancy tales of Fancy Fields, Mrs. George Willing's superb estate in Chestnut Hill, and then go on dreaming of others ad infinitum. One of them is that Mrs. Willing has an Italian gardener who creates his own designs and casts fascinating garden ornaments. He made the lovely stone pineapples which dot the top of the pink brick walls surrounding these colorful acres. Vases, lions and balustrades appear via Frank, who for thirty years has been ready and very willing.

**********

Henry McIlhenny, of Germantown, sails for France with his mother and sister aboard the trusty craft Queen Mary on June 22. After crepes suzette in Paris, this bright and colorful young man will take to his Glenveagh castle in County Donegal, Ireland, till the leaves crisp up in September. Crepes suzette are fine for a time, but when all's said and done, there is really nothing like potatoes!

**********

A guest bedroom in Mr. and Mrs. John B. Prizer's new house in Chestnut Hill suits me to a Victorian tee. Three of the walls are dove gray and the fourth, behind the bed, is done in white with a pattern of Staffordshire dogs, lambs and flowers. I can just imagine creeping down under lavendered sheets and drifting off into the 'eighties in no time at all.

**********

Ann Dickinson, a this-year's deb, is driving a garnet roadster with A.M.D. in pink on the door. Even at the wheel of this chic car, Ann looks as if she would trade it for a good horse any day.

**********

First it was a timid carnation...now the vogue is an immense gardenia. Why don't the June bridegrooms wear a peony as a boutonniere and be done with?

(*Evening Public Ledger* - June 9, 1939)

For about a year, I romped through the social fields of Philadelphia and environs covering debuts, weddings, opera, concerts, exhibitions, lectures, benefits, clubs, horse shows, dog shows, boating events - any occasion where fashionable people gathered. Along the way, from their ballrooms to their bedrooms, I picked up items for the column. They flowed like honey out of my typewriter. Simple, flattering, personal bits that would not have hurt a mosquito, written in days when people were not as afraid to have their living environment and appurtenances publicly described; indeed, they often were pleased with such description.

It might be past midnight when I had gone back to the office and written my story of the opera, a dance or a ball. The last train left for Chestnut Hill at 12:35 a.m. So I had found a little room in town.

Nobody thought I could find a room on my meager salary, but I did. It was on South 17th Street, near Spruce, on the third floor, with use of the bath on the floor below. There was a hot plate and the fire escape was a rope ladder. But it was "Seventh Heaven" to me, a pied-à-terre of my own at $3.50 a week.

Across the hall lived a Works Progress Administration (WPA) artist, Hilda (time has erased her last name). She was a lovely person, warm and talented, and we shared time and food together. Dr. Albert C. Barnes, the art collector, had bought one of her pieces of sculpture, a little animal, for the Barnes Foundation that he established in Merion, Pa., which was a real distinction for Hilda.

While we were neighbors, Hilda was working on an elongated mother and child figure, the parent bending backward and the child doing likewise, making a visual circle of childhood play. Years later, I saw a reproduction of that statue in a shop window, but I could not find the name of the artist. I'm sure it was Hilda's work. I lost track of her. The last I heard, she was designing fabrics in

New York. But the months of living across the hall from each other linger. With little money and sharing simple food, we were so transported by our respective work that we hardly noticed our surroundings - ambition and aspiration running high.

Changes were afoot at the *Philadelphia Ledger*, which apparently had not been doing well. Stanley Walker, the famous city editor of the *New York Herald Tribune*, was imported to replace the managing editor. I can see that editor walking out the door of the paper after 25 years there, and the sight has always lingered as an example of the transitory quality of newspapers and their employment.

Why Stanley Walker came to Philadelphia is a mystery. Perhaps it was the same spirit that brought him from his native Texas to New York, where he became a highly successful city editor and the teacher and mentor of scores of bright young newspapermen. Perhaps this short, wiry man with an acquiline profile and amazingly keen eyes thought it would be a change from the atmosphere and pace of New York. Or again, maybe he thought it would be an "entertaining" experience.

Asked to an evening soiree at the home of Emily Balch, a Virginian who formerly edited one of the first "little magazines" in the South, and later married a member of a well-known Philadephia family, Mr. Walker reportedly stood in a corner and demonstrated a game of matches, popular at Bleeck's Artists and Writers Club, a hangout for the New York press, across from the *Tribune*.

Stanley Walker brought a number of people with him. On the City Side came Tom O'Hara, brother of the author, John, and Gilbert Milstein, a promising newsman. Tom later went on to the *Herald Tribune* and Gilbert became a TV writer. They were young men then, under Mr. Walker's aegis. To the women's page of the *Ledger*, he brought three women: The first, Haydie Yeats, former editor and, I believe, a founder and developer of the A & P *Family Circle* magazine; Ruth Howell, a former staffer on the Washington Star and editor of a dance magazine, who worked under Mrs. Yeats, and a reporter from New York named Charlotte Huber.

By this time, I had suggested and was doing a series called "Top Flight Women in Philadelphia," brief interviews with a picture of prominent people. The following piece on Mrs. Nicholas Biddle was typical:

*EVENING PUBLIC LEDGER*, NOVEMBER 15, 1939

## TOP FLIGHT WOMEN
in Philadelphia

---

### Mrs. Nicholas Biddle

Tall, olive-skinned, with dark, lanquid eyes and sleek, center-parted hair, Mrs. Nicholas Biddle "does things" for long hoop earrings, a Spanish shawl and brilliant, exotic clothes that might well send Carmen back to the cigar factory. In her debutante dancing days, she even did Spanish and Hoya dances.

Moreover, in spite of her Quaker ancestry, she thinks it would be "tops" to be an opera star. And well she might. Her beauty is renowned, she has been painted or sculptured by Joseph Sacs, Julian Story, R. Taft McKenzie and Donoghue Chandor; looks best in her favorite red, leaning against the jaguar skin on the sofa in her husband's den.

She has accompanied her husband, Lieutenant Colonel Nick Biddle, great-grandson of Nicholas of banking fame, on hunting expeditions, and is no mean shot herself, although she's given up "roughing it," except for Southern shooting trips and a little Sunday morning winging of pheasants, with the pointer, Belle, and the Labrador, Duke, to retrieve.

The colonel's collection of Alaskan moose from his latest trip will be shown officially at the Academy of Sciences tonight. Mrs. Biddle, the former Sarah Lippincott, hates monotony in anything. She lets the cook order, entertains casually in the combined living and dining room of their 250-year-old farmhouse, Springhead, in Jenkintown. There, when anybody wants a drink of water, he may go and dip up one from the old bucket by the well.

Casual rather than purposeful, she accomplishes her ends without heroics. She is secretary of the women's auxiliary of Abington Hospital, and is on the Women's Committee of the Art Museum, and last year headed the Salvation Army's drive along York Road.

A member of the American Swedish Society, she really knows something about Sweden, and she and the colonel were in the party of Philadelphians who last year presented bronze tablets commemorating the landing of the Swedes in America to King Gustaf.

Beautiful clothes are her weakness; she loves jewels, particularly rubies, emeralds and sapphires, and won't look down her aquiline nose at sables or costume jewelry. She doesn't favor perfume.

She always knocks wood when she boasts, but the set of ladder-back chairs in the den, with copper plates announcing that they have seated the Wharton and Fisher families for four generations, haven't a nick or a dent in them, so boasting is not a weakness. She keeps her own counsel, reads some, mostly biographies, and pals with her five children.

The first crisis came when Charlotte Huber was assigned to do a "Top Flight Woman" one week, and I another. To me, it was like having someone steal a part of my entrails. Charlotte Huber was a medium-sized, French-looking woman who wore turbans with her brown curls coming out the front. She had been on New York publications and typified the new, slick, lighter touch writing then prevalent there. (We later became friends.)

Mr. Walker stopped the anecdotes in the "Just Gossip About People" column, which, in their way, already had attracted New York attention. The occasion was when I had written this; it bore the head "Regal Foxes."

Once upon a time there were two perfectly beautiful black pointed foxes. They lived in the forest and never even heard of the Acorn Club, the Philadelphia Orchestra or the Metropolitan Opera...But one day they became the regal furs worn by Mrs. Henry Brinton Coxe. Need we tell you they have had a social whirl ever since? At present they are keeping company in the evenings with a handsome gown of black lace...

The item appeared in the *New Yorker* with the footnote: "No, you need never tell us anything else again."

The anecdotes in the column discontinued, I began to gravitate toward the women's pages for assignments. I think Mrs. McCabe was sorry to see me go. But she always had my welfare at heart. And there was more writing opportunity on the women's pages.

The Lafayette Restaurant was near the *Ledger*. At the end of the day, sitting in the lounge-bar with its stuffed pheasant perched high over the mirror behind the bottles, I began to realize what kind of mind I had. It was a whimsical mind, yet critical, a mind interested in the poetic and dramatic. Some formulated intelligence, biased and immature as it was, began to arise in me, not just a pattern of what I had been taught, but how I individually, at that particular time of my life, saw the world. Needless to say, it has changed somewhat since. It was a limited viewpoint, but it was mine. It had some connection between myself and my environment. And it was as if, from the midst of a cocoon of tradition and circumstance, I had suddenly broken through into the sunlight.

# 12

## Sequins on Fur

A NOTED FASHION DESIGNER in the early 1940s said, "Look out for the world when it begins to sew sequins on fur." The United States was on the upswing in 1940 and most of '41. Rising from the ashes of the Depression, it was blossoming with new manufacture and luxuries. Theories, which sometimes become submerged in the harsh realities of war and poverty, were rising like mushrooms in a shady spot. The country stretched itself and smiled again in its legendary sun of prosperity. And in few places was this feeling of exultation more evident than in the women's pages of newspapers.

I was caught up in this kaleidoscopic scene. It was wonderful training for a young reporter. Almost every day into Philadelphia came persons on tour, stylists, cosmetologists, educators, entertainers of all kinds, cranks and freaks. I must have interviewed 200 people of varied interests during this period.

Haydie Yeats moved through the small golden oak office of the Woman's Page like a tornado. She was a good five-feet-ten with a mane of light brown hair. She wore a long polo coat, Indian turquoise and beaten silver jewelry and carried an expensive cigarette holder. She was charged with abounding energy and enthusiasm and her walk was a stride. I particularly remember a few of the stories I did for her.

The first assignment I had from her was to go to the Jersey Coast and take pictures of people on the beach. The photographer was named Gus Pasquerella. It seems a good time to speak of photographers and how much, through the years, I have learned from them.

With the exception of a very few editors, I believe I have learned more from photographers than any other source in the newspaper business. They are a special breed, practitioners of a medium that does not lie; they look truth in the face. A second's delay, a single misstep, and they miss their moment in history, a moment that cannot be recaptured by reminiscence or padded by imagination. The particular angle and attitude from which they see that moment is an individual one with each man, but to capture it is the ruling mandate of their lives. Often in keen competition with their fellows, they jostle for place to photograph the beauty, joy, tragedy and degradation of the world. They are an independent lot; you cannot tell a photographer directly what to do; if you are wise, you will only suggest. The immediacy, the courage and the agility that they teach a young reporter are inestimable. Most of them are in a continual state of complaint against their immediate boss, the City Editor or the general management of the paper as a whole; if all else is alright, they can take it out on the camera, its cost, method of operation or performance. Beyond the hurry and confusion of their lives is usually a cherished, normal home life, with occasional trips to far off places. Most are at least partial artists. Gus Pasquerella was a fine photographer. The lesson I learned on that first assignment with him had to do with women with fat legs. A woman might be lovely to the knees and then show a pair of over-sized shanks. Faced with such a situation on that Jersey shore, Gus took me aside:

"Make her kneel down," he said, "and her legs won't show." Bent on her knees to make sand castles, the lady looked great.

Then there was the morning when, slapping my 5-foot, 2-1/2-inch height on the shoulder to nearly spin it across the foot, Haydie Yeats said, "Taussig, go up and interview John Fredericks (the well-known milliner who was in town) in 3 minutes."

Mr. Fredericks was helpful. "I was in another city recently," he said, "and a young woman asked me how many hats I thought a woman should have. I told her, one to wear and two for illusion."

The third story I particularly remember was an interview with Mrs. J. Bertram Hervey, president of the Philadelphia Federation of Women's Clubs and Allied Organizations.

"Taussig," said Haydie Yeats, "I want you to go up and see Mrs. Hervey and ask her what she thinks about this new bill that is being considered by the State Legislature for castration."

Keeping a poker yet knowing face, I nodded and went into the City Room to look up the word in Webster's dictionary; I had never heard of it. To my horror and embarrassment, I learned it was emasculation by removal of the testes. The bill recommended it only for degenerates. Mortified to the marrow and in a quandary as to how to approach Mrs. Hervey, I took the trolley car to West Philadelphia where she lived. She answered the door in person, a pretty woman dressed in a tea gown printed in spring flowers.

"Come in, Miss Taussig," she said, "I'm delighted to see you," and leading the way into the living room, "I have just had my living room done over in the Tudor manner, don't you think it's attractive?"

I looked around at the room, paneled in oak and hung with dark blue velvet curtains; it was very English. But decoration was not on my mind at that point, and I sat down gingerly on a velvet-cushioned chair, trying to muster my forces for the interview ahead. Mrs. Hervey paved the way.

"You must have something to drink, some refreshment," she said, and disappeared through the dining room into, I suppose, the pantry, from where she rolled out a large tea cart, supporting a number of bottles of liquor and soft drinks. Tall glasses bearing some designs accompanied them. The popular idea of the Press is that they are always thirsty, particularly for alcohol.

"I have just had my highball glasses painted with the wives of Henry the Eight," said Mrs. Hervey blithely. "What will you have?"

Never drinking very much and stupefied by the present situation, I said I would have a little Coca Cola.

"And the glass?" Mrs. Hervey asked.

I settled on Katharine of Aragon.

Mrs. Hervey obliged, and we sat sociably chatting, the interview weighing like lead in the pit of my stomach. Suddenly she jumped up. "Oh!" she exclaimed, "I forgot the cheese and crackers," and again she made for the pantry.

This time she emerged with an enormous tray of crackers encircling a centerpiece of sliced cheese. Glad of any delay, I looked down at the tray she held out, preparatory to selecting some cheese to go with the crackers. I noticed some design on the tray under the spaces between the cheese. Mrs. Hervey apparently saw me looking. Cocking her head on one side, as lighthearted as a March robin, she announced, "Henry is on the cheese tray!"

After that, I had little difficulty in asking Mrs. Hervey, president of the Philadelphia Federation of Women's Clubs and Allied Organizations, what she thought about the bill for castration of degenerate males in the Commonwealth of Pennsylvania.

Ruth Howell was a contrast to Haydie Yeats. A well-built woman with a calm New England face, hair parted in the center, she was a controlled, able editor. She gave my catapultic drive a background of assurance and greatly encouraged me by calling me "the girl with the golden pen." Perhaps imagination is not a denominational quality, and in some way I had been able to make the transition from the approbatory approach of the Society Page to the more realistic and critical outlook of the Women's Page.

I particularly remember one golden autumn afternoon, when I interviewed Marian Anderson for Ruth Howell. It was one of my first interviews and, literally thousands later, I still think Miss Anderson is the most impressive person - male or female - I have ever met.   Her stature derived from her belief that her then magnificent contralto voice was given to her by God and was His instrument.   It is a belief that few human beings hold; I believe Enrico Caruso felt likewise.   But when it is truly believed, it produces an Olympian character who radiates an ultimateness that is not found in the average individual or artist.

There were not as many press conferences in those days.   You sought out your subject and, if you were enterprising and fortunate, you found him.   I found Miss Anderson at her mother's little house in Philadelphia where she had been born.   The brief interview, as it appeared in the *Evening Public Ledger*, tells the story better than I can rewrite it:

## MARIAN ANDERSON HOME, GETS BIGGEST THRILL
### by Ellen Taussig

"Nobody knows the trouble the world's seeing---but Jesus."

The poplar trees on S. Martin St. rustled harmoniously because they shaded a great secret.   In a wee blue-shuttered house---762 to be exact---one of their children had come home.   A little girl who, after singing before England's King and Queen and being decorated by the First Lady of her own land, still lists as the most thrilling moment of her career as a "voice heard once in a century" the time she saw her name on a pamphlet announcing that Marian Anderson, 10-year-old contralto, would sing at the corner Baptist church.   For, you see, the little girl was really only 8.

### HOME AGAIN

Today, following her sixth annual concert at the Academy of Music on Thursday night, a record never before achieved even by the great Patti, she had come home to the neat little parlor of her mother, formerly a laundress, where a radio which "often brings Marian home" is the center of interest.

Dressed in a sheer gray wool ensemble, with her stately head wrapped in paisley silk, the feminine Caruso of the era acclaimed the world soul sick because it had bowed down to golden calves.   "While formerly religion had played a great part in this country, many people being united by the thought of God, if not in specific belief, they have now turned to idols---money, power, sects and charlatans."

### PREDICTS REVIVAL

Miss Anderson predicts a great revival of hymns in these wartimes, both in church and on the stage. "Hymns give people assurance and confidence."

Greater understanding of her people is the great need of the colored race at this time, in her opinion. "My people are often mistaken in what they aim to convey; judged unfairly. You can't judge an individual, even by seeing a million people."

### POPLARS ARE PROUD

The sun was lowering on Martin St. Sixty concerts lay ahead of its little girl.

Calling "Good-bye, Pet," to her aged mother, her arms full of white chrysanthemums, she paused on the stoop. "No, I'm not going to lighten my program because of the war. I find people want to forget the trouble they've seen, and this can be accomplished by serious songs which absorb sorrow rather than the frivolous."

The poplar trees waved a proud adieu. After all, they had shaded greatness.

After I had returned to the office and written this story, Ruth opened a bottle left by a press agent of a liquer called "Forbidden Fruit."

I can still sense the golden radiance of Miss Anderson's presence, her touching devotion to her mother, the small purposefully furnished parlor, the scent of the baskets of salmon gladioli that I sat among, like a rabbit, in the back of the car, as I talked to her on the way to the station. And the heavy, sultry exoticism of "Forbidden Fruit."

The stories behind the public lives of the successful often are both amazing and touching. Like Sophie Tucker stepping down the alley from the Forrest Theater stage door to meet me, wearing a print blouse, black skirt, short fur jacket and moderated coachman's hat, (then in vogue), and fuchsia lipstick. She had no time for war or its songs.

"I never had one on my program and I don't intend to start now," she said. "Dozens of the same old kind have been submitted to me recently. People go to the theater and cafes to relax. I'll leave the war to the radio (no TV yet) and press."

Sophisticated songs with a bit of philosophy tucked in the vest pocket is what people liked, Miss Tucker had found.

She was performing six nights and two matinees at the theater and also did nightly shows on the Hotel Walton roof. It seemed requisite; among her near relations she had 14 dependants.

"This interview has been so nice and short," remarked Brian Aherne, after I talked with him and Joan Fontaine for about twenty minutes. "The last person who interviewed us (obviously a magazine writer) came and stayed three days, and at every meal he picked up his plate to see where the china was made." Evening paper reporters don't have time for plate juggling.

How far the world was flying above--or below--reality perhaps is illustrated by my little session with Elsie the Borden Cow:

### ELSIE, GLAMOR GIRL OF THE HERD, GRANTS AN INTERVIEW
#### by ELLEN TAUSSIG

The lowing herd USED to wind slowly o'er the lea--but that's old as the hills.

Today a pedicured cow winds languorously down the runway of a leading department store, giving an admiring populace the once-over. Interviewed in her Early American boudoir at Gimbel's, Elsie, the World's Fair glamor heifer, is a striking example of just how far a girl can go---if she has beauty, intelligence and poise--and is crème de la crème in pasture circles.

#### ANCESTRY COUNTS
"I do think ancestry counts in the long run," she breathed delicately, chewing one of the 17 varieties of dehydrated hay and ground grains especially prepared for her. "The birthrate in our family has always been good. My mother's name was 'Perennial Lobelia'; my father's, 'You'll Do's Volunteer'---I was his 167th kiddie," she smiled, dropping feathery lashes over orbs bound to hit the bull's-eye.

"I was chosen over 150 other purebreds at the fair; there wasn't even a contest--the others just never had a chance," and she gave one of the four velvet negligees (or throws) especially created for her in New York, a slight hitch of natural triumph.

#### FAMILY PORTRAITS
Elsie's belief in heritage is further confirmed by the oil portraits of her Uncle Bostwick, in rear admiral's attire, and

Aunt Bess, as a clover-bearing bride---hanging on the maple-paneled walls of her deluxe apartment.

"Your life has been very varied since?" we inquired with natural awe for the great (and the hoof).

"I've been entertained extensively," she snortled, "at a cocktail party at the Hotel Roosevelt, the annual ball of the swank New York Seventh Regiment, and as hostess at the American Newspaper Publishers Association. My first motion picture, "Little Men," in which my daughter, Beulah, and I co-star with Kay Francis and Jack Oakie, will appear shortly."

### MOTHER AND CHILD

Like many a career woman these days, Elsie has left hubby Elmer back on the farm in Plainsboro. But Beulah, her six-month-old offspring, bawls in a pen close to Mama. Beulah's a copycat, has a green wrapper like Mother's big one, nozzles a large rubber ball and a rock salt ice cream cone. She was born in Hollywood, and Elsie wouldn't budge into the special chartered train back home until she saw Beulah being led into another compartment in the car.

At that, she didn't lie down from coast-to-coast, worrying about how her babe was doing. On the movie set, Beulah got tired and lay down for a 15-minute rest. The director wouldn't think of disturbing her, although that little stretch cost the studio $1000.

### MUST KEEP UP

After you've once jumped over the moon, you have to keep up, Elsie asserts, flourishing her olive-oil-polished hoofs and horns. Her boudoir, lit by milk-bottle lamps, is perfumed with rose-odored deodorant. She gets a soap-flake bath once weekly and a thorough brushing thrice daily.

"Brush, brush, brush for beauty!" she bellows.

Elsie produces four gallons of milk a day.

Meantime, Stanley Walker, now editor of the *Ledger*, was perusing Philadelphia. Apparently, it was too much for his sense of humor. The withdrawn self-importance of the city, its calm and serenity in the face of the rest of the world, its emphasis upon and reverence for the Establishment, was something that permeated the very atmosphere of the city to a degree he was unable to contain. Mr. Walker began to laugh at Philadelphia. He began a little paper within the paper each Saturday, called *The Fellow Traveler*, which caught, in a humorous way, the communistic undertones that were surfacing on the national scene at the time. It included a series called "Great Women of Philadelphia and Environs" which parodied the "Top Flight Women" profiles that Charlotte and I were turning out. An example from the first issue of Jan. 6, 1940, follows:

### GREAT WOMEN
#### Of Philadelphia and Environs
(A series of intimate cameos and panoramas)
(Photo captioned Crazy Clare)

Two word description of Clarissa Trubitsch Baumgarten (Crazy Clare), the grande dame of Meeting House Lane: Problem Child.

Of course, when Clarissa was a little girl they didn't call them problem children, but that's what she was and is. Anything to be different. Born with two silver spoons in her mouth, of impeccable ancestry, Clarissa early in life showed signs of that roaming nature, that love of far horizons, which later took her the ends of the earth.

Her home, Red Gods' Roost, is a veritable treasure trove of trophies. It is a mecca for explorers, many of them moochers and nuisances of various sorts, all of whom are made welcome. With her first husband, Mike McGloin, Clarissa hunted Kodiak bears in Alaska; with her second, Reggie Ogden Primrose, she hunted the elusive springbok on the veldt; with her third, Oskar Olaf Svenson, 3rd, she led an expedition to capture the monster Galápagos turtles; with her fourth, Vladimir Trubitsch, she chased the rare Polish bison; with her fifth, Moe Baumgarten, she wrought havoc among the tigers of Bengal.

With her sixth - but why go on? She is shown here with Mitzi, her pet puma, which she and a boyfriend caught in the Grand Canyon - Ibid.

Stanley Walker lasted on the *Ledger* 8 months. It was said that he had nothing more than a "gentleman's agreement" with the management there. At any rate, he returned to New York, where he had made his name and where he truly belonged. Mr. Walker ignored the old saying "When in Rome, do as the Romans, etc." Atmospherically, he belonged in Philadelphia about as much as a bar belonged in the State House.

Generally speaking, it has been my observation that newspapers and their editors cannot change the character of a city. They can suggest new types of approach to the news; introduce trends and raise the standard of reporting and writing, but they cannot change the fundamental quality of the town where they operate. Only time can do that. Factors which formed the city and have been prevalent there for generations lie beneath its daily life and cannot be summarily uprooted. Papers have to tune in on a city's character and report its news - as it really is. Newspaper readers in Philadelphia do not want to be treated like New Yorkers, nor do those in Chicago as readers in Washington. They want indigenous reporting.

Purple prose was fading from the newspaper business and a slickness, a somewhat jaded realism, was replacing it, had indeed already replaced it on the better papers of New York, particularly the *Herald Tribune*. But it had not, to any extent, reached Philadelphia. To present things obliquely, perhaps even laughing at them en route, was not the Philadelphia way. Philadelphia was tradition grounded, and believed it had a social structure to uphold and support. Indeed it did possess qualities that were submerged under the great panorama and forward thrust of New York. Philadelphia believed in the past and the forms that had evolved from the past, and as again, Nathaniel Burt in *The Perennial Philadelphians* has pointed out, it was, at that time, content and satisfied with them and venerated them. Philadelphia was not like Taos or Greenwich Village or the Left Bank. Philadelphia braided its hair with garlands from England and was not too concerned, indeed shied away to a certain extent, from the latest hair pomade. It might be conspicuously shiny. But beneath its inability to laugh at itself, Philadelphia was above all else - sincere.

# Part IV

# Ripening of a Greenhorn

# 13

## The Whole, Wide World

PEARL HARBOR CHANGED ALL that. One of grandfather's six grandsons, Ensign Joseph K. Taussig, Jr., USN, 21, six months out of the Naval Academy, was Officer of the Deck of the Battleship *USS Nevada* for the forenoon watch on December 7, 1941. During the attack, he lay grievously wounded at his battle station - which he refused to leave - directing an anti-aircraft battery that led the heavily damaged ship out of the harbor, the only battleship to escape.

And out of the City Rooms of newspapers across the land, young men went to war. In the society departments, patriotism channeled through the Red Cross, the USO and benefits, began to feature prominently on the social calendar and new opportunities open to women due to the war were reflected in the women's pages.

I had become established as a women's page reporter on the *Evening Public Ledger*. In the summer of 1941, however, when an opening occurred by the departure of one of two women on the general news staff who left to be married, I was advised to take it, and eagerly accepted. An opening caused by death or marriage was practically the only way a woman could get on a general news staff in 1941. They were a rare breed. The City Side was an opportunity to look at the whole news scene through the eyes of an individual, rather than that of a woman, in short, as far as one's horizon permitted, to report on "the whole wide world."

So I slipped into the bride's desk. My assignments, in addition to internship as a general news reporter under the tutelage of Evelyn Shuler, the top woman, included an antiques column and the contribution of features to the magazine section.

The life of a city passes through the City Room of a newspaper, indeed that of the world, now even the universe. In former days, large newspapers had a local room, where the huge bulk of the area's news was handled, and other smaller rooms for state and national, financial and sports, and women's and society pages. Today, all general news is usually edited in one large space, with finance, sports and women's interests in separate areas. The society page, so alive for the first half of the century, now is practically extinct; few papers even give it a heading. The sociological change of the country has engulfed it.

Into the City Room by satellite, wireless, telephone and reporter come moon flights, shuttles, war, flood, famine, Washington, the

Pope, Hollywood, Las Vegas, courts, schools, wrecks, assassination and rape. It is here riots are recorded, reputations are lost, minors saved, heroes acclaimed, quintuplets born, the great eulogized, animals lost or found and the weather forecast. Here come the politicians, the publicists and the general public seeking to legislate, cite, disseminate or repress the news of the world.

The clock, of course, is the sentinel of the City Room. Under its impassive face, the men and women who put out the paper struggle to work in the early morning or spend the night hours completing their stints, with only pages of words to show for it; pages that may be used within the week to wrap up fish or batten packing boxes - yet in turn, which may influence the course of individual or communities' lives. Every day's paper is a segment of history.

A clock that ticks off a baby's first cry, a man or woman's last breath, the entrance of an era or a decade of decline. A graduation, a wedding, an anniversary, a promotion, an award, a scandal, an ostracism, a sentence, an imprisonment, a hanging, the electric chair. Spring, summer, autumn, winter; flood, snow, hurricane, tornado pass beneath the City Room clock's face. It records the life span of the newspaper itself, and even after the sheet has expired, and it has been taken down, the countless pages it has sired remain as the history of its time.

In the midst of the City Room, as its very heart, sits the city editor, usually a man, over whom this plethora of events, hopes, fears and causes break unceasingly, with no indication of how big a tidal wave will rise the next minute. I have seen many city editors. Most have one or more assistants, but the city editor himself, is supreme, responsible for the delivery of the news of the city. Someone has said his tenure is seven years. Indeed it is remarkable that he survives that long. There he sits, day by day, mentally and emotionally attuned to this catastrophic tide - yet never physically a part of it; he is entirely dependent on reporters and must sift and weigh, clarify and condense or expand what they tell him. Perhaps no other occupation, barring medicine, calls for such trust in the human race.

In many cases, the pressure makes way for pills, not drugs, but aids for digestion, high blood pressure, nerves; it would seem almost inevitable for these men who live the life of a city daily, without moving from a swivel chair or just walking a few steps to a neighboring desk. The fortunate get out before it destroys them. But there's really nowhere in the newspaper business for a city

editor to go except to a managing editorship. Like a 4-star general
or a 5-stripe admiral of the fleet, it is the only respectable goal.

The sense of humor of a city editor is not something to dally
with. Senses of humor differ widely anyway among people, let
alone those in such a heterogeneous post. You learn not to try a city
editor out; better stick to the story, which indeed may be humorous,
but don't match your reaction with his. You can fall flat on your
face.

The ripening of a green reporter can be both painful and
amusing. I learned the importance of punching in punctually at 8:30
a.m., reading my assignment for the day from the large book in
which it was entered, and then going out and having breakfast
before starting the day's work. I learned to meticulously keep an
expense account of the many trolley fares, telephone calls and tips
that a reportorial day could produce. And I learned the ethics of the
newspaper business, a business so different from anything else in
which I had any experience that one could wonder if ethics were
involved. But they are; even the "freedom of the press" involves
ethics.

The two tenets: the words "Off the Record" are sacred, and
there is the right of domain. If a person interviewed states that what
he says is off the record - unless the reporter prewarns him that he
cannot withold anything that is said - the reporter is bound to
observe that binding phrase. Secondly, a man's house is truly his
castle, and a reporter cannot enter unless he is permitted to do so.
Physical violence to obtain a story, also of course, is out of bounds
as it is in all situations of civilized society.

One of my first assignments on the city side of the *Evening
Public Ledger* was to interview the banker, Thomas William
Lamont. I always have had difficulty in balancing a checkbook, and
just why a fledgling reporter would be sent to interview this
knowledgeable financier, a partner in J. P. Morgan & Co., is
typical of the amazing scope to which reporters can be subjected.
This scope also is partly responsible for their cockiness - there is
nothing to do but be cocky when one is thrown so definitely out of
one's water. I cannot imagine what questions I put to Mr. Lamont.
Two or three times along the way, he muttered: "Off the Record." I
did not know what it meant; the tenor of my society and women's
page assignments had never been sufficiently rarefied to elicit it. So
on concluding the interview, I delivered to the newspaper every
scrap of information he had told me. Fortunately, nothing I had
asked or that he had said had world-shaking implications. At dinner
that evening, however, describing the interview to Mrs. McCabe

and Evelyn, I was roundly scolded. It was explained to me that I had broken one of the few cardinal rules of the business, and that I must never, never do it again. I did not forget.

In theory, of course, the right of domain can be challenged. One of my larger assignments for Morris Litman, the city editor of the *Ledger*, involved the estate of the late Joseph W. Widener in Elkins Park. The imminent question was whether the late Mr. Widener had left his collection of art, 300 paintings, sculptures and tapestries, to the Philadelphia Museum of Art, or had it already gone to the National Gallery in Washington? There was a report he had felt the collection would be accessible to more people if placed in the Capital, and again, that Mr. Widener was not satisfied with the social reception his family had received in Philadelphia. The collection included works of Raphael, Rembrandt, Bellini, Van Dyke, Titian, including his famous "Venus and Apollo," and Donatello. Dr. Abraham S. W. Rosenbach, the renowned Philadelphia bibliophile and bookseller, had estimated its value at $7,141,060. Others had gone much higher.

Peter A.B. Widener and William Elkins were butchers and butter-and-egg men, respectively, in the Reading Terminal Market. They invested in public transportation, became millionaires and began to "go about" in Philadelphia. A story goes that a Philadelphian of more distinguished lineage, meeting Mr. Widener at a party, exclaimed, "Well, well, here is my old friend, Widener, the butcher." To which, Mr. Widener replied, "Yes, and if I didn't have any more sense than you have, I would still be back in that stall."

The Widener family homestead, "Lynnewood Hall," was a Georgian mansion designed by Horace Trumbauer, with its formal French gardens laid out by Jacques Greber, redesigner of the outskirts of Paris. It was well staffed and I spent a day and a half intermittently ringing the bell, asking admittance, being turned down and finally, resorting to tipping. On the afternoon of the second day, I was admitted to the great hall to see Peter A. B. Widener II, grandson of the family's founder. It was hot and Mr. Widener was in his shirtsleeves. We sat on a bench in the hall which was hung with heavy portieres. Pent up with hours of reportorial assault on the house, in nervous excitement I greeted Mr. Widener with: "Hello, Mr. Widener! How about a drink?" Mr. Widener, whom I am sure was accustomed to the vagaries of the press, was very polite. He said: "No, I won't have one, thank you, but would you like one?" Mercifully, I declined.

The bench on which we sat had a view of the stairway leading up to the art gallery, the doors of which were firmly closed.  I interrogated Mr. Widener on the destination of his father's art collection; he was noncommittal.  Speculatively, I eyed the doors of the art gallery.  One good sprint up those steps and I would know if the collection was there or already had gone to Washington.  However, some remnant of gentility restrained me from taking the leap.  Perhaps the final block was that I felt there were footmen back of those portieres who would tackle me down if I did so.  I left without my story.

"You got nothing," said Morris Litman in disgust, when I returned to the office, "nothing."  Soberly reporting the interview at another dinnertime with my mentors, Mrs. McCabe and Evelyn, I learned not to open an interview asking for a drink.

I was to return to the Widener house in later years, however, and emerge a victor.

Incidently, Mr. Widener did leave his entire collection to the National Gallery.  A forerunner of his largess was his $100,000 collection of acacias, allegedly the finest in the world, and for years, the pride of the Philadelphia Flower Show.  I interviewed Arthur Hauenstein, superintendent of the Widener greenhouses, who had worked with the genus since 1905.  The 588 plants of 16 varieties of the Australian species - many more than 15 feet tall - were sent to the National Gallery in the Spring of 1941, in full bloom.  After the blooming season, they were moved to the Washington Botanical Gardens.  Earnest Black, one of the staff of 32 at the Widener greenhouses, had had charge of the acacias since 1906.  Mr. Black was buried the day those trucks rolled South.  As for the acacias, they were used at the Gallery again in 1942, then moved back to the Botanical Gardens once more.  Many were lost during the first two years.  By the third year, all had joined their former caretaker.

**********

The *Evening Public Ledger* was not in good health.  After Mr. Walker came Cummins Catherwood, an auburn-haired, moustached man of military carriage, with money, who walked through the City Room in a velvet-collared overcoat and derby.  More demanding than his commanding presence, however, was the protest of the American Newspaper Guild, C.I.O., against the laying off of 30 employees whom management thought superfluous.

Harry Nason, a brilliant editor, formerly on the *New York Sun*, was brought in.  I was told that he was one of the few men in the business who could visualize a page in type before it was set. When Pearl Harbor was attacked, he did something he had always wanted to do; he published the banner headline in white against a black background. It was immensely striking. But even his originality and energy could not stem the tide. The paper went steadily down. Court proceedings were in progress and staff morale deteriorated. Men sitting at the copydesk, played cards.

Out on assignment toward the end, I telephoned in a story.

"Taussig is still working!" exclaimed Nick Carter, then an assistant city editor, in amusement.

I had come a long way to be able to work on a newspaper and I didn't intend to give up the ship as long as it was afloat.

To describe Rutledge (Nick) Carter would take a Faulkner and a Damon Runyon, with perhaps a little help from A. A. Milne thrown in. In the first place, he was a "Virginia" Carter, the genuine article of note and plantations, although with the exception of an uprightness of bearing and the unassailable air of people who come from a satisfactory line and know it - genealogy was not on Nick Carter's, at least conscious, mind. If one saw him, as I did on three newspapers, with a green eyeshade askew over his forehead, heard his chuckling and witnessed his valiant endeavor to keep his trousers up over his practically nonexistent hips, the uninitiated might wonder if Nick had a mind or if it had partially wandered off. How wrong the uninitiated might have been.

Long ago, probably prodded by shelves of good literature in some oak-shaded Virginia house, Nick had left the Plantation, physically and figuratively, and followed the trail of his heart to write stories for newspapers. Readable, entertaining stories written in an able, crisp way that makes such men and women invaluable, respected members of a newspaper's staff. Nick could take the most tangled, detailed, chaotic tale and whip it into highly readable shape, perhaps with more agility than anyone I've known. He had a sense of narrative and humor, yet never went overboard, sending it out from the keys of his typewriter with a light touch that piqued yet never weighted the reader.

Socially liquored he was sometimes pugnacious, and in one of his enthusiastic moments threw a drum off the roof of Philadelphia's Adelphia Hotel. At some juncture in Buffalo, disagreeing with the city editor, he asked him if he'd like to "step outside."

Nick Carter died of tuberculosis in Arizona. I always was glad I kissed him goodbye as he drove away to the West.

**********

On the final day, January 5, 1942, the newsboys offered to take the loss of selling the paper for a couple of cents less.  But the court was adamant.  Faced with financial collapse, the *Philadelphia Evening Ledger*, offshoot of the illustrious *Philadelphia Public Ledger*, once the pride of the Curtis family, faltered and died.  The lights were lit in the City Room, but there was no one there when Evelyn and I returned from dinner.  A notice posted on a pillar said the paper was dead.  Slowly we went around turning out the lights.

# 14

## Detour and Reroute

THE CLOSING OF THE *Evening Public Ledger* left 1500 people out of work. Evelyn started an employment bureau in her apartment. I got a position in the mail department of the Immigration and Naturalization Service which, due to overcrowding in Washington, moved to Philadelphia during the war. By this time, I had been in the newspaper business three years and felt very much a newspaperwoman. Anything outside of it was foreign land. I wore tailored suits and hats and mentally was skimming a few inches above the earth, exultantly looking for stories. Now I entered a vast, somewhat impersonal organization, whose only news function was to bring in or deter immigrants from entering the United States. Used to the familiar Washington background, the Immigration and Naturalization Service did not want to come to Philadelphia. The Service was filled with employees, many of long-standing, who felt uprooted from the federal scene, their native element.

My compatriots were no more interested in the delight of the newspaper business than I was interested in the mechanization of federal bureaucracy. But I must work. In the Service's mail department, I sorted letters under the management of a former drum major in the Marine Corps. The general tone of the office may be illustrated by the following incident:

We had an errand boy named Harry, in his teens, and one day he stood at a counter in the mail room doing nothing.

"What are you doing, Harry?" asked the drum major in a loud voice.

"I'm thinking, Sir," replied Harry.

"What the Hell do you mean by thinking?" inquired the drum major, "don't you know that's how we got into all this (FDR's administration) mess?"

Within a short time, I was promoted to another department where I performed an operation involving seven phases, including typing, pins and paper clips; it was my first real association with paper clips. In this department, however, I had an intelligent and interesting boss.

"Federal service, Miss Taussig," he said, not in criticism of my work, "can be rewarding if you can master details." He was a fairly young man and apparently had done so.

I remember too, a beautiful, stunningly dressed woman supervisor who arrived from Washington and stood in the office directing the moving of files. She too obviously had profitably mastered federal detail.

At this point, I began to write about my surroundings and rolled out a little brochure called "How to Click with Uncle Sam." A synthesis follows:

## HOW TO CLICK WITH UNCLE SAM

So you're going to work for Uncle Sam, the grandest uncle in the world. Of course he is, but you're human, and you don't want to get lost in his voluminous pockets.

What has Uncle Sam to offer you, a prospective Federal worker? *An atmosphere of democracy, security and A-1 working equipment.*

Remember that Uncle Sam needs you, but he doesn't know you at all. More than anyone else in the country today, he is going to take you at your own valuation.

If you have any special aptitude at all, don't go into Government service with a blanket mind. Despite the war emergency, the manifold opportunities, the equality of remuneration for numerous different types of jobs, there exists a special job for you, your wartime niche.

So when you apply to Uncle Sam for work, tell him all, your talents, experience and preferences. As the Government field of activity expands and its need for workers increases, these preferences may be practically polite requests.

Ask Uncle Sam for what you think you are worth right off, and don't start at a figure below it. Even if you prove your merit on the job, it takes time to get a raise put through in the Service; forestall any period of chomping at the bit.

Once in your new post, be absolutely loyal to the whole setup. You would be to any business firm, wouldn't you? Well, even if you do think Mrs. Roosevelt is on the road too much, keep quiet about it.

Don't look back. Uncle Sam, your fellow workers or the world at large are not interested in how you increased the volume of sales for that asbestos firm you salesmanaged before you signed up. In Government service, you're at the hub of a *new* life - nobody knows how new yet.

When you first enter a Government bureau or agency, it's going to seem elephantine. This is the political forest, with its underbrush of red tape that you've heard of. Eternity's long, so what's the rush?

As a United States Government employee, Uncle Sam is going to ask you for *service, accuracy,* and *the ability to adjust to his pace, methods and your fellow employees.*

Like the Christian church, the United States Government asks service, by which both groups mean that the individual surrender his ego to the general cause. By this surrender, the two organizations affirm that the individual and the masses are both best served, and the cause promoted.

The offices of a Government service emanate this atmosphere of surrender to a higher authority, in place of the aggressive force of individual acquisition found in competitive business or professional concerns.

With thoroughness rather than speed in mind, Uncle Sam has made an art of detail, the mastery of which makes or breaks the Government apprentice.

In one Service, acknowledgement of an order to search records for specific information, the forwarding of the request to the correct department and the fee to the proper treasuries involves the execution of eight separate typed documents and the use of two pins and two paper clips. Erroneous handling of any articles involved can lead to catastrophe.

When one realizes, however, that the information checked is one digit in the life of one unit of a population of approximately 132,165,000 (1940), each of whose rights must be considered as the requested information is withheld or dispensed, the case at hand seems more tolerable.

Entering a Government Service office, Uncle Sam's pockets seem dark, deep and suffocating to the newcomer. A sense of bottomless routine from which escape is uncertain prevails.

Here are three rules on how *not* to get lost:

1. Take one thing at a time, whether it's a file number or a Congressional bill. 2. Pay meticulous attention to detail. 3. Keep your own pace. If you really want to get ahead, the last rule, reasonably followed, will swing the unit You, whether you work for yourself, Uncle Sam or your boss, along to success.

To the thousands of persons now entering Federal Service, who formerly had so called "creative" jobs, the routine positions in which many find themselves seem chain gang activities with a goal too remote to inspire.

As in other cases when life becomes too technical, one can only urge return to fundamental principals which outlive regimes and systems.

If the creative-minded person will give up his individual urge for the time, he will find rhythm in his routine work. The files of numbers, the indexes of names, even the consistent pounding of a date stamper does produce a certain rhythm which can render the employee in tune, at least, with the intricate mass of detail and distant purpose of his job.

There is no use working to get through in Government service. It gets you neither rhythm or new work. Unless the intelligent employee finds some rhythm and meaning behind his job, it becomes a purely mechanical process, dangerous to him and to the State because his heart is elsewhere. Most Government agencies are fully staffed. There will be no extra work just because you rush.

But in Government work, as in all others, in the face of any system or instructions, the worker must maintain *at least his own pace*. If the work seems to drag excessively, perhaps he has considered the job at hand so simple that he has slackened his normal rate of working speed. The quickening of pace to the height of individual capacity increases interest in any job.

The beginner in Federal work needs to remember that, as in all other trades, everything he does fits him for something better. A worker fully capable of answering the outgoing correspondence which he is given to fold, will know the form and style of these letters when his opportunity to write them comes.

If you are just plain dissatisfied and feel that you're in a rut in Government work, you'll never find a more serene spot in the business world to figure out just why you are there.

And granted that you are an ambitious person, that you really don't want to get lost in Uncle Sam's pockets, know that *it's the keeping of that ambition alive that counts,* and that there are now unprecedented opportunities in Government work. Uncle Sam does not seek initiative. But he recognizes it when he sees it.

Uncle Sam is not indefectible. The newcomers from the outside business and professional worlds are bringing new blood to his slightly hardened arteries. They are contributing the snap of competitive occupations, the style of rival trades, where individual personality is such a vital factor. They are donating that very personal initiative that *WON'T* get lost.

(You said I'd make the best of what I had, Mademoiselle Audi. Well, you can see I was in there pitching!)

From this department, I progressed to an office where I composed letters answering inquiries. This was more challenging. The atmosphere, however, was soporific. One day a friend of the woman with whom I shared an office came and stood in the doorway.

"How are you feeling, Louise?" she inquired of my officemate.

"I don't feel so well," the officemate replied, "I think I'll go home and get into bed and read."

"Why do you read," asked the caller, "why don't you just turn on the radio and save your eyes?"

My tenure with Immigration and Naturalization was about six months. Julia Shawell, a reporter on the *Philadelphia Daily News*, which with the *Philadelphia Evening Bulletin* were the only two evening papers left in the city, recommended me for a position on the *Daily News*.

Once again - I was to breathe oxygen.

# 15

# Ground Chuck

THE *DAILY NEWS* WAS at 22nd and Arch Streets, just beyond the Red Light district. It was a several-storied building and the city room was on the third floor. A smaller paper than the *Ledger,* it was the least pretentious of any I have worked on, yet one of the friendliest. The smaller papers as a rule are more family-like and warmer than the larger ones.

The City Room was connected by a door with the composing and pressrooms, which at times, of course, gave running accompaniment to the editorial production. Floors were uncarpeted, and at one end was a long table-desk with slots for typewriters, at which sat the indoor reportorial staff of five persons. To the left, directly in front of the door leading to the composing room, was the copydesk, and beyond to the right, were the shadowy offices of the drama critic and the sports and financial editors.[1]

Tabloids, one might say, are the "ground chuck" of the newspaper business. One has to be brief, vital and to the point to make one's way into the hands of the subway reader, who was the principal buyer of the *Philadelphia Daily News.* There was an earthy vigor about it; it sought the facts and presented them with full force, unworried about subtler shadings or intellectual ruminations. Its editorials often were outstanding; it fought the cause of the working man. By his very tastes and preferences, however, it had limitations.

Managing editor of the *News* was Dean McCullough, a short, stocky Pennsylvania Dutchman, whose family had large newspaper interests in Lancaster, Pa. The words that set Dean on fire were "love nest." He adored any story about one. In the hot Philadelphia summer, he and his copyreaders, three or four of them, worked in their undershirts. But when the day was over, it was another story. I can see Dean now, making for the washroom with a cake of a gray soap that he and his men used to take the carbon off their fingers. A little while later, he would emerge handsomely dressed; one would never have known he had any association with carbon. He would

---

[1]The Philadelphia Daily News, now one of the Knight-Ridder Newspapers group, is lodged in a modern office building at 400 North Broad Street.

cross the City Room and make his way down to the Bellevue-Stratford for the cocktail hour.

Newspaper people are compulsive workers; they have to use what they have. But once the day is done and the energy spent, they can - until tomorrow at least - look at the world without their compulsion. It is difficult to describe the keen pleasure a newsman or woman feels when the work is over, and - just for a space - he can sit back and watch the world go by without recording its passage, and think and dream subjectively for a little while.

Dean was quite different from the older man who assisted him at the desk, who every payday deposited $14 at a neighboring bar for a week's supply of evening gin; a kindly and charming man.

The City Editor of the *News* was Robert B. Vale, a Quaker, about 70-years-of-age, with an oval face and a long upper lip. He was able to give an air of restraint and dignity to the handling of the sins and foibles of the human race that wafted across his desk, and he did discriminate. I can remember E. A. Mallowan, the top rewrite man, answering the telephone one day, and turning to Mr. Vale:

"It's Tom Brown (let's say) from the *Bulletin*," Amory announced. "He says there's a case of indecent exposure at 12th and Market streets."

"Thank him very much for letting us know," said Mr. Vale, "but tell him we don't want it."

Quakerism and innate lower class values protected the *News* from going overboard. The working man would read of robbery, rape and murder, but the decadent social behavior of mankind was taboo.

Mr. Vale was a polite editor to work for. I was still in the painful learning process. One day he sent me miles over to New Jersey to talk to a man who had lost his son in the war. The man was elderly. I asked for a picture of his boy and he declined, although he said he had one.

"Just let me see it," I said, and he went upstairs and brought it down. Once I had the picture in my hands, I ran out the door and up the street.

Upon my return to the office, Mr. Vale looked very grave indeed. The father of the boy had called up the office.

"Ellen," he said, "did you take that picture from that old man?"

"Yes," I said, "here it is."

"Well, it's going straight back," he said.

I was not made to take the picture back personally, but it was a rousing lesson.

Amory Mallowan was a big, dark-haired, white-faced man who sold insurance from his typewriter at the *Philadelphia Daily News*, in between rewrites. Next to him sat Lou Jaffe, a former sportswriter for the *Ledger*, who despite arthritis in his arms, was able to type. Lou was a courteous, delightful person to work with, so gallant in his persistence of remaining in the business.

The night City Editor was Jack Morris. When I first went on the paper, I reported at 5 a.m. for morning rewrite. My baptism to a tabloid occurred the first morning, when Jack gave me a picture of some GIs looking over the top of a trench. I wrote the usual type caption that the Ledger would have published and passed it over to Jack. He glanced at it and shook his head.

"Let me show you how to do it," he said, and rolled out this one:

### GRIM REAPER PEERS OVER TRENCH, ETC.

Yes, I was on a tabloid newspaper.

Then there was Julia, a dark-haired woman with sapphire eyes and a presence; full of Catholic faith, professional drive, warm of heart and a fine friend. She was interested in causes. Julia had had her own Hollywood column on the *New York Graphic*. She kept abreast of world affairs and was wonderful at organizing facts. I remember one morning Dean McCullough asked for brief sketches of Generals Patton and Wainwright, or perhaps it was Bradley. Without any clippings, Julia sat down at the typewriter and produced them. She was square and helpful to work with.

The country - cities and individuals - were immersed in the war effort. There is something poignant in this surrender of once treasured trophies to the cause. Julia and I worked on this story:

## ANCIENT WAR CANNON ENTERING THIS SCRAP

### by JULIA SHAWELL AND ELLEN TAUSSIG

Everyone thought their day was done. There they stood rusting out their memories of the Civil, Spanish and World War I, wars fought to make the world safe - for something.

Today, the 30-odd cannons, howitzers and fieldpieces guarding posts of the American Legion, Veterans of Foreign Wars and other patriotic oganizations and parks about Philadelphia, may contribute the knock-out blow in a battle to hold the world together.

### OFF TO "GUN PARK"

Starting today, under the supervision of William C. Leinhauser and Leon Schlesinger, company commanders of the American Legion and Veterans of Foreign Wars, respectively, these 30 old weapons of war will commence to thunder and roll, via truck, into Reyburn Plaza, which will temporarily change its name to "Gun Park," in their honor.

There they will stand in state until 1 p.m. Sunday, when they will be carted off for scrap, climaxing the Philadelphia Newspapers' United Scrap Metal Drive of the past month.

Greater love hath no gun than this, than that he be melted down for his country.

### TONS FOR PRODUCTION

"It is estimated that about 250,000 pounds of metal will be released for national defense production, upon the scrapping of these landmarks," Judge Vincent A. Carroll, commander of the Civilian Defense Corps and originator of the scheme, announced today.

"The brass content of these old weapons is higher than any other articles of scrap contributed in the scrap campaign so far. The bases of two 1-1/2-ton Naval guns, at the American Legion, Roche Post, 6400 Paschall ave., weigh 400 pounds apiece alone, and are estimated at approximately 75 percent brass. Several of the pieces weigh 1500 pounds each, bases included."

Perhaps no individual, relatively speaking, gave more than a Philadelphia woman, of whom I wrote:

*PHILADELPHIA DAILY NEWS*     TUESDAY, OCTOBER 20, 1942

### UNHEARD MUSIC AIDS WAR EFFORT
#### By ELLEN TAUSSIG

Mentally rising above her own tragedy of complete paralysis, Bertha E. Mullins participates in the national defense effort.

Sightless, deaf and without sense of touch, the invalid learned that the world was at war from her mother, Mrs. Clara Mullins, 125 E. Meehan ave., Mt. Airy. Mrs. Mullins placed her lips on her daughter's forehead and whispered the sorry words to her. It is only thus, and through musical vibrations, that Bertha Mullins can communicate with the invisible world.

Eager to aid and undaunted by fate, which has kept her bedridden for 21 years, the paralytic outlined a plan for a series of musical concerts, the fifth of which takes place on Thursday at 8:30 p.m., at the Germantown Y.M.C.A., 5722 Greene st., for the benefit of the Red Cross. The Germantown male chorus will be featured.

Miss Mullins' interest in music, which she senses through vibrations from a radio loudspeaker placed on her chest, has brought her many musical acquaintances. Through letters dictated in soundless speech to her mother, and with the aid of a friend, Benjamin Frazier, an employee of the Germantown branch of the Philadelphia Gas Works, the invalid solicited and obtained voluntary donations of hall space and talent. Friendly volunteers supervise the actual events for her.

As it will not be broadcast, Miss Mullins will not be able to hear this Thursday's concert, even by vibration. But she does not expect to listen to any other musical program at that hour. She will just lie quietly in bed, as she has done since a child of 10.

But now she feels she is doing her part.

**********

Far more experienced than I, Julia got the top assignments. One day, however, on her day off, a big story broke. The Cruiser *USS Boise* carrying 10,000 men sailed up the Delaware to dock in Philadelphia. It was the first time the ship, plastered with battle stars, had touched port since leaving the South Pacific. Sailors waved from her rails, her portholes and her masts. It was a great sight to see a particularly little sailor shinny down a rope to hold her fast. But once the ship was moored, the press was not permitted aboard until Admiral Ernest J. King, commander-in-chief of the U.S. Fleet, should arrive from Washington. Cooped back of wire, we waited at least two hours, eating Milky Ways and, we of the evening papers, partially frenzied, as one after another of our evening papers' deadlines went ticking by.

At last the admiral, a tall, thin, severe-looking man arrived and was piped aboard and greeted on deck by the Boise's captain, Edward J. (Mike) Moran, "Fighting Mike Moran." He escorted the admiral below deck, and we, about 30 newsmen and photographers, were permitted to come up the gangplank to the upper deck. Inez

Robb, the famous *New York Daily News* reporter, and I were the only women.

After a brief delay, the admiral and captain emerged from the hold. They walked to the landside rail and partially turned their backs to us. Then, somewhere from the midst of the crowd, came the words "Well, Boys, take what you can get!" and I scuttled across the deck to the rail. I seemed to have been the only one to have done so; the instructions had been meant for the photographers.

But newsmen and women stick together, and within seconds, two or three other reporters joined me. Faced with the admiral, who looked as if he had just had a couple of lemons in hot water, I asked him if he had any comments on the conduct of the men on the ship.

"The ship needs no comment," said Admiral King, looking at me as if I were a spring caterpillar, "she speaks for herself." With that, I beat it for the gangplank, to try to catch my imminent deadline. Halfway down, I met Ashley Halsey, the public relations officer, who had been temporarily absent from the ship.

"What is this I hear," said Ashley, "I just leave the ship for a few minutes, and I hear some woman had broken loose!"

"They said take what you can get, Ashley," I explained, as I hurried past him on the way to a telephone.

The last editor was out when I got back to the *Daily News*, and the only one at the city desk was Amory Mallowan. I was crushed; I felt I had made a fool of myself before officials and compatriots. I'll never forget what Amory said:

"Kid," he said, "don't *ever* feel badly if you've done the best you can for your paper."

I was not thoroughly consoled. I resolved to go down to the Bellevue-Stratford and get a check cashed and eat and drink my way through it.

It was dusk when I reached the hotel and the pink-shaded lights in the lobby were lit. As I stood waiting in line at the cashier's cage, I suddenly noticed directly before me a pair of large, square Navy shoulders. Circling surreptitiously around them, so I could see their owner's face, I realized it was "Fighting Captain Mike Moran," himself. It was probably a toss-up whether I was more surprised to see him or he to see me.

It didn't take me any time to tell the captain that I was Admiral Taussig's granddaughter, and Fighting Captain Mike Moran left the line and came and sat down for the following interview:

*PHILADELPHIA DAILY NEWS*                NOVEMBER 20, 1942

### WHY BOISE MADE IT ---------
### MIKE'S FIGHTING JAW
#### By ELLEN TAUSSIG

Capt. Edward J. (Mike) Moran's long trick was over. He sat in the Bellevue-Stratford last evening, his square, sunburnt face - the face of a fighting man - shining with pride, his penetrating blue eyes glowing with satisfaction in the lamplight.

For, in his own words, the commander of the unbeatable Boise had sailed, fought and reached port with a crew "who in no case knew when they were through."

#### SILENT

When he brought his 10,000 ton cruiser that had bagged six Japanese ships to anchor at the Navy Yard yesterday; when he had received the congratulations of Admiral Ernest J. King, commander-in-chief of the U.S. Fleet, and when he had bid adieu to many of his crew of 600 as they rejoined anxious wives and sweethearts, the fighting captain was silent.

But last night, just after telephoning to his 11-year-old son and 13-year-old daughter in California, telling them he was safe back home, "although the newspapers beat me to it," he remarked, the widower captain relaxed a bit.

"Words at my command can describe in no measure my pride and good fortune to have been placed in a position to command such a gallant crew. In no case did they know when they were through," said the Boise's commander.

#### NINETEEN DECORATED

Indications of this bulldog spirit are reflected in the award of 19 members of the USS Boise crew, four of which were made posthumously to officers and men killed in action. In a number of cases, the medals were awarded at the instance of Vice Admiral W. F. Halsey, Jr., commander in the southwest Pacific.

Two Pennsylvanians are on the list:

The captain is proud in the case of Lieut. William G. Thomas, Jr., of 104 First st., Clover, Pa., who remained in the compartment to which he had been assigned, after it had been hit. Thomas instructed eight of his comrades to leave in safety, but he died at his post. He was posthumously awarded the Navy Cross "for extraordinary heroism in line of his profession."

The captain is proud of Second Lieut. Paul John Strecker, 902 Montooth st., Pittsburgh, Pa., awarded the Silver Star Medal "for distinguished service as helmsman." Strecker remained at his post in constant peril throughout the action.

"His disregard of personal safety enabled the commanding officer to control the ship quickly and accurately at all time, and enabled him to remove the ship from danger when it became necessary to break off action," read the citation.

**********

September, 1943, was a big news month in Philadelphia. It involved railroads. A great fire and a staggering rail tragedy took place there within seven days.

Large fires are a part of any general assignment reporter's lot. A reporter develops a sensibility toward fire from the destruction of families and their homes, the public buildings, plants and stores he has seen go up in smoke. I particularly remember a wax factory fire at which the sky was filled with saffron clouds of evaporated wax. But by far the biggest "blaze" (a newspaper term), I have ever witnessed was the burning of Philadelphia's Broad Street Station.

Designed by the noted architect Frank Furness, the Mooro-Gothic towered brick station, with its great arched train shed, had been a landmark of the city's comings and goings since 1881. It faced City Hall in the center of town.

Any fire alarm is sounded in local rooms of newspapers. The number of alarms, location and building are registered by the City Editor, who dispatches staff to the scene. A six-alarmer is big. The Broad Street Station was an eight-alarmer.

It began at 9:38 a.m. on Sunday, September 13, in a compressor or engine room adjoining the station's baggage and mail room. It raced through a block-long section of trackage and shed. By noon the area about the station teamed with an army of engines, trucks, ladders and ambulances. I shall never forget the labyrinth of hoses, some as thick as boa constrictors, on the blocked-off streets and pavements.

Three hundred and seventy-five persons were affected by the fire, most of whom suffered from partial asphyxiation from the smoke, but returned home after treatment. Hospitals received 21.

At 2 p.m., the fire was under sufficient control to allow me to mount the long flight of stairs leading up to the second-floor train shed. Thin wisps of smoke were coming up *through the cracks in the cement floor* of the section of the station leading to the track gates. An astonishing sight.

By the following morning 1,000 workmen, recruited from five states, had cleared much of the debris off the tracks, and with 400,000 feet of timber hammered together a temporary platform at train level at 16th Street, the next block.

Hourly service to New York was resumed at 7 a.m.

The greatest tragedy of human life I have ever covered was the Frankford Junction wreck of September 6, 1943, less than a week before the fire. Even today, the Frankford wreck ranks among the seven major railroad wrecks in the United States since 1876; it was the worst disaster in a quarter of a century. Seventy-nine persons were killed and one hundred and twenty-five injured.

It was Julia, however, who shouldered the almost intolerable burden of the wreck. Sent to the scene, she reported on the most rigorous assignment I have ever seen a woman undertake. I was sent to the Frankford Hospital, the nearest one to the scene, where a panorama of war stretched down its corridors and across its grounds. But Julia first: here in part, is her report:

*PHILADELPHIA DAILY NEWS*          TUESDAY, SEPTEMBER 7, 1943

In the nation's worst train disaster in a quarter of a century, 69 persons (later 10 more were listed) were killed and more than 125 injured here last night, as nine cars of the sixteen-car Congressional Limited derailed at Frankford Junction. Bodies were spewed out of completely demolished day coaches. Some were electrocuted as a great wired signal bridge crashed and knifed a steel car in two.

The accident, at 6:08 o'clock, was caused by a burned-out journal on the lead truck of an old-type day coach, severing the long speeding train. The locomotive and six coaches continued down the track past the junction station as the seventh jumped the rails into the air, striking the signal bridge top and carrying the eighth car, also a crowded day coach, with it. The ninth, first of two diners, overturned, spilling the passengers and kitchen crew, while the second diner and four Pullmans were torn off the tracks and the 5th and 16th Pullmans remained on the rails.

Among the dead were ten railroad workers who were speared and felled by flying ties and steel as they trudged the right-of-way on their way home from work.

All through the night hundreds of men cut away the metal prison of the dead, while 117 ambulances which had answered the general emergency calls bore victims to 20 hospitals throughout the city... priests, their clerical collars wet and their eyes bloodshot from the dust of the wreck, administered last rites to the dying and spoke absolution over bodies pinned in the upturned coaches...

The Philadelphia Navy Yard and Cramp's Shipyard sent dozens of welders to work on the mass of metal that pinned down the victims. The Philadelphia Electric Company's giant-sized floodlights made lurid day of the scene as darkness fell.

**********

I stood in the corridors of the Frankford Hospital looking into emergency rooms where burns of victims were greased and wrapped in cotton batting. Others lay on litters stretched on the tree-shaded lawn of the old hospital, awaiting their turns. Circulating among them were the white starched uniformed nurses of the institution, their little lozenge-shaped goffered caps, like French pastries, perched on their heads, the only light touch in a field of suffering.

My task was simple compared to Julia's. I have never forgotten my admiration for her performance. Could I have done what she did? I don't know. I doubt it, at that stage in my career. Yet faced with calamity and death, fire and flood, something within a reporter snaps into place like a cocked revolver. This is it, this is what you are here for and it will not come again. The opportunity is now; it will pass. A sense of armament very like the military takes over. One moves. It's an onrush, a torrent, a cataclysm - but it's up to you. There is no escape. In some way you have to see and tell of it.

I remember during the war being faced with a labyrinthian *OPA* report. To my unmathematical mind, it was Greek, impenetrable. I called up my City Editor and told him.

"Well what do you propose to do about it?" he asked. No "Bring it in and I'll help you," or "Go ask Ted" - just it's up to you.

I found the federal reporter, a marvelous man with long experience in Uncle Sam's antics. He helped me out. I finished the job by hook or crook. A reporter is expected to deliver.

Has this mandatory reportorial thrust only a purely selfish motive? Probably yes, at the moment it happens. But its ramifications are not confined to self. In case of a joyous or tragic event, other people - from a handful to the country at large - are waiting to learn of it. Their reaction may be rejoicing or mourning, but by it, they are informed. They know of life or death, success or failure, victory or defeat. They are not left in the dark. They know.

# Part V

# Big Time

# 16

## An Artful Craft

IN 1943, AFTER A YEAR on the *Philadelphia Daily News*, I applied for a position on the *Philadelphia Record*, which was owned by J. David Stern, who also had owned the *New York Post*. Walter Lister, who had been City Editor of the *Post* under Mr. Stern, and had come to work on the *Record* as Managing Editor, interviewed me. I got the job.

My first morning on the paper I met Fred Shapiro. He was an assistant city editor, training and encouraging young reporters who eventually fanned out to papers across the United States. My heart opens as I write of Fred Shapiro. There was something staunchly appealing about this little man, who looked like the Queen in "Alice in Wonderland." He had a high forehead and receding hairline, keen brown eyes behind glasses and a firm mouth in which he perennially clamped a cigar that he gently chewed. He had a nasal Philadelphia voice and small white hands. They were a newspaperman's hands, and Mrs. McCabe and an editor under whom I worked years later, Paul Neville, had the same kind. They were the hands of people born to deal in print, narrow with slender though not necessarily long fingers. Mr. Shapiro handled copy with those hands as if he were putting the pastry trimmings on a mince pie. One felt that in that rather lion-like head for his size was the ability to bring forth clarity out of any confusion he found in the copy before him.

He was a wonderful teacher, the best I have known, and whatever technique and succinctness of expression I have achieved stems back to him. All editors, even some very good ones, cannot teach; it is an exceptional gift. In some wonderful way, Mr. Shapiro helped clear the brambles from my overactive, impressionable and enthusiastic mind. He is one of the people in my life who has counted. I suppose one might say that I loved him, as a human being, a searcher for simplicity, a way-shower in reflecting the torrential and nefarious life of the city around us.

My first assignment from Mr. Shapiro was to go to the Chester County Courthouse for a hearing of a boy who had stuffed, I believe fatally, his grandmother in a closet. West Chester is beautiful hunting country, and the courthouse was picturesque, with a cobblestone courtyard and pigeons feeding about it.

I have always tried to get the whole picture in a story of where it took place and the surrounding atmosphere. I suppose it is the fiction in my bones, but I have never been content with just bare bones of a story; when confined to them I feel partially suffocated. So I returned to the office and wrote the story which included a description of the courtyard, the pigeons and in some miraculous way, under the circumstances, the word beauty. Fred Shapiro examined my first effort in his little white hands. Then he called me over and made suggestions. Along the way, pointing to the reference to the courtyard, the pigeons and the word beauty, he said: "Now this courtyard and those pigeons - get them further down in the story, also the word beauty; very few people know what it is." It was my initial experience with his keen, discerning mind.

The *Philadelphia Record* was the most literary paper I have ever been on. With a battery of seven or eight picked rewrite men, stories sometimes were rewritten three or four times before they suited the demanding taste of Mr. Lister, channeled through Mr. Shapiro. A Democratic paper backing the Roosevelt regime to the hilt, fostering the cause of the working man, it really was a crusading sheet. It sought stories for their own sake, and if they were not readily at hand, it went out to look for them. The *Philadelphia Record* went in for fire, theft, assault and murder, but its approach and sensibilities concerning them were different from a tabloid like the *Philadelphia Daily News*. The *Record* aimed for the educated as well as the uneducated liberal. The writing and photography must not only tell the story with conciseness, but must also have artistic merit. It was there to paint a picture from the soul of educated newsmen, who loved to respond to the scene around them, and who gave to their product - from their very solar plexus - the attention and creativity that distinguishes the artist from the craftsman.

Of course there were different kinds and degrees of talent on the paper, but I believe nearly everyone there was dedicated to the proposition that "Here is a sheet that can reflect dramatically, artistically and factually the city and the world around it."

The war gave intensity to that scene, as did the fact that the *Record* was a smaller newspaper than the Republican *Inquirer* and the *Evening Bulletin*; the terror spirit of the underdog also motivated our days. And overall was the sharp, dramatic, driving mind of Walter Lister.

He was very democratic, joining us at dinner at the neighboring Horn & Hardart where we would discuss the events of the day and facets of the business. While there was strict discipline on the

*Record*, as on all papers, there was also a spirit of liberality in its administration, as well as its policies.

Of discipline on newspapers, it should be said that on the good ones it rivals that of the Army. There is no time or place for argument or back talk in the face of electrically moving news. What is new one moment, may not be news the next. So for the reporter it is, as in "Charge of the Light Brigade," "Theirs not to make reply, Theirs not to reason why..." One complaint, one exhibition of balking, and there is always another reporter "waiting in the files" to take an ornery or even a questioning reporter's place. The newspaper business is no business for one who cannot take orders readily. There just isn't time for questioning.

Most people who stay in the newspaper business love it. It would be impossible otherwise. The speed, the tension, the hours, the weather encountered, the rebuffs, the criticism could not be sustained unless one is truly devoted to the craft. There is nothing just like it, and once a true reporter has savored it, he never gets over it; he is one as long as he lives, whether he continues to report or not. The newspaper business is *impression* and *expression,* a powerful twin inducement. An experienced newsman or woman has opened his pores, as Walter Winchell so aptly put it, for so long to the world; he has heard the beat at the heart of events; he has seen the great fall and the meek inherit the earth - and vice versa. He has become an organ of observation and communication, and cannot be reconverted.

# 17

# "Praise the Lord and Pass the Ammunition"

TO TELL THE STORY of reporting on the *Philadelphia Record* from 1943 until 1947, is like diving beneath the surface of memory and selecting pieces of coral from an underwater reef. The war events, the human interest stories, the causes, the crime, the personalities and the oddities formed a drama that could happen only once in a generation, and the experience of which was so varied that indeed, it was all one generation could experience and sustain.

War was the main thrust, but there still was patriotism in World War II. On the homefront, crime had not become so prevalent that it seemed futile for newspapers to select and develop special crime stories for readership. Military leaders were heros. The country swelled with pride at the repeated launching of ships. Labor was putting its foot in the stirrup and would soon be riding high on the horse. Women were feeling their oats and beginning to sow some. A cocky, sure America may not have been singing "Look for the Silver Lining," as in World War I, but it did chant "Roll Out the Barrel, We'll Have a Barrel of Fun, Roll Out the Barrel, We've Got the Hun on the Run." A prosperous America.

For the launching of the *USS Oklahoma City*, the sponsor, a spare woman with hair screwed back in a Psyche knot, was a "dry," who wrote the Navy Department saying she wished to christen the ship with water from some Oklahoma tributary. The Navy declined. Tradition holds that a ship be christened with spirits - preferably champagne. Sailors have been known to decline to sail on ships not so christened, considering them bad luck. The lady from Oklahoma yielded and arrived in Philadelphia in a mink coat, hatless and submissive. A new angle was struck in World War II for photographing ships and the Liberty Bell. Some photographer ingeniously had gotten under the bell and persuaded his subject to look up at the clapper, thus photographing part of the interior of the bell in preference to just the exterior. A ship too, when christened, frequently was photographed from the ground, the photographer looking up and catching the figure of the sponsor and the ensuing spray from the champagne.

I covered the *Oklahoma* launching with Jack Snyder, a veteran photographer, a literal, forceful man with great talent. We were down on the dock looking up at the Oklahoma lady as she was about to swing the bottle, Jack, his camera poised, I all attention.

Noticing us standing there, she leaned over and called to Jack: "Young man," (he was fully 45) "get away - you'll get it splashed all over you!" Jack, his mouth punctuated with expensive gold teeth, looked up and smiled:

"We like it, Ma'am," he said, "we lick it off our coats."

Handsome, white-haired, blue-eyed Fleet Admiral Chester W. Nimitz arrived in town for a mass interview. The war was at its height and we were all anxious and inquisitive. As I was leaving the room where the interview had taken place, a public relations officer spoke to me: "Well, little lady," he said, "you asked him everything except if he beat his wife, didn't you?"

A glorious story at the end of the war was the homecoming of General Carl A. Spaatz to his Boyertown, Pa., birthplace. From a second story bedroom in a crowded country inn, I described the scene by telephone to Nick. Here's some of it:

*PHILADELPHIA RECORD*                    JUNE 11, 1945

BERKS WELCOMES GEN. SPAATZ HOME WITH 3 PARADES
Relatives Lead Celebration; Mother Calls Him "My Baby Boy"

By ELLEN TAUSSIG
Record Staff Reporter
(as told to Nick Carter)

BOYERTOWN, Pa., June 10 -- Gen. Carl A. Spaatz came home today to be called "my baby boy" by his mother, to eat Berks county sausage and to be greeted by more folks than Boyertown ever saw before.

It was quite a day for the 54-year-old general who, as head of the U.S. Strategic Air Forces in Europe, commanded more fliers and more aircraft than any general in history.

He met some 5000 home folks - and Boyertown has a population of only 4000 - he greeted again a bunch of the "boys" with whom he used to play pranks in his boyhood, he ate heavily of Berks County home cooking, particularly sausage. Then he went to Reading and Pottstown to greet 95,000 more persons who think he is just about the greatest fighting man in the world...

The general had not seen his mother, Mrs. Anna Spaatz, 78, since 1941. She lives in a little white cottage with green shutters on Philadelphia Ave. with her daughter and son-in-law, Mr. & Mrs. William Steinmuller.

There were a dozen relatives in the house waiting for him, and there were bowls of flowers. Tables were piled high with canned peaches, cherries and other fruit sent by neighbors.

Spaatz, forgetting all about his military bearing, almost ran up the steps to grab "Mom" in his arms. She almost cried and said: "You're just my baby boy, you know." She called him "Buz," too. That's what all his boyhood chums call him.

Photographers gathered around and as they snapped pictures there was a series of flashes. Mrs. Spaatz jumped slightly. "Gosh, don't jump at the lights, Mom," the general said. "They won't hurt you."

Then the mother became bashful. With so many folks around, she didn't cuddle as close to her son as the photographers thought she should.

The general pulled her closer. "You know, Mom," he said, "this is no time to get fickle."

Mom looked her son over. She saw only one thing wrong. His socks were hanging down. But Spaatz explained he couldn't get garters in Europe. Ruth, his wife, had given him a pair when he came back to this country, but he had forgotten to put them on.

"My, my," Mom said. "He surely looks fine. I thought he would look older." The general smiled.

The big party was at the Boyertown Inn, which boasts of being 150 years old. Spaatz and all his relatives were there for dinner. More than 5000 gathered there and traffic was halted for four blocks in every direction.

Spaatz waved as the crowd cheered, clapped, and shouted: "There he is. There's the general."

When the general sat down for dinner he found quite a feast. There was fruit cup, chicken gumbo soup, spring onions and radishes, tenderloin steak two-inches thick, Berks county sausage, French fried potatoes, lima beans and peas and carrots.

The general hardly looked at the two-inch steak.

"Give me that sausage," he said, "and plenty of it."

He bit into the sausage and audibly smacked his lips. "Now," he said, "I'm happy."

He didn't even touch the steak and that was a disappointment to Clyde Houck, the manager of the inn, who had been saving it for the occasion. When Houck was a kid, he played ball with the general.

For dessert Houck offered almost every kind of pie. The general chose coconut custard.

Houck's wife, Florence, took the occasion to remind the general of the time he took her coasting when they were both in their teens.

"Remember," she said, "you hit something and I hit my head. I saw 15 million stars."

The general blushed.

Throughout the meal the band of Charles B. Yerger Post, American Legion, of which Spaatz is a member, played. Then the general went on the inn's porch to make a speech. He received such an ovation he had to wait a long time. He spoke briefly and to the point. He said:

"I feel very deeply about this gathering. I appreciate your coming here. We have fought a hard and cruel war. But it had to be done.

"The German nation was like the chestnut trees on our mountains. Once they were touched by blight, the blight had to be wiped out."

Then he gave a message to all the children gathered there to admire and cheer him. He told them:

"Grow up strong and self-reliant. Never accept aid for anything you can do yourself. Grow up to be manly men from Boyertown and Berks county."

Spaatz was happy and having a good time. He said as much. But he had to leave. There were a couple of other towns that wanted to see him.

Ten thousand persons turned out in Pottstown to greet him.

Reading saw the greatest turnout in its history, with 85,000 persons lining the streets.

*********

Perhaps the key wartime stories I covered were the return of Grover Bergdoll, a draft dodger of World War I, from prison to his home, and the GI who returned from Newfoundland to his wife, with a baby by an Army nurse.

Bergdoll had served his time and returned to his home on the outskirts of Philadelphia. I arrived in the morning to find John LaCerda, a crack *Philadelphia Evening Bulletin* reporter, safely ensconced in his Ford at the entrance of the property. Beyond, roaming about the Bergdoll country place, were dogs, most of them half-breeds, alert, barking and for all we knew, predatory. LaCerda was taking no chances. Having been accustomed to dogs all my life, I cautiously advanced through their ranks, and for a day and a half, attempted to get in the Bergdoll house for an interview. The afternoon of the second day, I got into the hall. Bergdoll was on the second floor and kept out of sight, but we exchanged conversation through the stairwell. I never actually saw him.

Mr. Shapiro was a thorough editor, and that evening or the next, for some unremembered reason, he sent me to Broomall to see Bergdoll's brother. Broomall was a desolate place outside Philadelphia, known principally in those days for a mental institution located there. The house of Bergdoll's brother was a large one with a porch. The photographer and I approached, and I suppose I rang the bell, standing back from the door as I had learned to do in unknown situations or when dogs barked inside. The brother appeared. He had on a woolen cap which smacked of the French Revolution, and under his arm was a shotgun.

I never remembered what I said, but years later, Julia, who too had joined the *Record* staff, told me that the photographer had returned to the office and reported that I enunciated: "You wouldn't dare do that to the granddaughter of an Admiral!" I was not shot.

I loved the newspaper business, and I used everything I had from energy to relatives to brass to flight in its pursuit. I have cajoled, bribed, stolen, queried and shouted to get my story, but I have never been immoral to that end.

The GI who appeared home to his wife with the baby by the Army nurse was an all-time high of war drama from a human interest point of view. The young man did not go directly to his wife, but brought the baby to his mother's house. The GI made overtures to his wife, who quite naturally, turned him down flat. She was in her early 40's, he slightly younger. They had never had any children of their own.

Several reporters were sent to try and "crack" the story, and unquestionably they did, what might be called "soften it up" somewhat. But finally, I was sent to talk to the wife. She had chased Jean Barrett, the *Record's* top woman reporter, off her porch with an umbrella. The wife worked in a Five & Ten Cent Store selling greeting cards. I found her, introduced myself, hung around and obtained a promise from her that if I would leave the store, she would meet me at the backdoor at closing time. At that hour, I was there, but the lady in question ran across the rooftops of the store and neighboring ones and escaped me. I lost no time in getting a trolley to her home in the Northeast and arrived before she did. A young girl, perhaps a relative, let me in. Shortly afterward, the woman arrived and raised cain at my being there. Perhaps it was the memory of the woman who got John Wanamaker's to take the scarves back by raising her voice, but anyway, I raised mine. I asked this woman who she thought she was? Eventually, I had to leave the house with a vague agreement of future contact, but no story.

The next day was Sunday, and we had the name of the GI's sister-in-law. I went to see her. We discussed the situation, and I learned that the wife had joined her husband and the baby and gone to the seashore. The sister-in-law provided the telephone number, and over the wire the wife told me she already was knitting a sweater for the little one. A story that had all the facets of a reporter's dream.

It was now afternoon, and I hurried to the house of the GI's mother to get pictures of him and the baby. Armed with a bunch of them, I stood on the corner of still another Northeast residential neighborhood, at least five miles from the paper, wondering how I would get back for the 7:30 p.m. deadline. I stood and I prayed "God, send a taxi down the street!" And within minutes, in a neighborhood not addicted to cabs - one rolled down.

It was a touching, eventually compassionate story that I shall never forget.

*********

LOVE, so often associated purely with romanticism, appears in many forms. It often comes forth in strange and amazing ways that on occasion, transcend the human state, and indeed seem to redeem it.

Charles Cooey, a delivery man for the Sisters of the Good Shepherd Convent in Germantown, Pa., for many years, was a case in point. The sisters maintained an institution for unfortunate or wayward girls, and conducted a large laundry which gave employment to the residents. In Chestnut Hill, our bed linen was sent to this laundry, and Charlie called for and delivered it in a big black truck. He was a delicate looking man of average height with gray-black wispy hair and mustache. His regular calls were a part of our life.  It was one of those strange coincidences that years later, after we had moved from Gravers Lane, Charlie's and my paths would cross again.  The circumstances of our meeting were as different as those of my life had become.

While on the *Philadelphia Record*, into Surrogate Court came a will for probate that aroused the invincible quality of love as clearly as any example I have witnessed.

It seems Charlie's wife had died, leaving a will that all his savings - which he apparently handed over to her down the years - had been placed by her in a bank account in *her* name.  Charlie, of course, had known nothing of this, until after her demise.

Very few sisters at the Convent of the Good Shepherd today remembered Charlie Cooey.  One who did, however, said it was known that his wife was "very controlling about money," and that he "usually had only some small change in his pockets."  She added that Charles was a "very docile man," and "served the convent well."

Under the terms of the will, Charlie's life savings were left to a nephew and niece of his wife.  I was sent to the convent to ask him how he felt about it.  Charlie looked at me with wan, patient eyes and said:

"I know she did it for my own good.  She was afraid it would get lost, or someone would take it or something.  She did it for me."

There was nothing you could have said to dissuade Charlie Cooey from belief in his wife.  It was not possible to enlighten him that she had fleeced him.  In his face and words, the accumulated devotion of years stood firm against assault, firmer than death or Surrogate Court.  He may have lost his money, but he still had his love.

**********

Another transcendence of love was that of Mary O'Brien, mother of three boys, who lived in South Philadelphia.  The oldest boy named John, Jr., age 16, went wild.

Mary and her husband, a truck driver for a hauling company, were decent people.  John Jr., went to St. Patrick's School in center city and was a good student until he hit 13.  Then he got restless. He started throwing stones at other people's windows, trespassing on railroad property and playing hooky from school.  He began to go with older boys whose reputations were bad.  Two arrests and warnings.  Finally, when he was in the seventh grade, St. Patrick's sent John home for good.

After he entered Aubenried Junior High School, John's scrapes became progressively more serious. In September of 1946, he was arrested for the first time as a "bender," caught with some other boys racing a stolen automobile through the streets. He was sent to the House of Detention where he was cited as a "model boy," and sent home.

Recently, John had decided to quit school and went to work as a stock boy with the Crescent Ink Company in town. He seemed to be doing quite well. One evening, John and four other boys, one 18, and the rest also 16-years-old, stole two cars and began racing with short bursts of speed, hurtling through ordinarily quiet neighborhood streets, until one roaring car could draw ahead of the other. The two sedans were speeding at 60-miles-an-hour in one of these heats when the one O'Brien was driving, according to police, struck 14-year-old Agnes Joan Banker as she stepped from the curb within a block of her home.

Joan's body was hurled to the top of the speeding car, where it hug for nearly a block, while the driver careened the vehicle to shake it off. The car, a front fender dented and the hood streaked with blood, was found later. John was arrested the next morning as he was leaving his house for work.

I was sent to see John's mother: "I'd rather he'd hit something and killed himself than have had something like this happen," she said, her lips trembling. "The poor little girl." Not - "Oh God, my son!" but "the poor little girl."

When I returned to the office, Fred Shapiro called me over.

"Was there anyone else with you, Ellen, when this woman said that?" he asked. He could hardly believe it.

I was angry. Apparently he was doubting my word.

"No, Mr. Shapiro, there was no one there, but that's what she said."

He took my word for it.

When John O'Brien was convicted of second degree murder some weeks later in Quarter Sessions Court, the *Record* ran a long editorial on the case, headed "Calling All Science: Solve The Case of John O'Briens." Its sentiments are as good today, as they were 40 years ago. It concluded:

THE *PHILADELPHIA RECORD*                    DECEMBER 13, 1946

It was a fairly simple job for detectives to trace John after he had killed the little girl, and to solve the crime he committed.

It will be a mighty hard job to trace the exact course of John's life up to three years ago and solve the strange mystery of what happened to him -- to find the influences that changed a good boy into a bad one. To arrest them, too.

This is definitely not a case that society can be blamed for, if all the facts we know are true. For there are many John O'Briens in Philadelphia and throughout the world. Boys and girls of good families, raised in respectable homes, who turn sour and bitter in their adolescence.

Science - whether it be in the branches of medicine, sociology, psychiatry - must be put to work to solve the mysteries of the John O'Briens.

If they succeed even partially, it will be so much more significant than SOLVING crime. It will mean PREVENTING crime.

********** 

CRIME on a newspaper can range from stories with ironic humor to the most horrific tragedy. One which I covered that exemplified "humor" was of an upstate Pennsylvania farmer who hired a black man to murder his wife. At the trial, she appeared, looking fetching in a new costume each day, visibly if not audibly laughing in the face of her husband. The black man had kidney trouble, and had to occasionally be excused from the witness-box. I forget the outcome, but the circumstances were hilarious.

The *New York Daily News* sent Grace Robinson, a distinguished veteran reporter, to cover the trial. I can see her now, white-haired, wearing a cape. The *News* had begun a system whereby reporters could telephone their stories in onto a record at the office. We still used rewrite men. One of the ones whom I dealt with was facile, capable Franklin Gregory; we did many crime stories together.

When it comes to unmitigated tragedy, I recall the morning I was sent to the Philadelphia dumps. On the ground, surrounded by winter-worn grasses, in a pile of ashes, lay the twisted, burned body of a man in a pool of blood. I thought later, had that body been more than a charred, black shape - I could not have stood it. It is such events that try the mercy of God and the stamina of a reporter.

After you have experienced a certain number of things like that - things beyond your frame of reference, even beyond what you might imagine could happen - you stretch, and you stay stretched.

A space of "any eventuality" forms in your solar plexus. You realize that so-called civilization is a form within the framework of life. You are neither optimist nor skeptic - but ready, seldom surprised, and geared to the tragedy as well as the wonder of life.

## 18

## "She Christened A Ship!"

AS IN LIFE, TRAGEDY is only a sometime part of the newspaper business. My return to the Widener estate from which I had come empty-handed on the *Evening Public Ledger* is an example of the variety and humor of a reporter's days. Now five years later, the estate had been sold and some of the furnishings were about to be put up for auction.

I went to "Lynnewood Hall," the Widener house in Elkins Park, with Mike Pearlman, one of the best photographers I have known. A medium height, stocky man with a round, smiling, white face, he enjoyed life and his work. He was simple, straightforward and an artist.

Mike only had been through grade school, and he was so proud when his daughter received her high school diploma that he hung it over his bed. Mike had something that high schools can't furnish - talent. Whenever the subject permitted, his pictures had a Corot-like quality; one felt this man, relatively uneducated in the formal sense of the word, lived in a world of muted beauty which he communicated by means of a camera.

We were admitted at the front door by Mr. Widener's former butler, a tall, slender, oval-faced man, obviously English, who announced himself as "Mr. Turner." He was coatless, wore snappy suspenders and a sapphire and emerald stickpin in his four-in-hand necktie. We were ushered into the drawing room where, as throughout the house, everything was ticketed for the approaching sale.

"Have a seat on a $10,000 sofa," said Mr. Turner.

I gingerly seated myself on the damask and gilt piece, and Mike took a matching chair.

"What is the value of this sale?" I asked Mr. Turner.

"It could not possibly be estimated - incalculable," was his reply.

Feeling our way, we advanced into the dining room where an enormous oblong table was covered with fine glass and china and silver.

"Do tell me about some of the wonderful meals you have served on this silver and china?" I asked the butler.

He looked at me obliquely.

"The grouse, the pheasant, do tell," I repeated.

FROM three wars with 14 battle stars, the USS TAUSSIG (DD-746) named for Rear Admiral Edward D. Taussig, USN, who claimed Wake Island for the United States, at rededication ceremony at San Diego Naval Base. From left, Captain Joseph K. Taussig, Jr., USN, (Ret.), grandson; Ellen Taussig, oldest grandchild and sponsor, and Commander Robert E. Adler, USN, skipper. U.S. Navy photograph. (right) Admiral Taussig as a captain.

107

"Young woman," he said, "let's keep this on a higher level."

I swallowed hard.

Descending to the ground-level floor, we found the kitchen, equipped with huge copper pots, their bottoms partially covered with monograms. Then we returned upstairs and went to the second floor to see the bedrooms. The bedroom of the late Peter A. B. Widener, founder of the fortune, was furnished in a suite of mahogany or some other fine wood, inlaid with mother-of-pearl.

"We must have a picture of the bedroom of the founder of the Widener fortune," I said to Mr. Turner, but as there was only a bare mattress on the bed - "but we must have the bed made-up."

"I don't know if there is any linen," said Mr. Turner, "I think the family has taken it all, but I will go and see what I can find."

Mike and I were left alone in the bedroom. As I have intimated before, photographers are an independent lot; nothing irritates them more than to be talked down to, and Mike was reaching the saturation point.

Mr. Turner shortly appeared with several pieces of unbleached muslin which had been used to cover downstairs furniture.

"This is all we have," he said displaying them.

"Well, we'll have to make it do," I said, "let's make the bed."

"I don't know if I know how to make a bed," was Mr. Turner's reply. Mike flushed heavily.

"Well I do," I said, "you get over on that side, and I'll get on this one, and we'll do it together."

Although Mr. Turner complied, at this point Mike needed an outlet.

"Look here," he spoke up, pointing to me, "she christened a ship!"

Mr. Turner turned and looked at me. I don't know if he had ever been a seafaring man, or had relatives who sailed before the mast, or whether it was just a lingering loyalty to the British Navy, but from that moment on, his manner changed, and we received cordial treatment.

Mike had had enough. And I had not only gotten into the Widener house, but helped make up its founder's bed.

Yes, Mrs. McCabe, "there is always a tomorrow in the newspaper business."

**********

There was new life too, to report, abundant life. The arrival of the Cirminello quadruplets at the Pennsylvania Lying-In Hospital in

Philadelphia in 1944, overflowed with it. Mr. and Mrs. Cirminello had been informed by doctors that her delivery would be a bumper crop, and the paper had gotten wind of it.

I was sent to the alley back of the Lying-In section of the hospital at night, and was instructed to watch the window of the elevator shaft, and report when it reached the ninth-floor delivery room. This would tell us that birth was afoot. Toward midnight the elevator mounted to the ninth floor, but it was nearly 12 hours before the babies were born.

Emma Dash, an able compatriot, wrote the story which began:

At 10:30 a.m. yesterday (Nov. 1, 1944), the incubators were in position. The instruments were ready. Nurses and doctors were alert.

At 10:40 a.m., a spinal anesthesia for a Caesarean operation was administered to a small, pretty woman in the immaculate delivery room of the Lying-In Hospital at 8th and Spruce Sts.

At 11:12 a.m. baby No. 1 arrived. A girl, she weighed 3 pounds, 8 ounces.

By 11:14 a.m., babies No. 2, 3 and 4 had arrived. They weighed respectively 2 pounds 14 ounces, 3 pounds 8 ounces and 3 pounds 5 ounces...

That's 13 pounds, 3 ounces of babies! - three of whom arrived within 2 minutes!

The first quadruplets in the history of Philadelphia had been born. The first Caesarean operation in the history of quadruple births had been successfully performed.

The mother, Mrs. Kathleen Hatcher Cirminello, 30, of 251 Harrison Ave., Upper Darby, was "doing fine."

Then somebody thought about the father, Joseph Cirminello, who once weighed 155 pounds but had lost 12 pounds during his wife's confinement, and who was restlessly pacing the corridor outside the ninth-floor delivery room.

Naming of the babies, he said, would be left to his wife. "That's the least I can let her do."

"My wife is the bravest woman in the world. At first we were afraid to tell her that X-rays (in August) showed quadruplets were on the way. But when it was all over - and she did hear the news - she just smiled and said:

"Well Joe, I heard an awful lot of crying, but I wouldn't believe it until you and the doctors told me how many there really were."

I covered the activities of the stunned father and some of the onslaught of perambulators, afghans, bed jackets, toys, dietary products and deluxe diapers that poured into the burgeoned family. Mr. Cirminello, a corporation analyst of Italian descent, had a penchant for Italian food, and he seemed to attempt to stem his nervousness by eating.  Soda mints were in order for this responsible father, as the babies thrived and preparations were made to bring them home from the hospital.  It was a beautiful story.

**********

EVEN more numerically gifted - if not recipients of so many offspring at one clip - were Edmond and Elizabeth Macatee of 5908 Greenway Ave.

On August 10, 1946, Mrs. Macatee presented her husband with twins in Lankenau Hospital, 14 months after she had given him triplets.  All were girls.  The Macatees also already had one son, Raymond, age 3.

I found Mr. Macatee, a Philadelphia Transit Co. motorman, who had been granted a 90-day leave to meet the crisis, hanging out a fresh load of wash in his yard.  I gave him a hand.

With his wife in the hospital, Edmond Macatee had a heavy schedule.  It follows:

| | |
|---|---|
| 7:30 | Rise and dress Triplets |
| 9:30 | Breakfast |
| 10:45 | Bathe Triplets, place in playpen and do housework |
| Noon | Lunch and naps |
| 3:00 | Give Triplets milk and place in playpen |
| 5:30 | Supper |
| 6:30 | Bed |
| 10-11 | Give Triplets glasses of water |

Mr. Macatee was cheerful but looking ahead:  "I'm just wondering how I'll be able to do that for 5 of 'em," he said.

Currently, it took more than 200 diapers weekly to supply the household.

Son Raymond was forthright.  "I think we've had enough babies around here already," he said.

As for the food bill - Edmond Macatee was counting on Providence.

Nor shall I forget a single birth that took place in a run-down section of the city on a quiet Sunday.  I had been on assignment in the neighborhood, and as I walked along the street, two or three young children leaned out of a second-story window:

"There's a lady up here who has a baby," called one. "She had it all herself."

Puzzled and wondering if help was needed, I mounted the stairs to the second floor where the children - who had evidently witnessed the birth - admitted me to an apartment. Seated on the side of a bed was a strong-looking woman, holding a baby. In a bucket under the bed was the afterbirth. She and her child - whom she had delivered with the help of a razor blade - were in good shape.

Hurrying downstairs, I found a telephone in a neighboring store and called the paper.

Assistant Editor Si Shultz was on the desk. If I had reported an aerial attack on Independence Hall, he could not have been more startled:

"What did you say, Ellen?"

"I said this woman delivered her own child!"

There was a shocked silence.

"You don't mean..."

"Yes, Si, I just saw her and her baby."

Terror shook the City Desk. In the background I could hear other male consternation, and I realized afterward, what a very feminine event birth really was, and how in awe the average man was of it; how much he relied on outside help.

Our investigation of the case at the Department of Social Welfare disclosed that "Mary Smith" - her name is lost to me - had previously delivered another child of her own.

Such miracles and amazements do live and breathe along city streets.

\*\*\*\*\*\*\*\*\*

Of course, there were personalities, varied and wide in range of activity and interests: Katharine Cornell, the Great Lady of the Theatre, who, when the photographer wanted her to pose against the window so that the light would silhouette her lovely figure, understood his professional motive perfectly and graciously complied.

Jack Snyder and I went to see Mae West in her dressing room at the Broad Street Theater. She was dressed in a lace-trimmed, sun-toned negligee which matched her perfectly beautiful apricot-tinted skin. Her golden hair was piled on top of her head and her teeth were dazzling white. As she reclined on a chaise lounge, I thought Jack Snyder was going to fall off his chair. Offstage, Miss West faithfully maintained the half-tart, half prima donna attitude of her stage performances.  There was no dropping of the curtain and the raising on her real personality.

We chatted about this and that, including black lingerie, moving as close to lively subjects as we felt a family newspaper would bare; but we evidently went too far.  Upon writing the interview, I turned it in to the City Editor, but it never saw the light of day.

Newspapers are very expansive in some ways, and surprisingly conservative in others.  Crime, theft, murder, assault and rape are not performed by *the paper,* but by *unruly, lawless citizens;* if caught, their statements are usually part of the legal process.  But risqué remarks by a performer like Mae West, if published, reflect the leniency of the newspaper toward upholding conventional thought and moral tradition.  Papers in the '40s were careful not to bring into the American home an approbation of lewd thought or morals.  The picture of course, has somewhat changed.

**********

There also were the oddities.  My assignment to fly in a small plane around William Penn's hat and distribute pamphlets on the city below.  I had never been up in a plane.  Driven to a suburban airfield, I climbed aboard a two-seated Piper Cub.  As I have always disliked heights, I cannot describe my terror, but I had been offered the assignment, and I would not have thought of saying no.  As we swirled around Billy Penn's hat, I threw my lunch as well as pamphlets on the City of Brotherly Love - until all were gone, and returned to earth, a weak but unflagging reporter.

Newspapers were careful about what they said of the towns and villages in their circulation area.  This was another lesson I had to learn.  On being sent to a coal mining town upstate, I reported, as was really the case, that the paint was peeling off the houses.  No sooner had the paper reached the town than officials were on the telephone bawling us out.

"Why didn't someone catch it?" asked Mr. Shapiro, who apparently had been away from the office, or hadn't caught it himself.

A lesson to me, in certain situations, not to scrape all the varnish off the truth.

Newspapers are full of light and shade, of sunshine and thunder, fire and water, storm and calm.  When there are no news or pictures they must be sought, and one of the most delightful pictures I ever participated in was taken on a somnolent Saturday afternoon

in Philadelphia's City Hall.  I was in the building for some other
assignment, when in the main hall, by the ornate staircase that winds
through the massive structure, lay a cat.  A few steps above her
unknowing head sat a pigeon.  The resulting picture, which made
Page One, was captioned "Saturday Siesta at City Hall," and the
cutlines read:

> "Nearly everyone in City Hall went to the shore
> yesterday afternoon, except Minnie, the official cat, (center),
> who dozed in a first-floor hallway.  But Minnie is not her
> usual alert self, for resting comfortably, as shown in insert,
> on a nearby stairway, napped this pigeon, unmolested and
> unaware of the City Hall program to exterminate pigeons.
> Ho Hum..."

The fact that the city was trying to exterminate the hordes of
pigeons circling around City Hall made the photograph particularly
timely.

It is such small incidents and images that are the filaments of
journalism, and that make one realize that news and art can be
closely allied.  But it takes the "seeing eye" to spot them.

Reporting, in the final analysis, is the alertness to the scene
around one and the desire to communicate it to others.  As one
develops in the business, one becomes increasingly sensitized to that
scene so that eventually even small situations or things yield their
story essence.  And so at last, the camera is focused, the interest and
perception fuse to reveal a story, a reality in even a minute
phenomenon or event.  Concern as to the size or importance fades
under the impact of the depth with which the trained reporter can see
the commonplace.  All senses are involved, all doubt dispelled as he
reacts completely to the scene around him.  It was years later when I
realized this, but it is most satisfying when a reporter becomes
aware that he is so "tuned in" on the scene around him that they
"breathe" together.  Perhaps, more than a master's degree in
journalism - this realization is the final sheepskin.

Thus the artistry and form behind a collection; the magnificence
of a flower show; a child's experience with a pet are captured and
intensified to the point where their telling becomes, shall we say, an
art?  At least, an illumined craft.

# Part VI

# Survival

# 19

## Strike and Rebuff

BUT ALL WAS NOT well on the *Philadelphia Record*. In 1946, the American Newspaper Guild, CIO, apparently decided to make Mr. Stern's paper a testing block to gain $100-a-week salary for a reporter after three years employment. A series of heated union membership meetings began.

The *Record* had what was known as a "closed shop"; one could not be employed there unless one joined the union. The staff became divided into pro and con strike contingents. At the final meeting, I joined Nick Carter and a group of contras in opposing the strike. I got up and made a speech which was severely criticized. Comparatively fresh from the demise of the *Ledger,* I told the meeting that newspapers were fragile and could easily be destroyed. It was hot and heavy as compatriots took sides against compatriots. In the end the pros won. Labor leaders from throughout the country had come to rally and reinforce them.

It was a sunny morning, November 11th (Armistice Day!) when the *Philadelphia Record* began the fight for its life. About noon, a staff members representative moved into the switchboard room and disconnected the trunks.

Out of the building we filed, about 500 employees, among them middle-aged, overweight copy desk and rewrite men who hadn't walked further than the subway for years. They joined other younger members of the staff in circling round and round the building. The management, whose slightest whim we would have obeyed with alacrity 10 minutes before, stayed inside and continued to operate the paper. The strike went on for nearly three months. A sound truck stood in front of the building, like a calliope playing a ditty - "The Union, the Union, I'm sticking to the Union..." Strike signs were supplied for marchers to wear bearing such unsavory announcements as "Mr. Stern, your Scabs are showing."

A floor in a building across the street in the next block was engaged by the union as headquarters. Free food was served to supplement the $5 a week the union supplied an unmarried striker; more for one with a family. The understanding was that those who did not strike could never work again on a union paper. Bravest of us all was Stanley Thompson, Assistant City Editor and rewrite man, who left and went to work for the National Association of

Manufacturers; but most stayed and marched. Their life in the newspaper business, which they loved, seemed at stake.

It was a particularly cold winter in Philadelphia. The Pennsylvania State Employment Service gave us $25 a week unemployment compensation. We were required to picket four hours daily. It was a toss up with our meager income whether to eat or drink to keep warm.

Humor, however, arises even in the coldest and blackest days. Mother and I were buying a little house on Panama Street at the time, and the curtailment of my salary made my share of the payments difficult. I had found a part-time job writing with the Penn Mutual Life Insurance Co. way downtown. One day it was very cold and I stopped at nearby Gimbel's to buy a pair of "snuggies" before going uptown to the picket line. Coming up Broad Street on the subway, I got off at Race Street, the *Record* stop, to go into union headquarters or the ladies room in a neighboring restaurant to put them on. Suddenly I realized I would not have time; it was nearly my appointed hour of 4 o'clock on the line. The only other private place between me and the line was a subway telephone booth, occupied by a woman. I waited; she continued talking, she went on and on as the minutes ticked off. After signaling her without results, I became desperate. I simply opened the door, squeezed in, put the snuggies on and ran to the picket line. The event was "lingerie" news in the strike newspaper that week.

Another strike story was of Charlie Fisher, a columnist on the paper. Somewhere in the depths of those frigid, lean months, Charlie had got together enough money to take a companion to the Ritz-Carlton to dinner. Unquestionably receiving the same attention from the maitre d'hotel that he had been given when the paper was in full swing, Charlie grandly ordered pressed duck. It was an ironic but chuckling fact that at a nearby table sat Mr. Stern and a guest.

The *Camden (N.J.) Courier and Post*, also owned by Mr. Stern, were involved in the strike. One night a group of us were trucked over to Camden to join their picket line. We were told to walk in chain gang formation, near enough to the striker in front of us so that the printers, who were not on strike, could not get through to the building. It was rough work for women, but no one was hurt.

But tragedy does not last forever. One evening near midnight, *Record* printers came into Rubin's Bar, across the street from the paper, the obituary of the *Philadelphia Record* in hand. Ready for the first edition of February 1, 1947, it read:

## STATEMENT BY THE RECORD

This is the last issue of the *Philadelphia Record* under my management. Publication is suspended as of today.

This step has been taken only after careful consideration and discussion with my associates.

The strike against the *Record* by the American Newspaper Guild, involving more than four hundred people, has gone on for nearly three months. It has been impossible to obtain a fair settlement which would assure this newspaper of its ability to discharge its obligation to the public.

This is not only because of the Guild's excessive demands. Guild policy has tried to restrict the rights of management to a degree where it has become too great a burden to operate a completely independent press.

I will not attempt to give the reasons for this strange attitude of Guild leadership. I only know that the *Record*, Philadelphia's liberal newspaper, has been chosen by this one Union as a target for its unusual theories.

No other of the numerous unions with which the *Record* has had relations for so many years has adopted such an attitude.

The assets of the *Record* newspaper will be sold to the *Evening Bulletin,* which is issuing an accompanying statement.

PHILADELPHIA RECORD COMPANY
J. David Stern, President


## STATEMENT BY THE BULLETIN

Following the decision of the *Philadelphia Record,* and *Morning Post* and *Evening Courier of Camden,* to suspend publication, the owners and management of the Bulletin have committed to buy all of the newspaper assets of the *Philadelphia Record,* and the *Morning Post* and *Evening Courier* of Camden and radio station WCAU.

We regret to see established newspapers suspend. The *Bulletin* will at the earliest date extend its service by publishing a Sunday edition including the features of the Sunday Record. The other services rendered by the *Record* and the *Courier-Post* of Camden we hope will be resumed under independent ownership.

For the time being, by agreement, salaries and regular wages are being continued to those presently at work.

The operation of radio station WCAU is not affected by these arrangements. It will continue to render service under the direction of the present management which is in full control of the station.

BULLETIN COMPANY<br>Robert McLean, President

Approximately 1400 employees - editors, rewritemen, reporters, photographers, pressmen, delivery men and hoppers, and scores of office personnel on the three newspapers were on the street, out of work. It was the second death of major newspapers in the Philadelphia area within five years.

The American Newspaper Guild was founded in 1933. The first contract it ever negotiated was between the *Philadelphia Record* and the Newspaper Guild of Philadelphia and Camden, covering 150 editorial employees, the Guild's sole jurisdiction at the time it was signed, April 7, 1934. By 1946, now a CIO union, it had a membership of 25,000 in editorial, business and other departments of newspapers throughout the country.

The day of the sale of the *Record* and the *Camden Courier-Post* to the *Bulletin,* Guild officers of the closed papers issued this statement:

"The strike against the *Record* and *Courier-Post* will continue despite suspension of publication by both.

"The suspensions are temporary. The published statements by both the *Bulletin* and Stern management indicate clearly that publication of all three newspapers will be resumed even though ownership may change.

"Any new owner of either the *Record* or *Courier-Post* will have to deal with the Philadelphia-Camden Newspaper Guild in settling the strike under the law.

"Strike benefits will continue as before. So will unemployment compensation."

The *Camden Courier-Post* was bought by Harold Stretch, advertising manager of the *Philadelphia Inquirer,* but the *Philadelphia Record* was never revived.

The issue, however, did not die there.  And the demise of the *Record* presaged one of the great labor reforms of the century.

On February 10 and 11, the House of Representatives Education and Labor Committee, which had planned to open hearings on a sheaf of labor bills, put them aside to devote its first public session to an investigation of disputes between publishers and their employees.  Chairman of the committee was a young New Jersey Republican named Fred J. Hartley.  He said the recent epidemic of strikes by the CIO Guild had presented an "unexpected crisis."

The hearing relating to the *Record* lasted two days.  An interrogation mark as to Communist influence in the strike of the Stern newspapers hung over it.  Witnesses, in order, were Sam B. Eubanks, executive vice president, American Newspaper Guild; Michael Harris, president, Philadelphia Industrial Council, CIO; Arthur Riordan, secretary, Philadelphia-Camden Guild, Local 10, American Newspaper Guild, CIO; and J. David Stern.

Mr. Eubanks suggested that Mr. Stern's motive in selling his newspapers was "financial gain."  Mr. Harris said Mr. Stern refused to "bargain in good faith."  Mr. Riordan told the committee in effect, that it was not the policy of the Guild to oust Communists from the union.  He declared that there undoubtedly were Communists in the Guild, although "very few."  To attempt to oust Communists, he asserted, might lead to the ouster of "Republicans and Democrats." He was "proud," he added, of a provision in the Guild constitution which admitted members "regardless of race, religion or politics."

"Mr. Stern, for many years one of the foremost 'liberal' and pro-labor publishers in the country...time and again stated obliquely a belief that Communists had sought to use the Guild as an instrument to bring about his ruin," reported the *New York Times*.

"I have always given into the Guild because I thought that sometime, some way it would come of age...," Mr. Stern said.  "I was the first publisher to recognize the Guild.  I talked it over with Heywood Broun, an old friend of mine, who was the first president.  I believe I am the author of severance pay which I had met up with in the French newspapers when I was on a visit to Paris.  I thought it was a very good thing."

He declared his difficulties with the Guild were coincident in their beginning with the start of his editorial attacks in 1936, on the efforts of the Communists to arrange a common front with "liberals."  Liberalism, he emphasized, was "the best protection existing" for conservatism, and suggested that radicalism, as typified by Communism, was aware of this and, therefore, was the implacable foe of liberalism.

Of the Guild leaders, Mr. Stern said:

"They just wanted to destroy my papers. And they did. And that's that. The membership was misrepresented. The leadership was motivated by something entirely foreign to the matter of the Guild. The circumstantial evidence is very strong."

The Communist publication, the *Daily Worker of New York,* was the only paper to support the strike, he noted.

Of his central recommendation, Mr. Stern said: "Although my newspaper career is over, I have this suggestion to make to your committee; that no editor or creator of opinion of any newspaper, magazine or radio station should be compelled to belong to any organization, whether trade union or any other ... That is the one constructive contribution I hope will come out of this great tragedy in my life."

The Taft-Hartley Act, also known as the Labor-Management Relations Act, was passed in June 1947. It established control of labor disputes on a new basis. Besides enlarging the National Labor Relations Board, the act provided that the union or the employer must, before terminating a collective bargaining agreement, serve notice on the other party and on a government mediation service. The government was empowered to obtain an 80-day injunction against any strike that endangered national health or safety. Among other things, the law outlawed the closed shop, limited the union shop agreement to one year, and permitted the union "dues check off" to continue only with the written consent of the employee; it also provided that a union before using the facilities of the National Labor Relations Board, must file with the U.S. Department of Labor financial reports and affidavits that union officers are not Communists. In addition, the act forbade unions to contribute to political campaigns.

There were other plans for the bill following the hearings; Chairman Hartley stated that the Committee would prohibit editorial writers and those who do other than straight reporting for newspapers from becoming members of the American Newspaper Guild. This, he said, was a direct result of the *Record, Camden Courier-Post* strike. There was no question in his mind, Mr. Hartley declared, that here was a communistic influence in that deal.

The Labor Management Reporting and Disclosure Act of 1959 amended some features of the Taft-Hartley Act, but attempts to repeal it have been unsuccessful. Even in 1947, this act bridled the union - already gaining the saddle - from running away with the national industrial horse.

# 20

# Noblesse Oblige in the Bowery

IMPOVERISHED AFTER MONTHS without pay, and jobless, with only three major newspapers left in the city, the newsmen and women of the *Philadelphia Record* went out to look for work. I doubt if even half ever worked on a newspaper again. Some took highly remunerative public relations and advertising posts. Some went to other newspapers in other cities, and a comparative few joined the other Philadelphia newspapers, or those of the area. It was like a club; the strikers were divided into two groups - those who had voted for the strike and those who did not. The former were blackballed on Philadelphia newspapers.

I was fortunate. I was hired by the Camden, N.J., *Courier-Post*. After J. David Stern, Sr. sold the *Record* to the *Bulletin,* he also sold the *Camden Courier-Post* to Harold Stretch. The managing editor of the *Courier-Post,* Frank Ryan, and his staff were retained. A few of the *Record* staff were hired. I shall never forget the afternoon when the telephone rang and I learned that I was among them. Again my heart resounded, as once more I breathed the oxygen of newspapering.

It was not my first encounter with the Camden newspapers. In June of 1946, J. David Stern, Jr., editor of the *Courier-Post,* had asked to borrow me to do an investigation of the Camden County Children's Shelter in Pennsauken, New Jersey. Fred Shapiro, as he expressed it in a memorandum, "lend-leased" me.

The Camden series which uncovered deplorable conditions resulted in the speedy dismissal of Mrs. Grace A. Riggins, the superintendent. David Stern, Jr. had liked my work, but I remember something he taught me in the course of the Camden exposé which was a valuable lesson.

South Jersey, for which the *Camden Courier-Post* was the principal newspaper and political spokesman, was a highly political area. The investigation of the detention home was an exciting one, ringed with controversial political issues and opposed by the natural defense of a financially run-down city. I can remember in the course of the assignment stuffing documents from the detention house files inside my clothes when an occasion permitted it.

I wrote four stories which were illustrated with pictures of desolate bedrooms, untidy clothes closets, broken drinking fountains, tin cans and slop buckets for urinals, etc.

The first article went off with a bang; I had poured my heart into it. But in the second one, there was a letdown. Mr. Stern called me in and said it was not as good as the first one.

"I guess I let down, Mr. Stern," I said.

"You can never let down on a job, Ellen," he said.

It was good advice.

Camden, N.J., was a has been city in 1947. With a population of 130,000, it was poor and shabby. Traces of what the city had been were found in the large Victorian houses along Cooper Street. Riddled with politics, it was, however, the political center of South Jersey and the *Camden Courier-Post* was its spokesman. Yet the paper was the most truly gentlemanly sheet that I have ever been on. It was located in the "bowery" of the town, at the bottom of a street lined with bars, short order lunch counters and bookies for New Jersey's numerous race tracks.[1]

The flavor of the atmosphere might be illustrated by a conversation overheard at lunch time in a neighboring lounge bar:

Two girls were sitting in a booth near me looking at the bartender. I had noticed him when he crossed the room, particularly his brown shoes; they were so old that the leather looked like crushed chrysanthemums.

Behind the bar, he picked up one of the shrimps from a free lunch platter and began eating it. This had drawn the girls' attention.

"My Gawd, Eddie's eating!" exclaimed one of the damsels.

"Leave him eat!" replied her equally amazed companion. It apparently had been some time since they had seen Eddie consume anything but drink.

The *Courier-Post* was a very old paper and had seen newspapering in the days of its highest color and greatest excitement. Wire services, which often supplanted the dispatch of staff reporters to the scene of a story at distant points, had dulled the keen edge of newspapering.

Frank Ryan, the managing editor, was the man responsible for the aura of the *Courier-Post*. A keen, diplomatic and kind man with a sense of noblesse oblige, under him the paper was more like a club than a newspaper.

---

[1]The *Courier-Post*, now a member of the Gannett Newspaper group, is located in a handsome, modern building in Cherry Hill, N.J.

Unseared by the recent strike and sale, the *Courier-Post* remained a haven of old-time newspapering and a sort of employer-employee Utopia of trust and confidence. Typically, there were no timecards to punch; one was just expected to measure up. And the staff did, with every bit of its will and art.

Liquor flowed in and around the paper, and once there was an actual physical altercation in the City Room. But the people who worked there *loved* newspapering. They had survived where others had fallen by the wayside and were bound by common experience and loyalty. Underneath the *Camden Courier-Post* were the arms of Frank Ryan, and the rapport he accomplished was unique and memorable.

The City Editor was named Jimmie O'Keefe, and he spent more time talking to contacts on the telephone than any editor I have ever had. He knew what was going on in the farthermost reaches of the counties within our circulation area.

It was at the *Camden Courier-Post* that I first became aware of counties. In a large city like Philadelphia, neighborhoods outshone them, and the names Chester County, Montgomery County, etc. meant little unless one sought one's birth certificate. An exception was Bucks County, which was acquiring a special aura as a settlement of artists and theatrical people. But in smaller cities, it is in the surrounding counties where a large part of a newspaper's circulation is achieved. There is a village-like, small town, suburban and rural aura about counties encircling the smaller cities which adds an entirely new dimension to a reporter's activities. The counties are really the heartland of America. It is there one realizes the land was here before man, and it made man rather than man made it. Moral and civic virtue and sin and error are more sharply defined in towns and villages than in cities. Each one is a miniature example of the opportunities, accomplishments and shortcomings of democracy.

I think this story of Max and Emily Pfueller and their 18-acre farm near Cedarbrook, N.J., in 1947, gives the county flavor:

"I never called work trouble," remarked Max Pfueller, 75, leaning on his plow. "I didn't get tired. I had to succeed or get out."

As he spoke, the farmer looked across his well-tilled, 18-acre farm on Beebetown Road, near Cedarbrook, N.J. "But you have to have a doggish determination," he added.

Neighbors called Max "dumb Dutch" when he brought his wife, Emily, now 73, and their six children to live on the run-down farm in 1921.

Immigrating to America from Saxony in 1891, Max, a molder by trade, met Emily, also a Saxon, at a dance in Philadelphia.

In 1919, the Philadelphia infantile paralysis epidemic drove the Pfueller family to New Jersey. They settled first in Chesilhurst.

Two years later, they moved into a five-room shack on the farm, which then numbered 10 acres. Water came from a pump.

Pfueller knew nothing of farming. His own father had been a bricklayer.

"The only connection I ever had with a farm was when I stole apples off the farmers' trucks in the old country," he said.

Both Max and Emily have been American citizens for many years but their English is still broken.

In between catching the 7:40 p.m. train home from a Philadelphia foundry at night and returning by the 4:50 a.m. train in the morning, Pfueller set about making the shack livable.

Then the entire Pfueller family set to work raising guinea pigs. With the profits, Max bought a plow, a harrow, a wagon, farm tools and a horse and cow.

Next, he went out and looked at the land. It seemed dry and lifeless...

"And it was," recalls the farmer. "It was exploited - dead."

A man with six children couldn't take a chance on land like that. Max continued his job as a molder. In the evenings and on holidays he planted. Emily and the children did the farming.

Directly across the road from the Pfueller farm were eight acres of virgin woodland, half timber, half swamp.

"The mosquitoes from the swamp were so thick we had to grease ourselves all over before we worked in the fields," says Max.

"The first year," he adds, "I planted twice as many potatoes as I dug."

"See that spot there," he adds, indicating a row of stocky raspberry bushes. "I'll never forget my pleasure when I saw crabgrass come up there. Farmers usually don't like crabgrass. But to me it meant the earth had come to life."

It took more than cultivation to revive the farm's depleted soil. Every week, sometimes twice, the Pfueller children hitched Jim, the horse, to the wagon and went to the woods for leaves and nettles.

"Some people don't have the patience," explains Max, "but leaves and nettles make wonderful fertilizer."

The rich loam, combined with green manure, nourished the tired earth.

The fourth summer, timid, pink raspberries appeared in the "bald spot."

Emily made a sunshine cake to celebrate.

His own 10 acres in hand, Max, still working at the foundry by day, purchased the eight acres of swamp and wood across the road.

The land was irregular, he recalls, and in the center stood a sand hill, rising sentinel-like from the insect-breeding waters. A narrow creek, clogged with fallen trees and underbrush, also traversed the property.

For months, Max and his sons moved loads of yellow gravel from the solid sections of the property to the marsh.

"Four hundred and fifty loads, I remember them," says Max. "The bog was so deep we had to put down planks for Jim to walk on. Then we heaped on three tons of lime and $40 worth of seed."

It was a great day when the first three caracul lambs arrived by express from Texas.

Max paid $200 for the trio, and $24 expressage.

And as the years progressed, a peaceful herd grazed dark against the green of the pasture that was once the old swampland. Max built the sheep a shack of fallen cedars.

The sheep were typical of Max's taste in stocking and planting his acres. With the longstanding patience the development of the land required, he developed fondness for variety in farm living.

"If you're interested in something you naturally want to make it varied, you don't let it get monotonous," he explains.

Catalogues and magazines expounding farm staples and rarities flooded the shack. Emily was kept busy dusting them.

And instead of the usual crate of Plymouth Rocks or Rhode Island Reds, Max ordered a batch of Black Leghorns.

Rabbits, black, and brown Belgian ones, as well as white, followed. Soon a hive of bees.

When the Depression came, Max stopped work at the foundry, and devoted all his time to farming. As the land prospered, the Pfuellers sent crops to market, berries, tomatoes, lambs and chickens.

The milk of an extra cow that Max purchased was not sold.

"We kept that for the boys," says Max. "Boys need milk."

Although Max later bought a dump truck and a car, which he converted into a tractor, he has never gone in for mechanized farming.

He is using the same harrow, plow and wagon he got when he started farming.

**********

The little state of New Jersey is a varied place. It has been called the highway between two states - New York and Pennsylvania. But it is far more than this and has a kaleidoscopic character: Wonderful farmlands for fruit and vegetables; longstanding race tracks with thriving business; the deluxe suburbs of North Jersey; the bridged Delaware at Trenton with its sign "Trenton Makes, the World Takes," and the stretch of Atlantic Ocean beaches, excelled nowhere in this country - make New Jersey unique.

Although settled earlier than New York or Pennsylvania, the general New Jersey aura is less pretentious and status conscious. Impregnated with the activities of General Washington, an outstanding event of which was the crossing of the Delaware River in a boat during the Revolution immortalized in Emanuel Lentze's painting - New Jersey neither seems to dwell overly on history or its mercantile and commercial accomplishments. It appears too busy to look back at its own image. Swept by interstate travel, it pulsates with the life of the two states bordering it, yet achieves an identity of its own. Eluding the blue laws of Pennsylvania across the river, it has maintained a jaunty, come-what-may attitude toward life. It is more casual and truly natural then Pennsylvania; less consciously proud than New York.

Although changing social conditions and political corruption have damaged New Jersey, it had, as early as the 1940s, one of the most unified and organized systems of handling social welfare in the country. The Department of Institutions & Agencies, during my tenure in Camden, was under the leadership of Commissioner Sanford Bates. All social welfare agencies throughout the state were under his aegis.

Geriatrics was a subject that was just coming into the limelight when I was in New Jersey. I had the privilege of interviewing Dr. Ellen Potter, deputy commissioner of welfare in the department, a pioneer in the promotion of long-range federal, state and local planning in the care of the old and chronically ill. She was then 77. At 69, she had fought the retirement to which she was entitled at 65 - "I was still too full of beans (Old New England for full of pep) to accept."

Born in New London, Conn., Dr. Potter was graduated from Women's Medical College of Pennsylvania in 1903 and after general practice became medical director of her alma mater, and later, Pennsylvania state secretary of welfare and superintendent of the New Jersey Woman's Reformatory and State Home for Girls.

Ellen Potter had made an historical speech before the National Conference of Social Work at Buffalo in 1946, calling for the

creation at state level of "a master planning body" to dramatize the
need for facilities for the chronically ill.

Her speech was the flower of two decades of planting and
nourishing an idea, revolutionary in the social work field - "the
substitution of solidarity for isolated individual effort" in the
treatment and prevention of chronic illness.

Shortly afterward, the American Public Welfare Association, the
American Medical Association and the American Public Health
Association issued a joint statement on "Planning for the Chronically
Ill." They recommended that "coordinated and comprehensive
planning" be undertaken at all levels of federal, state and local
government. Dr. Potter's appeal was vindicated.

I interviewed Ellen Potter in her sunny five-room Trenton
apartment.

"I think the principal reason I've kept in harness so long is that
I've tried to make up my mind quickly, and not to have a state of
conflict within myself," she said. "After I've made a decision, I've
tried to avoid looking back and wondering if I did the right thing."

"I've developed a philosophy about work, after 45 years of it.
It's to do the best you can on the job you've got and let Heaven take
care of the rest."

Of her work at the New Jersey Woman's Reformatory and State
Home for Girls she said: "It takes a strong personality to stand the
pressure of a correctional institution. If you're too easy, your
charges get out of hand, if you're too hard, it's even worse. And
maintaining a balance wears one out."

Reformatories were drab in the '20s. But the physician adopted
the principle that cooperation is essential even in penal
surroundings.

She eliminated the "chain gang" uniform in use, and asked her
staff to produce inmates whom they considered "leaders" at the
institution. The staff frankly was puzzled.

"There is Lois," suggested one matron, "she's the one who is
always getting the others into trouble."

"She's the one I want," rejoined Dr. Potter.

Lois, it developed, was an architectural student. The new
superintendent enlisted her aid in organizing the drafting of a pilot
plan of the reformatory. And inmates who had rallied to Lois'
leadership in misdemeanors, jumped just as eagerly on the new
bandwagon.

"You have to challenge an inmate's interest and give her
diversity," said Dr. Potter.

**********

During her 17 years with the New Jersey Department of Institutions and Agencies she had ample opportunity to formulate and study needs of caring for the aged.

"What to do about mother or dad, Dr. Potter?"

"Isn't the first obligation to the rising generation?" she asked. "In the old-fashioned family, there was always room for three generations, provided there weren't too many in the ranks. But today, families and homes have shrunk.

"If the home setting is small, it is to the interest of all, whenever possible, that the aged parent be provided with a setting of his own, pleasant and convenient enough for a grandchild to visit."

The association of grandparent and child was, in her opinion, a mutually beneficial one (I knew that!); but she considered the housing of a deteriorated aged parent with the family's young as "unfair."

She listed three main psychological factors to be considered in making mother or father happy in old age: prestige, security and affection, given and received.

Well known guidelines today, but Ellen Potter was a trailblazer.

Years later, I did some writing for a Dr. Theodore C. Krauss, medical director of the Rosa Coplon Jewish Home and Infirmary, Buffalo, N.Y., and assistant clinical professor of medicine, State University of New York at Buffalo. Empathy is perhaps the greatest personal characteristic a physician can possess, and Dr. Krauss had great empathy for older persons. He had cherished his own parents and the feeling overflowed to all older people. His opinion on work for the elderly is interesting.

"More and more people in their retirement years begin to realize that they still have enough to continue working, in spite of the fact that chronologically they have reached the final milepost which consigned them to retirement. Statistics show that at age 65 today, the average person has a life expectancy of about another 13 years, and many of these may prove useful working ones.

"Should the elderly person be physically able to leave his home and go into the community, certainly this should be encouraged. But sensible limitations should be in effect. It is fine to work, but let us limit working hours to perhaps four instead of eight, or every other day instead of every day, depending upon the individual and his ability to perform.

"If possible, the work done should not have to be 100% for financial gain, but should be work which will give satisfaction and a feeling of fulfillment and self-sufficiency."

**********

So much for the humanitarianism and philanthropy in which I participated in Camden. A seamy side of my days involved covering Divorce Court in Chancery Court, as its called in New Jersey. Throughout my years on newspapers, I assiduously avoided "beats," regular assignments on one subject. I liked kaleidoscopic variety, a colorful, revolving carousel of events delighted me. In my years as a general reporter, among the few beats I had were that divorce court, and in later years, the subject of alcoholism. Nor have I ever had an interest in becoming an editor. The intricacies of the "block" - the metal frame on which newspaper type used to be set in the composing room before the advent of cold type - and composition of a page had no charm for me. As the years progressed, however, through exposure I developed a certain eye for merit and mistakes in makeup and how much it can contribute to or detract from a story.

Advisory Master Burton was the judge under whom I covered most of my stories in Camden Divorce Court. A young man with wavy blonde hair and wearing a beautiful star sapphire ring, he was a dignified figure as he faced the torrent of breakups, fights, arguments, investigation and expository photography of divorce action in the area. The variety of cases was astounding, reflecting the outraged and defensive emotions and disillusionment of plaintiffs and defendants.

Yet humor worms its way into the corners of life's dreariest scenes. One of the most unusual cases I covered was that of a ranking military man, who returned to the States from the Middle East to face divorce action by his wife. Her claim was evidenced by photographs taken of the solider in Turkey. They showed a room with sofa pillows encircling the periphery. The defense argued that this was the custom of Turkey and had no immoral implications. The plaintiff argued otherwise. It's a long road from Camden, N.J., to Turkey and the trial brought a bit of Eastern spice into the courtroom. There was also the spouse who threw his mate on a hamburger grill, and another who bought a dog to protect him from his wife.

Then there was the former GI whom Judge Burton, upon examining his Army record, questioned concerning his discharge.

"Yuh Honor, you see I has flatfeet," explained the defendant.

"I don't see how flatfeet has any connection with statutory rape," replied the judge.

During the six months I covered this court, I observed the marital state in perhaps its lowest estate.

**********

IN THE LIGHT of the crisp, blue-covered report of the Visiting Nurse & Health Association of Camden County, Inc. for 1980, it is difficult to envision the level of home nursing service in parts of the Camden area in 1947. One realizes that despite an early founding date (settled in 1681, laid out in 1773 and incorporated in 1828) and the subsequent level of industrial and civic development of an area, the veneer of civilization can be very thin.

It must be recognized, however, that the health sciences have expanded greatly in the past four decades, gaining much wider emphasis. Yesterday's options are, in theory at least, today's mandates.

The maintenance of a hospital in a community and even limited public nursing service (as distinguished from private) can preclude a realization of the vast field beyond their periphery needing nursing care. Above all, however, in a poor community, the public dollar, with its potential of support of more attractive causes and of patronage, can exercise a stranglehold on humanitarian outreach. This supposition was graphically illustrated in the city of Camden and environs during my tenure on the *Courier-Post*. Again, through the power of the press, the soggy dough of a dimly perceived public need was given yeast - and rose.

When reporters reach the Golden Gate such leavening they have effected through their newspapers surely will be of help to entrance.

I am not a "cause" person. To observe, particularly the inspiring, beautiful or just plain interesting, has been my thrust. But when any reporter comes face to face with criminality, cruelty of human neglect, merely as a human being he rises in revolt to it; he becomes a crusader in spite of himself.

The following account illustrates what a community can do - given a shot in the arm (or a boot in the rear - clergy, excuse me!) by a newspaper.

CAMDEN, N. J., Chattanooga and Knoxville, Tenn., were the only cities of 100,000 population east of the Mississippi, without a visiting nurse association in the 1940s. More affluent neighboring towns like Collingwood, Haddonfield, and Merchantville-

Pennsauken each had a visiting nurse association which gave bedside care, but only in their respective communities. The once-grand, now industrialized yet impoverished city of Camden was vulnerable without one. Longstanding attempts by individuals and groups to establish a V.A. in the area were well-meaning, but failed.

In December, 1946, the Business & Professional Women's Club of Camden tried again. They asked the National Organization for Public Health Nursing, recognized authority in the field, to survey the situation and recommend what was needed.

The national organization agreed to do so, if the Camden County Council of Social Agencies consented. The council was willing.

Serious gaps in essential nursing service in Camden city and county were disclosed by the survey, which especially emphasizing the "acute" need for the care of the sick at home. Organization of a visiting nurse service was advised, which would be available to anyone who needed it, regardless of race, creed, color or economic status. It would operate in Camden city only until funds and personnel were available for county wide expansion.

NOPHN recommended the association be organized under voluntary auspices, such as community groups, as distinguished from official or public sponsorship such as the health department. The report on the survey had been presented to the Council of Social Agencies and the Community Chest at their annula feeding in April, 1948. It aroused little interest and no action.

**********

The Business & Professional Women, however, did not lose heart. They turned to the physicians of the area, the 240 members of the Camden Medical Society; 109 answered the club's questionnaire, 86, or about 76 percent, approved the formation of a visiting nurse association.

The doctors said it most frequently was needed in chronic, post-operative and post-natal cases, but also for the application of dressings and administration of internal irrigations; in cardiac, pneumonia and skin disease cases and for general bedside care.

Reassured of the validity of their cause, the Business & Professional Women enlarged their committee. Representatives of individual social agencies, clubs and educational groups were enrolled.

This was the situation in January, 1949, as the *Camden Courier-Post* sent me out to look it over.

Three year old Tony, who has a congenital dislocation of the hips. He has been in a body cast since last October, strapped in a frog-like position.

All day long - and through the night - the little boy lies on a metal frame in the dining room of his home. He is dependent on others for every function.

Tony's mother has six other children, ranging in age from two to 13 years. Her hands are full - to overflowing.

The child needs nursing care. But he's not getting it. Because there is no visiting nurse station in Camden.

**********

Mrs. O. developed cancer of the jaw. It swept across her face - destroying one entire side.

Her children could not endure the sight of their mother. They were unable to assist her. Nor did they know how.

A district nurse from a neighboring community learned of the case and called on Mrs. O. as often as her already crowded schedule permitted, instilled the children with fortitude and instructed them how to help.

But Mrs. O.'s suffering was intense. Particularly during days when the nurse could not come and the children were at school - and there was no one to change the dressings, provided by Camden county chapter of the American Cancer Association.

Finally, she was admitted to an institution for incurables.

**********

John J. is 83. He lives in the heart of Camden with his only son, a policeman. He suffers from old age complications, particularly a kidney complaint.

John's daughter-in-law is a high strung woman, with young children. She's fond enough of "Dad," but an "old" child on her hands stretches her nerves to the breaking point.

The Js can't afford a private nurse for Dad - and Camden has no visiting nurse service.

**********

The case of Mary Y. is hard to believe of a community the size of Camden.

Mary, 80, lived on the third floor of a rooming house in North Camden. She had not left that room for more than a year.

One day, it was announced the place was sold. Neighbors reported Mary's plight to the Department of Public Welfare.

The case worker found Mary seated in a sagging wicker chair beside a two-burner gas plate. But no gas flowed through the pipe. Mary had just finished lunch of a hot dog and a cold tomato.

Her withered frame was clad in clothes she had not removed for an indefinite period - filthy underwear, dingy underskirts and tattered black sweater.

Vainly, the Department of Public Welfare searched for a nurse to bathe Mary.

After two days, a neighbor volunteered. But she didn't wash Mary completely - at first.

"We were afraid is might kill her," says the case worker who assisted, "so we just gently washed sections at a time. It took a day and a half."

**********

There were approximately 45,000 persons suffering from chronic diseases or permanent impairment in Camden County. Chronic invalids numbered about 3,000.

The reason?

First an increase in longevity, but nearly half the chronically ill were under 40; about one-third were children under 16 years, chiefly with orthopedic disorders, and nearly a fourth of them were under six years.

The survey had disclosed there were 11 public health nursing agencies offering part-time service in all parts of Camden county; seven of them were in operation in all or parts of the city of Camden. These agencies employed a total of 79 nurses, 36 of whom worked in the city, 43 in outlying areas. In addition, 44 industrial nurses were employed in the county, the majority of whom served in the city; their duties, however, were confined to their respective plants.

Despite this battalion of "shock troops," as the public health nurse is called on the health battlefield, homebound sick, chronically ill, handicapped and aged persons - in need of anything from a bath to a penicillin injection - could not get help unless they could afford - and obtain - a private trained nurse. On the county's current welfare rolls, 2,700 were chronically ill persons over 65 years of age.

With the city's hospitals crowded to overflowing (the largest one had a waiting list of 150), the situation was reflected in local mortality rates. Camden topped the national average in all but three of the 10 leading causes of death. Perhaps most shocking of all, over 2-1/2 miles or 27 percent of Camden city was totally without maternal and child public health nurses from city or state.

NOPHN summarized it thus: "From this it can be seen that Camden city and county are fairly well supplied with public health nurses...but with the division of responsibilities among many different agencies, the result is a lack of essential public health nursing care for the community.

"The most serious lack of a complete absence of part-time nursing care - except for patients insured with certain life insurance companies (i.e. Metropolitan and John Hancock Mutual Life) - for persons sick at home and in need of skilled nursing sevice."

The service advised that in addition to the establishment of a Visiting Association, Camden county begin to develop a more unified and comprehensive public health and public health nursing program.

We asked: "Would coordination of these 11 agencies provide care for that 27 percent of the mothers and children in Camden city now lacking it? And would bedside care for the homebound sick then be available?

The answer was "no." NOPHN estimated that one public health nurse for each 2,000 persons is needed, including care of the homebound sick, and one public health nurse is required for each 5,000 persons, where care of the housebound is not included.

Thus with a population of approximately 225,800 Camden county and city needed a total of 113 or 34 more than employed, of which Camden city's quota would be 59, or 23 more than then available to its people.

On February 26, 1948, about a month after the *Courier-Post's* series, a Visiting Nurse Association of Camden City was launched. A new board of directors "took over the ball" from the survey committee sponsored by the Business & Professional Women's Club. The new board embraced one or more representatives of the clergy, civic groups, social agencies, clubs, the National Association for the Advancement of Colored People, the Parent-

Teachers Association, physicians, dentists, nurses, patriotic groups and medical auxiliaries.

The outcome is history.  In 1980, the Visiting Nurse & Health Association of Camden County, Inc. made 21,643 home visits, representing 3,264 persons needing single or multiple calls.  The spirit in which these calls were made is reflected in the statement of staff nurses in the Association's annual report:

"We may not change or alter the life of the person or family we are seeing, but hopefully we will bring understanding and knowledge where there is fear and ignorance, comfort where there is discomfort, independence rather then dependence, and maybe even an enrichment of life at death."

# 21

## "It's Mah Heart, Suh!"

DESPITE THE WONDERFUL esprit de corps of the *Camden Courier Post* itself, the depleted city was depressing. So after about a year there, one day I went over to the *Evening Bulletin* to see Walter Lister, who had become Managing Editor after the demise of the *Record*. Mr. Lister said he had nothing then, but to come back in about six months.

As I was leaving his office, an old friend, Mrs. Charlotte Trotter, the Society Editor of the paper, saw me passing through the City Room. In a day or two, I received a telephone call from her in Camden, asking me if I would come to work in her department for $10 more a week than I was receiving in my present post. In one of the mistakes of judgment of my career, I accepted, and left a general assignment position on the *Courier-Post* to return to my embryo, a Society Department. It seemed that I had to *experience* the fact that one cannot turn back the journalistic clock.

I was hired for the *Evening Bulletin* by the Feature Editor, Paul Cranston, who also managed the society department. Mrs. Trotter was the spirit of grace, but I sat there in the Bulletin society department like one stunned by a blow on the head. General news events marched around me and by me like mute soldiers; it was like returning to my adolescence.

There were, however, two exceptions, initiated by Mr. Lister himself. The Republicans were holding their national convention in Philadelphia in June, 1948. John LaCerda, the *Bulletin* reporter with whom I had covered the Bergdoll story on the *Record*, suggested to Mr. Lister that the *Bulletin* try to obtain the tentative draft of the *GOP* platform and run it on the first day of the convention, rather than the third. The idea appealed to the managing editor. It was my day off, and I was in the bathtub when he telephoned. Wrapped in a towel, I answered to hear:

"Ellen?"

"Yes, Mr. Lister."

"How soon can you be down at the Bellevue-Stratford (about 10 blocks from my house)?"

"About a half hour, Mr. Lister?"

"Make it 20 minutes," he said. "Meet Jean Barrett there, and she'll tell you what to do."

I was at the hotel within the specified time and met Jean Barrett at the Walnut Street door of the crowded lobby. Jean, a former Ziegfield Follies showgirl, who had become a fine reporter, also had come from the *Record* to the *Bulletin*. Drawing me into a corner, she handed me the badge of a woman delegate to the convention from Florida, May Kramer.

"You're to go up to the 18th Floor, pose as this woman, and get your hands on any papers you can," she explained. "Then get out of the room. John LaCerda will be at the door outside the meeting room to help you."

It seemed LaCerda had tried to pose as a delegate, but there were no male ones missing; Mrs. Kramer, however, was not present. Then Jean had been tapped for the job, but was withdrawn when it was found that a member of the platform knew who she was. It was up to me.

I pinned Mrs. Kramer's badge over my heart and pushed my way through the lobby crowd to the elevators. It was evident it would be a long time before I was able to board one. Speed was imperative. Rounding the side of the lobby, I found the marble staircase which reached 18 floors to the room where the delegates were meeting to consider the draft of the Republican platform. There was no alternative; I would have to walk. As I gained about the 11th flight of the fortunately shallow marble staircase, I overheard two women delegates through the open door of a bedroom as I passed; all Republicans do not come from the North, these two women were Southerners.

"Mah, I'd like some ginger ale," one said to the other, who assented.

Nobody but I knew how I would have like to have paused for a ginger ale at that point!

It was a particularly hot June day, and my healthy heart was beginning to pound a little. Upon reaching the 16th floor, I was able to get the elevator to the 18th, but I was still pretty pale when I reached it, which incidently served me well.

Presenting myself at the door of the meeting room and displaying my badge, I was immediately admitted and chose a seat near the window at the end of chairs. I carried a large and expensive pocketbook that my Mother had given me in honor of my being hired by the *Bulletin*. By the window, I fanned myself with a bit of Kleenex, as I and approximately 75 other delegates faced the Platform Committee.

In a short time, large piles of legal-sized documents were wheeled around by cart and distributed to the gathering. A glance showed them to be the tentatively drafted platform. Waiting a couple of minutes, I folded the document and placed it across my chest beneath the voluminous handbag. Then rising to my feet and fluttering the Kleenex, I started for the door. A thin, middle-aged man approached me with an inquiring look:

"It's mah heart, Suh," I said in a deep Floridian accent, "It's the heat...I just can't stand it..."

Staggering toward the door with his assistance, I was greeted outside by a contingent of Blacks who anxiously were awaiting inclusion of some clause in the draft. My guide murmured something about my indisposition to the group, and they made an aisle for me, directing "let the lady out!...she's gonna' faint. She ain't well - she's sick!" Outside the door was LaCerda. He joined me in going to the elevator, and I slipped him the Republican Platform of 1948 - that 2,400 word document, in mimeograph form. It had been so guarded that Bellevue-Stratford pages had carried the copy from floor to floor, traveling upward by the marble stairs, just as I did (although I doubt all at one time), rather than take a chance on having it stolen in the elevators.

LaCerda ran ahead of me to the office to write the story, and in the Three Star edition that afternoon, the *Bulletin* printed part of the platform; the entire 2,400 words appeared in the Four Star Final.

When I went back to the office, I went into the society department. Mr. Lister came in shortly.

"It's no more than I expected, Ellen," he said. From a man whose praises were not given lightly, that far exceeded the subsequent $50 bonus.

"As a senator, I think it was a hell of a thing to do," said Sen. Henry Cabot Lodge, Jr., according to *Newsweek*. "As a former newspaperman, I think it's wonderful."

**\*\*\*\*\*\*\*\*\*\***

On another occasion, I was sent to Freehold, N.J., to work on the sensational White Russian story of August, 1948.

The leap of Mrs. Oksana Stepanovana Kosenkina from the third floor of the Soviet consulate in New York on August 12, 1948, further inflamed a growing national consciousness of Russian activity, both espionage and repression, in the United States. It would burst into full conflagration under Sen. Joseph McCarthy in the 1950s.

Mrs. Kosenkina, a Russian citizen and teacher, had been taken from the Valley Cottage farm for anti-Communist Russians, operated by the former Countess Alexandra Tolstoy, about 30 miles north of New York City, on Aug. 7, by Soviet Consul General Yakov Lomakin and aides. She had been in the consulate from that time until her leap. An international struggle for her custody was in progress.

Although the Soviet consulate told police the teacher had not been held against her will, she apparently dreaded exportation to Russia, where she was quoted as saying that her husband, also a teacher, was seized by Soviet secret police in 1937, and she had not seen him since.

"I was struggling to break out; I was like a bird in a cage," she was quoted as saying after her leap. "I had to get out!"

At the time, Mrs. Kosenkina was at the Valley Cottage farm, another Russian teacher and his family also were sheltered there: Michael I. Samarine, his wife, a daughter and twins. The *Bulletin* learned this family had been moved to the farm of a White Russian chicken farmer in Freehold, N.J., 13 miles south of the once fashionable resort of Lakewood, with its well known hotel, "Laurel-in-the-Pines."

Walter Lister pulled me out of the social nest in which I was embedded and once more sent me into "the whole wide world" on the story.

The closely guarded hospital room of Mrs. Kosenkina in Roosevelt Hospital, the mounting struggle for her custody, and her refusal to see anyone from the Russian consulate made every line obtainable about the status of Russian refugee teachers in the United States of significance and high news value. The eyes of the country were on the hospital room and anything pertaining to or related to it.

The *Bulletin* was the first large metropolitan paper in the country to run this story, which surely cast some light on the Red/White Russian activity in this country. It should be noted that some of this account was lifted from the local paper in Freehold. In days when metropolitan paper reporters were sent personally out of town on assignments more often, in their eagerness to "get the story" they sometimes just plunged right into it physically, so to speak. It was an ironic fact that on-the-spot, small local papers could have it before them. Therefore, it was wise to take a few precious moments to get those locals. Even if they did not have the story, they might have valuable bits of information or leads that would save much legwork and time.

Next to the Holy Spirit, news probably is the freest thing on earth, free of any particular form in which it must be passed on -

word of mouth, sight, sound or print. And like electricity, it cannot be contained indefinitely.

Years have blurred my memory of Freehold, a great sulky race track center, the surrounding farms of which were impregnated with White Russians. I can dimly see the town lined with hotels, boarding houses and bars, but more clearly the land of the chicken farmers. I remember running over fields in search of one Harry Schbanoff. A giant of a fellow in his middle 60s, Schbanoff, an ex-Russian revolutionary, had hidden the Samarines for nine days.

His story, gleaned largely from the local Freehold paper which had several hours jump on me, was at least an echo of that of Mrs. Kosenkina in her New York hospital bed.

Incidently, it was to that superb rewriteman, Stanley Thompson, who had left the *Record* rather than strike and who now, too, had come to the *Bulletin* - he later became City Editor - to whom I telephoned the story which is synopsized here.

Schbanoff, an American citizen, had lived in Freehold for 38 years and operated a medium-sized chicken farm with a few cattle on the New York highway a-mile-and-a-half north of Freehold. He met Countess Tolstoy, who operated the Tolstoy Foundation with headquarters at 289 Fourth Street, New York, for the first time through his efforts on behalf of a Frenchman detained at Ellis Island.

His visit to the Cottage Valley farm and the nearly 90 refugees from Europe he saw there deeply impressed him. He promised the Countess he would do anything he could to help her.

On July 29, the Countess called, asking him to come to New York. He was at the Tolstoy Foundation headquarters the next morning. The Countess told Schbanoff that Oksana Stepanovana was in her office - this was eight days before she was abducted by the Soviet consulate - and another Russian teacher, Michael I. Samarine, also had come there. The Countess then voiced her suspicions that one or the other could be a spy.

"Samarine had told the Countess he was afraid to go back to Russia because of the death or severe punishment he heard would await him," Schbanoff explained. "He wanted to stay in America.

"If he were not allowed to stay, Samarine said, he would kill himself and his family, his wife, and their three children, a daughter 12, and 12-month-old twins...."

The Countess admitted she had heard this from many others, but from her considerable experience felt Samarine meant what he said. She said she was 95 per cent sure he was going to be allowed to remain in the United States. She asked Schbanoff to hide him a few days, before the ship on which he was to sail departed from Russia.

Arrangements were made for Schbanoff to meet Samarine in a cafeteria at Broadway and 140th Street, and they went to the teacher's house nearby. There Schbanoff explained to him his efforts to hide him would be "dangerous and risky," and that he would have to work hard in the United States at work he was not used to. Samarine reiterated he would kill himself and his family rather than return to Russia.

Schbanoff was impressed. After returning to the Tolstoy Foundation and discussing the matter with the Countess, he agreed to take the Samarines to his farm in Freehold.

"I looked at the clock," he said, "and realized it was pretty late. I would have to go back to Freehold and get my truck and I would not be back until late that night. Samarine said: "The later the better."

After returning to the farm for his truck, Schbanoff drove it back to New York City.

"There was no place to park at Samarine's home," he explained, "so I parked a block away and went to his house. We started to prepare furniture and trunks. Then I sat and waited.

"After midnight or later, I brought my truck to the front door and we loaded everything into it. Samarine sat on the front seat with the twins, his wife and daughter sat in the rear.... A few blocks before we came to the Lincoln Tunnel, I told Samarine to ride in the rear of the truck and let his wife up front. He did. We got home at about 3 a.m."

During the week that followed, everything was quiet, Schbanoff said. But on Saturday, Aug. 7 - the day the nation was to get its first intimation of the struggle that was to develop over the custody of the Samarines and Mrs. Kosenkina - Schbanoff and his wife, Alexandra, went to Perth Amboy, N.J., to market.

"While we were away," Schbanoff reported, "a strange man called a member of my family, since we have no telephone, and asked if we could hide the Samarines somewhere else because they were now in danger. When I came home I learned about the call and was surprised."

Schbanoff telephoned the Tolstoy farm and talked to the Countess. She told him that Mrs. Kosenkina had been kidnapped from the farm and taken to the Soviet consul in New York City. For that reason, she wanted the Samarines hidden somewhere else. The original telephone call had come from one of her agents.

The next day at 6:30 in the morning, the Countess came to the farm with three men. One was the agent who had made the telephone call. He spoke Russian. The others spoke English and Schbanoff believed they were FBI agents. They entered the farmhouse without knocking. Samarine left with them, his wife and children remaining a few more days before departing.

Schbanoff, one of about 300 chicken farmers - many of them Russian - in and around Freehold, said that for himself, he was not a member of any White Russian underground or political group. His only remaining affiliation with his homeland, he declared, was his church membership.

Americans were ingenuous about Soviet aims and activities in the late '40s. But the Kosenkina/Samarine story of '48 was a partial eye-opener of what was simmering beneath the surface. It came to a boil the following March, when 11 leaders of the U.S. Communist Party went on trial in New York City.

After 9 months, they were convicted of advocating violent overthrow of the U.S. government; 10 were sentenced to 5 years in prison each, and the 11th to 3 years. The Supreme Court upheld the convictions June 4, 1951.

That was the year in another city, on another newspaper, the Communists and I would meet again.

But now, I realized that if I remained in the society department of the *Evening Bulletin,* I would lose my impetus for general news. Motivation and desire must be nurtured. Like other human characteristics, they too can erode. My motivation would be stultified; I would be frustrated.

At the end of five months, having delivered two major news stories to the *Bulletin,* I went to Mr. Lister and asked if he could not move me permanently to the City Side as a general assignment reporter. But politics can be stronger than news or fiction. He shook his head.

"It's not what I want, Ellen," he said, "but I can't."

Mr. Cranston, who had engaged me for the society page, would not let me go, and at the time, Walter Lister did not have the authority to go over his head.

I liked Walter Lister. He had hired me on the *Record* and I had worked for him for four years. I had been through a strike in which I voted for his cause. To him I said among the bravest and most gallant words of my working life.

"People, Mr. Lister," I said, "are always more important than things." I meant that if he were not in a position to help me, his professional welfare was more important than if I got the job.

"People don't walk off the largest evening paper in the United States," Barbara Barnes, the *Bulletin* feature writer, told me when I said I was leaving.

"But I'm going, Barbara," I said.

So I walked out into the afternoon light on Filbert Street, again a reporter without a newspaper.

# 22

## Heading West

IT WAS 4-1/2 MONTHS before I found another newspaper to work on. Newspaper jobs were scarce in the East. My friend, Virginia Wilton, the advertising manager of the *Courier-Post,* helped me make an elaborate dossier, illustrated with top stories I had covered during my 10 years in the newspaper business. I took it to Washington, proudly drawing the attention of the head of the Associated Press Bureau there to my series on the Camden County Children's Shelter. He was unimpressed.

"We want someone who can get the facts and run fast to a phone," he said.

One of the most precious things in my possession today is a slip of ruled paper from a notebook with this message to the city editor of the *Washington Times-Herald.* It reads:

"Eddie Folliard: Help this girl get a job in Washington. She's at least as good as _____ (a nationally-known reporter) was, will work harder."

It was signed - Fred E. Shapiro.

But Mr. Folliard could not oblige. I went to New York where I did not find a newspaper job, but where the former advertising manager of the *Philadelphia Record*, now working for the Hearst Co., got me one writing public relations releases for *Harper's Bazaar* and *Yachting*, under John A. Clements, a public relations man at Hearst.

"I'm worried about you, Ellen," he told me when I questioned the fact that it was not a newspaper, "take this; it will tide you over."

After a short while, Mr. Clements sent me down to Washington to do a survey of surveys, which were beginning to blossom. I stayed at the old Willard Hotel and had a meal or two at the atmospheric Occidental nearby. After that, Mr. Clements got me a job with a budding mothproofing company, writing promotional pieces. I remember on one occasion, the head of the company had to borrow 10 cents from someone in the office to ride uptown on the subway.

After completing the few weeks of work there, one morning, back in New York, I was walking up 57th Street, very near the end of my resources. I had two choices: I could continue writing public relations releases or I could contact the last newspaperman I knew who might know of a job - Nick Carter, recommended by Fred

Shapiro, he had been hired by the *Buffalo Evening News*, at the time one of the richest newspaper in the country.

"You've spent 10 years in the newspaper business and you love it," I reasoned with myself as I walked up the street, "are you going to let it all go down the drain?"

I had reached Seventh Avenue, with its drugstore on the southwest corner. I went in and found a telephone booth.

"Give me the number of the *Buffalo Evening News*, please," I told the long distance operator, as I rummaged in my change purse for the silver to stay in the newspaper business.

**********

Nick Carter said he would see what he could do and to call him back in a couple of days. I went back to Philadelphia and waited. When I spoke to him again, he said there was an opening in the Society Department for someone to eventually fill the Society Editor's place; she contemplated retiring.  I could call Mr. Alfred H. Kirchhofer, the Managing Editor, for an appointment.  I called.  Mr. Kirchhofer said he would pay my railroad fare to Buffalo for an interview.

"Buffalo's a long way away, Ellen," my mother said.

"It's a newspaper, Mother," I said.

Philadelphians did not often leave their native city.  It was beloved by them.  They valued their roots the better they went down through the earth of time of signers of the Declaration of Independence or the Constitution of the United States.  Of course there were many gradations on the way to the present, but such descendancy was considered the cream of the 175-year-old crop. They lived, worked and socialized in the sultry-aired city with its beautiful rolling, environmental countryside; its emblems of history at every turn of street or lane.  They dwelt in contentment under a Quaker canopy that Penn had raised, with its ideals of simplicity and peace.  If an aristocracy had risen in its ranks, it rose largely from participation in the development of a new country and its civil liberties, industry and commerce.

A contentment of domain pervaded Philadelphia in the early 1940's, it was satisfied to live largely within its own boundaries or surrounding suburbs.  With areas within those boundaries becoming run-down and failing to keep pace with progress; throttled by a longstanding corrupt Republican political regime that had no roots in the Declaration of Independence or the Constitution or landed or industrial gentry - Philadelphia existed, lulled by its colonial dream and unheedful of the future.

Our city had yielded both the capitalism of the nation to Washington (1790); the superiority of its port to New York (with the opening of the Erie Canal in 1825), and finally, in 1833 under President Andrew Jackson, the holdings of the Bank of the United States, headed by Nicholas Biddle, which, at the time, was the veritable treasury of the country.

But Philadelphia did not yield its social posture, which according to Nathaniel Burt (*The Perennial Philadelphians*) became even more locally dominant after relinquishment of its third and final national asset.

**********

Nevertheless, a change was in the wind sweeping over the mellow yet fading old city. Even in the mid-'40s, there were stirrings of what in the '50s would become known as the "Philadelphia Renaissance."

While on the *Record*, I had covered a Philadelphia Planning Committee meeting, attended by about 30 dissatisfied men and women with a distant vision.

"What a shame the riverfront doesn't have promenades along it, as Penn planned," commented one of the group of the Delaware's factory-lined banks.

A sturdy woman in a tailored suit and what we used to call a "built-up" hat - high crowned with angular bows of ribbon on it - got up: Dowager Frances Wister, booster par excellence of cultural institutions and philanthropic causes.

"Why don't we move some of the industry?" Miss Wister asked.

There was a pause of incredulity. (Yet years later, that was just what Philadelphia did!)

And with the conclusion of the war, even the social picture began to change. Philadelphians used to marry Philadelphians, Baltimorians, or occasionally, New Yorkers or Bostonians; now with the interchange of college students throughout the country, they began to intermarry with the United States. A broader horizon was opening up.

**********

But I was 43 and had lived in the aura of an older Philadelphia. The city shaded my roots. I loved it, the sultry air, the tree-lined squares, the narrow streets and rolling countryside, which now, in addition to youthful memories held those of stories I had covered on four newspapers - five including the one across the river in Camden. I was proud of my city's historic past and traditions.

So when I boarded the coach of the Lehigh Valley night train to seek another newspaper in Buffalo, N.Y., a city totally strange to me, I was being venturesome; in the back of my consciousness too, was an unspoken resistance to leaving the East, which for me was that crowded corridor between New York and Richmond. I had never imagined leaving it.

I was prepared, however, by my love of newspapering, which coursed through me more strongly than precedent, sentiment or the past. I must use whatever God had given me - beyond my birthright.

\*\*\*\*\*\*\*\*\*\*

In the early morning hours, the train passed through the beautiful rolling country of the Genesse Valley. Everything seemed larger than in eastern Pennsylvania - from the land to the trees, most of which had been left at fields' edge. Even the sky seemed more expansive in the rising morning light. As we neared our destination, the torch of a steel foundry stack flared in the air; multitudes of tracks wound serpentine on either side of the train, and at last, to the north, there was a great expanse of blue water - Lake Erie! "BUFFALO...BUFFALO" called the conductor, as the train began to slow down, inching into the Lehigh Valley Station. I was indeed, far from home.

The Lehigh Valley Station was a handsome one, with lots of brass railings and fittings. Two or three porters drifted around in the early morning light, and I checked the two suitcases I had brought; I was determined to get this job. I went into the women's room and straightened myself; I was wearing a black taffeta dressmaker suit and a small Milan straw hat, with a moss rose affixed to it; it had seemed an appropriate costume for a prospective society editor. Breakfasting in the station, I then walked the two short blocks up to the *Buffalo Evening News* for my 10 o'clock appointment.

The *Buffalo Evening News* was six-story building at the corner of Main and Seneca Streets. Founded by Edward H. Butler, Sr., in 1880, it had become a Western New York institution, a strong independent political force, with Republican leanings, and a veritable upholder of the ethical standards of the seven counties which it served.

I passed through the marble-countered lobby with its vase of fresh flowers and grilled cashiers' cages, to the elevators, and thence to the third-floor office of Mr. Kirchhofer. Frances M. Hurley, his attractive secretary, who had been a clubmobile captain in the Red Cross overseas during World War II, greeted me in an outer office.

Shortly, I saw Mr. Kirchhofer, a tall, austere man with a fine, strong, Teutonic face. The position open, he explained, was that of a society reporter, who might eventually replace the Society Editor, who might retire in the not too distant future. Mr. Kirchhofer and I came to terms, and I got the position. From the first, we hit it off. Buffalo paid higher wages to reporters than Philadelphia then, but I didn't know it, and named a price slightly above what I had been receiving at the *Bulletin*. I got it without question; I could have asked for $25 a week more.

Margery Marble, the incumbent Society Editor, was then called in, and I was introduced. A slender, wiry, athletic woman, she was a wonderfully square shooter. After the amenities, she invited me to go to lunch at the Hotel Statler, the great 1100-room hotel in the center of the city. Ellsworth M. Statler had started his chain in Buffalo, in a hotel further downtown, which had been sold and was now called the Hotel Buffalo. We had lunch in the large Terrace Room of the big Statler, and Marge Marble briefly outlined the social scheme of things in Buffalo to me.

I was going to stay with Nick Carter and his wife, Belle. After luncheon, I inquired of Miss Marble how to get to the Ambassador Apartments where they lived.

"It's just a few blocks up the street," said this athletic editor, "you can take a bus, or you can easily walk."

I thanked her and turned in the direction that she indicated, north on Delaware. A wide street, it still had some of the 100,000 elms that had been planted in Buffalo beginning in the 1870s, of which Dutch Elm disease would eventually destroy more than half. But Delaware Avenue still maintained an aura of horticultural and residential grandeur. After a nearly-two-mile hike in the summer sun, I reached the Ambassador.

"Where have you been?" said Nick, as he looked up from the *Decameron*, "we've been waiting for you - we thought you were lost!"

"I got the job, Nick," I said. "We went to lunch at the Statler, and then I walked here."

"She walked, Belle!" said Nick, flabbergasted by such a feat.

But the long train ride, the excitement of the interview and the hike in the hot sun after a sumptuous lunch were too much for me. I made for the bathroom and lost it.

# 23

## Landed Gentry and City Culture

SO HERE I WAS, back on a society page with the same kind of job I had started in the newspaper business 10 years before and which I had left a few months previously.

I wanted with all my heart to continue as a general assignment reporter. But Shakespeare said, "There's a divinity that shapes our ends, rough-hew them how we will." I must wait.

Margery Marble and her staff welcomed me and treated me handsomely, and indeed my first assignment at the *Buffalo Evening News* could not be faulted by any reporter, especially one inclined to feature writing. The story of the Wadsworth family of Geneseo was a taproot of Upper New York history, with offshoots extending to Washington and national affairs.

The start and hub of these distinguished landowners in Western New York was the site of "The Homestead," of which I wrote:

The blue, the red, the gold of it! Autumn in the Genesee Valley...October at "The Homestead."

Great white, green-shuttered house of Mr. and Mrs. William Perkins Wadsworth at Geneseo, you are more than a country seat.

You are a way of life.

Living at "The Homestead" is living in the country, yet it is sophisticated living. Perhaps the greatest sophistication of all - the kind that sallies forth abroad, brings back armfuls and mindfuls of treasure, and then hugs the land close again.

The earth. Acres and acres of it, 13,400 to be exact, which homesteaders eventually have found to be the great teacher, cultivator and master artist.

Look over these broad green fields laced with weather-silvered fences where sheep graze (there is an autumn lamb this season), and ask yourself, "Did the great French landscapist Corot do better?"

"The Shining Valley," the Indians called it, and it shines on under the haze-filled noon and the harvest moon these days.

And horses. For next to love of land, the Wadsworths have placed horses. Many Wadsworths have gone forth to the wars from "The Homestead." But they have returned to the call of the horn, which they followed casually before

1876, formally with the Genesee Valley Hunt ever since, war years excepted.

"The Homestead," which we are about to enter, stands within a half mile of the spot where James Wadsworth and his brother, William, built a cabin when they came to the valley in 1790.

Nearly fifty years later, an English traveler described the view thus:

"The broad meadows of alluvial soil, covered with the richest grasses, as watered by the winding Genesee River, are studded with trees beautifully and negligently grouped, among which are scattered large herds of cattle..."

A cobblestone house succeeded the cabin, and was replaced by "The Homestead" in 1804.

Come with us under the portico of the great house under which - or its equivalent - the Bishop Prince de Talleyrand, Mark Twain, Arthur Brisbane, William McKinley, Sen. Mark Hanna and Theodore Roosevelt - to name a few, have come.

Mind you clean your boots on that horseshoe scraper before you enter the glassed-in vestibule and hang your hat on the rack fashioned from antlers - among the goodly number of everything from snowcaps to pith helmets hanging there.

Your coats - on that line of pegs made of upturned deer feet, if you please.

**********

The valley and its gently rolling fields embrace the house. As you stand in the blue-walled hall running the length of it, and look westward, there is a view of the country of the Genesee through the rear door leading out to the Georgian-railed veranda.

Over the stoop of "The Homestead" have come brides from the metropolises of the East...

Naomi Wolcott of Connecticut, Pioneer James' bride...Emmeline Austin of Boston, Mass., wife of William Wolcott Wadsworth, son of James...Elizabeth Perkins, wife of William Austin Wadsworth, a Bostonian too...Martha Scofield, first wife of William Perkins Wadsworth, and his second wife, the late Penelope Crane of Buffalo.

Each of these women has brought her taste, and often some furnishings, to the great house. So it stands today, pervaded by an atmosphere of variety, lingering grandeur and hospitable comfort.

The original part of "The Homestead," which includes two parlors, a library and dining room on the first floor, comprised about 18 rooms. James built it for Naomi. Throughout the years here have been rambling, commodious additions until it now numbers more than 40 rooms.

Legend has it walls of at least some of the original structure were both bullet and arrow proof. At any rate, owing to the 3x12-inch oak planks used as studs in the walls - and petrified by age - special wiring was necessary when electricity was installed.

Maj. Wadsworth - he too served in World War II - admits that penetration of the walls take "a devil of an arrow, and that they would probably bend a rifle shot."

**********

Join us in the drawing room to the right, facing North. The picturesque curls in an etching of Naomi are in harmony with the garlands of pink, blue and white roses and mallows, green entwined, wreathing the cornices and woodwork of the white walls.

The mantel in the Adam manner is flanked by two French cabinets displaying pastoral patterned china.

A painting of the historic Big Tree, giant oak which stood on the Wadsworth property and under which Robert Morris procured the title to Genesee country lands from the Senecas for the Holland Land Co., hangs over the mantel in the rose drawing room, as it is called.

The arboreal motif is echoed in the exquisite inlaid pattern of autumn leaves of a rare fruitwood desk at the window.

The delicate presence of miniatures pervades these parlors.

Nearby is a hand illumined verse, which reads in part:

> Piping down the valley wild
> Piping songs of pleasant glee
> On a cloud I saw a child
> And he laughing said to me

Pipe a song about a Lamb
So I piped with merry cheer
Piper, pipe the song again
So I piped, he wept to hear.

The dining room at "The Homestead" is a room of portraits. Paintings of some of the men and women who have played a vital part in settling the land and running the great house hang high against gilded burlap-covered walls above the handsome oak mantel and linen fold paneling.

Among them is Jeremiah Wadsworth, commissary general under Gen. George Washington, uncle of James and William, who sold them the idea of emigrating to and developing the Genesee Valley.

The late Elizabeth Perkins Wadsworth, one of the house's greatest horsewomen and hostesses, as a dark-haired matron in an orange, oriental-looking gown, holding a fan. Her husband, William Austin Wadsworth, who founded the Genesee Valley Hunt 85 years ago, resplendent in his Spanish-American War uniform.

The dining room is completely ringed with flowered plates, giving a homelike touch beneath the formality of the portraits.

Pioneer Gen. William Wadsworth, who fought so gallantly at the Battle of Queenston and eventually fell at the Battle of the Wilderness, and his brother James grace the smoking room, the veritable "heart" of "The Homestead."

Hung in what is believed to be the original dark blue, dogwood patterned paper, its turkey-red carpet invigorating in contrast, the room is the epitome of mellow, cultivated, hunting-based country life.

Swords, a rifle and dueling pistols, whose triggers Wadsworths have drawn, stud the walls. But the masks of foxes predominate - there are 11 throughout house and adjoining kennels. When and if a fox is killed the mask (head), brush (tail), and pads (feet) are trophies of the chase. The mask automatically goes to the master of the hunt who gives the brush to the man or woman first at the kill, and the pads to other people well up.

In the wide bay window looking out on a terrace is an interesting eight-sided desk, probably built for the room when it was done between 1870-80, as were the bookcases.

Hunting memorabilia from photographs of the GVH in the field to portraits of famous hounds deck the walls. And comfortable green and red sofas and chairs face the hearth - where a huntsman may - hot toddy in hand - stretch out and relive the morning's chase.

**********

If the blue hills encircle "The Homestead" out of doors - books embrace its interior. The library with its Grinling Gibbons carved overmantel, incorporating the Wadsworth crest, was carved from oak of the estate. The crest, bearing three fleurs-de-lis on a plain field reads, "Aquila non captat muscas" - or "The Eagle does not catch flies."

Lining the room to the ceiling is the literature of the ages, soft-toned leather bindings exuding that particular aroma that only fine leather can. Will you have Chaucer or Molière or Faulkner? Or perhaps you'd rather dip into a five-volume set of "The Silva (Trees) of North America," or "The Wild Flowers of New York?"

"The Homestead" itself is dramatic, and there are a number of secondary plots within it; i.e., the round glove table under the staircase on which rest perhaps 20 pairs of riding, gardening and walking gloves. A congregation of canes, crops, whips, leashes, umbrellas and field-sticks in the vestibule.

Sofa pillows on formal and informal sofas, big downy ones, minute cuddly ones, in paisley, brocade, velvet or needlepoint, including one that reads "Before You Mount - Look at the Girth."

Footstools, and footstools.

**********

You feel near the sky upstairs in "The Homestead." The dowled white, red-carpeted staircase, a later addition, mounts in state to three master bedrooms, each with dressing room; and a homelike sitting room done in Chippendale furniture, with mezzotints framed in wide gold mats - and a view surpassing them.

The four bedrooms with their great four-poster beds, and the dressing rooms with sleigh or other 19th-Century ones, are all in blue and white in tune with the hills, clouds and sky seen through their windows beyond. Four more master bedrooms stretch above. Every room at "The Homestead" has a bootjack.

Beyond too, is the stable built in Grandfather William's time, with its big pigeon house atop, 29 horses, and the stallion Gray Flares quartered there this autumn. Leeland Gardner is stable manager.

A 10-minute drive and one is at the Genesee Valley Hunt Kennels, for which Mr. Wadsworth, as MFH, is responsible. Twenty-nine dogs and 30 bitches are in the current pack.

**********

Like his family before him, William Perkins Wadsworth tills some of his land, more than 7,000 acres, and lets out the rest to tenant farmers. He works hard in his office, a yellow gatehouse, this one of the last of the great estate masters. It has been a tradition among the Wadsworths to help their tenants up, to discourage sharecroppers.

When day is done, he returns to "The Homestead," his blue eyes far keener than those of a city man, with the satisfaction that only living on the land can give.

I was to journey down to Geneseo several times in the coming years, and it was always an exultant delight.

**********

There was a pattern about society reporting in those days. Activities in which prominent men and women engaged were featured. Buffalo is a great church city, and every few blocks there seemed to be a large, beautiful building which gathered in the flock from the neighborhood around it. Many of these people were active in churches.

Religious services make possible the baptisms and marriages which are featured on a society page. But primarily, society news is devoted to secular activities. In the 1940s, a good society columnist could draw hundreds of readers to a newspaper. The *Buffalo Evening News'* competitor, the morning and *Sunday Courier-Express*, had an excellent columnist named Lucy Laureate. Mr. Kirchhofer was looking for a column that could match her.  It seemed in the cards that I should be asked to produce one.  It was to be called "These Interesting People."  It is interesting to compare this column in Buffalo with "Just Gossip About People," which I had written in Philadelphia 10 years earlier.  Here's a sample; trivia, it seems, is timeless.

THESE INTERESTING PEOPLE

3/4/50  Remembering the famous horseplay by Lady Robert Peel (actress Beatrice Lillie, to you), about "a dozen double damask dinner napkins," we dropped in at the Erlanger Theater the other night to ask her what kind of table linen she was using these days.

We found her 5-foot ladyship, wearing 1-1/2-inch eyelashes, perched in her dressing room during the intermission of her current show, "Inside USA."  The room was all draped in English chintz that Miss Lillie takes on tour to make her feel inside England in the United States.

"Will you be using double damask dinner napkins when you return to England for a vacation after Easter, Lady Peel?," we asked.

Lady Peel wrinkled her famous retroussé nose.  "No," she confessed, "that all changed with the war.  We had to get used to another kind of dinner napkin - and sometimes to no napkins at all.  The ones we did have were insignificant.  Nothing double about them.

"But since I've been in the States," she added brightening, "I've discovered some perfectly marvelous ones.  They are big and squashie and I have them marked."

"With the Peel crest, Miss Lillie?," we hastened.

"No, just with my initials, B.L.  When I go back home I shall take dozens and dozens of 'em - double paper dinner napkins - I'm really mad about them!"

**********

5/13/50  Like most well-bred horses Gifted Lady's Cameo and Spring's Serenade owned by Mr. Henry H. Minor of "Seven Springs Stables," Batavia, have brought their beauty kit with them to the Fourth Annual Buffalo International Horse Show.

Contents of the smart green and white box disclose that keeping beautiful is - as cosmetic experts advise - a matter of faithful routine. Horses, like ladies, its seems, do not attend a horse show, the equivalent of a formal dance to any mare, without considerable primping.

For example, the kit shared by Spring's Serenade and Gifted Lady's Cameo includes such beauty aids as talcum powder, sponges, show polishes, gay ribbons (for manes) and sleek brilliantine (for tails). All of which adds up to that well-groomed look.

**********

2/11/50  On one side of Delaware Ave. is a small "all night" restaurant. Diagonally across the street is the Buffalo Club. Employees of the diner, shining up their coffee urns, often marveled at the aroma of frogs' legs, sweetbreads and filet mignon emanating from the club's kitchens. As one diner employee put it: "The Buffalo's got everything."

But recently the club asked its compatriot, the Saturn Club, down for a Monte Carlo evening. And around 3 a.m., Buffalo Club President Dr. Herbert A. Smith suggested a round of coffee. But the club's kitchens had closed at midnight.

Undaunted, Dr. Smith drew out his wallet and extracted a crisp bill. He ordered a waiter to go out and fetch $5 worth of steaming coffee. Beaming - the little all night restaurant filled the order.

**********

2/25/50  Paul "Chips" Benning Davis Jr. was 6 on Wednesday. He woke early with the pleasant prospect of a party given in his honor in the Saturn Club. Guests would be his 25 kindergarten classmates in the School of Practice, Buffalo State Teachers College. Ice cream, cake and whistles loomed ahead.

At noon, Chips commenced dressing. He spent some time contemplating the flock of new ties grandfather and grandmother, Mr. and Mrs. Alfred L. Lyth, had sent him from Florida. Heretofore, Chips' interest in haberdashery had been slight.

As Lincoln was having a birthday anniversary this month, too, Chips chose a red, white and blue tie to complement his checked suit. Mrs. Davis found her son fully clad but surveying himself anxiously in her pier glass. Little lines etched his usually smooth forehead.

"Do I look my age, Mother?" he asked.

**********

4/8/50 Every Easter Attorney Jay T. Barnsdall Jr. has a standing order at a local pet shop for 100 rabbits. Mr. Barnsdall doesn't keep the rabbits - in fact he never sees them. Through welfare channels they are distributed to children, who would love a bunny - but ordinarily would not get one.

Mr. Barnsdall can't remember exactly when he started this pleasant custom. He thinks it was about ten years ago when he noticed the expression on the face of a friend's child as she received a Peter Cottontail. If Mr. Barnsdall has given 100 rabbits away each year for 10 years, that adds up to 1,000 such expressions on the faces of local youngsters.

**********

The tone was very much like that of "Just Gossip About People" in Philadelphia. But the reporter who wrote it had changed.

Buffalo and Philadelphia were two different cities, the latter about 125 years older than the former. Both cities, of course, had a gentry, but the Buffalo one was small and the society page opened its columns to successful professional and business people, far more than did Philadelphia. I remember how surprised I was to find a city directory in the *News* society department, in which names not listed in Buffalo's slim *Social Register* were checked. The rich and the newly-arrived, however, were not confused with old stock, with families who had settled in New England several generations before and, when it became crowded, made the trip Westward by oxcart, on horseback or by the Erie Canal. The first family to come into Erie County, in which Buffalo is situated, by a coach, arrived in 1804.

In contrast to the backdrop of the Revolution and the formation of the Union, Buffalo's scenario was first the clearing of forests; survival despite severe winters; the burning of the little village in 1812, a few years after its founding; and its place as the terminus of the Erie Canal, which opened in 1824. It became the gateway to the West. Some westbound travelers arriving in Buffalo, did not push on further. Seven generations later, this background, combined with success in rails - Buffalo became the second largest rail center in the country - the manufacturer of steel and above all, the shipping and storage of grain, had produced a rich and conservative gentry, which, as in all cities, had received body blows in the Roosevelt years.

The two-mile stretch of Delaware Avenue, once perhaps the closest thing in the country to Newport's Bellevue Avenue, was eroding. Some of the great houses were being given by their owners, tax free, to charitable or religious organizations, others were being converted into apartment or office buildings, and some were being torn down.

There is no better place to observe the history, manners and customs of a city than an auction. When I arrived in Buffalo, auctions of the contents of some of the great houses along Delaware Avenue still were in progress. Most were held in the houses themselves, but I particularly remember one held in the Twentieth Century Club, the largest women's club in the city. The sale was of furnishings, objets d'art and clothes of Mrs. Frederick L. Pratt, a great beauty and social leader, who fomerly had occupied a magnificent house with a pillared portico. It, like the house of Mrs. Pratt's parents, Mr. and Mrs. Charles H. Williams, next door, had been designed by Stanford White, who with Frank Lloyd Wright and Louis Sullivan had built several structures in the city. The Pratt family was the first to come to Erie County in that coach in 1804.

In two galleries, lit by Mrs. Pratt's own lamps, with bases of jade or rose quartz, were displayed photographs, books and her wardrobe trunk, her bed and clothes. Delicate French lingerie cascaded out of the drawers of the trunk, and on the bed were hats and furs. Picture frames, the contents of which generally were removed, stood on tables about the room. It was the most intimate public sale I had ever seen. The intimacy climaxed over the bed where the crest of the Jewett Family, Mrs. Pratt's maternal grandfather, hung. The motto on the crest brought a catch to one's throat; enscribed in French, it was "Toujours le meme" (Always the same).

"Are they going to sell that?," I asked Benjamin Lenkowski, the engaging auctioneer.

I can't recall what he said, but the next day the crest had disappeared.

What kind of a city had I come to? To what had I journeyed from historic Philadelphia, with its quiet, somewhat withdrawn pride in itself; its canopy of Quakerism; its dislike of show; and its almost reverence for the American Revolution. Some comparison between it - Philadelphia and Buffalo - is in order.

I think the dominant war of an area, the climate and of course, the environmental terrain, mold its character and thought. I must have read of the War of 1812, but I had no specific knowledge of it. I was imbued with the American Revolution. The signing of the Declaration of Independence and the Constitution of the United States were also high on my list of interests. Any Philadelphian who descended from a "signer," as those who signed the Declaration of Independence were called, or even the Constitution, had something to be intensely proud of, more recent and politically formative than even passage on the Mayflower. Descent from a signer unrolled a red carpet down the historic and social aisles for anyone who wished to tread it. It was a rare and distinguished heritage. Likewise, kinship with a signer of the Constitution, that document which gave the country its ground rules, was an inestimable distinction. Below these Olympian heights marched an army of descendants of patriots, enrolled in such organizations as the Sons of the Revolution, the Colonial Dames of America, the National Society of Colonial Dames and the Military Order of the Loyal Legion, among numerous others. Of course, there were Philadelphians who had no interest in such hierarchy, but it was an indigenous interest that contributed to the aura of the city.

The Civil War made a far greater impression in Buffalo than in Philadelphia, where persons who could afford it paid enlisted men to take their place in Union Army ranks. Buffalo was a terminus for the Underground Railroad, the Niagara River an ideal clandestine route to Canada and freedom; this fact has influenced race relations in the area down to today.

When it comes to terrain, the difference between Philadelphia and Buffalo is marked. The Grand Canyon and the Niagara Falls and Gorge region, of which Buffalo is on the periphery, are the two most impressive natural presentations in the United States, and probably the world. Immense, shallow Lake Erie, flowing into the broad and rapid Niagara River, a coursing, racing river which climaxes in the Great Cataract and then flows on between high cliffs to Lake Ontario, is catapultic and awesome.

How different in contrast, are the flat stretches of Philadelphia, embraced by its two sultry, slow-moving rivers, the Delaware and the Schuylkill. On climate: Buffalo weather is a Wagnerian opera compared to the Mozart sonata of Philadelphia.  Situated in the crotch of lake and river, Buffalo draws snow and wind like a basketball basket attracts a star player.  The arms of lake and river reach out and draw them in to its frosty bosom from the middle of November to the middle of March, when the cold breaks into a quick spring and a bright, unusually cool summer and short autumn.  On the other hand, Philadelphia, although blizzards are not unknown, has a reasonably temperate climate throughout the winter, and a humid, hot summer.

These three factors - historical outlook, terrain and climate - affect the people who live in the two areas.  Philadelphia has more to look back *at* than Buffalo, and it does so more.  Independence Hall and the historical buildings induce pride and unusual consideration of the past.  The warmer, sultry air affects the very pace of walk in Philadelphia.  Geared to cold winters and stimulating summers, a Buffalonian's gait is quicker; indeed a busy Buffalo business or professional man might be said to bustle.  The amenities are longer in Philadelphia:  a salesman making a call leads up to his sales talk with general conversation.  In the northern city, business people often get right to the point, with little social prelude.  The average citizen rises early and goes home to an early dinner, as lunch has been short, and the cold has given appetite.

Another interesting assignment I had on the society pages of the *Buffalo Evening News* was an interview with Dr. Lillian Moller Gilbreth, the distinguished mother of the best-seller, "Cheaper by the Dozen."  An industrial engineer and psychologist, she and her husband, Frank Bunker Gilbreth, had been among the first in the scientific management field and the very first in motion study.

A tall, slim, fit woman, then in her early 70s, Dr. Gilbreth wore a black tailored suit and a tricorn hat on her upswept white hair.  She told me about visiting a factory during the war; while talking with one of the employees on the production line, she asked him what he thought of when he executed his particular operation.

"I think of a foxtrot," he said, "One...Two...Three...Four."

"Why don't you think of it in waltz time?" asked the efficient Dr. Gilbreth.

An indication of how times have changed was Mr. Kirchhofer's comment on my interview.  I had written "Dr. Gilbreth made a fine 'figger' of a woman."

"Must we defile the dignity of our pages?" wrote Mr. Kirchhofer in a memo to Miss Marble.

*********

I was building momentum again.  After nearly a year on the society page of the *Buffalo Evening News,*  I asked Mr. Kirchhofer if I might be moved to the City Side where I had been for a number of years on the Philadelphia newspapers, with the exception of the brief interlude at the *Bulletin.*  His answer was no.  I had been engaged to eventually replace Miss Marble, who had not yet left.  That was that.  Again I faced an impasse as I had with Mr. Cranston.

I had not yet put down roots in Buffalo, and every time a train whistle sounded in the night, I would think of Philadelphia.  I went home every three months on the Maple Leaf or Black Diamond, night trains of the Leigh Valley, sleeping in the day coach with a pillow provided by the railroad and carrying a small amount of crème de menthe to induce sound sleep.  I carried this in a little bottle, and I often wondered what the many Catholic Sisters, who usually were traveling in the same car, thought if they saw me preparing for a night's rest.  At 5 o'clock in the morning, one got off at Bethlehem, Pa., to change trains for the final lap to Philadelphia.  From the platform, how familiar and friendly the waning stars looked at that hour.  They appeared smaller and less bright than those of the seemingly wider heavens of Western New York.

I had now saved some money and was relatively independent.  So I prepared to leave the *Buffalo Evening News* and go back to Philadelphia.  On a summer afternoon, a year after I had come, I was cleaning out my desk when I was called to Mr. Kirchhofer's office.

"Are you going?" he asked.

"Why yes, Mr. Kirchhofer," as I had already told him.

"Do you have another position?"

"No." I had made no effort yet to get one.

"Why don't you stay around until you do?" he suggested.

I was amazed.  I already had my unemployment compensation slip from the *News* bookkeeping department and had given my landlady notice about my apartment.  I paused.

"I'll have to go to the ladies' room and think that over," I said.

I went up to the office of George Esselburne, the feature editor, some of whose family had come from Philadelphia.  An understanding, gentlemanly man, we discussed the situation.

In a short time, I returned, and told Mr. Kirchhofer that I would go on a vacation for two weeks, and would then come back; but there would be no obligation between us.  If he had a position for me on the City Side, I would take it; if he did not, I would return again to Philadelphia.

In two weeks I was back, sitting by his desk. He again suggested that I return to the society department. Again I declined. It was the City Side or nothing, I repeated. He said he would see what he could do. I went back to the apartment and waited for several days. Hearing nothing I called Frances Hurley, and she said she would call me back. The reply came shortly: Nelson Griswold, the City Editor, said he would guarantee me 90 days work (the trial period for a city side reporter).

It was enough. Again, I had a chance to report on the whole wide world.

# 24

# I Drop Anchor

MY FIRST ASSIGNMENT ON the city side of the *Buffalo Evening News* was to do a series of stories on the historical markers around the city. There were about 30 of them. It sounded like a rather musty, static assignment, but it could not have been a better one for me at the time. Through it, I learned a good deal of the history of Buffalo and the Niagara Frontier: the gallant effort of the pioneers and settlers to establish first a village, then a city; the events and structures that the city held dear.

In writing of these markers, I learned the events that had shaped the city; the War of 1812, the settlers relations with the Indians, the Underground Railroad, with its access to Canada, and the city's great outreach - the Pan-American Exposition (1901) which ended in the tragedy of President McKinley's fatal shooting.

It was a different war from the American Revolution, on which Philadelphia leaned so heavily. That war was before the Niagara Frontier's time and remained in the public consciousness only as an historic conflict or one in which early settlers had engaged in before they came West.

But the burning of the village of Buffalo by the British - assisted by Indians - on the night of December 30, 1813; the principles and loyalties concerning the abolition of slavery; the consummate grief which caused the erection of a towering monument to the fallen President in the very center of town - these were the posts upon which Buffalo's civic consciousness had been built.

I learned:

1.  The city's main street developed from a fork of the old Central Indian Trail - it was 15 to 18 inches wide and footworn 3 to 12 inches, no runner or warrior could miss it - which wound from the Hudson River in Albany through the state to Lake Erie.

2.  Buffalo's first church (circa 1810), a "Congregational and Presbyterian" one, was heated by 4-foot logs and the congregation filled their foot-warmers with hot coals from a vestibule grate.

3.  The great Seneca sachem, Red Jacket, was a friend of George Washington.

4.  Mary Jemison, "The White Woman of the Genesee," was taken prisoner by the Indians when a child, conformed to their customs and was wed to a chief.

5. The midtown site from which both Lafayette and Lincoln spoke.

6. And, of course, I was reminded of Commodore Oliver Hazard Perry's victory on Lake Erie and his immortal words "We have met the enemy and they are ours."

All such things acquainted me with the city to which I had come and helped me to understand it.

**********

It should be mentioned at this time that in my nearly 40 years of newspapering I never owned an automobile, although I had driven up to the time I was 18. Soon after Daddy died I had gone to work in the city and had no need for a car. Trolleys and the subway were easily accessible in Philadelphia, and when I branched out to the suburbs or surrounding countryside I usually went with a photographer; or in the event one was not assigned to me, I traveled by bus. The distances a general news reporter travels in the Philadelphia area are usually less great than those in Western New York. In those days, too, there was an abundance of trains. I pursued this pattern, which I established early, throughout my newspaper years.

The reach of my non-vehicular state, however, was to be stretched beyond my wildest dreams by my next *News* assignment. In the middle of the broad, swift-flowing Niagara River, dividing New York State from Canada, is an enormous body of land called Grand Island. The *Buffalo Evening News* wanted a report on how the population and development of the island was doing.

Great stretches of unoccupied land covered at least two-thirds of the island, interspersed at broad intervals with small communities of mostly modest, modern houses. Between 1850 and 1900, in what had been called its Golden Era, the island was a fashionable summer resort, with large, hospitable houses of Buffalonians along the west shore of the Niagara River, facing the Canadian one. There had been hotels and amusement parks.

Now the grand old money had been depleted by time and the New Deal, and the majority of the residents (3,080, 1950 census) lived in small new homes. Sewers and waterlines had not yet been dug on many parts of the island. There were broad highways, however, the popular route to Niagara Falls being across one of the twin bridges connecting Buffalo with the island, and thence to the cataract. Bus service around the island was intermittent.

In many a newspaper office - long before the days of Social Security inducements or mandatory retirement - there was a veteran whose days of serious labor were over, but who still loving the business, wrote small bits and obituaries and drove other reporters to assignments.

On the *News,* there was Frank Balch, a dear man in his 70s, who sat at a desk by the front window doing the aforementioned writing or perusing the paper - always with his hat on. When not reading or writing, he gently dozed. Like a Kentucky racehorse, farmed out to pasture, it was considered that he had earned such respite; the company continued to include him as a member of its newspaper family and did not turn him out. Publishers of newspapers often provided lifelong harbor (sometime specifically in their wills) for such men.

So one morning, Frank drove me across the bridge from Buffalo to Grand Island. I had no map of it, I had no contacts there, I had nothing but the written assignment in my hand and the urge that had brought me so many miles to work on this newspaper. As I surveyed the broad stretches of land, traversed by largely vacant highways, Frank offered an explanation:

"You know," he said, "it's bigger than Manhattan."

He deposited me in a small community in the center of the island, where a post office and a church or two were located. Then he left. I was to return home by bus.

I stood still in the middle of the "town" a few minutes, looking uncomprehendingly at the vast uninhabited spaces around me. Then I sighted a small restaurant; I went in and sat down. After two plates of chocolate ice cream and pondering the situation, I decided to call on the priest of the nearby Catholic church, not for solace, but for guidance. The Father gave me the general layout of the island. Eventually, I rented a bicycle and pedaled those vast stretches, village dogs yipping at my heels.

Here is a synthesis of what I found - past and present - as I cycled my way the great length of Grand Island those summer days of 1951:

"La Grande Isle" Franciscan Father Louis Hennepin called it when he first glimpsed Grand Island in the Spring of 1679. The great white oaks were in bud. Blue herons were returning from the South. Marsh marigolds were sprouting.

Indeed, approaching its vast green length from the arch of the South Bridge on a misty summer morning, the island still resembles the work of the French masters - perhaps Corot.

It is larger than Manhattan Island, wider, but not as long. Manhattan is 12-1/2 miles-in-length and 2-1/2 miles at its greatest breadth; Grand Island, 8-miles-long and 6 miles at its widest point, with an average of 4-1/2 miles. Manhattan covers 22 square miles, Grand Island 27.

The population of Manhattan and Grand Island have differed greatly down the years, the former more than a million in 1950, the latter with a few thousand, under 5,000 to be exact.

Wings of international events of great moment have brushed over both islands. But until recent years, Grand Island has reacted largely in reverse of its metropolitan counterpart. New York chose to welcome the world. Grand Island, until comparatively modern times, has generally resisted it.

The history of this great body of land - denuded of its primeval white oaks, first by squatters for barrel staves and later by New Englanders for clipper ships - is in its way, almost as amazing as that of the island of New York.

**\*\*\*\*\*\*\*\*\***

After the War of 1812, the State of New York purchased Grand Island from the Seneca Indians for $11,000 with hunting, fishing and fowling rights. In 1825, one Capt. Mordecai Noah Myers, who had seen service at a cantonment in Williamsville, now a suburb of Buffalo, launched a movement to reestablish the government of Israel, the government of the Jewish nation, on Grand Island. About 2,500 acres were purchased there for "Ararat," a city of refuge for the Jews. The name derived from the mountaintop upon which Noah's Ark came to rest.

Jews throughout the world were called upon to pay a tax of three shekels (about 7.5 grams) in silver per annum to support the venture. The plan fizzled, and today the cornerstone of the visionary refuge rests in lonely state in Grand Island's Town Hall, while thousands of miles away millions of Jews have returned to their homeland of Israel proper.

When the United Nations was looking for headquarters after World War II, the Niagara Frontier Planning Boad presented plans for its establishment on Grand Island to the island's Board of Supervisors. They were turned down. Establishment of a regional airport on the island also was resisted. Board member Andrew W. Kirkwood, who also was justice of the peace, said that both the airport and the U.N. headquarters would constitute "a nuisance and an invasion of privacy."

Despite these rejections, how could so large an area, in such close proximity to both the American and Canadian shores, remain disassociated from the mainland for so long? How was it possible?

Up to 1935, one might say that the reason was isolation. Until the advent of the two graceful bridges connecting the island with the mainland, Grand Island was accessible only by boat, which for the average citizen was a ferry.

Again, by 1950, the native population still owned the majority of the island, an estimated 70% of which was open country or farmland. Approximately one-tenth was still in timber, the last of the timber wolves having been shot down less than five years before and hung up at the island's Rod & Gun Club.

Yet less than 12 native farmers were said to be making a living on the island. With the exception of one 1,000-acre owner, their farms averaged less than 300 acres; no new land had been sold on the island for farming purposes in more than 10 years. Land could be rented for from 50 cents to $1.00 an acre.

An established social hierarchy existed on Grand Island, birth on the island conferring a distinction that years of resident living or even intermarriage did not bring. As the daughter of a mother born to the island purple, and a father, who had sojourned there over a quarter of a century, put it when asked if she was born there:

"Yes, I was born here, but Daddy is a foreigner."

Newcomers on the island found that the old guard accepted them with some reservations. But while there was much intermarriage among native Grand Islanders, morals were notably high.

Grand Islanders had wanted the bridges for many years before they were built in 1935. Upon their completion, they felt there would be a great demand for residential land. Prices soared to as high as $500 an acre. Most of this land was undeveloped.

This lack of modern sewage disposal and water piping, combined with the natives' resentment of intrusion - particularly if it threatened loss of taxable land - had kept Grand Island in virtual Arcadian privacy. Water was delivered in tanks on the island; septic tanks were common, and the outhouse was not extinct.

Grand Island's fire hall in the center of the island had 120 volunteer firemen. There was no hospital, so the two resident physicians used those on the mainland. The county sheriff and four constables composed the police force. There was a resident chiropractor, corsetiere and interior decorator, but no undertaker.

Yet Grand Island reportedly was a clean place to live, cooler in summer than the mainland and 10 degrees warmer in winter, owing to flowing water - 90% of which does not freeze.

Winds are prevailing westerly by west nine-tenths of the time and it is not in the paths of fogs and storms which come down from Lake Erie upon Buffalo. It has less snow. Accessible? Buffalo and Niagara Falls both are only eight minutes away.

**********

Despite its recluse tendencies and lack of almost all but elemental glories, by 1950 the winds of change were blowing over the island. The bridges of course, had been the first onslaught, but early in 1941, Robert Moses, chairman of the New York State Council of Parks and entrepreneur of highways, parks, bridges and beaches, had drafted a bill for $1,900,000 to complete the long-discussed State Parkway along the west bank of the Niagara River. Funds did not become available, however, until 1944. But in 1945, 300 Grand Islanders voted opposition to the drive - 8 ayes, 242 nays and 50 noncommittals.

The contract for the first 4.75 miles of the 7-1/2-mile West River Parkway, a scenic drive along the river and a link in a thoroughfare encircling the island, finally was awarded in July, 1949. In the interval, the state proceeded with the acquisition of the necessary land. Some of the Grand Islanders, whose land was required as right-of-way for the new drive, settled at the state's terms. But more than 40 contested. It was reported that the cost of acquiring land for the parkway might reach nearly $1 million.

When I arrived on this remarkable island on which the clumps of new white clapboard houses stood out in relief, and the weathered farmhouses and barns sank into the background, it was the natural beauty of field and wood that still predominated.

It was the eve of the transfer of the highly successful bridges from the area's Niagara Frontier Authority to the State Thruway Authority. The transfer would be accompanied by $9 million in highway construction, the majority of which would directly benefit Grand Island.

Actual construction of the first half of the long disputed 7-1/2-mile, $3,500,000 West River Drive, with its splendid view of the Canadian shore, was practically complete and it would shortly be turned over to the state.

About $3.5 million already had been spent by the state in developing two recreational parks, Buckhorn and Beaver Island, at the north and south end of the island respectively, and elaborate further developments were planned.

The Town of Grand Island itself was building sewers in several locations. And the population had risen from a 1940 low of 1,055 to a record 3,081. A third addition to the Charlotte Sidway Elementary Public School, which had been erected after the advent of the bridges to replace several one-room schools on the island, was being built to accommodate a rising enrollment.

Real estate operators, who having exhausted most of the developed mainland were now obliged to seek out undeveloped acreage, were moving in; building permits to augment the approximately 900 homes on the island were soaring.

Today, 30 years later, Grand Island has a population of nearly 17,000. Its Chamber of Commerce, founded in 1948, tells us:

"Within its boundaries, Grand Island has two nursery schools, a day-care center, ten churches, a library, two parochial schools and a variety of fraternal and social organizations. Recreational facilities abound. Large open spaces invite horseback riding, snowmobiling and cross-country skiing. Also on the island are two state parks, two golf courses, a major resort hotel, marinas and a recreational theme park."

There also is a Research and Industrial Park, already the seat of several major companies. In its prospectus, the Town Board welcomes the world to Grand Island, in part, thus:

"We can offer you the financial assistance, labor resources, and tax incentives you need to locate and grow in our community. New York state offers a number of financial incentives that encourage firms to locate here. Grand Island Industrial Park offers its support in preparing optimal conditions, designed to promote individual effectiveness in attractive surroundings."

Time and the river flow on to ameliorate both the climatic and sociological course of La Grande Isle.

**********

Communism was a hot subject in the United States in the early 1940s. Senator Joseph McCarthy had heated it up to a fever pitch. Mr. Kirchhofer decided he would like to have a survey of its spread throughout the country, particularly in New York State. A project worthy of a veteran State Department staffer.

I was assigned. What I knew about Communism or Russia for that matter, with the exception of my visit to Freehold, N.J., at the time of the White Russian story for the *Bulletin,* would not have filled one of those wonderfully-decorated Ukrainian Easter eggs. I was familiar with Tolstoy's "War and Peace," but Karl Marx and I were utter strangers. Intellectually, the whole subject was as remote to me as Siberia. I had been to the Russian Tea Room Restaurant near Carnegie Hall in New York and that was about it.

Others knew, however, and they had written it all down. The challenge of reporting is not so much to *know* about a subject, as to learn *where* you can find out about it. Another thing reporting teaches: Nobody knows how little you know if you don't - either by inadvertent conversation or confession - tell them.

There is a tremendous difference in the frame of reference of reporters that springs from reading, formal education, experience, travel or just a plain mental alertness which has taken in the world around one since childhood. The rewrite men on established newspapers of the past, often without college education, had a wide frame of reference, usually based on the classics and working on papers across the country. Their general information may have been superficial owing to the pressure of time in the business and the tendency, through necessity, to move rapidly from one subject to another - but it was wide and comprehensive, and unpretentiously brought enrichment to their craft.

In a number of weeks, I produced a series entitled "*DOOR AJAR-U.S.* - A General Survey of the State of Communism in the United States and Civil and Political Events Which Have Accompanied It - Particularly in New York State." It consisted of 30 pages of copy, comprising six installments.

Mr. Kirchhofer was somewhat taken aback.

"I intended an article in broader strokes," he commented, as he perused my blow by blow account of the Reds' 30-year march. But he made few cuts or corrections in the articles, and they ran in April, 1951. While much was being written then about Communism from a national viewpoint, the series was believed to include the first account of its infiltration into New York State.

**\*\*\*\*\*\*\*\*\*\***

My 90-day trial period now passed, backed by some knowledge of Buffalo's history, physically exercised from bicycling around Grand Island, and intellectually tuned up by research on Communism, I was now running on all cylinders as a general news reporter, moored to a big, firm, steady, affluent newspaper, the *Buffalo Evening News.*

Still, at night, hearing the train whistles sound wistfully in the distance, I envisioned the Lehigh going southward down the track. How they made me think of home!

But another sound began to gain my attention: Lakeboats, leviathans carrying grain, ore and lumber down the Lakes to the Sea. Their whistles were strong and assertive, a part of the reality of my new life.

# Book II

# The Harvest Years

# Preamble

THE 25 YEARS I SPENT on The *Buffalo Evening News* unroll like a multi-patterned carpet: the gold of harvest fields of the luxuriant farms of Western New York; the green ecstasy of spring in a northern clime, and the burying snows and Biblical winds of winter.

It would be impossible to capture the complete pattern as it unfolds - the first street cleaner in April; Prince Philip borrowing 10 cents from an aide to look through a telescope at Niagara Falls; the child clown who must go back to school in the fall to become a better clown.

All these are secondary patterns and so multitudinous and interwoven, it would be a prodigious task to unwind them in orderly time. So I stand on major motifs - religion, education, sociological patterns, homes, entertainment, travel and the men and women whose personalities have stood out in the thronging crowd that compose a reporter's daily life.

Harvest years, of course, in turn bring reminiscence of earlier ones, and when an event or experience of my younger newspapering days arise en route, I recount it along with the latter recollections, of which they were the precursors and sometimes, guideposts.

# Part VII

# Crowns and Clowns

# 25

# The Woman I Love

MY FIRST ENCOUNTER WITH royalty was when Prince Bertel, Duke of Holland, youngest son of Gustav Adolph, later King Gustavus VI of Sweden, attended a reception given by the Holland Society in Philadelphia.  The years would bring several observations of these elevated, usually unapproachable figures, who stand almost niched in today's world, tenuous bonds with the political ascent of Western man.  For men and women who still respect a stratification of society, based on inheritance, they still evoke reverence and an historical significance, which is shared by academics who give no quarter to class distinctions.

Eventually, however, for the American of the United States an asbestos curtain lowers between him and such figures, much as he may be fascinated by their glamour and trappings.  The blood becomes warmer, and the whole panorama of the past 200 years, with its fresh concepts and freedoms, rushes to the fore.  A dignified and often glittering legend remains.

The next time I crossed royalty's path - or it crossed mine, whichever is most deferential - was on the Widener estate during World War II.

Edward VIII, by then Duke of Windsor, came to the Lodge there to review a contingent of U.S. Coast Guard dogs on a summer day in 1942.  The Duchess accompanied him.

Their car circled around the carefully raked gravel driveway before the Lodge and they alighted.  Here were my impressions of this pair who rocked the throne and romantic annals of Britain:

"His hair was the color of ripe wheat.  Perfectly straight and brushed back from a face very like his mother's, the Dowager Queen Mary.

"He wore one of the small imitation carnation boutonniere he made fashionable in the lapel of his gray suit, and his dubonnet-brown shoes matched the subdued nosegay.

"You could see your face in the shine of those shoes...

"She (the Duchess) was erect, graceful, her black hair parted in the middle and drawn down in waves to frame a strong, somewhat angular face, inset with dark larkspur-blue eyes.

"It was the eyes of the Duchess that held one. Majestic, direct, yet attentive.

"The Windors and their party mounted to a second-floor balcony, overlooking a wide lawn where the Coast Guardsmen and dogs waited.

"The Duke sat down (straddled) a camp chair, casually, with simple assurance. Everything about him was simple, the superfluities whittled off, a person who had found a pivotal point.

"He sat a little behind his wife. He gave her the stage; she was his spokesman.

"She stood at the rail of the balcony, and turning those magnificent eyes on us reporters, listened intently - without condescension - to what we asked."

(God knows what we brash bunch of younsters did ask!)

She didn't ask us what papers we represented or showed any differentiation among any of us (gratifying to a tabloid reporter). She just absorbed what we voiced and answered directly.

Yet writing a little memoir of the occasion at the time of his death nearly 30 years later, to me "it is the presence in the back seat, the afternoon sun streaming down on his (naturally) golden crowned head, that lingers in the memory as the curtain falls at Windsor Castle today (June 1, 1972)."

**********

Nine years were to pass before my next royal encounter. In October of 1951, shortly before leaving for the rooftop house in Kenya where she would learn of her father George VI's death and her own sovereignty, heiress presumptive Princess Elizabeth and the Duke of Edinburgh came to Niagara Falls, Ontario. Goodwill seemed to be the purpose of the visit.

The ten-car royal train arrived from Toronto in the early morning and by 10 o'clock the royal pair stepped out on a 16-yard red velvet carpet rolled out for them.

The Mayor of Niagara Falls, Ernest M. Hawkins, and Mrs. Hawkins greeted them. It is remarkable from my observation, how well mayors, often without benefit of higher education, do in the presence of VIPs. Perhaps the assault necessary to arrive at such office, and the confidence of having arrived creates an individual assurance that even thrones cannot tremble. In turn, the vast social gap between executives of even small municipalities is remarkably well bridged by the VIPs of any distinction. The right to govern is the common denominator. They ride together, talk together and dine together in a harmony which would be less compatible if both were not in the saddle in their respective spheres. Government is government, the power and responsibility of which is to be respected by the high and low alike.

The royal party drove from the station to Christ Church, situated on the road along the Niagara Gorge, 1-1/2 miles above the Falls. The vanguard of a crowd of thousands who were to see the royal pair on their 3-1/2-hour visit had begun assembling at the little church since 6 a.m.

It only seated 367, so just a small number of the approximately 1,500 waiting outside could be admitted. The press drew lots for admission to the choir stalls, and I was fortunate to be among those winning a seat in one. We were admitted before the royal party.

"When their Majesties come in, I think we'd better put our notebooks under the pew tops, don't you think?," a veteran woman reporter from Boston, Massachusetts, sitting next to me commented.

I don't know what I replied, but it would have taken wild horses to get that notebook out of my hand. I had not come so far in distance and professionally to be so deferential. I didn't intend to miss a flutter of Elizabeth's eyelashes.

The $64,000 question of the moment was who would sit on the outside of the royal pew. If Elizabeth did, she was attending as the future sovereign; if she let Philip do so, she were there as his wife. Feverently we prayed for the triumph of romance over dynasty.

She came into the church, a serious young woman with perhaps the most exquisite complexion I have ever seen, wearing a hunter's red suit trimmed with black velvet, matched by a toque worn well back on her curly brown hair. An elaborate jeweled ornament was pinned on her left lapel.

It was her back, however, that made you realize that she was a future queen. I shall never forget it; erect, authoritative, it emanated a dominance that had nothing to do with the Declaration of Independence; the Magna Charta perhaps, but its monarchical mien was absolute. It said "I am," and in response did not inquire who you were.

Prince Philip, who followed her into the church, was quite different. He projected the image of an assured individual rather than a ruler, of contact with the gathering around him. He was a lubricating complement to her.

She entered their pew first - he followed - and our romantic hopes were fulfilled.

As the royal entourage assumed their seats, the church chimes which had been ringing out across the more than 300-foot gorge above the river were silenced.

The service opened with the singing of "God Save the King" by the assembly inside the church and those occupying chairs or standing room on the lawn.

Upon his own request, Philip read the lesson. With his straight blond hair and regular features, navy-blue suit, white shirt, light-blue tie, a white handkerchief in his breast pocket, and an air of relaxed confidence, he was every inch a fairy tale prince.

"For whosoever exalteth himself shall be abased; and he that humbleth himself shall be exalted," he read from St. Luke XIV:1-11. His tone was even and firm and his classic pronunciation and distinct diction was a delight to hear.

Princess Elizabeth bowed her head slightly as her husband spoke.

The choir in royal blue cassocks, starched white collars and black ties then rose and sang Tchaikovsky's anthem, "Hear, Lord Our God, Have Mercy."

Mercy was needed for Canon Albert Franklin Holmes, rector of Christ Church, who with other clergy and wardens had greeted the Royal pair upon their arrival outside.

The occasion was almost too much for Canon Holmes; he looked flushed with ecstasy. But he rose to his ecclesiastical duty with both empathy and instruction.

Basing his sermon on the collect for the day, he said:

"No man can ever find peace of mind if he is not at peace with his Creator.

"The higher one rises in life the greater one's responsibility becomes; the more people are affected by our decisions, and in this complex life today, I have the greatest sympathy with our rulers because, upon their decisions, upon their wise planning may rest the peace of the world...

"What we all need today is the ability to make decisions with confidence and assurance and to live happily in spite of our responsibilities."

Canon Holmes said faith, prayer and the ability to "let God direct, guide and empower us" are the answers.

**********

Leaving the church, the Royal party drove down the River Road by the Gorge to the Falls. It was a day tailored to royalty. Brilliant sunshine flooded the region and, as the entourage passed along the highway, twin rainbows, one wreathing the Falls and another arching the magnificent surrounding parkway, appeared.

The crowd lining the road along which the Royal party passed was orderly and respectful, but not markedly enthusiastic. There were, however, dramatic exceptions.

Mrs. Amanda Misener, 99, of Niagara Falls, Ontario, who as an 18-year-old girl saw Princess Elizabeth's great-grandfather, Edward VII, when he toured the Falls, stood on a chair as Elizabeth and Philip drove by, so she could see them better. The Prince noticed this and gave her a special salute.

The bed of Mrs. John J. Bampfield, also of Niagara Falls, Ontario, to which she had been confined for several years, was wheeled to the roadside so she could see the royal party pass.

For others, they or their forebears had come a long way from this spectacle. For them, it was different; you don't embrace a past you have put behind you with your life effort. It was not the same as if they were watching her drive out of Buckingham Palace on a fall afternoon. For them, those days were gone forever.

Yet the paradox of Canada was and is that - even though those days are gone - she is still there. And when American power and personality and cockiness assert themselves, one can always lean back on the royal bosom with confidence. Politics and even progress cannot entirely erase the psychological bulwark of the Crown. It is still very, very old. One is not entirely an auslander in this new land, not totally "cut off."

At the Falls, the Princess and the Prince sat in the flag-encircled, circular amphitheater of the Oakes Garden Theatre, overlooking the cataracts. The theatre is the central point of the surrounding Rainbow Gardens, which stand on land presented by Harry Oakes, the man from Maine who became a British baronet, made a fortune through gold mining and eventually was knighted.

A great gallery of lawn swept up behind the stage, encircled at the crest by a pergola of British Columbian, hand-hewn cedar, which was terminated at each end by tile-roofed pavilions flying dove-shaped weather vanes. Adjoining the theatre, parterres, laid out on different levels, fanned out.

Mayor Hawkins spoke from the heart: "If you could look into the hearts of your people assembled here today, you would know how proud and happy we are to have you with us."

Listening to the mayor's welcome, the Princess noticed a wrinkle in the red carpet stretched before them. With a good Hanoverian hausfrau gesture, Elizabeth gave it a smoothing pat with her French-heeled oxford.

An indication of Prince Philip's alertness to the public was his greeting to Warden William C. MacDonald, a Niagara Falls alderman, who was among those presented and had also passed the offering plate to the royal pair in church:

"You get around, don't you!," the Prince jovially remarked.

The couple were then driven to Table Rock House where they alighted to go to the promontory to view the Falls. We were informed that we could not approach nearer than 30 feet to them, and the Mounties stood by to see that we did not. You don't traffic with the Canadian Mounted Police.

Elizabeth did it all. She listened with much interest to the mayor's description of the magnitude and possibilities of Niagara's power. Prince Philip, turning to an aide to borrow 10 cents to operate a telescope provided for sightseers, viewed the American shore. Royalty does not carry money.

Then slipping into special new raincoats - an "Edinburgh Rose" one for the Princess and a beige mackintosh for the Prince - the Royal pair took the tunnel trip under the Falls.

Prince Philip did more. Reportedly, since a boy he had wanted to drive a locomotive. So, a striped engineer's cap on his head, he piloted the royal train for about 14 miles en route to Hamilton, Ontario. Apparently there's a little housewife in the most exalted princess, a bit of boy in every prince.

# 26

# Princess Margaret

IF THE VISIT OF PRINCESS Elizabeth was il penseroso leavened with the blitheness of her prince - that of her sister, Princess Margaret, to Ontario seven years later, was an allegro one.

In the first place, it was August instead of October; their father George VI was dead and Elizabeth was queen. Margaret, herself, had had a blocked romance, but as she stood in the Oakes Garden Theatre, overlooking the Falls, in a printed chiffon dress with short sleeves, a full skirt, and a cap-style hat made of pink and white flowers, her image was gay and sophisticated, amused and interested.

The garden too, was filled with flowers such as she had known in England, standard heliotrope, roses, fuchsia, sweet william and alyssum.

"Observers thought the crowds were larger and better distributed than when Queen Elizabeth II, then princess, and Prince Philip visited here in 1951," wrote my compatriot Jean Reeves. "They attributed this to the fact that Princess Margaret has always been less austere than her sister, and that she is known to be fun-loving and high-spirited."

Her widest smile was saved for an Indian chief. After cermemonies, she descended from the stage of thc amphitheater to sign the historical Queen Anne Bible, presented to the Mohawks by the crown in 1712. The worn, 17-1/2 by 11-1/2-inch Bible bore the signatures of nine members of the royal family, dating back to Albert Edward, Prince of Wales, in 1860.

The Rev. Canon W. J. Zimmerman of the Brantford Reservation then introduced three members of the Mohawk tribe in native dress: Chief Councillor E. P. Garlow and Councillors Fred Hill and Walter Lickers, the latter wearing a war bonnet and supported by crutches.

Princess Margaret appeared fascinated with them all, but it was Councillor Lickers who especially seemed to take her eye. She conversed with them, smiling until her dimples appeared. Mayor Hawkins then escorted her to the Bible stand where she signed the book.

The Rainbow Tower carillon rang out with such airs as "Drink To Me Only With Thine Eyes" and "The Piper of Dundee."

\*\*\*\*\*\*\*\*\*

A state luncheon for 120 was given in the Princess' honor in the Sheraton - Brock Hotel Rainbow Room, with its magnificent 10-story view of both the American and Canadian Falls.

Again, the press had to draw for admittance, and this time I lost, although Chief *Buffalo Evening News* Photographer Barney Kerr was chosen "pool" photographer for it.

Maitre d'Hotel George Foster who had served her grandfather, George V, at a luncheon in England 30 years before, personally waited upon Princess Margaret. White-gloved waiters in scarlet and black livery served the other guests.

The care in composing and serving the menu illustrated the Province's earnest desire to revere and please her. When a royal official had called at the hotel weeks before, he informed Chef Louis Gamdanella that the Princess is very fond of seafood, particularly fresh lobster. So lobster was flown in from Nova Scotia, as was fresh salmon from the Gaspé Peninsula. Squabs were raised especially by a Peterborough, Ontario, farm to be six weeks old for the occasion. White asparagus was imported from France.

The menu, encased in a print reproduced from a painting of the Canadian and American Falls by French artist Hippolyte Sebron in about 1852 and marked with purple satin ribbon, was a treasure piece.

Wines produced from Niagara Peninsula grapes and selected by the Canadian Wine Institute were poured. Sherry preceded the salmon; a dry white table wine accompanied the fowl. A toast to the Queen was drunk with a special port.

Rumors reached beyond the dining room doors that the Princess had asked for gin. And the fact that she applied lipstick at table was duly noted by an alert press.

Comparing the visits of the two princesses, it is that erect, red-clad back, seated in the little church on the Gorge in 1951, that lingers deepest in the memory. It was Empire, incarnate.

# 27

# God Save The Queen

IT WAS IN JUNE, 22 years later, that I saw Elizabeth and Philip again. They came on a 12-day visit to Ontario in honor of the 300th anniversary of Kingston, a city of slightly more than 50,000 population on the north shore of Lake Ontario, 264 miles south of Toronto, and for the centennials of both Prince Edward Island and the Royal Canadian Mounted Police. They also would attend the opening of the new $3 million Shaw Festival Theatre at Niagara-on-the-Lake, a small town founded by British loyalists in 1790.

We, a contingent of the 1455 members of the communications media who were converging on Toronto to inscribe, photograph or televise anything we could get our pencils or lenses on - from marmalade to crown jewels - had been briefed by Lt. Col. J. A. McPhee, press coordinator for the royal visit, the previous afternoon.

"The Queen is not under contract to the media," stated Col. McPhee with true British authoritarianism and chutney bite. "The people would like to see her." Outlining our ground rules for the visit, he described it as the "green knees tour," meaning that the photographers would have to get down on their knees (to hell with their trousers) to photograph Her Majesty, thus permitting the people behind them to catch of glimpse of her. "Walk about" rules included the press staying 30 feet ahead of the royal party. The Queen, we were told, likes to hold private conversations with her subjects en route, so no microphones would be permitted in the coverage.

********

The silver, red-striped DC-8 bearing the royal couple from Heathrow Airport, London, to the Toronto (Malton) Airport cut the cloudless sky and touched down in the early afternoon.

Fourteen 40-foot pine trees stood in great concrete tubs before the mammoth black hangar and the flags of the Canadian provinces flew from high standards before them.

A contingent of the Queen's Own Rifles in green uniforms darker than the pine trees stood just as straight before the flags, their black beaver hats with horsehair cockades bristling in the hot June sun.

On a long red carpet stood Canadian Governor-General Roland Michener in a black suit and holding a black fedora, and Prime Minister Pierre Trudeau, his hair blowing exuberantly in the hot breeze, with their wives and other dignitaries. Madame Trudeau was startlingly beautiful in a yellow dress and picture hat.

When the plane was sighted the scarlet-coated, beaver-hatted Royal Canadian Regimental band played "God Save the Queen." A crowd of about 8,000 stood by. As the plane touched down, everything stopped. There was a moment of absolute silence, as officials moved to open the door. People drew in their breath. Then the door was flung back, the runway affixed and the Queen of England stood in the opening. Her dress was a flowery summer one and she wore a wide, upturned Breton sailor hat. She raised her arm in the age-old greeting. It was a fictional moment.

There was no fairy tale, however, in the firm progression of the trim figure followed by Prince Philip, as she reviewed her Own Rifles and circled the entire fence line greeting people with whom she seemed in touch. She stopped here and there to chat with older people like Mrs. Alice Fleming, 71, of Toronto, who remembered her grandparents, King George and Queen Mary.

Observant as ever, Prince Philip in passing warned 8-year-old Hugh Kendall, son of Dr. and Mrs. John Kendall of nearby Burlington, to take his finger off his camera lens if he wanted a good picture of him.

The atmosphere on the airfield had switched from a deferential silence to a warm, excited family relationship. Quite different from nearly a quarter of a century before.

I wrote this assessment:

"It was nearly 22 years ago, as a *News* reporter, that I last saw Queen Elizabeth. She wasn't a queen then, only a 25-year-old princess, but she came to Niagara Falls, Ont., and attended services in Christ Anglican Church, along the Gorge.

"She had been married nearly 4 years and had two children. She showed, we observed, 'a serious demeanor.' Elizabeth became queen a few months later.

"Today, two decades later, the demeanor of the queen is still serious. But it is more motherly.

"The somewhat rigid mental and physical posture of her girlhood, inculcated by her stately grandmother, Queen Mary, has softened. She tends rather than commands her flock.

"As then, Prince Philip stands by her in obvious empathy and support. Some of his democratic warmth has rubbed off on her.

"The effect is of a Royal couple in sociable, concerned contact with their public, replacing a more distant and objective attitude from the throne."

**********

The Queen and her consort stayed in a suite at the Royal York Hotel overlooking the harbor which was filled with a variety of craft, from sailboats and ferries to lakeboats, many of which dipped their colors to her as she gained the hotel. The huge 45-year-old hostelry was being renovated to the tune of $13 million, a project then still in progress. Two key features had just been completed in time for her visit: A magnificent 3,000-pound pressed crystal chandelier hung over a new double spiral staircase leading from the main lobby, redone in tones of red and gold, to the floor below. And large portraits of Elizabeth and Philip, framed in red velvet and gold, she in court dress and he wearing a kilt, highlighted the entrance.

I had been to see the office manager, Gordon Viberg, before the royal party arrived and asked him, among other things, what brand of preserves he would serve the Queen of England?

"You are the first one to ask about marmalade," he said. "We serve Chivers brand, and we'll serve the Queen the jams and marmalade we serve at the hotel." He had a good deal on his mind besides jam - like the state dinner for 1,400 the following evening.

The royal party dined privately in their suite that evening, at the great mahogany dining table with its 20 velvet-covered armchairs.

**********

There is no tardiness in engagements on a royal tour. The itinerary brochures schedule events at as little as 5-to-10-minute intervals. They are illustrative of the meticulous, disciplined attention to detail which makes British pomp and ceremony possible.

Queens earn their keep. The next day made a kaleidoscope look static. A day of cannon shot and bagpipes, of leopard skins and diamonds, of spit and polish.

It began when a red-wheeled landau drawn by four white horses called for the Queen and her consort at the Royal York. As the sun stuck the shining brass helmets of the Governor General's Horse Guards in their scarlet coats and bearing lances, while they waited for their sovereign before the hotel, one traveled back eons in time. Perhaps it was the lances that did it, but a fictional shiver ran through me, and I'm sure others of the crowd estimated at 300,000 to 400,000 - "the largest crowd I've ever seen here, and I've seen a number," according to Metropolitan Police Inspector Robert Buchanan. The Crown had gained in esteem and affection since that autumn day in 1951 at the Falls.

The Horse Guards escorted the carriage to Queen's Park where Premier of Ontario William G. Davis welcomed Elizabeth before the old Gothic Parliament Buildings.

Citing the indebtedness of Canada to its British heritage; the benefits of its parliamentary system of government; the derivation of its legal system from the principles of British Common Law, and Ontario's Human Rights Code as "a contemporary projection of the light of liberty first generated by Runnymede with the signing of Magna Charta," Premier Davis said in welcome:

"To people of all origins in Ontario, Your Majesty by personal example casts a civilizing influence upon all our deliberations in meeting the challenges of an increasingly complex world. While Your Majesty's position commands respect in itself, it is Your Majesty's gracious and humane occupation of that position which evokes devotion and loyalty on a very immediate and personal level."

The Queen responded: "Under the protection of the law and the system of parliamentary democracy, people from all over the world have been able to choose various ways of being Canadian, respecting others but not forsaking their own inheritance. The shelter of confederation has given all the parts of the Canadian community the chance to grow into a mature and independent nation."

**********

In the face of Ontario's evolution as Canada's wealthiest and most industrial province, Elizabeth then added one interesting insight: That while the people of Canada "owe much to their own efforts..." they also inherited a great deal from the pioneers who came before them, who in turn, "learned how to survive in the new world from those who had flourished among the lakes and forest from time immemorial," a fact she declared, we must never forget. Thus, like her sister, Margaret, the Queen did not forget the Indians.

A new, fully equipped playground for the Hospital for Sick Children then was presented by the Premier to the Queen, on behalf of the government and people of Ontario. "I ask you most humbly to accept The Queen Elizabeth Playground," he said, "as a gift from your loyal and loving subjects...and as a permanent memento of your visit with us..."

Barristers in their black robes and white jabots were greeted by the Queen afterward in the garden of Osgoode Hall, the city's legal center. She was proudly shown a small room there, decorated with paneling from Old Bailey, London.

A civic luncheon for 1,400 in the Queen's honor followed in the grand ballroom of the Four Seasons Hotel - so new that a couple of pieces of styrofoam fell out of a chandelier in the dining room near the route the royal party would take - only minutes before their arrival.

Proud, excited British-boned women guests, many in wide droopy garden hats or flowered turbans, and carrying white gloves (a favor unquestionably granted in advanced prescribed protocol), lunched on melon ball cocktails, double lamb chops with mint sauce, potato croquettes, vegetables and lemon souffle with Canadian claret and champagne.

As at the dinner tendered by the Lt. Governor of Ontario that evening, the Queen's own footman in black and her page in scarlet livery stood behind her, not serving but assisting the hotel staff in her attendance. One may be sure that every dish served was tasted beforehand.

The humanitarian aspect of the royal visit came into focus when her Majesty called at Sick Children's Hospital and Mt. Sinai Hospital in the afternoon.

Elizabeth is at her best when confronting some issue of human concern; it softens the projection of royal image instilled in her by her grandmother, but in the presence of a representative gathering, the old rigor asserts itself. Both she and Prince Philip talked intermittently with the great circle of nurses lining the avenue between the two institutions, which face each other.

They greeted Mrs. Ralph Rice, head of nursing at Mt. Sinai, in her white uniform, at the center of scores of board members and medical staffers and their wives. Prince Philip particularly lingered in conversation with the head of nurses, apparently questioning her on the operation of the hospital.

As the Queen unveiled a tablet opening the new wing of the hospital, however, the inbred, authoritarian posture again reasserted itself. One felt the uncrossable span between her and the elite and reverential crowd.  An erect, vigilant figure, she pulled the cord unveiling the tablet, then seated in a gold velvet chair at a draped table, signed the register.  In those moments, the Crown of Britain shone.

A kingdom and its domains are composed of many elements, as well as territories, and like the Almighty and sparrows, the Queen has her eye on them all.  Before the afternoon was over, Elizabeth had released a batch of tagged small-mouthed bass at Grenadier Pond, symbolically inaugurating Ontario Conservation Week.  Anglers successfully landing these tagged fish in the future would receive a medallion commemorating the royal visit.  The Queen also met 100-year-old Mrs. Helen Vinnels, a native of Aberdeen, Scotland, who remembered her great-great-grandmother, Victoria.

I have been to many dinners, state and otherwise, but the one given by Lt. Governor MacDonald of Ontario for their Majesties that evening, outshone them all.  The storybook quality of the presence of royalty added something over and beyond any United States governmental function on any level.  The diamond tiara on Elizabeth's head seemed to literally bring it all into focus.

We, the press, were allowed to stand at the side of the red carpet stretched through the lobby of the hotel, down which she walked to the ballroom.

She appeared looking rested and radiant, gowned in a straight-line aquamarine and silver dress, reembroidered in aquamarine and turquoise; long diamond earrings and a three-strand diamond necklace falling  below the Gothic-spired tiara.  The Order of Canada and family orders were pinned at her breast.

She came first, of course, the Prince and the Lt. Governor walking slightly behind her.  At this point, we were relegated to the balcony with the musicians, overlooking the ballroom.  It was a pleasure to sit with my old compatriot, Ruth Seltzer, society editor of the *Philadelphia Inquirer* - a reunion so far from home.

We looked down on a splendid gathering, the royal party and dignitaries at a long table on a dais to the right, and the assemblage of 1850 men and women in evening dress at table below it.

The linen was pink and the centerpieces of roses and daisies.  The menu:

Aspic de fois gras
Consommé Rothschild
Tournedo Marie Antoinette
Bouquetiere de Legumes
Hearts of Palm Mimosa

Strawberries Sabayon
Friandises
Coffee

The wines were cream sherry, Canadian Burgundy, extra dry champagne and cream port. Both the Queen and Prince left spoons in the coupé glasses - apparently a British custom, but not sanctioned by Emily Post.

**********

Fifteen years had passed since Margaret rippled the scene by applying lipstick at table at Niagara Falls; now her sister, the Queen, did likewise, unnoticed except by the most observant reporters.

Elizabeth rose for the toast, raised her glass, then as de riguer, placed it upon the table, untouched. Neither the Queen nor Prince smoke, but throughout the tour smoking was permitted after the toast. She told the assemblage that no one coming to Toronto after an interval of 14 years could fail to notice "the changes, the growth and the general improvements of standards," a material development only to be expected in this age of technological development.

"The only danger is to mistake material growth for social improvement," she said..."at the center of it all are men and women and children. They are still the same size, they still function in much the same way and their ordinary human needs are not much different...

"The real measure of success of any community, whether it lives in a modern, urban industrial world or in primitive conditions," the Queen declared, "is the sense of freedom, the ability to participate in self-government and the social and cultural development which makes all its members feel that life is worth living..."

The Queen said she had been "moved and touched by the special warmth of our reception by Canadians who cherish links between Great Britain and this country," and that it was a particular satisfaction to her that the crown can be "a powerful link between all the nations of the Commonwealth."

"But it is as Queen of Canada that I am here," she stated. "Queen of Canada and of all Canadians, not just one or two ancestral strains," she emphasized. "I want the Crown to be seen as a symbol of national sovereignty belonging to all. It is not only a link between Commonwealth nations, but between Canadian citizens of every national origin and ancestry.

"The Crown," affirmed Elizabeth, "is an idea more than a person and I want the Crown of Canada to represent everything that is best and most admired in the Canadian ideal."

The Queen, Prince Philip and their party then left the ballroom to cross the street, through lines of Troops of the Argyll and Sutherland Highlanders of Canada, to the Canadian National Railway Union Station, where the royal train awaited. Person or idea, it is dubious if as many diamonds had ever crossed a Toronto highway or that any Canadian mogul had put in a fuller day than Elizabeth, Queen of Great Britain and Northern Ireland.

# 28

# The Tour

THE 15-CAR TRAIN pulled by three diesel locomotives bearing the Royal Standard would carry the Royal party to seven Ontario cities and towns, en route to Niagara-on-the-Lake including the tricentennial celebration at Kingston, where the day's schedule, if anything, would top that of Toronto.

"Canadian National will note a Royal passenger extra in its train orders this month," announced the railroad in candid, democratic fashion," but somehow this does not convey any of the extensive planning that goes into organizing transportation for Queen Elizabeth...  More than 200 CN employees are involved in the movement of the train, directly or indirectly, as it moves across Southern Ontario..."

"It is not just the addition of one extra train," noted J.J. Menary, the railroad's coordinator of the train.  "In most cases a pilot train will run about 30 minutes ahead of the Royal Train at any given time, and special operating procedures will govern other trains operating in the vicinity."

Some of the procedures were:

Opposing passenger trains at a double track area must pass the Royal Train at "slow speed" - no more than 10 miles an hour.

Opposing freight trains must be off the same track at least one hour in advance of the train's passage.

Passenger trains heading in the same direction must be at least one hour ahead; freight trains, four hours.

While the Royal Train was stationary at terminals or intermediate tie-up points, all other trains in the vicinity must operate at "reduced speed."

Roadmasters and track supervisors would check the track prior to the train.  Even right-of-way fences would be checked to ensure that livestock would not wander onto the track.

Slowdowns of one-or-two-miles-an-hour would be made at specific locations, so crowds gathered there could see the Queen and Prince, who would be on the rear platform.

**********

Inside the Royal coach, the atmosphere was more homelike. The recall of Chief Steward Wilfred Notley of Ottawa, after 47 years of service, gave a local continuity to the journey. The steward had served on six royal tours, including the 30-day visit of Elizabeth's parents, King George and Queen Elizabeth. This was the fifth time he had served their daughter. The Order of Canada for "distinguished service" was awarded Notley just before the royal visit. A staff of three assisted him.

As chief steward, Notley would receive the Royal couple on board the train, prepare the daily menus made up each day according to suggestions from the Queen and Prince Philip, order the dinner wines and oversee all food preparation.

The Royal dining car was furnished with an oval table, four high-backed dining chairs, and a mahogany buffet on which was a silver tea service set on a large tray. Linen was white and the china service, Royal Doulton, also white, but with a band of blue and gold. Glass was crystal and the flower centerpieces were changed at each meal. Napkins and candles matched the centerpieces.

At the end of the dining car was a comfortable lounge area with a writing desk and chair, a bookcase containing a selection of books and magazines and two special high-back, regal looking chairs covered in rose velvet for their Majesties, as well as an occasional chair or two.

The Royal Sleeping Car was divided into two bedrooms and baths, a small pass-through in the wall enabling the Royal couple to converse if they wished. Six other sleeping cars, two staff business cars, a lounge car, a baggage car, a crew car, a diner and one electrical generating unit were included in the 1,418-foot train.

**********

After visits to seven cities and towns in two days, the Queen and her consort arrived at sundown at Niagara-on-the-Lake, the town at the southern tip of Lake Ontario, the home of descendants of British Loyalists who founded it in 1790 and long a fashionable summer Canadian resort for families; a town which, like Stratford, Ont., with its Shakespearean theatre, literally sprang into public prominence with the summer production of the plays of George Bernard Shaw in its old Court House. The new $3 million Shaw Festival Theatre the Queen was about to open was testimony to their success. But success is a relative accomplishment, and at this point, a word about the town itself, seems requisite.

The ignorance of much of the Eastern Seaboard about Niagara-on-the-Lake until recently is an example of its own provincialism. Yet unquestionably, the fact that this rare and sequestered spot was not well-known before say the 1970s, can be laid at the often exquisitely-designed door of the town. Before that, Niagara-on-the-Lake had nothing but itself to acclaim, and that was the last thing it would have thought of doing.

If American "get-on-ness" had not come in and seen the potential of the Shaw offerings, already being staged with understated dignity in the old Court House, it is dubious if the town ever would have garnered international fame. But it did, in the person of an American summer resident, Calvin Rand, whose family had been among the summer colony for three generations. Grandson and son of a leading Buffalo banking family, Mr. Rand was interested in "cultural exchange" between the United States and Canada. The development of a first-class theater around the well reviewed company in the Court House seemed an excellent means of so doing. With large grants from the Provincial government and wide and generous patronage, Calvin Rand had brought it off. Although it was theatre, the Shaw Festival became a rock of reality in the midst of an ambiguous sea.

Indigenously, Niagara-on-the-Lake and Bermuda share much in common: Both are places where Britons have ruled; both are at least partly surrounded by water; both have square, stalwart, impregnable-looking houses with fine architectural detail, and both exude a wistfulness that comes from separation from England and a pull toward America. They are literally pulled both ways.

As one turns off the road along the Niagara River and goes down an incline to the beginning of this 213-year-old town - very old for the Niagara Frontier - one has a feeling of entering Brigadoon.

My first encounter with Niagara-on-the-Lake was in writing about its annual Simcoe Ball. Soon after its founding, the little town became the first capital of Upper Canada, as the land west of the Ottawa River was then called. The first Lt. Governor was John Graves Simcoe, and in 1793, he and his wife, Elizabeth, gave a ball in honor of the birthday of George II (1760-1820), a ball which has not been forgotten. It was a glowing memory among the inhabitants who survived the burning of the town in the War of 1812, and 150 years later in 1963, there began an annual reenactment of it - from a minuet by candlelight, "serving wenches" and roast beef to an old English drink called shrub (1 gallon sugar syrup, 2 gallons brandy and 20 lemons - all mixed with 3 gallons of white wine).

An entry from the diary of Mrs. Simcoe describes the original ball which gives a glimpse of social life along the Niagara Frontier at the time:

"In the evening, there was quite a splendid ball...What excites the best feelings of my heart was the care and affection with which the ladies meet each other, although there were a number present whose mothers spring from the aborigines (Indians of the country).

"They appeared as well-dressed as the company in general, and intermixed with them in a measure which evinced at once the dignity of their own minds and the good sense of others."

At the "reenactments," the question of attire is not left to the whim of the guests, who are asked to come in costumes of the period or evening dress. A guide to "deportment" accompanies tickets. Governor and Mrs. Simcoe are enacted by a representative couple from the area.

Following a reception in the supper room of the Court House, the guests repair to the candlelit ballroom where they remain standing until a drumroll announces the entry of the governor, accompanied by members of his staff and their ladies, all of whom compose the Reenactment Group. The Lord Mayor of Toronto and his wife also usually attend.

The Historical Society emphasizes that the ball is "an historical reenactment; it is not a fancy dress party." A military quadrille, quite a new dance as early as 1790, and the Triumph, a line dance of the 1840s, are engaged in, as well as the minuet.

Supper is served at 9:30, contemporary Fort York Guards carefully tying napkins on the governor and his party and serving them. The roast beef is borne in with perhaps a bit of an old song like this one by Richard Leveridge (1670-1758):

When a mighty roast beef was the Englishman's food,
It enabled our hearts and enriched our blood,
Our soldiers were brave and our courtiers good,
Oh! the roast beef of old England!

(It should be added here that it would be hard to beat Canadian beef, the flavor of which, many believe, surpasses that raised in the United States.)

A concession to the 20th century is made with ballroom dancing after supper, with intermittent entertainment by the Simcoe Dancers, girls from the Niagara District Secondary High School. They dance such old time favorites as Petronello, the Eight-hand Reel and the Gay Gordons, in which the assemblage is invited to join. Free instruction is offered before the ball to guests wishing to take part in the old dances.

It was into such a town, weighted with British tradition yet supporting the peculiar alchemy which is Canada, that Queen Elizabeth and Prince Philip came, a town her great-grandfather, Albert Edward, then Prince of Wales, had visited in 1876, and etched his initials with a diamond ring on a glass pane of the china cabinet in the dining room of the grand old Breckenridge-Hawley house on Mississauga Street.  A town where her grandfather, George, then Prince of Wales, and Princess Mary, Elizabeth's mentor, also had visited nearly 70 years before.

# 29

# Royal Box

NIAGARA-ON-THE-LAKE was prepared for the Queen. It had been at it for eight months. In a report on its plans for the royal visit, I wrote:

"Niagara-on-the-Lake is pleased and honored but not awed by the royal visit. And it is preparing to greet its official head of state in its own manner, without striving for out-of-place grandeur.

"As you walk the quiet tree-shaded streets scores of houses built before the mid-19th century, with boxwood and roses (they'll be in bloom for the Queen) in dooryards and gardens, you sense excitement underneath the traditional reserve. Visits of royalty have been among Niagara-on-the-Lake's most cherished memories, bowing only to the lore and legend of the War of 1812."

For such figures are symbols, at least, of a monarchical form of government under which Canada exists today.

**********

So the Royal coach eased down through the cities and towns of Ontario to this historic one - not "This blessed plot, this earth, this realm, this England," but a place yearning toward it against the pressures of time and distance.

Motoring from St. Catharines along the lake to the Welland Canal, the cherry trees abloom on its banks, and the John Hancocks of ships from around the world and the date they were there painted in bright colors along its lock walls, the Royal party came to Niagara-on-the-Lake, where old-timers were keeping an eye on Jean, the Scottish wife of Frederick W. Curtis, the barber. When King George VI and Queen Elizabeth (whom, you'll remember, is also Scottish) passed through in 1939, Mrs. Curtis broke the silence of the tree-shaded main street with a rousing greeting - "Hooray for Glamis! Hooray for Strathmore!," both spots dear to the Queen's heart. Mrs. Curtis still treasured the memory of the Queen's gracious recognition of her exuberance.

It was toward sundown when the Queen and Prince and their party of about 40 drove down Queen Street, that main thoroughfare of the town, with its memorial clock tower built after World War I;

hanging baskets of flowers ornamenting the light standards and the fronts of the shops, past the great, square, white houses with their classic doorways and fragrant gardens to Fort George, British bastion before the War of 1812.

There were those like English-born Maj. B. Handley Geary, V.C.M.A., living in a white, green-trimmed house on Victoria Street with a little flag of the Province of Ontario aflutter from the porch, who felt that a monarchy is best. Maj. Geary was the town's only holder of the Victoria Cross, Britain's highest military decoration.  He would be presented to her Majesty during ceremonies at Fort George.

"Naturally, I'm very happy to know she's coming.  I think she's charming," he said in his study filled with mementos of World War I, in which his East Surrey Regiment defended and held Hill 60 at Ypres with great courage and heavy losses.

"I think the Monarchy is the best part of our Constitution because of its permanence, its reliability and the fact that it is nonpolitical.  I think no elected head of state can represent all the people of a country..."

**********

While pomp and circumstance could be played down to fit surroundings, in anything connected with a royal visit protocol is as inflexible a necessity as high tea.  Buckingham Palace and the Federal and Provincial Governments issued specific protocol notes on a variety of matters, from dress to toasts, in regard to the Queen's visit.  Among them:

DRESS:  "In regards to ladies clothes, short afternoon dresses are correct for daytime functions.

"It is no longer obligatory for short gloves to be worn at daytime functions, although many ladies will feel more comfortable with gloves; if worn, they need not be white and should not be taken off before the wearer is presented to the Queen or Duke. Hats are normally worn until 6 p.m.  They are optional but preferable.

PRESENTATIONS:  "Each guest bows or curtsies and shakes hands with Her Majesty, then does the same with His Royal Highness and then passes on.

"Ladies presented do not make a full curtsy, but half a curtsey, i.e., the right foot is placed behind the left heel, the knee bent slightly and the head is held erect as the presentee shakes hands...

"The bow for gentlemen is a neck bow and the body is held erect while the head is inclined forward..."

Protocol also dictated that neither the Queen or Duke ever accept "gifts from firms engaged in trade or commerce." But presents from "Governments, civic bodies or associations were usually accepted."

The only presents offered by private individuals, personal friends excepted, were:

Food if perishable; flowers; "very small presents of purely sentimental value offered by children, veterans, etc...when a refusal would lead to hurt feelings."

Books of "a non-controversial nature...when offered by their authors, provided they are of reputable character;" but manuscripts of books or music were not. However, pictures generally were satisfactory, if offered by the artist, including photographs and drawings.

Live animals were declined.

One can imagine the offerings and resultant situations of the past that had served to necessitate such specifications.

**********

Upon the Queen's acceptance of Niagara-on-the-Lake's invitation, the town swung into action. From Buckingham Palace came Philip Moore, deputy private secretary to the Queen, and Brig. Gen. P.S. Cooper, Her Majesty's Canadian secretary, to discuss plans with Niagara Town Clerk J.Y. Fleming.

Her Majesty's likes and dislikes were discussed and it was learned that the Queen did not like seafood, so none was included on the three menus submitted to her. But she was anxious to see the orchards of the region, which extend right down to Lake Ontario, a mass of delicate pink and white bloom at that time of year, against the blue water.

When it came to gifts, the Town moved, within the boundaries of the aforementioned protocol, in an indigenous manner. There was something infinitely touching in the principal gift to the Queen, a decanter of pearwood from the nearby farm of Alderman William Griffiths, which Wilson Johnston, a local carver, had been commissioned to make. Pearwood is heavy and dense, and the interior of the bottle was treated to hold liquid. Both it and its case featured carving of the town crest, grapes and the principal fruits of the region - peaches, pears, apples and cherries. Two books by Peter John Stokes, restoration architect at Upper Canada Village and of extensive restoration in the Niagara-on-the-Lake area - "Early Architecture of the Town and Township of Niagara" (Niagara Press) and "Old Niagara-on-the-Lake" (University of Toronto Press) - also were presented.

As protocol dictates, the pre-1801 Union Jack flew from Fort George. The fortification is a series of low log buildings of simple dignity, far less elaborate than the stone one at Fort Erie, some 20 miles to the south, built in 1764. Just across from it was the new Swedish Modern Shaw Festival Theater, the two buildings - the historic fort and dramatic playhouse - like a parenthesis figuratively, enclosing the town's past and future.

The Queen, wearing a lime-green silk ensemble and matching cloche trimmed at the back with a large white rose, and Prince Philip, in a light gray suit with blue and white striped shirt, took their places in a canopied pavilion before the fort's primitive blockhouse, overlooking the parade ground. They sat in simple Windsor chairs, accompanied by Lord Mayor Jacob Froese of the town.

Elizabeth smiled broadly and fondly as the coach in which her grandparents, the Duke of York and his Duchess, Mary of Teck, the future King George V and Queen Mary, had ridden through the town in 1901, drove up. It had been meticulously restored by the Niagara-on-the-Lake Foundation. And who do you think was in the coach? Even in this, one of its finest hours, Niagara-on-the-Lake would not forget them: why Lord and Lady Simcoe, of course, portrayed by Brig. Gen. Willis Moog (Ret.), custodian of Dundrun Castle in nearby Hamilton, and Mrs. Moog.

However, Frank McD. Hawley, wiry, debonair vice-president of W.S. Tyler Co. of Canada, Ltd., as the boot, in maroon and white livery, really had an edge on all except the Queen. For on a glass pane of the china cabinet in the dining room of the house built in 1800 in the town, which he had had restored with museum techniques as his dwelling - a signature had been etched with a diamond ring - "Edward, P.W., 1876." Records show that Edward VII, then Prince of Wales, lodged there overnight.

**********

The Simcoe Dancers, in scarlet coats and swaying skirts, performed on the greensward and words of Gen. Isaac Brock, hero of Upper Canada in the War of 1812, whose statue tops a huge obelisk above his tomb overlooking the Gorge, were declaimed by Paxton Whitehead, artistic director of the Shaw Festival Theatre.

By far the most strangely touching of the ceremonies, the resounding climax, was a spirited enactment of 1812 War tactics demonstrated by the Fort York Guards in period uniforms - Fort George had no military guard protection - from a handbook of the period. At least 10 cannon shots and numerous rounds of flint-musket fire banged and crackled across the compound.

The Duke of Edinburgh laughed heartily, and upon its completion - "This is longer than World War II," commented a member of the crowd - both he and the Queen came down and reviewed the guards. The moment was moving, a faded yet heartfelt gesture of a country, which had fought and gained the right to remain British, offering a memento to its contemporary sovereign, from leagues across the sea.

During the ceremonies a brief shower forced Elizabeth and Philip to take shelter in their closed car nearby. As she gazed out the window at the teeming crowd of all ages, many waving Canadian flags, she looked tired beneath the lime green bonnet with its white rose. Her expression was one of calm duration - but intermingled with love.

*********

By evening, she was again radiant. In a pale green metallic gown, encrusted with a design of rose raindrops, a single strand diamond necklace with pendant drop and long diamond earrings, she and the Prince and their party were entertained at a civic dinner in the Pillar & Post Inn, where they had rested in a suite furnished with handcrafted reproductions of Upper Canadian furniture made of 100-year-old pine in the inn's own workshop. The quarters included a Franklin stove, cobbler's bench, coffee table and handmade patchwork quilts.

Here again, Niagara-on-the-Lake stuck to its own guns rather than attempting to imitate or import continental resplendence. The Queen's personal Canadian Flag was broken upon their arrival.

Printed cards had been issued on protocol to the 250 guests attending the dinner, informing them that, among other things, they were to rise and face their Majesties upon their entrance to the main dining room; to stand while the blessing was asked by the Rev. Hugh Maclean, rector of 169-year-old St. Mark's Anglican Church nearby; to rise and stand during the toast, and to refrain from smoking until after it.

Old pine tables were set with bright plaid placements, woven in Canada; but Wedgwood china in the Argyle pattern, plain white with a green and gold border, had been imported from England.  Forty young college students in period costumes of Upper Canada Gordons served the meal:

> Peninsula Melon Supreme
> (with strawberries and cherries)
> Newark Filet of Beef
> Loyalist Baked Stuffed Potatoes
> A Bouquet of Vegetables
> Strawberry Ice Cream
> Coffee            Liqueurs

Bright's President's Extra Dry Champagne was served at a reception in the gallery before the dinner, and Bright's Solera Sherry and Chateau Gai Gamay Beaujolais was poured during the meal.

Only a two-member press pool received access to the dining hall, so I, with scores of others, circled about the inn awaiting a glimpse of the guests and picking up any bits we could of what was going on inside.

The Royal couple sat before a 10-place head dining table of century-old Canadian white pine, in 17th-Century chair reproductions of similar wood, handcrafted by Mr. Johnston (executor of the decanter which was then duly presented).  The coat of arms of Ontario was carved on the chairs.

The more than 50 newsmen and women, many from overseas, not admitted to the royal dining hall, nevertheless fared well.  They supped at the Buttery, a charming floral basket-hung restaurant, on: "The Queen's Day Buffet" - cold roast beef with mustard sauce; royal game pie; Old English steak and kidney pie; Canadian ham with beer glaze and fresh salmon with watercress sauce.  This was topped off with fresh fruit in Cointreau; strawberries and cream in meringue shell and English triffle.

Toward the end of the meal a toast was raised: "Here's Health Unto Her Majesty!"  A current as old as Britain swept over the crowded second-floor room as flushed and elated, all raised their glasses.  No one could possibly have doubted their sincerity and devotion.

An audience - many of the women in floating chiffon and the men in white dinner jackets - greeted the Queen and her Prince in the Shaw Festival Theatre, a brick, wooden and glass structure designed by R.J. Thom of Toronto.

In sophisticated, modern contrast to the afternoon setting of the old fort, the 822-seat theater is in warm earth colors with a semi-circular garden lobby which opens onto terraces and broad green landscape beyond. Plantings of dark fir line the driveway.

Elizabeth and Philip sat in special armchair seats in one of two boxes in the theater, which has a very lofty rake. They faced a massive modernistic wool and sisal curtain.

By some fortune, I and three other reporters were lodged in the box on the other side of the theatre, giving us not only a fine view of the stage, but a perfect spot from which to see the royal enclosure. Elizabeth read the handsome blue suede-covered program of the play - Shaw's "You Never Can Tell," an 1896 comedy of an English seaside town, intently. During the performance, Prince Philip nonchalantly rested one foot on the railing of the box.

Mrs. Rand took Mayor Froese's place with the royal couple and her husband during the second act of the play. Champagne was served between the acts, and Elizabeth and Philip went backstage and greeted the cast after the performance. The audience remained seated until she returned to the theatre proper, and left to the playing of "God Save the Queen" by the Canadian Brass of the Hamilton Philharmonic. As she walked through the crowded but closely guarded lobby, the Queen smiled with pleasure. Evidently, she had thoroughly enjoyed herself.

The royal party drove to the St. Catharine's Canadian National Station where they had left the royal coach. And so across the vast, uninhabited stretches of the province the train bore its sovereign to other cities and towns of Canada, sounding an authoritative yet wistful whistle across the night. And the Town of Niagara-on-the-Lake settled back into its historic yet prospering reality.

# 30

# The Queen Mother

NIAGARA-ON-THE-LAKE awoke again July 5, 1981, really awoke - not just artistically, financially or crowd wise, an established fact since the opening of the Shaw Festival Theatre - but the very roots of the town's English oak heritage stirred beneath the ground of its shaded streets and fragrant gardens - as again, it received royalty:

Her Majesty Queen Elizabeth, the Queen Mother. In 1939, she and her husband, George VI, were the first ruling monarchs to visit Canada. Now a widow for nearly 30 years, she came again to Niagara-on-the-Lake alone, for the 200th celebration of the little town, which here and there hung out the Scottish flag - yellow with Red Lion rampant, in her honor, along with the Union Jack and Canadian banners.

"I am deeply touched by your kindness in inviting me to join you on this important occasion," said the nearly 81-year-old Queen, known to millions as "Queen Mum," as she stood on a red-carpeted platform below the steps of the 133-year-old court house.

She was dressed in one of her usual summery chiffon ensembles of pale gray blue, and wore a toque of matching flowers restrained by a bit of veil. A great jeweled pendant pin ornamented her dress.

Upon arrival, she sat in a Louis XV chair of black walnut - Niagara-on-the-Lake is very particular about the chairs that their visiting royalty rest in - covered with off-white damask, which Robert Kroeken, a regional cabinetmaker, was commissioned to execute. The town wanted the Queen's coat of arms carved on the top rail, and Mr. Kroeken, wondering slightly what Louis XV would have said, with the Queen's permission, complied.

The Queen had attended morning prayers in 171-year-old St. Mark's Anglican Church. She had asked that it be a normal "every Sunday" type of service.

Afterward, at the clock tower in the very center of town, she had reviewed the Lincoln and Welland Regiment and received a 21-gun salute by the 10th Field Battery, 56th Field Regiment (R.C.A.).

The staggered cannon fire, intermingled with the drums of the Niagara Regional Police Pipe and Drum Corps in their blue tartans and great black busbies, the white tassels falling from their pipe-tops matching their spanking puttees, shook the air of the town.

In honour of the visit to Niagara-on-the-Lake by
Her Majesty Queen Elizabeth II and His Royal Highness Prince Philip,
the Buttery this June 28th, 1973 presents

### The Queen's Day Buffet

Assorted Appetizers               Assorted Relishes
    Green Salad           Waldorf Salad
Cold Roast Beef with Mustard Sauce    Royal Game Pie
Olde English Steak & Kidney Pie   Canadian Ham with Beer Glaze
    Fresh Salmon with Watercress Sauce
Fresh Fruit in Cointreau    Strawberries & Cream in Meringue Shell
    English Trifle
Assorted Cheeses    Fresh Fruit    Beverage

$ 6.75

"Here's Health Unto Her Majesty"

The Buttery,
Niagara-on-the-Lake,
Tel: 468-2564.

*THE Press supped when Queen Elizabeth and Prince Philip dined at Niagara-on-the-Lake, Ontario, in 1973.*

Anyone concerned about the survival of Britain could be reassured by the force with which Sgt. Robert Little of St. Catharine's laid his stick on that drum, and Drum Major Constable Don Mealy's wielding of his mace.

A light rain had fallen just before the Queen Mother's arrival from the church, but the crowd lining the street, abloom with red and white petunias cascading from baskets on the light standards and in tubs at the curbs, sat unmoved under umbrellas and slickers. There was muted conversation, like a drone of bees, and an assurance among the older women of fellow sisters about to receive a member of their order.

Church bells rang intermittently.

Then there she was in their midst!

There she stood, facing the crowd, many in T-shirts and shorts, slacks or jeans, the personification of feminine grace - nearly 81-years-old, but 81 years graceful.

**********

The Queen Mother Elizabeth differs markedly from all other members of the royal family I have witnessed. She seems to make no effort to impress her royal image on the public; she takes that image for granted.

Her expression is one of happy sharing that says - with really a slightly mischievous air - "I think the world is cheerful and lovely - do join me in its enjoyment!"

Utterly unselfconscious, she takes everyone in, never looking *down* but always *at* the people. Her viewpoint is horizontal. She chats and smiles, sustaining a continuity of social manner and pleasantness throughout her appearances.

The former Lady Elizabeth Bowes-Lyon, daughter of the 14th Earl of Strathmore, has needed no ERA - she has always known her place - queen, wife, mother, grandmother and now great-grandmother.

For the shops along Queen Street bore witness to another milestone in her life, their windows full of books, china, tea towels, boxes of shortbread heralding the approaching wedding of her eldest grandson, heir to the British throne. She already had Lady Diana Spencer under her wing at Clarence House, unquestionably giving her royal flying lessons.

The Queen Mother expressed gratitude for "the vision and persistence of courageous pioneers," and warmly praised the accomplishment of "this vigorous young country."

She unveiled a tablet declaring the 115-year-old Niagara Apothecary Shop a national historic site. Then she rested before lunch in the Prince of Wales Hotel, where Edward VII also had stopped.

*********

An attar of Victorianism permeated the lobby of the hotel through which she passed. Pictures, busts, "Her Most Gracious Majesty, 1840" - a print of Victoria holding two roses, her shining center-parted hair done in braided coils resting on her neck...a replica of Franz Winterhalter's painting of the Royal Family, 1846, from the Royal Collection. Busts of Victoria as a girl and an aged queen.

A likeness of King Edward VII in the uniform of field marshal, white coq feathers drooping from the dress hat in his hand. And in a corner, an oval-framed photograph of his grandson, Edward VIII, as a very, very young soldier, whose abdication had - against the now Dowager's Queen's personal desire - placed her husband, George VI, and herself on the throne.

Perhaps, like the rain, it all made the Queen Mother feel somewhat at home. But Elizabeth Bowes-Lyon does not live in the past. She obviously lives in the lives of those around her.

She lunched on medallions of veal, and chicken with sauce Bernaise and an elaborate torte, special creations of the hotel, then went to Fort George, largely a reconstruction of the original built between 1796-99, its primitive bastions reminiscent of simpler, more gallant wars. Hundreds of scouts on jamboree lined her path.

Seated on the parade ground facing the fort, she removed her right glove and enthusiastically applauded a choir, piercingly loud bellringers and a shorter enactment of a War of 1812 military drill. Then mounting a platform, she accepted a lap robe woven by Carol Bannister of neighboring Queenston and three "bicentennial" potted pink roses.

"I can't say how touched I am," the Queen Mother said feelingly. "In winter, wrapped in this beautiful blanket and in summer when these roses bloom, they will be memorials of a very happy day here in Niagara." Her simplicity and appreciation were in themselves, touching.

She stepped down from the platform to greet Walter Sharp in a wheelchair, whose father had trained the Royal horses. Mr. Sharp is a second cousin of the Duke of Wellington.

"Will Ye Nar Come Back Ag'n" piped the Niagara Regional Police Pipe and Drum Corps as she left the fort.

The Queen Mother looked as fresh as when she had arrived, as five hours later, she left the town, sitting erect in the limousine, giving a final familiar wave to the crowd particularly gracefully, her hand raised slightly backward at the wrist.

**********

And so they pass - the long procession of the Crown of 1000 years - these men and women born to lead, to rule for a time, but always of necessity, to walk largely alone. The heroic personal adjustments of temperament many have made can only be surmised; the continual demands of their state are more obvious.

Standard bearers of a political form that now only tenuously clings to the earth, they continue to fascinate and command our respect.

# 31

## The Circus

SURELY, THE CIRCUS is one of the phenomena of civilized man. Its courage, dedication and endurance of hardship shines forth in the performance of its people. It is a life with daily physical danger that the average citizen experiences possibly once in a lifetime. It is a life on the precipice, gallantly and exultantly lived.

To the average citizen, the circus is fascinating but incomprehensible. How anyone would eschew a home and physical safety to become a public spectacle, often in danger, is a mystery. Yet in that very mystery - the continual challenge of gravity and a gypsy-like yet severely disciplined structure of living from one end of the country to the other - lies its appeal; it provides an escape and enchantment to lesser mortals who do not fly through the air in a trapeze with ease and are alarmed by the barking of a dog.

The circus has gone through various phases, but surely its very essence, a fantastically varied community, adventurous journeying and perennial expectation and exhilaration was in the air the morning of May 3, 1943 when I was sent by the *Philadelphia Daily News* at 4 a.m., to see the Ringling Brothers & Barnum & Bailey Circus come to town. It was like this:

Just as the world's big top, the sky, lightened a bit this morning, a string of silver cars bearing the circus rolled into town.

With only seven scant hours to unload the human, animal and material contents of 41 coaches and freighters, the greatest show on earth will open at G and Luzerne Sts. at 12:30 today.

Long before the fantastic cargo-laden cars pulled in at 4 a.m. at the Fairhill freight station, an eager knot of men and boys - and what's the difference when it comes to a circus? - had assembled on the small hill overlooking the tracks.

Amid a general champing and stamping, the doors of the boxcars were thrown open. From the depths of hay-filled interiors, Trilby, 45-year-old elephant, was the first to breathe in the Philadelphia air. Sleepy circus hands crept out and stretched. Glowing eyes from the depths of strongboxes indicated that the tigers were awake. Peanuts,

the camel, made her debut.  And in a private coach on a
siding, a 72-year-old lady slept peacefully on.

Edith Ringling, daughter of a Zumbro Falls, Minn.,
Methodist minister, has been trouping with the greatest show
on earth for 35 years.  She sleeps much sounder in the bunk
of the 38-year-old car she tours in than in the massive Italian
bedstead of her 20-room pink marble mansion in Sarasota,
Fla.

I talked with Mrs. Ringling.  She personally had
inspected the six-pole top, the real old-fashioned tent being
used this year.

"The show has reverted from more or less of a girl show
into a real old-time circus again," said this three-score-and-
ten-year-old executive with eyes as steady as any of her
jugglers.

Many of the old hands who traveled with the big top,
prior to the streamlining of the past five years under the
management of John North, are now back on the job.

"Remember me?," ran one application to Mrs. Ringling.
"I was lame and slow when I worked for you five years ago,
Mrs. Charles.  Well, I'm even lamer and slower today.  But
how about it?"  He was back.

After half a century of parachutes, peanuts and panthers,
Edith Ringling still believes "that if you're honest with
yourself and the world, nothing else matters."  This is her
only employment policy.

The tailored, upright lady with flawless teeth and high-
piled white hair has seen a lot of bravery in her time.  But
Paul Humpero beats all.  A group of midgets entered the tent
for their "Snow White and the Seven Dwarfs" act. Lady, the
tiger, broke loose.  One of the dwarfs was about to faint
from fright.

Humpero, 40 inches in height, knew that his buddy had
heart trouble.  He knew if he hit the sawdust, he was as dead
as yesterday's mouse.  Humpero took his little rubber mallet
and walked right up to Lady and biffed the tiger right on the
nose.  It worked.  So he did it again before the keeper
arrived.

"I have never forgiven myself for not getting the Carnegie medal* for Paul," said Mrs. Charles.

**********

Most intriguing of all the sights before one reached the Big Top were the sideshows, which included the freaks. A barker dressed for Ascot, standing on in a sort of elevated rostrum at the entrance of this lesser tent, regaled the crowd with the amazements and wonders therein for the price of perhaps, 50 cents.

One of my assignments on the *Ledger* women's page was to interview the women occupants of the freak tent. The dignity of some of these people is what lingers in my memory. Those were the days when an interview included asking the person interrogated a host of superficial questions, i.e., their hobby, favorite color, jewel; their favorite foods, exclamations when provoked, etc. Probably this was partially a reaction to the life and death questions World War I had evoked. Today, Raquel Welch is asked her opinion of U.S. foreign policy. But the vein was lighter at the turn of the '30s. The theme of my interview was what the ladies of the circus did in their spare time, which was indeed short, as the sideshow ran 12 performances a day from noon to 1 a.m. Of course there were short breaks and the Winter months vacation, but these were not always easy.

Katie Sandwine, the 57-year-old strong woman, whose repertoire included bending a bar into a horseshoe, breaking an automobile chain in two, and letting two men clang an anvil placed on her abdomen while she lay on a cushion of nails - tried retiring, but it didn't work.

"I like people too much," she told me. "Where does housework get you? It doesn't bring in a thing."

Katie performed in a leather loincloth, topped by a black satin jerkin. Off the job, she favored tailored suits, enjoyed Hungarian music and fresh vegetables.

Patricia Smith had swallowed swords for seven years. It fascinated her while attending school and she taught herself with only one casualty, which landed her in the hospital for a brief period. A native of Lexington, Ky., Mrs. Smith and her husband,

---

*A medal established by Andrew Carnegie for recognition of deeds of heroism.

also in show business, planned a white cottage in the cotton that Fall, when her daily round of gulping 2-foot swords, scissors, neon tube and an exploding bayonet was over. She loved to cook, like to watch polo and personally rode and swam. Hawaiian music helped her relax. She wanted to open a restaurant and tourist camp, adjoining the proposed cabin.

The snake charmer, Senorita Josephine, came from Mexico, where she too learned her trade as a girl. The secret of handling a snake is "kindness, good feeding and keeping their mouths clean," she told me, (not elaborating on how the last attention was accomplished). Also "warm blankets for cool days, and a tub of tepid water for humid ones."

Senorita Josephine lived in Los Angeles in a Spanish house with a Mexican-decorated parlor. She loved orchids and eccentric hats, played the mandolin and purred "Caramba," which means something in Mexican which is cowing to snakes.

Betty Broadbent, the tattooed lady, found riding in a Wild West show unsteady work, so the year the Lindberghs were married (1929), she began to get herself tattooed, personally selecting from magazines and newspapers many of the pictures that covered her bosom, back, upper arms and legs in four colors.

The intricate layout featured the American eagle across her chest, Madonna and child on her back, a couple of cherubs down her spine, a Wagnerian group, Poor Butterfly getting the cold shoulder and Col. and Mrs. Lindbergh.

Drawn in two or three times weekly in outline, over a period of six to seven months, the entire scene was then filled in during a five-year period. The red tones were retouched occasionally, but the rest was permanent.

Mrs. Broadbent liked to embroider and overhaul furniture, and enjoyed avacado pear salad. Her favorite sport was playing "Button, button, who's got the button?" with her Australian Sealyham Terrier, "Aussie," named after the Southern Cross in Australia where she bought him.

Giantess Gracie Fisher, a statuesque 8 feet, and her 8-foot-2-inch husband had a requirement when they registered at a hotel; they asked the management to install four single beds, two placed end to end making a Fisher single. Blankets uncut at the bottom were best for them.

Mrs. Fisher liked to keep house in their Sarasota, Fla., apartment and enjoyed cooking, particularly making chicken and dumplings. Her hobby was taking snapshots, and she liked opera music and red roses.  Like Mrs. Sandwine, the strong woman, in private life, she too, wore tailored suits.

Alice, the fat lady, kindly sent me a Christmas card the year I talked to her.  The 685-pound woman sat in complacency on a chair at her stand (motion picture theatres put a special chair in the aisle when she attended a performance), emanating a sort of gentle calm and dignity.  Collecting road maps was her hobby; she had them from every state in the Union and had traveled in all but five.  In her leisure moments Miss Alice did fancywork, specializing in vanity sets and bureau scarves.  She enjoyed fishing and liked chicken and teabud roses.

When it came to dignity, the Doll Family - all under 4 feet - personified it.  It was a dignity that left no room for condescension from a taller world.  The family wintered in their seven-room Spanish stucco house in Sarasota, with a big, cool front porch where Daisy, the matriarch, served ice tea to guests.  She cooked for the entire family on an up-to-date gas stove, the legs bobbed six inches.  After lunch, the Dolls went cruising in their 16-foot green and tan boat, "Little Skipper."

Daisy also designed and made the evening gowns for the three women in the troupe, whipping them up on an electric sewing machine.  Incurably romantic, she loved soft waltzes and serenades; liked daisies and collected dolls from all parts of the world.  She never whistled in her dressing room and her expletive was "Gee Whiz!"

All the people of the sideshow had assurance - the assurance of having found their place in the world.  In the final analysis, perhaps that is what makes people feel assured - to find and know their place.  It may not have been the one they would have wished for, but it sustained them, lodged them, fed and clothed them against dependence on others.  With perhaps an unconscious show of spirit - at a lonely height, far above the thousands who came to see them - they met life by offering what they had - and triumphed.

**********

One of my earliest memories of the circus was Ellis Gimbel, in Piccadilly collar and cutaway, entertaining 10,000 underprivileged and orphaned children there of a May afternoon.

The atmosphere in the great tent was nearly explosive with the excitement of the children, which in sheer volume at least, surpassed the thrills offered in the rings; and the white-aproned attendants peddling great swoops of pink cotton candy and peanuts.

Of course there were the strongly scented areas.  Whether you like it or not, the circus is partly smells - sawdust, greasepaint and animals - where one fed peanuts to the elephants and was careful the llamas did not spit in your face; the giraffes munched hay, the lions prowled and the great gorilla lounged in their gorgeous wheeled, red and gold cages.

**********

With my love of the varied and dramatic, it was natural that I should follow the circus to Buffalo, where I covered not only Ringling Brothers & Barnum & Bailey's, but also the Hamid-Morton Circus, which performed for the Shriner's and other humanitarian groups to benefit hospitals, homes and charities.

From a reportorial viewpoint, I was fortunate to be on hand for two landmarks in the Ringling Brothers & Barnum & Bailey circus's history.  The prelude to the folding of its tent "forever," and the 100th anniversary performance in Buffalo of "The Greatest Show on Earth," when it came to Memorial Auditorium, the first, the end of an era, the second a triumph over time and "progress."

On July 5, 1956, I saw the circus struggling for its life on a rough, rain-muddied lot in Niagara Falls, N.Y.  The afternoon performance was canceled.  It was a sorrowful sight to see men, wagons and animals straining to set up the auxiliary tent, which had been rushed from Sarasota in the wake of the original one the wind had ripped just as the evening show was starting, four days earlier in Geneva, N.Y.

Plagued by weather, railroad delays and shortage of labor, ten days later, the circus folded its tent and returned to winter quarters in Florida.

"The tented circus as it now exists, is, in my opinion, a thing of the past," said John Ringling North, board chairman and nephew by marriage of Mrs. Charles Ringling, in making the announcement.

Yet 14 years later, I was covering the 100th anniversary of Ringling Brothers & Barnum & Bailey's Circus:

"The Old Girl is not suffering from tired blood, lack of Vitamin B or stiff knee joints," I noted.

"In her centennial performance at Memorial Auditorium in Buffalo, N.Y., she lives up to Robert Browning's promise that "the best is yet to be."  She put on not only "the greatest show on earth," in her own words, but the best in the experience of a veteran reporter.

"In a day of pornography and self-indulgence, the Circus wisely has kept both its decorum and, of necessity, its superb physique.

"Her anniversary program - almost as good as the show - informs us that the R.B. & B & B show is the first in American show business to observe a centennial. It's done up gold, alright: 26 acts in 2-3/4 hours, many with three troupes of performers in each, 20 of these troupes appearing for the first time. They come from all over the world, but the Balkan countries have contributed particularly heavily."

The internationality of circuses is reflected in the fact that 17 of the 24 acts, "varied and beautifully costumed even to the fresh white tie on a seal or a pony's plumed coronet," in the Hamid-Morton show one year, also hailed from Europe. Perhaps the age-old spirit of these countries in the face of conflict generates both a danger-defying courage and a need for entertainment to offset the threat.

**********

Particularly touching are the circus children, formerly reared in tents and bespangled with days that the average child experiences once a year. The delight of their elders in their art and their assurance seems to have rubbed off on them, sometimes down many generations - an aspiring, disciplined, exuberant life.

There was in my rounds, for example, Diane Theron, "dainty as a snowdrop, airy as a butterfly," whom I saw make her solo debut on a two-wheel bicycle, two weeks before her third birthday in 1958.

Sawdust was old stuff to Diane, of the brown velvet eyes and the gold ponytail. Roars of lions and crowds, her lullaby.

Since 18-months-old, she had been held on the shoulders of her sister, Germaine, now 8, who in turn, stood squarely on the shoulders of another sister, Esmeralda, 12, as she rode a trick bike around the ring.

The French Cycling Therons act was composed of Diane, her parents, sisters, uncle, aunt and cousins. It dated back to her paternal grandfather, Josef Theron, a professor of mathematics at Louvaine University, Belgium, who in the 1890s attended a European performance of Buffalo Bill's Wild West Show.

Afterward, Buffalo Bill on horseback and Grandfather Theron astride a big wheeler raced each other 100 yards. Grandfather won. That did it. He dropped math and started his own cycling act.

The Therons came to America in 1956, played with Ringling Brothers & Barnum & Bailey, and then switched to the Hamid-

Morton troupe.  Esmeralda and Germaine made their debuts at age 2, respectively.

Little Diane took her work seriously.  Before circus time, she played with the other circus children.  But when ringtime approached, she was ready and eager.  Her playmates often helped her into her costume, made by her mother, Louise, ( a cousin of Maurice Chevalier).  It was an airy dress with a coronet of flowers for her hair.  Then she took a small camp chair to the ringside and awaited her turn.  In the ring Diane lapped up applause the way a kitten does cream.  She bowed, kissed her hand to the audience like a veteran, and with Parisienne eclat.

At nearly 36 months, she had toured the United States, Canada, Mexico, Havana and Puerto Rico.

Like her sisters, when she was old enough, Diane would attend school in each city the troupe toured for a week or two, a privilege allowed to circus folk.  But that April day I saw her in 1958, she was just soaking up the limelight.

**********

When I saw 5-year-old Coco III, or "Coconut," in the trailer of his famous clown father, Coco II, he was as free as the winds of humor and the smiles of mirth.  But he probably knew more about human nature and the public at large, and what tickles its funny bone, then some people ever do.

Coconut, the adorable little red-headed clown who tagged along after his father - the only clown who had received the Order of the British Empire - would have to enter Ashland, Ky., Elementary School at the conclusion of that year's circus tour.  Only when he had graduated - and only then, could he follow in the footsteps of his grandfather, Coco I.

The transition from sawdust to school was bound to be a severe one for Coconut, whose real name was David Polakovs, fourth generation of a distinguished clown family.  Think about it.  What could a boy who had lived in an ordinary street in an ordinary house possibly have of interest to communicate at recess to one who had been performing with a circus since he was 18 months?  Perhaps the language of childhood is so simple and pure it transcends sophisticated nuances, and a ball or a top or a train have universal interest in its ranks.

Coconut's entrance into the circus was one of expediency, as his father told me:

*COCONUT III, only clown to receive the Order of the British Empire, and son Coconut, age 5, fourth generation of a clown dynasty, in their trailer between Ringling Brothers and Barnum & Bailey Circus performances in 1970. William W. Dyviniak photograph.*

"The circus was touring Denver, Colorado, and my wife, Hazel, (Coconut's mother accompanies him on tour), had brought the children - we have six - to visit.

"I wanted to talk to her between (benefit) performances in a children's hospital, but they questioned her bringing David in.

"So I told them he was a performer, put a little greasepaint on his face and - still in diapers - he came into the act. He's been in it ever since."

It was a touching sight in the trailer to see Coconut's little nose transformed from that of a typical American boy into one of man's earliest professions, that of court jester. Only now of course, clowns are jesters to the world.

"Get out your nose," Father Coco told him, addressing himself to his makeup box, and David took a round ball of pink putty and began to soften it up.

"I make him up, and will, until he's about 8 or 9," said Coco senior. "Then I'll let him into the makeup box on his own to find his own mask."

"No two clowns have the same face. The wig, the nose and the suit, they're all handed down from one generation to another. But the face must be original."

When the nose putty was soft, Coconut put it on and his father shaped it exactly like his own. Then he painted a duplicate of his own mask on the small, eager face.

Grandpa Coco had sent the red, real-hair, hand-tied wig that raised alarmingly at the jerk of a small wire to his grandson from England. It also matched Papa's.

The red, rowboar shoes like Dad's, the baggy plaid trousers, the polka-dotted shirt and the gay coat came next. Finally, the sailor's hot with "COCONUT" written across the front. Tears and laughter are very close and somehow it made the eyes mist.

The great Coco's advice to his son: "First, keep clean - no smutty gags. Next, don't interfere with politics, and lastly, all people are the same, regardless of race, color or religion (one finds "human rights" in surprising places!) Your business, Son, is to make 'em laugh!

# 32

## Demise of a Duchess

RENEWAL IS A FRESH, spring word that is echoing down the streets of most U.S. cities. In its wake, some of the very structure and tradition of a city falls. Only time will tell if renewal justifies itself.

In every city there is what might be described as a heart or core. The Erie County Savings Bank at Shelton Square was perhaps the primary valve in the heart of downtown Buffalo, the McKinley Monument rising in a circular park in the center of town excepted. But the Erie County Savings Bank was the living heart.

I wrote her eulogy:

A Buffalo duchess will soon return to the dust.

Arched of brow (windows), ornamental of coiffure (turrets), and buxom of figure (granite walled), the old Erie County Savings Bank Building will bow to progress.

For 74 years, this temporal grande dame, whose style of architecture is Romanesque Revival, has shared winds on her roof, snows in her eyes, and pigeons on her balustrades with her spiritual neighbor, St. Paul's Cathedral.

Side by side on separate triangles, which are unique characteristics of downtown Buffalo, they have stood.

By May 1, the 15 remaining tenants of a one time 60 in the building will have vacated her spacious, towered offices and travertine stone, Mexican mahogany-wainscoted halls, leaving her hollow.

The last retreating footsteps will have echoed down her nine-story marble staircase, with its bronze balustrade featuring the fleur-de-lis of royalty.

That golden opulence of the bank proper, into which three generations of Buffalonians have walked to deposit or withdraw the material fruit of their lives, will be darkened, its Moorish mellowness deserted, its gold leaf ceiling dimmed, its autumnal-toned marble pillars left guarding only emptiness.

Silent will be the two great marble clocks which for years have ticked off accruing interest.

The bronze lamps in the customer's desks will be extinguished, and the bronze wastepaper baskets will stand empty of ripped open pay envelopes.

Her tills, coffers and vaults unloaded, the duchess - relieved of responsibility - will figuratively breathe a deep sigh - and wait.

Already the shadow of her demise looms in the distance. A giant crane, like the one which will batter down her walls, rests in the adjoining Main Place excavation (hub of the renewal effort), of which she will become a part.

Why? hundreds of Buffalonians asked.

One gets numerous answers.

The need to do something in the downtown core area to improve it.

More efficient operation of the bank which, as it had expanded in the past 15 years, had been obliged to take over space at numerous locations throughout the building.

The tile is crumbling.

Valuable space wasted owing to turrets and odd corners.

The plumbing is vintage 1893.

Thomas Edison helped plan the electrical system, but today it's inadequate.

A ravenous breed of summer mite has invaded the banking floor for many years, and still 'outwits' the best professional exterminators.

Air conditioning installed in 1937, the heated sidewalk of 1957, undersized elevators obtained in 1925, and an 8-year-old gas furnace all need rehabilitation 'to be made operable at today's norms.'

(The duchess tosses her turrets at the word 'norm.' Designed by George B. Post, architect for the Equitable Bldg., New York, first office building in the metropolis to have an elevator; the Produce Exchange; the Stock Exchange and the buildings of the College of the City of New York - decorativeness rather than normality has been her forte.)

Harold L. Olmsted, well-known artist and architect, who had done his best to save the duchess, understood: 'The whole place, upstairs and down, reeks with honesty and open-minded intelligence from its delightful pavement blocks to its heavily paneled doors and wainscots, its lovely windows and the views they so adequately and amusingly frame...its charming variance in plan from the usual.'

But there were other voices: "If it were the Tower of London, it could support itself as a tourist's attraction," Harlan J. Swift, the duchess' eighth president, said in part, in a letter to friends of the bank. "But it is not, and cannot support itself as anything except a beloved landmark of a bygone era in Buffalo history."

The eulogy continues:

The Erie County Savings Bank Building has always been different from most banks in the area. Continental in appearance, its atmosphere is that of a place where large affairs are conducted in a dignified manner.

Next to pigeons, law firms - some with four or five-member titles, i.e., Moot, Sprague, Marcy, Landy & Fernbach, have been its principal tenants.

It's a 'Good morning, Tom,' or 'How do you do, Sir?' not a 'Hello, Charlie,' in the elevator, sort of place. No slapdash or chatting with the elevator girls. Decorum, and above all, permanence.

In the cellar of the bank one feels fortressed. Descending to it, down slate steps wavy with age, one reaches the boiler room, the heart of the duchess.

"This building was made," says Milton W. Treach, superintendent and chief engineer..."You'll never see another building like this."

The bank walls are nine feet at the base and taper up to three feet. Great brick arches span the distance between the four massive pillars which support the middle of the building, and huge boulders stud the stone and brick foundation at intervals. Overhead is a spaghetti of multicolored pipes.

Mounting to the ninth floor, turret windows give on a fascinating upheaval of tiled roof, carved stone images and finials, where, as on a mountain, the snow lingers in the crevices long after the pavements below are cleared.

And so in mid-Summer of 1967, the ravaging of the duchess began.

Edward E. Gabriel, president of the Niagara Wrecking & Lumber Co., foresaw no difficulty in the task:

"We have the original working plans," he told me, "and it's just a question of working in reverse." (That's what he thought.)

"She just doesn't budge," noted George L. Sheridan, a vice-president of the bank in charge of her.

Nevertheless, the grand old building already had experienced a foretaste of what was to come.

"When they drove the sheet piling in under our north side during the Main Place excavation, however, she shivered with every wallop of the pile driver," recalled Mr. Sheridan.

They held an auction of the duchess' fittings in June. At first they could not sell the magnificent marble staircase (about 180 steps) with its wrought iron balustrades, because they needed it to climb from floor to floor. But they sold practically everything else, from the monogrammed brass doorknobs which locked on both sides and had discreet keyhole covers, to the marble walls and flooring.

One could feel the pressure of time throughout the sale, the hurry to get her down. Utility and removability rather than craftsmanship were the determining factors of purchase.

The ratio of time, money and a craftsmanship (which has practically vanished) it took to build her, to the prices they paid for the baroness' entrails was traumatic to witness.

The great mirrors on the banking floor went for $5 each; they gouged out the 2-1/2-ton main vault for a $1,000 bid, and the big Victorian mailbox in the lobby brought $10.

"It's this way," said Auctioneer Rosen, "this is old stuff. A man pays $1 for something, and he has to hire labor at $4.50 - $5.00 an hour to get it out."

The duchess refused to give up her heart - the 15-foot gas furnace (kept at 80 pounds constant blood pressure in winter), and the auxiliary coal one that could be stoked up to 120 pounds. Eventually they were sold for scrap.

She was now ready for the wreckers.

*********

The duchess did not bow easily.

Every evening for more than three months a battle was fought in Shelton Square between her and two carnivorous cranes. The latter attacked with two primitive means of offense: A pair of jaws and a rock - or in modern wreckers' parlance - a clambucket and a busting ball. The former weighed in at 3 tons, the latter at 3-1/2.

The fight was one of the toughest in veteran wreckers' memory. For a wrecker to admit resistance is like a weight lifter confessing his muscles are getting flabby.

It began at 4:30 in the afternoon and continued through 7:30 the next morning, five days a week. A crowd of variable size would gather to see the kill. It was the show of the town. Whole families arrived in station wagons from the suburbs. A middle-aged couple might bring chairs. A friend would explain to a blind man what was happening.

As Mr. Gabriel had said, the original plans of the building were made available. When the crane operations of the 25-man demolition crew began to munch at the building, however, it was evident that plans and reality did not agree.

The roof with its turrets and gargoyles and finials was the toughest. A finial lifted intact like a birthday candle to the ground measured about 3-1/2 feet high and weighed an estimated 600 pounds. Not to mention the cones on the towers which looked like cake frosting aloft, but on the ground measured 20 feet high and 15 feet across. Cast iron and steel.

As the wrecking progressed, scores of 200-pound red granite carved images, 5-feet thick, set in the walls around the crest of the building came tumbling down, their carnival faces of joy and sorrow biting the dust. The very stones of the building were resistant. The walls, which tapered from nine feet at the base up to three feet, were composed of foot-thick red granite stones weighing up to three tons each. Interlocked, they had to be lifted out like lumps of sugar, piece by piece. They did not sound like sugar when they dropped.

**********

The evening before the opening of the Mall, of which the new streamlined Erie County Savings Bank towered at one end of Shelton Square, I was walking up Main Street when I caught a glimpse of history. It's a winged thing, and you have to catch it on the fly; you can easily miss it. But as I came closer to the new building, I saw a man sweeping up the pavement with a brush. He was an Indian whose ancestors, a hundred years before, had sold sassafras, arbutus and violets here, on Shelton Square. Now in the shade of the new, modern bank, with its flat roof, its central heating, its adequate electrical system and its modern plumbing, he was sweeping up the last of the duchess' dust - and the past, in the wake of renewal.

POSTSCRIPT:

One of the Biblical concepts is that nothing is ever completely lost. "Ashes to ashes, dust to dust..."/"swords into ploughshares..." etc. Even the rubble of buildings is used in some other location for "fill." Resurrection in some form seems an innate part of life.

Nelson J. Reimann, president of Morris & Reimann, Wreckers Inc., who had dealt death to literally hundreds of buildings - from churches, convents, schools, railroad stations, markets, stores, banks, auditoriums, factories, warehouses and institutions, to bowling alleys, taprooms, drugstores, soda parlors and greenhouses - had kept the glint of immortality in his eye.

The understanding in the wrecking game is that after an owner has removed his goods and chattels from a building to be torn down, finders are keepers of whatever remains on the wrecking site.

Bowing to this principle, Nelson Reimann, who began knocking down buildings when he was 17 during the Depression, had garnered a great quantity of memorabilia from the roofs, walls, attics, cellars, rubble and ground of structures he had demolished before and during the Downtown Urban Renewal Plan activity in Buffalo.

With it, Mr. Reimann had distilled an attar of Western New York life over the past 150 years, into his summer place at Sunset Bay, near Silver Creek, N.Y.

"All you've got to be is a little handy and have a little time," this burly, genial man told me in one of the understatements of the year. Then, more realistically, "I'm always looking for it!"

It had begun 10 years before when Mr. Reimann tore down the old brick Merchant's Refrigerator Plant at Michigan Ave. and Perry St., Buffalo. He had eight truckloads of the bricks hauled out to the 100-x-200-foot, double corner lot he had bought a stone's throw from the lake.

Shortly afterward, Holy Cross School in Buffalo and the Linde Air Products Co. building in Tonawanda, N.Y., succumbed to the Reimann bulldozer, providing a quantity of lumber, mostly hemlock, which was dispatched to Silver Creek.

Nelson Reimann designed and built the eight-room house, and with the help of one assistant, had the roof on in nine weeks.

"The neighbors were great," he told me, "when a tough job came along, they just pitched in and lent a hand."

It was fortunate that about this time, the David Electric Co., at Genesse and Spring Sts., Buffalo, gave up the ghost. Extensive wiring and a number of lamps found their way to the new Reimann house.

The structure to house the area's memorabilia of a-century-and-a-half now was ready.

More public and private buildings had been torn down in Western New York in the 1960's than ever before. The area was in its first massive "second time around."

Wreckers wear the buildings they have demolished proudly like escutcheons in their consciousness. "It's making progress for the city," Mr. Reimann said; but he refused to let at least fragments of the past be carted away to oblivion. In a crunching, devastating business - before or after the onslaught - he saw and saved.

Granite balls from the entrance posts of the old Roswell Park Hospital stand at the entrance to the Sunset Bay driveway, which is curbed with Medina stone window-sills from several properties.

Segments of the marble footing of the old Lehigh Valley Railroad Terminal on which three generations of Buffalonians waved farewell or welcome home, which reached its personal terminus in 1962 and where Mr. Reimann recalls "each column was a truckload," made a perfect patio by the Lake.

And a walk of red flagstone from the subbasement of the old Lang Brewery, where the kegs were stored, winds along the house past a sitz bath from a Delaware mansion, now used as a flower planter.

The center of the house at Sunset Bay is the family room and lounge. Here Mr. Reimann's eye for immortality has run rampant, plucking the overripe fruit of felling accomplishments from churches to taprooms, not to mention finds from nooks, chinks, crannies, corners and cubbyholes of attics, cellars, barns and outbuildings.

A collection of copper articles fetched from village and farm shine from the living room hearth. And a miscellany of humbler antique pots, pans and other household utensils - from a washboard to an oil lamp - form a frieze over the doorway leading from the family room to the garden.

"In the Endless Days of Our Great Grandmother" reads a painted sign beneath them.

Farm and carpenter's tools, from a hacksaw to a hoe are identified by another: "In the Tireless Days of Our Great Grandfather."

The sacred joins the secular aloft in the family room. A bevy of bells from the altar of St. Michael's Church, which was razed by fire in 1963, shine there. "They were bent when the roof caved in," explains Nelson Reimann, "but we straightened them"; there's a handbell from leveled Cardinal O'Hara's School and a little bell from the former Convent of Perpetual Help.

A revolving sign for Schlitz beer serves as a chandelier.

Refreshment is on hand at a tap flowing from a huge cooling unit in the lounge, fetched from a bowling alley Mr. Reimann axed. "We Drink What We Can. The Rest We Give Away," a sign declares. You may enjoy the draft at tables which found their way from a West Ave. ice cream parlor or a Genesee St. saloon.

If tea's your cup, the tea cart was once a nationally-known cosmetic firm's display case, salvaged when the old Hengerer Department Store warehouse hit the Washington St. dust.

Lighting is heterogeneous: A candleholder from St. Michael's; a brass altar light from a West Seneca church; old railroad crossing and brakeman's lights; a processional light from St. John Kanty's School. And a variety of lanterns.

They shine on a miscellany placed about - a top hat left in the attic of a noted doctor when his house was about to be torn down; a hashish pipe found in some rubble; the doorbell from a house of entertainment; a framed $1 bill, which was found stuffed in a hole of an old building behind City Hall, and an incense burner from the debris of St. Brigid's Church. Nelson Reimann and his wife, Marie, have burnished the burner to a golden glow, and also hung it aloft - in thanks for their lot and their luck.

Mr. Reimann fenced Sunset Bay's front lawn with an ornamental cast iron fence that he found in a garage at Main and Dodge Sts. "People just shove these irreplaceable things into a garage or barn," he explained, shaking his head.

High above it all fly the Stars and Stripes from a flagpole the top of which Nelson Reimann - who refused to totally pulverize the past - rescued when Memorial Auditorium was given a face lifting.

# Part VIII

# Ladies and Lakes

# 33

## Four First Ladies

MY FIRST ENCOUNTER with a First Lady was when Mrs. Franklin D. Roosevelt walked into the meeting room of the Women's Division of the CIO Convention at Philadelphia in the mid '40s. Among the small group of women who accompanied her was a good-looking black woman, an unusual escort for a President's wife in those days. In 1939, Marian Anderson had been refused the stage of Washington's Constitution Hall.

Dressed in those conventional clothes and a conservative nest-like hat, this tall willowy woman with gray-green eyes and beautiful hands mounted the rostrum and in that cultivated, carefully enunciated manner, addressed the gathering "Ladies of the CIO." The O was pinched in the English fashion and came out "OWE."

The flower-hatted assemblage had learned to expect concern and inspiration from Eleanor Roosevelt in her public addresses, but humor was not generally associated with her. This time she delivered it with a surprisingly light touched modernity.

"My secretary and I were flying into an airport in California," she recalled of a recent trip, "and as we neared it, there were several thousand of our boys (pronounced "boise") standing in the field below us.

"We had on our Red Cross uniforms ("un-e-forms") so of course they didn't know who we were."

The ladies of the CIO waited in breathless amazement at the lack of omniscience of the military.

"And as we neared the ground," continued Mrs. Roosevelt, "all the boys raised their hands and called 'Hello, Baby!'"

The ladies of the CIO were caught off guard.

The next occasion on which I saw Mrs. Roosevelt was a more serious one. FDR had only been dead about a year. One day Fred Shapiro called me over:

"Ellen," he said, "there's a report that Eleanor Roosevelt is considering getting married. The man mentioned is Senator Townsend of Delaware. I want you go go find him and ask him."

The ancestral home of Senator John G. Townsend (Rep.), former governor of Delaware, was at Selbyville, Del., about 15 miles from the railroad. I took the train down and upon arrival at the Selbyville station looked vainly around for a cab. Finally, a farmer with a wagon filled with crated chickens drove up and agreed to drive me there.  I hopped up on the front seat next to him, the chickens expressing all kinds of political views in the back.

It was still morning when I arrived at the house, but the Senator had already gone.  I learned afterward that he breakfasted daily on clabber biscuits with an aged relative in the town.

It was afternoon before I found him in a wooded retreat near Rehoboth Beach, a distance of another 15 miles, this time by taxi.

A tall, handsome man with a crest of white hair, lively blue eyes and a healthy pink complexion, the Senator looked pleased as a fighting cock when I asked him if he had romantic intentions toward Eleanor Roosevelt.

But the Senator, an astute politician, was also a gentleman.

"Why don't you go and ask Mrs. Roosevelt?" he said.  "If she would tell anyone, I think she would tell your paper (the *Democratic Record*)."

It was a bright spring afternoon a few days later when I crossed Gramercy Park and entered the apartment house where Mrs. Roosevelt lived when in New York.

The doorman telephoned up my paper's name, and the reply came down that Mrs. Roosevelt was not at home.  I then asked to speak to her secretary.  The message relayed by the doorman was that "the secretary to Mrs. Roosevelt's secretary says the secretary is sleeping."  I sat down on a bench in the lobby facing the door to wait for Mrs. Roosevelt.

In about 20 minutes, a tall, slender figure, wearing a widow's bonnet with a veil almost to her waist, just like Grandmother Taussig wore the rest of her life after Grandfather died, was silhouetted in the doorway by the sunlight in the park.

Eleanor Roosevelt looked particularly tall to me (who am 5 feet, 2-1/2 inches) that afternoon.  I rose and met her in the middle of the hall, introduced myself and said I had come to ask her a question.  Incidentally this was in pre-television days, and interviews with public figures were more tempered than they are today; but there still were some brakes.

She looked down at me from that gracious height and said- "Oh, but I never give interviews here."

"We tried (as we had) to get you at Hyde Park, Mrs. Roosevelt," I replied.

"Oh, but I never give interviews there," she answered.

That was her mistake.  Nothing from nothing leaves nothing.  It was clear that I was being put off.

"The matter is urgent, Mrs. Roosevelt," I said, and indicating the bench, "won't you sit down."

I think we sat. I could feel the muscles of my face tightening, but I went on.

"Mrs. Roosevelt, my paper has received a report that you are considering marrying again. Is that so?"

She started up and turned flashing green eyes on me: "You go back and tell your newspaper," she said with vigor, "that if I have any information like that to give - I shall do so!"

Then she turned and walked to the elevator. (While awaiting her return, I had tipped the operator to loiter upstairs, once she arrived.)

I followed.

"The man mentioned, Mrs. Roosevelt, was Senator Townsend of Delaware."

I had passed my zero moment, and her fire was beginning to cool. "The poor man!" she exclaimed, "I was with him in the United Nations." (Senator Townsend, too, was a delegate.) She was still aghast, but no longer furious.

The elevator came, as all elevators eventually do, and she got in. I felt I had followed as far as I physically could. But the image of Fred with the radar-like mind and unlit cigar back on the City Desk rose before me. What else would he have me ask?

She entered the elevator, but the operator considerately dallied with the door.

"Do you believe in doing it a second time, Mrs. Roosevelt?" I inquired from the hall.

"NEVAH," she said with spirit as the door closed.

And she never did.

**********

Mrs. Roosevelt was an Olympian, a towering female Colossus, beyond the height of ordinary women.

But speaking of average women, no matter how elevated their place, I think Mamie Eisenhower was the greatest "lady" of the four president's wives I have met. Someone has defined a lady as one who always makes others feel at ease. Mrs. Eisenhower qualified.

Although she had had a careful, privileged upbringing, she did not take her ladyship so seriously that she could not tune in on the world at large. She was an American woman at her best. She was not afraid of the public or of association with those apparently beneath her. She just was.

I met her when she accompanied Gen. Eisenhower as he toured New York State for the presidency in his special train, "Look Ahead Neighbor," in 1952.

Jack Meddoff, the *Buffalo Evening News* political reporter, and I were sent to Rochester to join the tour. At the Rochester station, a contingent of Republican women met the train and they preceded a public relations woman and myself into the private drawing room car occupied by Mrs. Eisenhower. There were about eight in the group, their leader's arms laden with American Beauty roses, and they blocked a full view of the back of the car.

Mrs. Eisenhower sat in a chair at the front end of the car and, as the rose brigade paused before her, she peered through their phalanx and inquired who was the woman way back there? I was identified as a *News* reporter. She then said that she wished to be introduced to every one in the car before the presentation ceremony. Reporters *never* forget consideration like that.

After the speeches and delivery of the roses, I had a short interview with Mrs. Eisenhower. Five-feet-four, piquant rather than pretty, with those insouciant bangs masking her high forehead, her image was that of a woman who has always been sheltered and cared for. Mamie Eisenhower knew how to pour tea before she got to the White House. She was in command, but she exercised her authority with a light touch.

She had lived in at least 25 houses or apartments in her 26 years of married life, so I asked her what made a home real?

"First the people, secondly the curtains, I never found one set that could fit another pair of windows," she said. "I think family pictures do a lot to make a room liveable, and I like little boxes."

How does a general's wife treat him when he comes back after a backbreaking day?

"Leave him alone," she warned. "When the General comes home tired, I often just get my knitting out, and he may read or we may listen to TV or to the radio and we don't talk at all."

Mamie Eisenhower wouldn't comment on what she felt was the role of the wife of the President of the United States.

"I haven't crossed that bridge yet," she said, "but I can usually adjust myself to circumstances."

It's doubtful, however, even after the General became President, that she thought of herself as anyone but Mamie Eisenhower. For her, it was enough.

**\*\*\*\*\*\*\*\*\*\***

By 1959 Jacqueline Kennedy had been a newspaperwoman and photographer on the old *Washington Times-Herald*. But when I met her that year, six years after her marriage to John F. Kennedy, then a Senator from Massachusetts, she bore no resemblance to a journalist. The essence of a newspaperwoman - the opening of the whole personality to the scene around her, without reservation of class, color or creed; the capacity to mirror what she sees and to interpret it as a sociological phenomenon (albeit there is no real objectivity, the observer colors the scene by his own mores) - such a capacity was not evident in Mrs. Kennedy. In later years, she made great strides in aligning herself with the public - but this was 1959.

Senator Kennedy had come to Buffalo with his wife on a May day to attend the annual Grover Cleveland Dinner of the Erie County Democratic Committee. He had not decided yet if he would be a presidential candidate. Mrs. Kennedy accompanied him.

Before the dinner, Rita Smith of the *Buffalo Courier-Express*, and I went to the Statler-Hilton where the Kennedys were stopping, to talk to her. We sat in her bedroom. The conversation was constrained. Seated before us was an unusually pretty woman with rather windblown, dark hair, intent brown eyes and a wide mouth. It was a mild spring day, but the atmosphere in the bedroom was not warm.

One had the feeling that Mrs. Kennedy was still deep in private life, that she didn't want any of the whole political business and that she didn't want us there.

One had the feeling of being in the milieu of a woman's magazine. Asked if she wanted her husband to run, Jacqueline Kennedy in turn, asked "Where?"

Then she giggled and said: "Ask him that. If he does it's fine." And she smiled sweetly.

On helping her husband if he did run, Mrs. Kennedy replied: "You can always help a man by taking care of him, seeing that he eats, that he had adequate rest and that his home is a peaceful haven for him, you know."

What a long way she came, even beyond one of the most dramatic demonstrations of courage in time of loss the country has ever seen, as she followed the President's bier on foot down Washington's Pennsylvania Avenue. The growth was tremendous, and she also gave the country a model of social and artistic standards that have seldom been equaled.

**\*\*\*\*\*\*\*\*\***

The aura around Patricia Ryan Nixon was quite another one. One felt the keen edge of an individual with an awake mind who had come up the road with energy and labor. I first met her in 1956, when she came with her husband, then Vice President to campaign for the Presidency.

The image she presented as she stood at the Buffalo International Airport fence to greet about 200 people who had come out to see her, with her left arm laden with red roses, was of an almost movie star pretty woman, a little too thin and a bit angular, perhaps; but on the whole, one who would have fitted nicely into a "Song of Music" or a "Mary Poppins" role.

She was warm and straightforward with the press. "We work as a team," she replied simply, when asked what she considered her greatest contribution to her husband's career. She declined to comment on whether she believed the Eisenhower-Nixon ticket would win again.

"I never talk of political matters," she said. "I visit with the women of the towns. But I'll tell you this," she added, "the campaign enthusiasm is greater than in 1952."

She came to Buffalo again in 1960. It was a cautious, somewhat defensive Mrs. Nixon who faced a mass press conference in the Executive Motel, as her husband made his first try for the Presidency.

"You never know what's going to happen, but up to now we are very encouraged," she said. She repeated the teammate bit.

Asked her campaign technique, she said (a clue to the future), "I think if you have a good spirit in your heart, you do things that are right and you want to please people. That's all you need to know. People know you're not putting it on for show; you can't fool people anywhere in the world"

She already had seen some of it: In Caracus in 1958, she sat looking straight ahead without flinching or showing alarm when a mob dented the limousine in which she and her husband were riding, and smeared its windows with eggs and spittle.

"She was as brave as any man I've ever seen," said an aide who was with her.

Mrs. Nixon came again in 1968 when her husband, following his defeat by John F. Kennedy, ran again for the presidency. He had not been in public office for eight years. But the Nixons had broadened their horizons and Mrs. Nixon showed it. They had been to the Soviet Union and to South Vietnam.

In a private interview at the Statler, this time she was dressed in red, white and blue, but more sophisticated clothes than eight years before. She had becomingly gained 10 pounds. She was unequivocally confident. She said, in effect, that there was a difference the second time around. She certainly reflected a difference.

Asked the perennial question of what her role would be if her husband won, she said: "To support his program. I think that's the right thing for a President's wife to do." She didn't seem to have any doubt that he would win. There wasn't room for even the faintest shadow of failure - past or future. Mrs. Nixon was assured.

As the First Lady, she came to Buffalo on October, 1972, to lead the annual Pulaski Day parade in an 18-block march through the Polish district. I marched the 18 blocks, keeping as near to her as protocol and police allowed.

Patricia Nixon had come a long way since we first stood together by the wire fence at the airport. And somewhere along the way, she had found something that went beyond her husband's program. She was campaigning for him, of course, but she was doing it as a person in her own right.

As she walked through the streets of Buffalo, she was no longer dressed in red, white and blue. She wore impeccable tweeds, matching her own fair coloring. Her coiffure, which had amazed all with its perfection on sites ranging from airports to balls around the world, was as usual. She walked with an air beyond assurance, an air of arrival. But it didn't stop there; having walked past constriction and assurance, Patricia Ryan Nixon was free to be herself.

**********

Every President's wife brings an individual quality to the White House. Mrs. Nixon brought a rare one. It was not the top brass, protected lady quality of Mamie Eisenhower. It was a direct relationship of a woman - who appeared to want to see herself as an average American - with the people.

She had her own gesture of the hand for greeting the public. The Queen of England raises her hand in royal recognition of the crowd, the hand remaining fixed, with the fingers elevated. Patricia Nixon raised her hand in a similar manner, but she didn't stop there. She moved her fingers gently from side to side in a motion that extended "the divine right of kings," from curb to curb.

Personally, Patricia Nixon never wanted to be a personage - but she became one, with perhaps the most natural, widely appealing approach to the man on the street and the woman at the

*GREETING Patricia Nixon at Buffalo Municipal Airport, on her first presidential campaign trail in 1956.*

curb that we have witnessed. She often said her only goal was "to go down in history as the wife of a President." She emerged a warm, interested, democratic individual, drawing public response beyond her position or politics. She really cared about that man and that woman on the public thoroughfare. And as her appeal was not based solely on being "the wife of the President," but on herself; she weathered scandal and tragedy, and still stands a respected and affectionately regarded figure throughout the world.

She paid a brief visit to the headquarters of the Committee to Re-elect the President in the neighboring suburb of Amherst on her Polish visit. As she came in the door, I was standing near it. She walked past me toward a group of women waiting for her with the perennial red roses. Then, some recollection must have flashed across her mind. She turned and greeted me.

# 34

## Credo And Cross

I HAVE SEEN MANY so-called religious people. I have seen them in groups and individually. I have seen bishops, priests, ministers, rabbis, nuns, missionaries, evangelists, Jehovah's Witnesses, Jews, Roman Catholics, Episcopalians, Presbyterians, Baptists, Methodists, Lutherans, Unitarians and individuals who purport to have had special revelations.

Spirituality is a gift. There are many secular people who spend their lives devoted to, and working for spiritual causes, often making inestimable contributions, although they themselves are not spiritual. They are giving the cup of water in Christ's or some other spiritual leader's name, but for themselves that water has not been turned into wine. For that to happen, one must receive a gift.

I cannot say if continuous giving of bread and water (in substantive, psychological or theological form) will bring spirituality to the giver. But I do know there is a particular light that shines in the eyes of some people. It is, in my judgment, a sign of spirituality. But with a change of credo in a person's life, I have seen what light they had become dimmed, like a lowered lamp. One wonders if the credo were restored, would the light shine again?

Spirituality that shines through the eyes does not originate in outer sight, however. It is something from within that shines out despite physical fact. I have had the privilege of knowing several normal people with this ineffable light in their eyes, but the most spiritual looking person I ever met was a blind woman at a University Club gathering. I had never seen her before and knew nothing of her. But as you saw her, she had it - a greater degree of spirituality than I had ever witnessed. She could not see you, she said nothing of a spiritual nature, she was just one of the guests among the group. Yet you realized immediately that you were faced to face with a spiritual person; there was no mistaking it. I have never seen her since, but I have never forgotten her.

Here are some religious people I have met over the years:

### A REAL PERSON?

Dr. Albert G. Butzer was the minister of Westminster Church, Buffalo's most "fashionable" Presbyterian Church. The words church and fashionable never seem to go together, but it's a secular fact that in every city and every denomination, one church seems to draw a congregation most active in the social life of the community.

A man of great charisma, idolized by his large congregation; a member of prestigious boards, his sermons broadcast every Sunday from the pulpit were the "in absentia" worship of hundreds of people of all faiths throughout Western New York.

I had interviewed Dr. Butzer upon his 30th anniversary at Westminster, and was much impressed by his career and its accomplishments. When the interview appeared, he sent me two dozen sweetheart roses with a charming note.

But the word "fashionable," intertwined with church, still left a lingering question in my mind. Was Albert Butzer real? Did his success rest on the ability to preach, to build, understand, support and console the 2500 parishioners under his aegis?

The question was not answered for me for about five years. Buffalo had been a very ethnically divided city, divided more sharply than New York's East and West Sides by Main Street, the demarcation line between the foreign population of working-class, and the so-called Establishment. The division was accentuated in the 1870s, by the arrival of literally thousands of Polish immigrants, who came to work in the railroad factories and steel plants. Germans had preceded them in the area, but as they prospered, they too, moved westward.

But in 1873, Albert Butzer was born on the East Side in a largely German neighborhood called the "Fruit Belt," because its streets were named for fruits - Peach, Cherry, Mulberry, Grape Streets. To the residents of West Side Buffalo, the Fruit Belt was the end of the world.

In July, 1967, Dr. Butzer went home to the house where he was born. The *News* did not hear of it until a day or two later, but the editor was so intrigued with the idea, the clergyman was asked if he would repeat the trip. Dr. Butzer agreed, and I accompanied him. It was the first time he had been in the house in years.

"I just felt nostalgic," he said as we approached the house. "And besides, Wednesday was my 74th birthday. It's like looking down the lane of the past," he said, unlatching the gate of the small gray house with coral trim.

He walked up the steps of the porch, its trellis covered with roses and morning glories. Mr. and Mrs. Don McCullough, the present owners in today's largely black neighborhood, welcomed him. It made a lovely picture as the clergyman crossed his arms so he could shake hands with each of them at the same time.

"This is your home anyway, yours and your children's home, whenever you want to come," said Mr. McCullough, a retired employee of Pratt & Letchworth Co.

"It used to be just a cottage," Dr. Butzer said.

Mrs. McCullough showed him through the first-floor rooms.

"We had a piano like that," Dr. Butzer exclaimed. "I took lessons...They set the alarm clock and made me practice an hour. On snowy afternoons, when the teacher was a little late, I'd hope she wouldn't come."

Off the parlor was a small dormered bedroom.

"My elder brother, George - there were seven of us - slept here," said the clergyman. "There was just enough room for a double bed."

"You have a lot of things in the kitchen that we didn't have," he said looking around. "You have a refrigerator. My mother, Wilhelmina, used to put things out of this window."

At the back door, Dr. Butzer looked out "Well what do you know!" he said. "It's the same old backstairs."

Turning to Mrs. McCullough: "It was a big event when my father - his name was Louis - added the second story. When that happened, we got the bathroom. Before, we got baths every Saturday afternoon, in a tub in this kitchen. No fooling!"

Mrs. McCullough smiled.

"We used to hang our clothes around an old-type stove - right where you have this space heater - to warm them in the winter" Dr. Butzer said. "There was no central heating."

He paused and his eyes were laughing. "As Bruce Barton said, many of us were brought up as underprivileged boys. But we didn't know it, because no one told us."

Everyone sat down in the cozy parlor.

Dr. Butzer's recollections turned to Tilman's Drugstore at the corner of William and Emslie.

"When I was in the ninth grade at School 31, I went to the drugstore at 7:30 every morning and swept it out. Then I came back after 3 and worked until 5:30, and all day Saturday.

"During college vacations, I was a guide at the Larkin Co. The Larkins were later members of my parish," he said of Westminster, from which he had retired five years before.

He was called to Westminster in 1932, while serving as a minister in Ridgewood, N.J.

"I didn't want to come back here," he told me. "I'm an East side boy, you don't want me at a church on Delaware Avenue, I told Horace Reed and Edward Barcalo, when they asked me.

"They told me I'd find many parishioners were former East side boys," he said. "It was true."

He rose to leave.

"They brought us up to work," he said, taking a final glance around the parlor. "You had nobody back of you but yourself. If you wanted to get anywhere, you had to get up your own get up and go."

He was real, alright.

## SHEPHERD OF THE LAKES

On a brisk October morning in 1968, the Lake Boat *Nipigon Bay* nosed into Lock 4 of the Welland Canal. Capt. Melvin W. Buckland, the wiry, sandy-haired skipper, his eye on the steering pole of his 622-foot ship, called the orders to Wheelsman Bernard Courmoyer.

"Steady now," said the captain.

"Steady now, Sir," replied Mr. Courmoyer.

"One more degree," said the skipper.

"One more degree starboard," repeated the man at the wheel.

"A wee bit to the starboard," said Capt. Buckland.

And the vessel came to a stop beneath the great lock walls.

The Rev. Cameron Orr, chaplain of the Welland Canal Mission for seamen of all nations and beliefs, which was celebrating its 100th anniversary, came aboard. A long-legged, sinewy man wearing a white safety helmet, he carried a 60-pound (early morning weight) case filled with hand Bibles and tracts for this ship and the three or four others he would board that day, as he did six days a week from April, when shipping on the Lakes opened, to December when it closed down.

As he boarded the ship, Rev. Orr was greeted by members of the crew, some of whom he had known for years. And as he progressed the length of the great vessel, he conversed with the men he met. The crew of a ship passing through the locks has no time for a religious mass meeting. Every man must be near his post. It was upon the brief, personal encounter that Chaplain Orr counted. In this manner, he spoke with about 5000 men a year.

"Glad to see you, sir," said the chaplain extending a hand to a deckhand. "I saw you last on the *Port Colborne*. Have you a Bible? Well, I want to give you this little one." Taking a testament out of his case (it lightens as the day advances), Chaplain Orr opened it, selected a special verse - "Your verse," he told the man - read it and offered a prayer for him and his family.

"May this be your chart and pilot to eternal life," said the chaplain, handing the deckhand the book.

He greeted a 20-year-old oiler from Port Basque. It seemed he had lost the Bible the chaplain had given him on a previous visit. "Well, here's another," said Rev. Orr, and the two men went to the rail for a brief talk.

"It doesn't seem to matter if they want to listen," said an officer of the *Nipigon Bay*, "he gets their attention. I've discussed problems with him. He has sons, so do I. It helped talking to him."

Chaplain Orr lunched in the officers' cabin mess before descending into the engine room to greet men there. As the ship rose in one of the massive locks, he said grace: "You always eat better after grace," he said, as he dipped into a thick soup.

"We try to touch the men where they are," he told me. "It's Christ, not the Church, that puts it in you. If He's not in there," tapping his chest, "if there's no Church in the heart, you just go through a form."

"Religion is a form of godliness, but a denial of the personal power. Therefore Christ is a do-it-yourself kit between you and God. It's done at the Cross transection - it's done at the Cross."

***********

How did Christ get into the heart of Chaplain Orr?

Born at Newcastle-on-Tyne in Northumberland, England, of Scottish ancestry, he was dissatisfied with the lack of opportunity in England in the financially dark days of 1929. At age 21, he emigrated to Ontario where he worked on a farm for several years. The Oxford Movement was his go-between. "After hearing a group speaker," he relates, "I knew I didn't know that God and what He meant."

One afternoon, as he was plowing a field, "the conviction of past sins came down before me - as a sheet came down before me. It wasn't very pleasant; I knew I must have it removed. In faith, I asked Jesus to cleanse and to convert me."

Immediately, Cameron Orr recalled, a desire to tell others awakened in him, and he knew he must prepare to do so.

"I had $6," he recollected, and only knew that God called me. I went to Toronto Bible College - conversion is an entrance requirement - and for three years worked my way through, waiting on table and giving out handbills, etc. Each summer, I'd earn enough to add to this, and return in the fall."

In the summer of 1937, he was appointed missionary to sailors on the Kingston, Ontario, waterfront, and a year later for the Sailors Mission, Toronto, for both of which he received money and credits at the college.

Upon graduation, he entered McMaster University, Hamilton, Ontario, to study for the Baptist ministry. But news of the vibrant force in this wiry Scot - you could feel it as you talked with him - had reverberated throughout the province. And during his first year at McMaster, the Welland Canal Mission issued a call to him to become its missionary - only the second in its history.

Cameron Orr left the university, resigned his church and took his converted heart to the Welland Canal. When I met him, he had been with the mission for 29 years. In the summer months, he also preached in churches throughout Ontario about the mission, which is supported by donations from church groups and individuals.

The mission of Rev. Orr was not an "orthodox" one. Yet probably few members of the orthodox clergy have had more influence on more of their fellow men. None certainly, have met their fellows more candidly.

Three hundred lake boats and 600 ocean-going vessels from 30 different countries passed through the Welland Canal the year before I saw Chaplain Orr. On ocean-going ships which circle the globe a sailing man may not see country, home or family for two years; a lakeboat man, for eight or nine months.

"The loss of natural living conditions affects them," the chaplain said, "loss of church - some haven't been in one in months - loss of community, relatives, friends and social life."

Utter dependence on God - through Christ - for redemption and the power to live was Cameron Orr's answer to this need. It had been his own experience, and he was spending his life telling others about it.

## LIGHT FOR AFRICA

Mrs. Mary Lane Clarke saw "the glory of the coming of the Lord" in West Africa.

At 87, she was still helping that glory to shine by translating her fourth book of the New Testament into the language of the Limbas, 12 tribal groups living in the Protectorate of Sierra Leone.

"It has been one of the most heartwarming and joyous experiences of my life," this evangelical matriarch of the Wesleyan Methodist Church, told me, a significant statement in a life that brimmed over with challenge and adventure.

I found Mrs. Clarke, a stately, prophetical figure, seated at her desk in Houghton, N.Y., 12 miles from Lyndon where she was born in 1874, and from which she came to Houghton Seminary, now Houghton College, as a child of 12. Valedictorian of her class upon graduation, she returned there to teach. And it was at Houghton that she met the Rev. George H. Clarke, an Englishman of furlough from missionary service in Africa, who was taking advanced study at the seminary.

In 1896, the hut-tax uprising and the massacre of several missionaries, including four women, occurred in Sierra Leone. The Rev. Clarke was recalled to Africa. Four years later, Mary Lane sailed there to become his bride. The wedding took place in the brick English Wesleyan Methodist Church at Freetown, capital of the mountainous, rocky country.

A British colony purchased from native chiefs in the late 18th Century, Sierra Leone had supplied slaves for the British colonies. It later became a refuge for liberated slaves from Nova Scotia and England.

The young bride spent her first two years as a missionary among the Temnes Tribe in Kunso, an unhealthy area constantly attacked by malaria. During her second term, she was stricken with black water fever and returned to Houghton. A Buffalo specialist gave no hope, but women of the Wesleyan Methodist Church there joined in prayer on her behalf. Mrs. Clarke recovered and never contracted any type of African fever again.

On her first trip to Africa, Mrs. Clarke and her husband had received a call from Paramount Chief Kalawa of the Limba Tribe, who was dissatisfied with the dark paganism of his people.

"It was during my nearly fatal illness that I felt called to go to these needy people," Mary Clarke told me. "My husband agreed."

So in 1908, the Rev. and Mrs. Clarke and their party entered the Limba country to establish a mission.

"Chief Kalawa had waited long and eagerly, and his welcome was most hearty," Mary Clarke recalled. "He wanted an early morning, afternoon and evening service on Sundays, and one every evening in the barry or public courthouse. He wanted his people to be educated and the sick to be doctored."

The missionaries lived in two grass-thatched huts given them by the chief a short distance from town, until Mr. Clarke could build a more suitable home.

"In front of the huts, at a proper distance on either side, was a large mango tree," recounted Mrs. Clarke. "The shade of one was used as shelter from both rain and sunshine for our open-air school, and the other by our nurse for her dispensary.

"Life was simple. The cooking was done largely in iron kettles on three stones, and a simple steamer or tin kerosene-can oven took care of the extras. Our diet was mainly rice and soup made of native herbs."

The Clarkes' first task was to learn the language of the country. Each of the 12 tribal groups among the Limbas have some slight distinction in dialect. Carrying a notebook and pencil everywhere, the missionaries compiled a dictionary for their personal use. Composed of more than 1000 words, it was published by the British Government in 1922, and was the first dictionary the Limbas ever had.

To carry the message of the Gospel to these heathen tribes, Mary Clarke began translating hymns.

"The natives chant at their work," she explained, "and I shall never forget the morning the stains of 'Nothing but the Blood of Jesus' drifted up from the rice fields for the first time...It was a moving moment."

But the Clarkes had come to Africa to found a Christian mission among the Limbas, and a mission can't grow without Gospels. So Mary Clarke began translating the Gospel of St. Luke into their language. The British & Foreign Bible Society, London, published it in 1911.

It was nearly 50 years later that I sat in Mrs. Clarke's parlor, where she was just completing the translation of a fourth book of the New Testament, the Gospel of St. Matthew, into the language of the Limbas. A lifetime of faith, danger, courage, patience and unquenchable dedication had intervened.

"I undertook St. Luke first, because if they were only to have one Gospel, it has more of the parables and miracles than any other," she explained.

George Clarke contracted African jungle fever among the Limbas and had to be borne 150 miles by litter to a coastal hospital, where he recovered. The couple returned to America in 1915, to live on a farm near Houghton. From there, he organized the national Young Missionary Workers Bank of the Wesleyan Methodist Church, whereby young people raised funds for the field. His wife took over the superintendency of the bank in 1917, a post she held for nearly two decades after his death in 1929.

In 1947, more than 30 years after her return to the Houghton area, Mary Clarke's second book of the New Testament in the language of the Limbas, the Gospel of St. John, appeared.

**********

At age 75, a whole new cycle in the life of Mrs. Clarke began. Throughout the years in that quiet college town, she had not forgotten Africa. She had longed, even prayed, to go out again - but her duty seemed at home. Now, upon retirement as superintendent of the young Missionary Workers, that duty appeared over.

But Mary Clarke was too old to return "officially" to Africa to "bear witness" to her faith. And she knew all her old friends among the Limbas were dead.

Nevertheless, the desire for a face-to-face evangelism triumphed. After 30 years absence from the Bak Continent, she took her own savings of $1000 out of the bank - "all the money I had" - and sailed.

"It was a memorable reunion," she recalled of her return to Sierra Leone. "The people of the town came right to the church; leave it to them to know how to do things. They presented me with white rice (a delicacy), sheep and two bunches of bananas in welcome."

"I recognized faces in the crowd - Sasipo, son of the late Chief Kalawa, and descendants of other chiefs I had known; I saw the faces of old friends in their grandchildren's faces."

She taught the Bible to senior girls at the Clarke Memorial Girls School at Kambia. Living in a lean-to next to the church of the Rev. and Mrs. George Huff, missionaries at nearby Kafago, she taught them the Limba language. She stayed 18 months.

Four years later, now 79, Mary Clarke flew again to Africa, now as a housekeeper to medical missionary Dr. Paul Parker. In between, she continued her evangelism among the Limbas. A year-and-a-half later, she returned home to Houghton for good.

Mrs. Clarke had begun translating the Gospel of St. Mark in the field. It too, would be published with the completed St. Matthew by the British & Foreign Bible Society.

Four characters in the Limba language had changed since her translation of the Gospels of St. Luke and St. John, and she had also revised them.

The secretary at which Mrs. Clarke sat was once owned by William Houghton, founder of the college, which had conferred an honorary doctorate upon her in 1951, the same year that the Wesleyan Methodist Church of America cited her for "distinguished service in many fields."

The shelves of the secretary held a collection of books on missionaries and a variety of well-thumbed Bibles. One - its black leather cover sharply defaced - was special.

On her final trip to Africa, Mary Clarke and a missionary nurse were driving through the bush country - "five miles from anywhere." She was holding that Bible.

The automobile swerved from its course and plunged into a neighboring field. As it zigzagged out of control, Mrs. Clarke recalled a fragment of Psalm 42, which she had used in other crises: "Yet the Lord will command his loving-kindness in the daytime, and in the night..."

"He answered in a very wonderful way," Mary Clarke told me. "If we had veered to the *left* - we would have been impaled on cropped stalks of bush. We swayed to the *right* into a ditch dug by construction workers."

She knew nothing until she awoke with a severe head wound, in a hospital more than 100 miles away. One light on the car had remained intact until help had arrived, which prevented the two women from being devoured by leopards and hyenas.

The attending physician, examining her thoughtfully, said: "Madam, there certainly is an Unseen Presence at work in your behalf."

Mary Clarke looked up at him without surprise. She had known that for a long, long time.

## BETHEL'S NEW HOME

Theories of raising children seemed somewhat academic as I sat behind a young mother nursing her baby, as what is believed to be the oldest Negro chuch in Western New York held its first service in its new building.

Surely, the saga of the Negro in the North since the Civil War is between the lines of this story of July 6, 1953:

The oldest Negro church in Buffalo rejoiced Sunday and entered a new house of the Lord.

Bethel African Methodist Episcopal Church, which began its mission of prayer in a little frame building at Washington and Carroll Sts., 122 years ago, held its first service in its new building, the former Covenant Presbyterian Church, Michigan Avenue and East Ferry Street.

The Bethel congregation, also believed to be the oldest Negro parish in Western New York, purchased the property from the Buffalo-Niagara Presbytery June 29 for $120,000. The transaction was effected under the leadership of Bethel's present pastor, the Rev. Harry J. White.

Since 1928, the Bethel congregation has occupied a church at 551 Eagle Street, that it obtained from the Atonement Lutheran Church, which now worships at 222 Northland Avenue, near Lonsdale Road, for $19,000.

The Eagle Street site is one of those acquired to make way for the Ellicott District housing projects. So when Covenant Church, which recently merged with Lebanon Presbyterian Church, Northampton Street and Wohlers Avenue, put its premises up for sale, the Bethel congregation promptly purchased it.

To appreciate the achievement involved in the purchase, it is necessary to glance at the venerable history of the Bethel congregation, and at African Methodist Episcopalianism.

The sect, which lists an international membership of 1,150,000, was started in 1816 in Philadelphia by a former Negro slave, Richard Allen. He had earned his own freedom from a member of a Chew Family, who permitted him to work on his own spare time. Allen paid $2000 for his liberty.

The Bethel congregation, which numbered 1000, was organized on April 28, 1831, when New York State had a population of 1,918,000. This was a year before the Village of Buffalo was incorporated.

The original humble meeting place on Washington Street was replaced in 1845 by a brick edifice at 17 Vine Street, built at a cost of $3000.

Both buildings were used as underground railroad stations for slaves fleeing from the South to Canada. Negroes coming North were brought in from Rochester and hidden in the church cellar. Late at night, small groups went down to Ferry Street, where sympathizers rowed them to the Canadian side.

The Bethel congregation worshiped in the Vine Street church 82 years until the building was demolished in 1928, during the extension of William Street, when it moved into the Eagle Street church.

**********

It was against such a background that Mr. White, 44, who came to the parish only a year ago, opened the initial service in the newly acquired church Sunday afternoon. Bethel's new church holds approximately 700.

Earlier in the day, Mr. White held a final Sunday morning service in the Eagle Street church, which seats 500.

Mr. White is a tall, slender man, more than 6 feet in height. He was graduated from Morris Brown College, Atlanta, Ga., and Greater Payne University, Birmingham, Ala. He received his honorary doctorate from Wilberforce University, Wilberforce, Ohio.

The mercury was up to 90 degrees and a transportation strike was on, but about 300 members of the parish, from matriarchs to youngsters, sat in the fine oak pews for the afternoon service, wearing festive, light clothing.

Despite the fact that the vivid stained-glass memorial windows of the church had been opened, fans were in evidence.

Fine organ music flooded the church. In marched Bethel's three choirs, the Gospel Choir led by Mrs. Muriel Glover; the Cathedral Choir under Jehrnard Williams' direction, and the Youth Choir conducted by Mrs. William Sloan. The singers were in black or white robes. White flowers banked the rostrum.

The whole congregation raised its first voice in its new church by singing "Holy, Holy, Lord God Almighty! All Thy works shall praise Thy name, in earth and sky and sea..."

"I was glad when they said unto me, we will go into the house of the Lord..." intoned Mr. Brown.

The Rev. Melvin G. Crawford, assistant minister of the congregation more than a quarter of a century, delivered the opening prayer:

"Here we are, Heavenly Father...we come before Thee with praise and thanksgiving...Through Thy tender mercy and loving kindness You have permitted us to come into this new sanctuary...It is Thou who hast made us and not we, ourselves...

"With Thee all things are possible...Without Thee nothing is accomplished...Give us a clean heart, O God, bless us, direct us and guide up for Jesus' sake..."

Mr. White explained there had not been time to move the hymnals from the old church to the new. But it didn't matter. Everyone knew the hymns by heart.

Addressing his audience informally, Mr. White had a bit of difficulty with the rostrum. "I can't lean on it - it is too low...the gentleman here before me evidently was a short man," he said to the parishioners' delight.

Turning from this brief levity, the clergyman then called the congregation's attention to the beauty of the new sanctuary.

"Isn't it lovely?" he asked.

A wave of rejoicing ran over the gathering.

Mr. White chose for his text the 35th verse of the eighth chapter of the Epistle to the Romans - "Who shall separate us from the love of Christ? shall tribulation, or distress, or persecution, or famine, or nakedness, or peril, or sword?"

"The way to heaven never has been easy," the pastor told his sheep. "The man who seeks an easy way will never arrive there. Each step on the journey is uphill - am I right?"

Bethel's congregation agreed.

Mr. White noted that a big task faces the congregation. An initial payment of $50,000 has been made on the new church, he said, with $10,000 more due in four months. This will leave a bonded indebtedness of $60,000.

Recalling a maxim he once saw hanging on a prospective employer's wall, the clergyman quoted: "Any old, dead fish can float downstream. But it takes a live fish to swim upstream."

"God gives big men big tasks...if you are a little man, he will give you little tasks. But if you are a big man, he gives you a big job to do." explained the pastor.

Mr. White expressed full confidence that Bethel--with God's help and effort on its own part--will attain its goal. The church, which has more than 30 active organizations, will continue to keep the former Covenant Church premises as a community center, as it has been in the past.

The edifice has a fine recreation hall, seating 300 at table, plus bowling alleys and other meeting rooms which have had wide use by neighboring groups. It is a Civil Defense Center and headquarters for a county-operated "well-baby" clinic.

An offering of $366.15 then was collected. An additional $500 offering had been made at the morning service in the old church.

Then the Youth Choir sang "The Lord Is My Life...whom then shall I fear?"

The Sisterhood of Bethel served refreshments in the new recreation hall after the service. There were congratulations, handshakes, smiles and a few tears of joy.

Richard Allen, founder of the AME Church, would have been pleased mightily.

# 35

# The Waterfront

## Spring

### I

IT WAS MAY, 1967, and the cherry trees were white, the peach pinkening when I went down the Erie Canal from Buffalo to Albany in a tugboat. The canal, now a part of the new York State Barge Canal System, would celebrate its 150th anniversary on July 4th.

The old Erie which helped to push New York State's financial development, opened Eastern markets to the farm products of the Great Lakes, fostered immigration to the old Northwest and helped to create numerous large cities, in 1918, was converted into the State Barge Canal.

But the spirit of this 348-mile waterway lives on in the minds of Upstate New Yorkers, in song and story and as an influence on the course of railroads and the Thruway traversing the state. And it survives in the lives of the cities and towns to which it gave birth and the deeds of people it transported along its route. It lives on as a vision that paid off.

One must not look, however, for the body of the old canal. It is like visiting an untended graveyard. You long to see some trace of it, and the stories you've read and songs you've heard rise and ring in your mind.

Your eyes strain through the swamp willows for it as you sail today's Erie Canal, but you are seldom rewarded. Here and there a depression in the fields...a section of battered stone wall...the phantom emptiness of abandoned locks. But even these are scarce. Much of the body of the old Erie lies beneath today's canal or is covered by highways. Yet along the banks of today's waterway, these occasional fleeting glimpses sustain the mystique of the spirit that remains.

To someone raised near the sea, the prospect of a journey on water that eventually will find its way there is open sesame. Even if one does not really reach the ocean, the knowledge that the water beneath one opens a landlocked concept in the mind. Inland, we forget that all brooks, streams, lakes and rivers ultimately join the sea.

We boarded the tug, *Margot Moran*, at the Black Rock Lock near Buffalo on Friday at 9:30 A.M. Capt. Chester E. MacDonald of Rome, N.Y., a dignified man with a nice smile, welcomed us aboard.

We met the crew. Tugs, like other lakeboats, are cosmopolitan. Mate Clayton M. Gillikin hailed from Beaufort, S.C.; Relief Engineer Esmond Rose from New England; Assistant Engineer Donald Velie was a Staten Islander, while Able Seamen Arne T. Halvor and Berger A. Nostdahl came from Brooklyn.

Leif Helgesand, the cook, who was to hand me wake-up coffee every morning through the door of my cabin, which Mr. Gillikin had kindly relinquished for me, came from New Bedford, Mass. But several of these names obviously bespoke original homelands on the Scandinavian coast. They were all friendly and courteous. There's a wholesome solidness about seamen and railroadmen. The fact that I was the only woman aboard was of little consequence; the true cosmopolite has seen so much of life that the minor unconventionalities leave him practically untouched. Side by side daily living in elemental surroundings also tends to sand down any rough edges of self-consciousness.

Battleships may be the greyhounds of the deep, but tugs are the bulldogs. The *Margot* was 90 feet long, 20 feet wide and weighed 141 tons. She had a diesel engine and transistorized radar equipment that could scan the shoreline at a distance of 24 miles, as well as AM, Mobile FM and ADF direction finder radios.

She was pushing a 229-foot, 1278-ton barge filled with 2440 tons of caustic soda from the Hooker Chemical Co., Niagara Falls, to Weehawken, N.J. Barge captain was Ralph C. Tobiassen of Portland, Me., the mate, Fred Parker.

**\*\*\*\*\*\*\*\*\*\***

Lake Erie, the shallowest of the Great Lakes, is subject to violent storms. A 38-mile-an-hour wind was kicking up the lake as we came out of the lock. It had a Wagnerian sound to it, and Capt. MacDonald decided to tie up at the Buffalo Terminal, back down the lake, possibly for a day or more, and ride it out.

One can imagine the frustrated feelings of a reporter, keyed up to the nostalgic trip, to learn she was to spend the night in her sailing port. But there was plenty to observe, learn and eat aboard the moored tug.

Cook Leif rang the dinner bell at 11:30 A.M. Crews of Great Lake vessels eat well; the steamship companies insist upon it.

Wisely they know that good fare will help ease the months - often from April to Christmas - when the men will be separated from their families, that as any army marches on its stomach, lakemen sail on theirs.

Stick-to-your-ribs soup, roast beef, loin of pork, chicken with curry sauce, corned beef and cabbage, sweet and white potatoes, vegetables and a salad, plus a good pudding, were daily dinner fare on the *Margot*.

Tugboat men are good company. Most come from families who have worked on the canal or sailed the seas of the world. They have pulled, pushed and nudged to berth or far distant points vessels ranging from naval ships, lakeboats and passenger steamers, to the massive cargo barges that take freight up and down the canal.

They are refreshed by the gossip of the world as they maneuver ships in New York Harbor. They are citizens of the world whose waters they have sailed. Their captains walk their decks with confidence, their crews with independence.

An able seaman, under contract with the United Marine Division, Local 333 AFL-CIO, earned $50 for a 12-hour day in 1967, and working two out of every four weeks Saturdays and Sundays drew double time, holidays time and a half.

The sun made a pale pathway across the water of Buffalo Harbor as it set on us "landlubbers," but the wind continued through the night. Yet the mystique of my mission lingered in my little stateroom. The rounded stern of the tug with its thick coils of rope (they're nylon now) out the window of the cabin, was reminiscent of pictures I'd seen of old canal boats. With legends and lyrics drifting through my mind, to the slap of waves and gentle whine of ropes we fell asleep.

**********

Cook Leif handed a white mug of coffee through the door a little after 5 A.M. The coffee was strong, and as I made my way to the galley, the air was fresh. Breakfast was hearty - eggs, bacon, potatoes and hot cakes.

We leave Buffalo Terminal at 6:15, with a little swell on the lake and a light wind from the northeast. We pass Port Colborne's white, red-roofed lighthouse at 8:55. A large colony of gulls crowds the seawall.

We are going through the Welland Canal first. The Erie Canal between Buffalo and a point west of Syracuse has a governing depth of 12 feet; the Welland, a 24-foot depth. The barge we push has a draft of 11 feet, which makes going on the Erie between Buffalo and the point near Syracuse too close.

Entering the Welland, we begin the day-long descent of its locks, the first voyage. No. 8 Lock on the Welland - 1380 feet - is among the longest in the world.

Great patience and control are required to operate through locks and canals. It is an inching, nosing, halting process that calls for steady nerves and hands. Two TV cameras on each Welland Canal lock inform the central office at Thorold, Ont., of every movement of every ship in the locks. Orders and responses are meticulously polite.

The descent had both medieval and international flavor. One after another the great iron, crossbeamed, riveted gates swing open to admit or release ships from around the world. We pass vessels from seven countries. The olive-green water ripples softly and the smell is of dampness.

Seamen Halvor and Nostdahl toss the ropes 20 feet or more to the linemen on the lock wall, who fasten them to the bits (posts). As tug and barge rise, the lines are thrown back on the tanker, where they land with a hollow thud. It's a picturesque sight, a sort of canal ritual.

Along the lock wall, in bright colored paints, ships that passed through have left their John Hancock, where they hailed from and the date they were there..."M-S PATIGMBES, 21-7-65, Antwerp...SALVINA, Sept. '66, W. Africa," and there are signatures of Oriental ships.

The sun is shining and Mate Parker, who has sailed schooners and rolls with the sea even when walking on land, hangs out a plaid shirt he's just washed. Community life goes on, too, as the cook of a neighboring tug, *Seneca Chief,* comes aboard to borrow a loaf of bread.

Whole families come down to the locks to see the ships; an observation stand at Lock 7 is crowded. Sweethearts stroll along the walls holding hands.

Rows of poplars stand at attention on the banks, and the cherry trees are white, the peach buds pinkening in small farms along the waterway. The very proximity of farmland to water is novel to one who was reared near bodies of water that ran through city parks or crashed on untillable sand.

At 8:45 P.M. we reach Port Weller and enter the opal shimmer of Lake Ontario. Niagara-on-the-Lake juts out in the distance, as parting the tranquility of the water like veiling, the *Margot* and her tanker push on toward Oswego.

Out of our porthole shine two stars.

**********

Now it's Monday. It's cloudy today, and there is a light north wind, as we head into the slightly choppy arc of the lake.

A tug is a big power in a small package; it's really built around its engine and fuel tanks. Instead of firing like an auto engine with every other stroke, the diesel engine of the *Margot* fires with every stroke, providing extra wallop. When the tug is pushing along at a peak 10 miles an hour, you feel pretty much as if you're sharing quarters with a chained panther. But you get used to it.

We are about 8 miles from shore and a little bird is flitting among the hatches of the barge. Capt. MacDonald says there are usually two or three aboard.

Oswego looks like a mezzotint as we cruise down the lake passed it . The *Margot* sounds her hoarse whistle - "I do like a good whistle," says the captain as we approach the green shuttered, white lighthouse at the entrance of the city.

At 12:30 P.M., we enter the locks of the 24-mile-long Oswego Canal, which links Lake Ontario with the Erie at Three Rivers, the junction of the Oswego, Oneida and Seneca rivers. Both the Oswego and Erie canals, from this point on, have a draft of 14 feet, so we can take this route.

Capt. MacDonald lowers the pilot house of the *Margot* hydraulically, to pass under the bridges above us.

Seven more locks. Each gate opens with promise of the future, and closes with finality on the past of our trip.

We pass a graveyard on a hill where surely an old canal boat captain or two rest after "the long trek"...a curved dam at Minetto with its glassy waterfall...finches skim over the water around us.

Clumpy inlands with old swamp willows shading carpets of wild white lilies. Here and there a bit of industry, like the asphalt factory at Fulton...nearby, a boy fishing.

New York State is making the bank of the Erie Canal more secure. Miles along the water's edge are being "rip rapped" - edged with crushed stone. Old barges are used to haul it, and it's usually spread with a mechanical grader.

The canal is immaculate. One hardly ever sees trash or garbage on its surface. It is policed by a fleet of lively little buoy tenders, blue and yellow boats which whisk along its surface like flies.

Pleasure boats on the canal have tripled during the last ten years. They sail its placid surface tooting and waving to the tugboat and barge crews, who "never know what they are going to do next." Tugboat captains look down on them with a resigned tolerance.

There is a swell but no tide in canals, except when they flow through rivers. But, as the wide world is learning, man cannot isolate himself from others. The wake of one canal boat affects another.

The sun is a flaming ball behind the spring wood, as we approach Lock 23, a particularly attractive one, near Brewerton. Five hundred feet of pine and hemlock line the lock, with its high-windowed powerhouse and circular beds of tulips on the grass. The national and state flags are raised.

The lockkeeper has an older Water Spaniel. Dogs usually make for the galley when a boat is moored in the locks. Tugmen like children and dogs; perhaps they remind them of home.

Now darkness closes out the view of the Erie Canal, except for lights on the boats and in the cities and villages en route. The tug runs all night. The moon beats a silver path to our porthole as we cross Lake Oneida. Tomorrow night it will be full.

**********

On Tuesday we're getting near to Rome. At least, we're told so. Out of the portholes of the mess at breakfast is a fog - as thick as Cook Leif's excellent pea soup.

"Haven't seen the bow since 3:20," says Tug Mate Gillikin, as he comes off the midnight to 6 watch to eat.

A spectral canal appears as the mist gradually lifts, the swamp willows palely etched in the water.

"The temperature dropped to 22 degrees during the night," reports Capt. MacDonald at the wheel, "and farmers are lighting bonfires around their orchards. Enough smoke makes cloud cover so the fruit won't freeze."

There is mystery and variety along the Erie Canal. Like life, one never knows what's around the next bend.

Bulk gas plants near Rome...a cement pipeline...Griffiss Air Force Base...ruins of an old bridge once used to shuttle cattle across...new skunk cabbage in the wood.

The canal's length is lessened by the shadow of trees at times, and you go down an open stretch between the reflection and the actuality of its banks. Rather like life, too.

At Whitesboro, it crosses its greatest competitor, the new York State Thruway, and you can see it almost all the way down to Albany from there.

A missile goes by on a truck near Utica. Old canalers would probably have thought it a massive Easter egg. We know better.

In the Mohawk Valley Hills we again descend through locks.

It is a beautiful warm day now. and Capt. Tobiassen is painting portholes on his barge and touching up rusty spots on the hatches with red lead.

The swamp willows are so heavy now that they actually touch the water.

Near Herkimer, a carnival is setting up its tents on the canal bank.

At 4 P.M., we reach Little Falls, the largest lock on the Erie - 40-1/2 feet. The town is set in a rocky crevice of hills and the houses climb them. The water reflects it all like a looking glass, including church steeples, a radio tower and factory stacks.

The Old Erie Canal is plainly visible here through the merciful new green of the trees running alongside it. A grass-grown ditch clogged with dead wood. But the mirage of story and song - some true, some not so much so - hover like a dragonfly over it.

Today's canal is literally carved out of rock, at Little Falls. But springs soften it; small white flowers grow out of the cliffs, gripped by white birch in leaf.

**\*\*\*\*\*\*\*\*\***

At Midenville, the canal course enters the Mohawk River and continues on down to Waterford, a few miles above Albany. Historic country. A post-Colonial white stone house with four columns - two plain and two Ionic - is visible through the trees; we suppose the other two original Ionic ones wore out.

Oil trucks zoom along the Thruway and a patchwork of freights rattle by on the New York Central.

We have strawberry shortcake for supper this evening, and the moon is full.

On Wednesday, it is clear and sunny as we take the last five locks to Waterford. Facing mountains, we are embraced by cow pastures, railways and highways, cherry trees in full bloom and peach beginning to blush - a fitting climax to the whole trip.

The bells of the *Margot Moran's* ship's clock which have serenaded our hours in the pilothouse chime gently 8:35 A.M.

Thus the spectral dry locks of the Old Erie descend into the juncture of Lake Champlain and the Hudson River. We think of glory that was Rome...

*Epilogue:* On the historic day in 1825, when the Old Erie Canal was completed, Gov. DeWitt Clinton sailed from Buffalo to New York City, where he emptied a barrel of water from Lake Erie into the Atlantic Ocean. I was only going to Albany, but I resolved to be as true to historic form as possible. So I left Buffalo with a partially filled bucket of Lake Erie water, and - for good measure - refreshed it with a pint or two from Lake Ontario as we sailed across it. During the trip, however, it occurred to me that I did not need as much water - the bucket was taking up room in my small tug cabin - so I filled a cosmetic bottle with the mixture and threw the rest overboard.

Upon arriving at Albany I hailed a taxi and asked to be driven to the banks of the Hudson where - while the driver waited - I tossed the water into the stream, which, in turn, bore it down to the Atlantic. I can't recall if I explained my mission to the cabbie, but one way or another, he had probably seen a lot of characters in the capital of New York State.

# Winter

## II

The clock in the pilot house of the *S.S. Chicago Trader* chimes eight bells.

A sparse string of lights lit by a cable from the shore trace their eerie way down the 54-feet-length of the vessel moored in the Buffalo River, at the foot of Main Street.

Autos on the Skyway high to the west make a moving, lighted trail. Lonely rays shine from the peaks of the grain elevators to the south.

Beyond, all is darkness and silence. The cold, ice-laden blackness of the lake.

The thermometer reads 3 degrees. Lake temperature: 32.

Yet someone is aboard the 60-year-old ship, one of the oldest freighters on the Great Lakes. Light shines from a few portholes of the aft cabin.

Shipkeeper William (Bill) London is aboard the vessel, owned by the Gartland Steamship Co., Division American Steamship Co.

But for three months, it's just the powerless 12,000-ton *Chicago Trader* - all her current and water shut down - and Bill London, the snow, the sleet and the wind. And this year, 400,000 bushels of grain stored in the ship's hold.

The oak-paneled cabin with its leaded-glass windowed cabinets and big, old-fashioned mirror is snug 75 degrees.

Bill London, 59, a 5-foot, 8-inch tall, 190-pound blue-eyed World War II veteran, with 25 years service on the lakes, sits by the kerosene stove that's his main source of warmth.

"It's tied up with the main tank of the boat," he says with obvious satisfaction, "so I don't have to go outside and get the oil. With these raw winds from the Lake, you have to keep the fire up day and night."

Right now the day's work done and a good dinner under his belt, Mr. London is reading one of his favorites, *White Fang*, by Jack London:

> "Dark spruce forest frowned on either side of the frozen waterway. (The trees had been stripped by a recent wind of their white covering of frost, and they seemed to lean toward each other, black and ominous, in the fading light.) A vast silence reigned over the land..."
>
> The text was appropriate.

The shipkeeper has been up since 5:30 A.M.

As soon as he arises - if the weather is warm enough - he opens the doors from the dining hall into the galley and mess to warm things up. The only heat in the galley is from the cooking range which runs on bottled gas.

"You can't leave the door from the cabin closed too long," Bill explains, "or the paint on the galley will freeze and peel off."

As all waterpipes on the *Chicago Trader* have been drained to prevent freezing, Bill uses water which is delivered to the boat in five-gallon tanks for all purposes.

He starts his day by heating enough water to wash and shave in a basin on the kerosene stove in the cabin. Washed and dressed, he goes to the galley, which has now warmed up a bit, and cooks breakfast - "Sometimes it's eggs and bacon, or sometimes it's rolled oats..."

Then putting on a jaunty plaid hat that looks more like the Ft. Erie Race Track than the waterfront, a heavy woolen jacket and galoshes, he takes a handful of keys from the boards hanging on the cabin wall, sticks them in his pocket, puts on lined gloves and steps out on the deck.

The sun is rising, and the gulls are wheeling and crying under the Skyway and out onto the Lake.

Beyond, the city is awakening. Lights are coming on in the office buildings, and the hum of traffic is picking up on the Skyway Bridge.

The shipkeeper walks to the portside rail and looks westward. Breathing in the air is like inhaling ice water. Great segments of ice form a frigid mosaic on the river leading to the ice-locked lake.

Moving gingerly to the portside, Mr. London lowers the gangplank and once more is in walking contact with land.

Then turning eastward, he confronts the 58-foot width of the boat, the walks or wings flanking her 31 tarpaulin-covered hatches, both wet and slippery.

A shipkeeper is more than a watchman. As the name implies, he must keep his ship from harm. To the outsider, this may seem a quite, even passive post.

But to maintain a 12,000-ton lake freighter filled with grain safe throughout a Buffalo winter requires vigilance, experience and good judgement.

The enemies are heat, cold and wind.

First thing Bill London does each morning is to check the winches that hold the powerhouse steel cables which moor the ship.

Has the southwest wind - which raises the water at this end of the lake - affected the ship? Are the lines too tight or too slack? Failure to adjust them accordingly can cause even such a cable to snap.

The next thing is to check the sounding wells, pipes that reach 31 feet down to the ship's keel, to see that there is no freezing water in the ballast (the tanks between the outside hull and the hold).

These sounding wells are located at intervals down the length of the ship, six on each side, and others at both bow and stern.

"The other morning we'd had sleet in the night," the shipkeeper recalls, "and the deck was so smooth and slick with ice I had to crawl along to it."

He takes a rope to which is fastened a 6-foot pole and lowers it one by one into the wells. The end of the pole is chalked for about a foot, so if there is any water in the tanks it shows up.

Then he checks the engine room, forward quarters and water tanks to be sure they are tight and dry.

"You have to watch out," says Mr. London, who is not a fearful man. "You're all alone on the boat. For instance, when you go into the engine room and the blindhold (the dunnage or storage room), you've got to be careful you don't slip and get hurt. You only have a flashlight; you've got to take your time."

Coming topsides again, Bill London gives those tarpaulins on the hatches a sharp look. If the temperature is freezing or below and the snow or ice on them is beginning to melt, that grain in the hold may be getting overheated, in which case it could spoil or even cause spontaneous combustion.

There also are the seacocks close to the ship's hull, valves for opening or closing the pipes which communicate with the sea when the ship is in service.

Is the gelatine-like sealer with which they are closed for the winter, holding fast?

Freezing water in the pipes, warming grain in the hold and leaking seacocks; any such developments are reported at once by the shipkeeper to his company or the grain's shipper.

Like any good housewife, Mr. London now returns to the kitchen to heat some more water to do the breakfast dishes.

By now, life has begun to appear around the ship. The tug *California* - the name on her bow looks ironic in the frigid setting - steams by to help move one of the 17 freighters in harbor this winter, further up along the pier.

Her captain, John Meyers, toots Bill London a cheerful good morning.

Repairs and maintenance work are done on the *S.S. Chicago Trader* in winter. Mechanics, electricians and other repairmen will be visiting her weekdays from now on.

Mr. London will be doing extra work too; company rules permit him to work a 26-hour week, over and above his shipkeeping duties.

"The job keeps me pretty busy nearly all day," says the shipkeeper, who already has thoroughly cleaned the crew's quarters preparatory to painting them sometime after Feb. 15.

"It has to be 65 degrees to work the paint," he explains, "so when it gets a little warmer, I bring a heater into the rooms one by one, leave it there a couple of hours and I'm able to get to work.

**********

As the four o'clock whistle blows, Bill London tours the ship again and locks up. The hatches closing cold, vacant chambers and passages where the workmen have been are locked and bolted.

Workmen troop down the gangplank, which then is raised for the night. The light fades once again, the deep, cold dark envelops river and lake.

The shipkeeper goes in to cook dinner, his big meal of the day. He eats well. The company stocks his pantry shelves with the best quality, rib-sticking canned food, a crate of eggs, and others of apples, oranges and pears. They usually last all winter.

Casimer Cichy of 124 Baitz Ave., a mechanic with the City Parks Department, with whom Mr. London boards on his infrequent stays ashore, takes him shopping each week for fresh meat and milk. And once a week, the shipkeeper goes back to his house for a shower.

"I'm a fair cook," says Bill London, one of a breed who are notoriously fussy about their food. "And I always have a nice supper."

Polish sausage, ground steak, ham, pork chops, sauerkraut, potatoes and corn are hearty fare for a man who tends a sleeping ship in the bitter cold.

At 6 P.M., Mr. London listens to the news and weather reports. The latter may determine whether he can spend a quiet or watchful night.

How is the wind? Is snow predicted? What temperature is expected?

At last, all information considered and any necessary precautions taken, Shipkeeper London is alone with the radio, TV, his books, his memories and his thoughts.

Is he lonely?

"No I ain't," he reports. "I like company as well as anyone else, and especially on Sundays, people do drop in and see me."

"It's a nice quiet life - nobody bothers you. These are good people to work for; if you do your job, there's no comeback."

Mr. London is a wheelsman on the Lakes in the summer time. Why doesn't he lay off in winter?

"There's no use working all summer and saving your money, then spending it in the winter and getting no place," he answers.

The Lakes have been his life; he knows them intimately:

"They're all bad," says Mr. London, who really is a cheerful man.

"Storms come up easiest on Erie, and go down fastest.

Long winter evenings at the foot of Main Street, he has time to mentally wander along the many waterways he has wheeled up or down...

All five of the Great Lakes and almost every port on them; rivers, channels and passages, each with their special navigational hazard from rocks, current and bends to shallows, bridges and other vessels and barges.

Time to recall the winter of 1947, when he was on the *S.S. Rufus P. Ranney*, when she was grounded in the ice outside of Buffalo for seven days.

The 1953 tragic sinking of the *S.S. Henry L. Steinbrenner* on Lake Superior, when his ship - four hours back of the stricken vessel - came on to pick up survivors.

And that sparkling summer day in 1959, when sailing on Lake Sinclair, his ship sighted the royal yacht *S.M.S. Britannia*, escorted by U.S. naval vessels.

"She was a pretty ship. She had brass portholes. We dipped our flag," says Wheelsman London gallantly.

Nine o'clock is Shipkeeper London's bedtime. He opens no portholes for fresh air. The door to the galley is closed, and the little kerosene stove burns on in the cabin as deep night cold closes in.

Weather reports are not infallible. It may be a peaceful night in Buffalo Harbor or then again, a storm could blow in from the Lake.

"The ventilators rattle, the ice creaks and it gets creepy at night - if you're not used to it," says Bill London, his grin indicating fears overcome down the years.

He sleeps with a shotgun by his berth, and a prayer in his heart that the pipes won't burst.

# Part IX

# Birthing of a City

# 36

# Coach From New England

AS EDITOR OF THE *Buffalo Evening News,* Alfred H. Kirchhofer circulated in the community. He joined key boards and committees of the universities, colleges, hospitals and foundations, giving him a wide view and broad contacts. He and his tall, dark, strikingly handsome wife, Emma - they made an impressive pair - also went out socially to clubs, cultural groups and private parties. At such parties, they met and mingled with the city's elite and the socially prominent. It was on one such occasion that a series on *First Families of Buffalo* was launched.

It was difficult to doubt the integrity of Alfred Kirchhofer. His strong featured, somewhat brooding face whose severity could be lit with an occasional understanding smile; his quiet, diffident manner and interest in and quiet concern for those he met, could not readily be associated with anything cheap or sentimental. Attentive to the most minute detail of personal contacts, he tuned in on the community, noting and selecting what he wished for his paper that he held up as a sort of beacon to Western New York. In Alfred Kirchhofer's mind, to appear in the pages of *The News* on legitimate grounds (not illegal ones, of course) was an honor which enhanced the city of Buffalo itself. It is unquestionably with this attitude and approach, and in such a social setting, that he persuaded Mrs. Livingston Fryer to cooperate on the story of the Pratt family, the first family to come into Buffalo in a carriage, and the first to have a carpet on their floor. The Pratts arrived in the autumn of 1804.

## FIRST FAMILY OF BUFFALO

As I sat on the Louis XVth sofa in the Aubusson-carpeted drawing room high in her penthouse apartment with Mrs. Fryer in 1960, the span between those two carpets seemed very wide indeed. The Pratt line had descended not through Mrs. Fryer, the former Catherine Appleton, daughter of Benjamin Appleton, a Boston, Mass., industrialist, but through her husband's mother, Melissa Dodge Pratt. The three-quarter length portrait of Mrs. Pratt by Philip de Lazlo, in luminous evening gown and tiara, on a wall of the room, further lengthened the vista of that coach, jolting across the miles of unpaved roads through forest from Vermont to the tiny settlement at the junction of Lake Erie and the Niagara River, more than 150 years before.  In that span, Buffalo had been born and flourished.

Enclosed in the folds of this historical cloak, the story of the Pratt family had become a part of the legend of the city, immersed in its civic and social structure.  There was little Mrs. Fryer had to offer to bridge that span: a book of genealogy and some general information, odd bones of a frame that had envisioned, led and graced the city for nine generations - a long time in that part of the land.  To flesh the frame was up to me.

Histories of the city, historical records, dissertations, maps, newspapers, portraits and pictures all helped to build the bridge, and several months later the series appeared.

The roots of the story, the exploits and achievements of the line as it descended more than a century-and-a-half to modern times, ran so deep I was at a loss as to what to entitle it.  The Pratts were a pioneer family that was certain, but they were far more than that. What to call them?

I consulted Mother, whose selective speech and ear for a line often had helped me.  And before she died that March of 1961 at age 82, I was able to take proofs of the first article to her in the hospital, bearing the banner, *THE PRATTS: SAGA OF AN ILLUSTRIOUS BUFFALO FAMILY*.

The Pratt series was the first of two from each of which I have chosen what, in my judgement, was the family in question's finest hour or experiences.

The saga of the Pratts begins, as does that of many Buffalo first families, in New England, specifically in their case, in Westminster, Vt.  Such Buffalonians never forget their New England roots.

Capt. Samuel Pratt, 40, a veteran of the American Revolution, returning home after a fur trading trip in Canada early in 1804, had passed a cluster of log cabins on the future site of Buffalo, at the joining of Lake Erie and the Niagara River.  Gazing around this pinpoint of civilization in the wilderness with that vision occasionally bestowed on the pioneer, he foresaw the area as the future center of large commerce.  He returned home, packed up his family and worldly goods, and with a caravan of two white-arched covered wagons led by a coach, began the trek West in September.

The record picks the little party up at Batavia, starting out on the 44-mile-as the crow flies - three-day trip to New Amsterdam, as the hamlet was then known.  A description of their journey follows:

Underneath the primeval elms, oaks and sugar maples, along a wagon track laid on an Indian trail, came the coach - the four horses floundering at times, in mud up to their bellies.

Inside, Esther Wells Pratt, 38, a small, fair woman with a British air, said to her son, Herman, 4:

"It's time to give your sister Esther your seat for a spell, Herman, like a little gentleman."

The coach gave a violent lurch, but five other occupants - Miss Polly Smith, a relative, with Mary Pratt, age 2, on her lap; Esther, 6, Benjamin W., 8, and Permelia, 11 - clasped one another as the wheels sank to the axles.

Again, the party of woodsmen who escorted the carriage on either side to keep it from upsetting, heaved to. From one of the two covered wagons, Capt. Pratt, a broad-shouldered, thick-set man came forward to help. As he stepped up to the wheels, he saw his wife's tired face. They had been obliged to camp the previous night in the woods and the horses had got astray. It was high noon before they were found, harnessed and ready to press on.

Now men and horses struggled together, and the high, leather-sprung coach - stately even beneath a splattering of mud - was on firm ground again. Capt. Pratt vigorously brushed off his hands and preparing to return to the wagon to join his other sons, Asa, 16, and Pascal Paoli, 10, he met his wife's eyes.

"It won't be long now, Esther," he said in reassurance. "We'll see the Lake before sundown."

Esther Pratt, wary of tears, looked straight ahead.

Young Herman, future Mayor of Buffalo, reluctantly gave his sister his seat.

The train of vehicles entered Buffalo by the Williamsville Road. The party picked its way down an unfenced, stump-filled, log-strewn Main Street, until it reached a small clearing in the woods to the west, at what is now High Street.

There through the opening, they first saw Lake Erie, that vast body of water which was to shape their lives and those of their children and children's children.

Slowly, they descended to the Terrace, a cleared section of land with a full view of the lake, and came to a halt before Crow's Tavern. A crowd of the less than a dozen white families in the village and a group of Indians had come out to meet them. The whites gazed at the coach with nostalgia; the Indians with awe. It was the first carriage ever to enter Erie County.

Samuel Pratt helped his wife and children alight. Erastus Granger, superintendent of Indian affairs, a young widower who had come to the village about a year before and lived in the pub, gallantly offered the newcomers his room, one of two in the tavern.

With dignity, Esther Pratt entered the room, followed by her brood of seven. The log walls, like those outside the building, were chinked and plastered with clay; the floor was of split logs smoothed with a drawshave. There was a fireplace with a stone hearth. A bedstead of rough-hewn poles stood in one corner.

Esther Pratt looked about her. Back in Vermont, the children's nurse had rocked the small ones to sleep with this refrain about a river in the West:

> To the Genesee,
> To the Genesee;
> We're all going
> To the Genesee.

It had sounded romantic. Well, they'd come West. Here it was. Esther Pratt wept.

Suppertime inevitably rolls around in a family with seven children and Innkeeper John Crow served a fine meal including venison, duck and wild turkey from the surrounding wilderness. Afterward, Indian blankets were provided, and Mrs. Pratt and the children retired.

Capt. Samuel Pratt, one of the very first keen-sighted pioneers who foresaw the mightiness of the West, and Erastus Granger, sat up late, planning the course of Buffalo history.

The first thing Capt. Pratt did was to settle his family in a log cabin on the Terrace. It, too, was crowded and uncomfortable, but they managed. Next, he built a small temporary store nearby, in which to conduct a fur trading business with the Indians.

By the summer of 1805, the captain had erected a 2-1/2-story L-shaped house on Buffalo Creek, and a better store. The house was the first dwelling of any size in the village, and the store was its first established mercantile business.

Boston carpet laid in the parlor of the new house was the first to cover a floor in Buffalo. And George Keith, the cabinetmaker whom Capt. Pratt had brought with him from Vermont, made a half-moon shaped table and bureau of black walnut. Inlaid with different kinds of wood, these two pieces were the first furniture manufactured in the village.

**********

Parental love was active in those days. With his wife and children suitably housed, Capt. Pratt's mind turned back to his parents, Aaron, then 63, and Mary Clark, 61, in Vermont They were considered old, as the average life span was then about 35 years.

It is gallant to report that Esther accompanied her husband on the arduous trip East again, and brought the aged couple back to Buffalo to live with them. Thus Aaron and Mary Pratt became the patriarch and matriarch of a Buffalo family now in its tenth generation.

Having gathered his own unto him, Capt. Pratt settled down to business. He had opened a store and - obeying a cardinal law of merchandising to cater to the largest population group - stocked it with merchandise pleasing to the Indians, who usually paid him in furs. The pelts were marketed in Europe.

Here's how the captain transported his goods to Buffalo: Sloop to Albany. Up the Mohawk and down Fish Creek to Oneida Lake. Down the Oswego River to Lake Ontario. By lake and the Niagara River to Lewiston. To Fort Schlosser by portage around Niagara Falls and up the Niagara to Buffalo.

When the main state turnpike was made a good road, the captain imported wares with Conestoga wagons drawn by five to seven horses. The journey from Albany to Buffalo took 28 to 30 days - depending on the season and the state of the roads.

Capt. Pratt was a generous, casual trader. He also was a diplomat. When Indians presented him with beaver skins - the claws weighted with lead - he never mentioned it. He just chopped off the claws, threw them aside and allowed liberally for their net value. He was popular with the Indians. They called him Ho-da-ni-da-oh, meaning that he was merciful, kind or liberal, also Ne-gur-ri-yu, the honest dealer.

The U.S. Government paid its dues to some of the Indians at stated intervals in those days. Capt. Pratt gave them exclusive use of the basement of his house for such occasions. He gave them pork and flour, too. They roasted the pork on sticks before the big cellar fireplace and mixed the flour into a kind of cake, rolled it in green corn husks and baked it in the ashes.

Esther Pratt found the fumes of "kinnikinnick" or Indian tobacco - a species of sumac with a little sweet Seneca grass, which they smoked in their pipes - difficult to take. But the Pratt family was on good terms with the Indians, including sachems such as Red Jacket, Cornplanter, Young King and Farmer's Brother.

*********

Esther Pratt was deeply religious. Her husband was not a church member but a practical Christian who respected religious observances.

A year after emigrating to Buffalo, the Pratts, with considerable difficulty and expense, brought the Rev. Samuel Whiting of Boston, Mass., to the little settlement. The Rev. Whiting was the first local minister to serve in the area apart from the jurisdiction of a missionary society. He lived with the Pratts for more than a year and drilled their children in the catechism each Sunday. He preached and taught school. Every itinerant minister also was welcome at the Pratt house. Mrs. Pratt and a neighbor, Mrs. Joseph Landon, established the first series of evening prayer meetings.

From the outset, Capt. Pratt concerned himself with the public good. The year he arrived in Buffalo, he and another early settler, Dr. Cyrenius Chapin, went to the Holland Land Co. in Batavia and procured a piece of ground as a village burying ground. It was named Franklin Square. He helped cut away the scrub oak and clear the ground and bury a fellow New England traveler, John Cochrane, in the first grave there. Then he purchased more than 100 acres on both sides of the Buffalo Creek. There he built a sturdy farmhouse, a little distance from the water facing the creek, to replace the smaller home he had built in the village.

The vigorous frontiersman obtained a grant from the State Legislature and established a common large-sized scow ferry run across the creek. He also bought black walnut timber from the Indians and spanned the stream with a toll bridge. The Indians paid no toll.

Capt. Pratt's efforts were not all successful. He suffered heavy losses when a large uninsured shipment of furs was damaged by salt water en route to Europe. And spring freshets washed away the toll bridge after his death. The War of 1812 was declared on June 19. Forebodings of British troops sounded through Buffalo village.

A man who had enlisted in the Revolution and served in Washington's army at the battles of Germantown, Fort Mifflin and Monmouth, Samuel Pratt took these forewarnings seriously.

"I must look up those spurs, my dear," he said to his wife of a pair of silver ones he had worn in his youth, "I may have to use them."

He died three months before the reality of distant cannon sounded across the village on the night of Dec. 30, 1812.

The *Buffalo Gazette* of Sept. 1, 1812, the village's first newspaper, in part put it thus:

"In the town, yesterday morning, Capt. Samuel Pratt, aged 48 years.

"Capt. Pratt was among the first inhabitants of this place. With them, he cheerfully encountered all the privations and hardships incident to the first settlers of a new country.

"The public spirit displayed by him in whatever related to the improvements of the village, and the convenience of the early settlers in his vicinity, will render his memory dear to all who knew him." He was laid to rest in the Franklin Square burying ground.

As the shadow of war hung over the village of Buffalo, Samuel Pratt, Jr., 25, eldest son of Capt. Pratt, became head of the family. It was the day, ostensibly at least, of patriarchal supremacy. A rather slender man about 5 feet, 9 inches tall, somewhat delicate in appearance, Samuel Jr. and his wife, Sophia, 19, had come to the village in the summer of 1807.

It was the summer Robert Fulton made the first practical steamboat trip from New York to Albany in the *Clermont*. Three generations later, this historic vessel with its side-paddle wheels was to cross the Pratt family line again.

The Pratt Jrs. came West in one covered wagon on a train owned by the captain and in the charge of a younger son, Asa, now about 19. The wagon train, bearing mainly Indian supplies, was en route from Boston, Mass.

In her arms, Sophia Pratt, daughter of Gen. Samuel Fletcher of Revolutionary distinction, held their 3-month-old son, Samuel Fletcher Pratt, a future founder of the nationally-known paint company, Pratt & Letchworth, and first president of the city's most prestigious girls school, the Buffalo Female Academy, now the Buffalo Seminary.

The little family stayed at Capt. Pratt's until a house could be readied for them. And the young pioneer, who had clerked at Townsend, Vt., now opened his own shop in the modest building formerly occupied by his father, later supplanted by the first brick building of any importance in the village.

In 1810 however, Samuel Jr. retired from business for a time to become sheriff of Niagara County, which then included the territory now comprising Erie County.

One can imagine how arduous the office of sheriff was on the frontier, entailing travel under hard road and severe weather conditions. Stumps from the primeval forest were scattered down Main Street as late as 1811. And even as the war opened, a good deal of land within the present city limits was dark with original woods.

But despite the propulsion of those days, as they helped give birth to a city, the Pratts relished good living.  Samuel Pratt, Jr. bought Holland Land Company Lot No. 39 for an undisclosed price.  Later he sold it for $2020.  Asked to drop the $20, he flatly refused.

"That," he said with finality, "is for a silk dress for my wife."

**********

Booming of distant cannon awakened Mrs. Elijah Leech in the middle of the night on Dec. 30, 1813, at the Pratt Farm on Buffalo Creek.

The daughter of the late Capt. Pratt had difficulty in alerting her husband.  For months there had been false alarms that the British were coming.  Children were put to bed partially dressed, and a few days' provisions were packed and ready.

Faithful servant Jack Ray, a fugitive slave, was awakened and ordered to harness up a team.  About daylight, the wagon was dispatched through the snow and mud - the weather was raw and disagreeable - to the village for the Pratt family.

Meanwhile, Judge Ebenezer Walden, a neighbor of Samuel Pratt Jr. at Eagle and Main, rapped on his window and said the British were almost here.

The wagon from the farm soon arrived, and Mr. Pratt helped his wife, Sophia, Samuel F. Pratt, 7, Lucius H., 5, and Sophia, 3 into it.  They were accompanied by a little Negro servant girl called "Tam."

Jack Ray whipped the horses into a run - and they escaped just in time.

They hadn't got very far, however, when Mrs. Pratt found they'd left the silver on the mantel.  Against her orders, Tam slipped off the wagon and ran back to fetch it.

She soon returned with the report that British soldiers and Indians were in the front room, had all the earthenware jars on the table and were enjoying the sweetmeats and mince pies.

A little later, Tam got off the wagon once more, and they never saw her again.  But they did sight a detachment of British soldiers marching on Main Street near High, their bayonets shining in the early morning sun.

Back at the farm, another team or two with sleighs or wagons was added.  The party crossed the creek and joined a throng of other fugitives hurrying up the lakeshore.

Shots reverberated in the distance.  They looked back to see
Buffalo in flames.

"Whip up the horses, Jack," ordered Mr. Leech.

Bob, one of the team, had been a favorite saddle horse of Capt.
Pratt.  Jack loved him.

The stocky figure of his late master too, rose before his eyes.

"I ain't gwuine to kill Captain's huss," he cried - sparing the
whip.

**********

Leadership in a community usually stems from public service.

Capt. Samuel Pratt took the welfare of struggling Buffalo village
to heart.  Following in his footsteps, his son, Samuel Jr., stood by
it in disaster.

After he had helped his wife and children into the escaping
wagon, Samuel Jr. stayed behind.

He thanked God that his mother, a widow of three months, and
sister, Marilla, were visiting in Batavia and spared this devastation.

How much of his pioneer father's vision of the little village as
the future site of a great city could he salvage for his family and
other residents?

Judge Ebenezer Walden also stayed  behind and the two men -
keeping out of British sight - went about putting out the fires kindled
by the enemy in numerous buildings, only to see them relighted.  It
was discouraging work.

Samuel Pratt Jr. commuted between the family farmhouse on
Buffalo Creek and the smoking village for several nights.  A helper,
who escorted him on one trip, was shot and scalped by an Indian
crouching behind a large beech tree at the foot of Michigan Street.
Samuel Jr. escaped before the savage could re-load.

The British burned and plundered Buffalo village for three days.
The large Pratt storehouse at the corner of Ellicott and Seneca
streets, a frame house of Widow St. John's near the corner of
Mohawk and Main, and the frame blacksmith shop, riddled with
bullets, were among the few structures left standing.

Capt. Pratt's storehouse was saved as a packing center for
plundered goods.

About 30 frozen dead were taken up from the streets when the
enemy finally withdrew from the pillaged village.  The blacksmith
shop served as a morgue.

In the meantime, the Pratt families, who had spent the first night
of their flight sleeping on the floor of a log house in Griffin's Mills,

the second on a log tavern floor surrounded by wounded soldiers, had reached Lima.

There they were reunited with the matriarchal captain's widow. She had heard of the British attack while visiting friends, but received no news of her family until the teams drove up five days later. As she counted her dear ones, she fainted.

The Pratt women had stout hearts. After a few weeks, however, Grandmother Pratt took children and grandchildren in a sleigh back to Westminster, Vt., from whence she had come through the wilderness to Buffalo nine years before.

A respite from frontier life seemed in order.

**********

Like a river, every family has its turning point. The day arrives when it must ask itself the question: Shall we follow the current around the unknown bend, or shall we backtrack into the pond of safety?

It would have been easy and comfortable for Esther Pratt to stay in her old Westminster, Vt., home, where she returned with the children and grandchildren after the burning of Buffalo.

By coincidence, the house she and her late husband, Capt. Pratt, had occupied in the little New England town by the Connecticut River, was available. They stayed there.

Mrs. Pratt had some income from the sale of New England wild lands and was not destitute as were many of the Buffalo villagers. The hamlet her husband had helped struggle to its feet was sacked. A number of settlers had moved east, even before the actual British attack.

Was it the memory of the captain's eager face as he envisioned a future city there, or some indefatigable strain in her own Yankee stock, or both, that recalled her?

The important fact is that six months later, at 47 years of age, she again headed westward. A report of the Battle of Chippewa detained her at East Bloomfield, Ont., and it was February 1814 before she arrived back in Buffalo.

But she did return. The history of her descendants and of the city might have been quite different if she had not.

Esther Pratt found the farmhouse her husband had built on Buffalo Creek still standing. Greenness of timber had saved it.

It was here, caught up in or at least faithful to the dream of her pioneer husband, that she lived for 16 more years, extending hospitality to every race, color and denomination of homesick wayfarer.

It was here that she mixed vinegar, butter and honey for Red Jacket when he had a sore throat and welcomed other Indian chiefs.

It was here in this house, decorated with evergreens and the parlor candle lit on the day peace was declared, that she saw her oldest daughter, Esther, married to Augustus C. Fox, a young settler who had given the British the slip as they sent him to find the key to a wine cellar.

And it was here, in the spring of 1830 - as the peach trees her husband had planted burst into mature and productive bloom - that she died. Buffalo's first great lady: Esther Wells Pratt.

# 37

## House Calls on Horseback

THE STORY OF DR. Bryant Burwell was available in quite a different and infinitely more personal and exact form.

Bryant Glenny agreed to let the *Buffalo Evening News* peruse the diaries of his great-grandfather, one of Buffalo's 12 doctors in 1824. The diaries, written over a 10-year span from 1837-47, were put down in pen and ink in six ruled-page, leather-bound volumes, the script now somewhat faded with age. I sat at a table in Mr. and Mrs. Glenny's apartment for some weeks excerpting bits of the "journals," as the doctor himself called them. The selection of passages of interest more than a century later was the key to this slice of history of medical practice and the way of life in Western New York, during the first half of the 19th century.

In preface, we noted "a doctor examines many lives, but it is seldom that the public is permitted to look into the life of a doctor." The diaries of Dr. Burwell, who was between 41 and 51 when he wrote them, give an intimate picture of the man, his romantic interests, his profession and his times.

In his own words, they are "the undertaking of preserving a complete record of my thoughts and the complex and varied phases of my affairs." As such, they are human and therefore timeless. I have chosen as the highlight the professional side of Dr. Burwell's life, selecting passages from years and months most conducive to this end.

It seems appropriate, however, to describe the newly-incorporated City of Buffalo (1832) at the time they were written and to introduce the author:

The streets of Buffalo were lit only by the dim lamps of oyster sellers when Dr. Bryant Burwell took up his pen to write of this decade of history.

Main Street was unpaved, save for a fifth of a mile. Water came from public or private wells, and fires were extinguished mainly from reservoirs beneath the streets in only the central part of the city.

The first fire-alarm bell was installed on the Terrace the year the diaries begin.

A single railroad, 20 miles in length, ran into the city from Niagara Falls. It had no connection whatever, with any other tracks.

Western travel - much to the benefit of the town - was still by boat in summer and stage in winter.

The population of Buffalo was about 10,000. Indians were still on the Buffalo Creek and Tonawanda tracts.

Mail took days, people wrote long letters and whole families arrived en masse for extended visits.

The atmosphere of the era was enigmatic sentimental and melancholic, yet vigorous, energetic and enterprising. There was a dauntlessness about it.

A preoccupation with death, the Bible, verse and personal charity were evident. Duty was a byword.

People spoke frequently, not only of the heart, but of the soul.

It was a decade of labyrinthine courtesies of thought and expression.

Yet amidst its storms, epidemics, heartbreak and triumphs - this new City of Buffalo enjoyed itself. It was a sociable place that rolled out the red carpet for the traveler. It religiously attended its funerals - but it also danced at its balls.

Dr. Burwell was born in the Town of Russia, Herkimer County, N.Y., in 1796. His father was a farmer.

Upon completion of the usual academic studies of the period, he entered the office of a Prof. Willoughby in Newport, Herkimer County, as a student of medicine.

From 1822 to 1823 he pursued his medical studies at Fairfield Medical College in his native county, and at Philadelphia in 1826 and 1827.

He started his Buffalo practice in 1824, leaving briefly to further his studies.

In his diary of 1839, Dr. Burwell reminisces on his start:

"I had just commenced the practice of medicine. I was then pretty much a 'greenhorn'...

"Poverty and I were brothers. I was just entering my 21st year. I had no library save Thomas Practice - no money beyond a few pence - no clothes - except a single thread - bare, homemade suit - no medicine except what was contained in a capacious pair of saddlebags, and no horse or vehicle or other mode of conveyance...

"Thus poorly equipped - thus watchfully provided for, did I commence my career in life. When I look back 22 years to that eventful period, I am astonished at my temerity and my success."

He was married twice and had four children by his first wife.

Bryant Burwell wrote in his diary in his "quiet room," sometimes before departing on his daily rounds, sometimes late at night. He made those rounds on horseback, by buggy, sulky and sleigh, on occasion traveling more than 50 miles a day. When necessary, he went by foot or even an improvised raft.

A religious man, an idealist and romanticist, he was somewhat socially shy. But he observed human nature keenly despite his abounding compassion and treatment of life's ills.

Here are excerpts from his travels and practice:

## 1837

January 1 - But two things can render the practice of medicine tolerable - the recovery of our patients and the generous payment of our bills. In both respects we are sometimes gratified, and alas! in both we are sometimes disappointed.

January 7 - Bled Mr. Woodruff's little child who is very ill with pleurisy. It is a very disagreeable affair to be compelled to bleed a little child. The poor little sufferers cannot comprehend...the necessity of the operation.

(Referring to a man who had just lost his third wife in 10 years) - She was not my patient - I am thankful for that - for nothing is so painful to me as to lose a patient by death.

March 14 - A fine, cool, pleasant day. I have been among my patients all day - some 15 families and many of them I have visited twice.

March 24 - (To a Mr. Abbott, who had evidently just passed his medical examination) - To every medical man that is an important period; and next to matrimony, perhaps the most so that will occur during his life.

April 30 - Attended Mrs. _____ in her first confinement - six months married! Not a word said.

May 28 - A cool and pleasant chuchgoing day - I poor devil, have been denied that privilege, being compelled to visit many patients today - I have therefore made myself useful, if not as pious as some others.

August 26 - The recovery of my patients is a thousand times more pleasant to me than is the fee I get for my services.

December 2 - Night at length came on! - and I finally went to bed!

### 1838

(In his journal on Feb. 3, 1838, Dr. Bryant Burwell tells of attending a Mrs. Gorham, who, apparently, had been poisoned.)

I proceeded instantly to administer albumen as an antidote. She took in rapid succession the white part of some half dozen eggs beat up in water...the patient was made to drink frequently and largely of diluted albumen and muscilage.

(The woman tells the doctor that within the past 15 months before this, she has taken corrosive sublimate, a virulent poison, once in ginger tea and again in a peach.)

(Dr. Burwell indicates traces of poison in the glass by the woman's bed to her husband, who says that it was "strange" how it got there.)

(The physician replies that "it was indeed strange, but that it could not have got there without feet and hands.")

Dr. Burwell to his diary - Would to heaven that I knew more or much less of this strangely, mysterious affair.

I feel it my duty to go to the District Attorney in the morning and state only such facts as I know to be true, and leave the affair with him to act as he thinks his duty requires him to do.

Feb. 5 - I have seen enough of human depravity within the past week to make any man, who has human feeling not quite contaminated by this vicious world, "blush and hang his head to think himself a man."

March 9 - The grand jury did not find a bill against Capt. Gorham...there is not in my mind any more doubt than there is that the sun shines...

(Upon Capt. Gorham leaving town, and his wife following him):

It is, I think, one of the strangest traits of human character that woman's love can so far blind her, as that she cannot see such faults as her husband has been guilty of...We may admire the ardor of her affection, but we must pity if not despise the weakness of her intellect.

April 15 - I am making full notes and going through my whole library on the subject of various dislocations of the hip joint, and also, of fractures of the neck and of the femur;

all preparatory to the suit of old Crooker against me for malpractice...

May 1 - Early in the afternoon...my brief of 60 pages of closely written matter being completed, I must say that I felt a degree of confidence and certainty of success...

May 3 - Today, my attorneys informed me that the case would not probably ever be tried...Consequently, I gave Dr. Lathrop (one of the most material witnesses), cash $5 and a new hat, $6 for his journey (50 miles from Fredonia) and trouble. I now consider the suit ended.

June 21 - I have been among the sick, dying and dead all day, and this evening I attended a sparkling wedding at Mr. Tillinghast. All was fashionable - and gay and mirthful.

Good heavens - what a contrast! What a variety of impressions a doctor gets in a single day! Day and night are not so opposite - O what a variegated scene is life.

Oct. 28 - We had a very stormy night - I was out on horseback visiting patients until 2 o'clock this morning.

This morning early I started for Hamburgh to see a Mrs. Rice, sick with bilious fever. She is very bad and will probably die - poor woman, how anxiously she watched my countenance, as I examined her...it is very painful to tell a patient...that she must die.

The judge passing sentence of death on a guilty man has a trivial duty in comparison with the physician, who possesses sensibility and pity for the sorrow of others.

Dec. 1 - In my profession an ocean of medical literature is around me and yet I have not time to read, digest mentally and arrange and clarify what is written.

## 1839

January 14 - All is again frozen - the weather is cold with a horrid easterly wind - I have many sick patients - business is laborious and responsible - I am almost sick myself with a bad influenza - but I must keep going - going until I am quite gone forever.

I am much attached to the practice of my profession; it has become a habit with me. The fears and hopes and despair and joy of a sick world are excitement enough for me. I need not court the jolly God for amusement.

Moreover, is it not a great and glorious privilege to be able, under the blessing of Divine Providence, to still the raging fever, to calm the frenzied mind, to mitigate or relieve the anguish of pain and torture; and to lay your hand on many cases of disease which -without skill would be futile - and say "this far shalt thou go and no further."

What on earth is a more glorious triumph?...The good physician was long since justly appreciated when Homer sang:

> The good physician, skilled
>   our wounds to heal,
> Is more than armies to the
>   commonweal!

February 2 - Today has been uncommonly stormy weather even for the most savage winter...Such weather as we have today is quite too bad for horses or other cattle to be about. Nothing but poor Doctors should be compelled to stir forth.

March 5 - And now at 11 o'clock (PM) I am called to attend Mrs. T.B. Good heavens, the women will kill me.

July 15 - Have talked - prescribed - explained and advised continually from early dawn until this late hour at night.

Constant and unremitting fatigue, great responsibility and anxiety - loneliness - solitude - but still a buoyancy of feeling worth them all - an inward and expansive cheerfulness which I trust will never forsake me - great hopes for the future - such is life to me.

August 1 - I have been to Clarence Hollow to see Miss Tiffany. She is quite ill; and in some danger of being lost. She is an excellent old Girl - and I cannot conceive of why old maids are deemed so very unmarketable.

December 29 - The greatest snowstorm I have known in this country during the 14 years I have resided here...I was obliged to visit my patients this forenoon on horseback...

It was in this year that Dr. Burwell composed this prayer:

O Thou great Bestower of health, strength and comfort, grant thy blessing upon the professional duties in which I may this day engage.

Give me judgment to discern disease, and skill to treat it; and crown with thy favour the means that may be devised for recovery; for with thine assistance, the humblest instrument may succeed; as without it, the ablest must prove unavailing.

Save me from all sordid motives; and endow me with a spirit of pity and liberality towards the poor, and of tenderness and sympathy towards all, that I may enter into the various feelings by which they are respectively tried, may weep with those that weep, and rejoice with those that rejoice.

And sanctify their souls as well as their bodies...


## 1840

January 15 - In the afternoon, I attended the annual meeting of the Erie County Medical Society. Some sport and sparring we had in discussing by-laws - Resolutions, etc.

January 30 - Nobody but Doctors can endure such a storm; even stage drivers are obliged to stay within doors...My house shakes.

If we are not burned up tonight; or blown to pieces by the gale; nor frozen by the intense degree of cold coming on...we ought to thank Heaven for its mercy.

(Same - 4:30 AM) - I went to bed at half past two o'clock - and in fifteen minutes afterwards I was again called up to attend Mrs. Giles Thomas...

March 19 - I was quite ill this morning with the headache - visited a number of patients and then started in the mud and rain for Hamburgh, 12 miles...I returned quite well - so much for exertion and perseverance.

August 2 - How much of anxiety have I not seen today. How many serious, solemn lessons on the uncertainty of life; on the futility of earthly happiness and unsubstantial nature of all things below, have I not heard among various patients...

I have extended myself today, to the full extent of my capacity to do for all...If I have done good and been useful...I am satisfied. If I have done aught amiss may heaven forgive me.

December 21 - Well I have been to a "party" tonight. I mention the fact because I have so seldom done such a thing heretofore...I went; was just beginning to feel myself at home and at ease, when I was called away to see an only son of Mr. George B. Gates, very sick with scarlet fever...Such is the fate of a Doctor: no rest; no recreation; no amusement.

## 1841

February 27 - I have just returned from visiting two little children with inflammation of the lungs. They are both younger than my babe; and their Mothers are quite alarmed about them.

How fierce and holy is a Mother's love! How tender and yet how strong the tie that binds them to their offspring.

March 14 - I went to Eden 18 miles last Sabbath; to Griffin's Mills in Aurora 18 miles last Friday and to Clarence Hollow 18 miles today. All the rides were cold and tedious. But I encounter them with cheerfulness; my health is good; my spirits fine...

June 16 - Professional business is tolerable - the Town being healthy. Green peas are in market today - When lettuce, radishes, currants, peas, cherries and cucumber shall be plenty in market - sickness will also be plenty in every street.

June 25 - I have indulged in a little miscellaneous reading this spring - and it has delayed much my promptness and attention to business.

The doctor was not without humor. In this year he comments:

The thanks and gratitude of patients and their friends are very agreeable to one who has a kind and benevolent heart towards all, even though one may be conscious that words are cheap.

To hear one say "O Doctor, I know not what I should do if it were not for you" is worth $20. "I am much obliged to you, Doctor," is worth $10 when uttered by a lady and $5 when spoken by a gentleman - "You shall be paid next week," is worth from two cents to a York shilling...

## 1842

January 30 - It seems as if I had enough to do the ensuing week to occupy ten men; O what a pity it is that I am compelled to sleep; I should like to work without one moment's interruption by night or by day.

March 1 - Quite a number of my patients are most dangerously ill - I fear I shall lose them. What anxiety and care I feel on their account. O God spare them if possible.

March 19 - It is Saturday night - my week's work is done and I believe, well done - Amen.

March 30 - Heigho! I am really weary. I was called
away at 1 o'clock this morning - and have but this moment
returned at 12 o'clock at night. What patience! What
suffering have I not again beheld!

Poor Mrs. S. It was her first confinement. Twenty-
four hours of pain and travail - and every hour much severer
than that which preceded it.

O woman! woman how much thou hast to bear! - How
kind and protective every man ought to be to all women.
Indeed he ought to reverence them - to love them - and by
every means in his power, to honor, cherish and protect
them, as heaven's best, best gift to man.

April 12 - Since dusk I have been nearly all over town
on horseback, the outer streets being too...muddy to ride in
my carriage.

June 1 - I am continually engaged in my profession; and
with the most glorious success. I have lost but one patient in
nearly six months - and my business has averaged nearly
$400 per month. I have, also, collected $100 per month in
cash besides, as much more in trade...

September 15 - On this day I have witnessed one of the
most melancholy scenes I have ever beheld in the sudden
death of Gen. Nelson Randall's only child, a daughter, five
years old.

She died by Laudanum, given by mistake by her
Mother...intending to give her a teaspoonful of Tincture of
Rhubarb, she gave her a teaspoonful of Laudanum. It was
taken from a vial marked "Tincture of Rhubarb," and hence
the most dreadful fatal error.

How it came in the vial no one knows, and we have not
dared to question the distracted mother - for she still
supposes that her child died in a fit.

The child died about two hours after she took the
poison...Did the mother know what she has done, her
friends believe it would drive her mad and destroy her. Her
friends intend to withhold the truth from her forever.

December 31 - I have been entirely alone during the year
and have charged $4896.75...collected $2630.25  This is
doing pretty well.

## 1843

January 10 - I rode in the rain all the forenoon, and have attended the annual meeting of our Medical Society this afternoon.

Dr. A. made a full and fair recantation of his quackery; expressed frankly his regret that in an unguarded moment he had consented to advertise his syrup for the cure of cough, colds, croup and consumption. The Society forgave him this unprofessional act on the condition that he should "go and sin no more.."

May 4 - I went over hill and dale, like a bird on the wing. My horse enjoyed this freedom and exercise as much as I did.

Another horse ride brought me to Col. Brown's on the banks of the Buffalo Creek, where I found the bridge impassable for my horse - I therefore left him to be stabled and fed, proceeded another mile on foot...where my patient resided.

I was obliged to cross the creek on a stick of timber 12-inches-square, about 40 feet long and about the same height from the water - I soon accomplished this with a steady eye and a firm and steady step. I was soon with my patient.

From thence I hurried on towards home, and was so fortunate as to enter the noble old forest, which the road traversed for 6 miles, a little before sunset.

How tall and reverend appeared those trees! with the bright sunshine gilding their tops. I repeatedly stopped my horse to let the awe of this forest, planted and reared by the Almighty, sink deep into my heart - and also to listen to its almost audible silence.

## 1844

Jan. 11 - (Quotation from Jean Paul) - "God is near the birth of every child. Who does not find him in this uncomprehensible mechanism of pain, in this sublimity of his exquisite machinery, in this prostration of our own independence - will never find him."

January 21 - I was enabled by neglecting my patients to attend Mr. Shelton's church this forenoon...

November 30 - Dr. Sprague's eldest son died last evening of inflammation of the bowels in a little more than 48 hours illness.

I think the calomel given him soon after the full fury of the disease burst upon him was awful! that the bleeding was omitted 24 hours too long - and that the anodynes were given far too sparingly. For the City of Buffalo, I would not treat one of God's creatures in a similar manner.

And yet to save feelings and reflections of the most bitter kind, I said at the Post-Mortem examination held this afternoon - that all had been done for him that could have been done, and I felt, alas! that I lied! May God forgive me.

### 1846

March 25 - (Letter to Dr. N.S. Davis) - In a city like Buffalo, with 30 or 40 practicing physicians, there must, almost necessarily, be some little cliques - and odd combinations - some jealousies and rivalries; they are amorphous compounds - always changing - redissolving - and recombining in some new form.

All deeply feel the evils which afflict our profession at present. We seek a remedy, if one can be found...I sincerely hope...that the deliberations of the convention (National Medical Convention in New York in May to which he was a delegate) will be characterized by the liberality of its views, the charitable concession of its prejudices and the sectional feelings, and the wisdom of its recommendations.

# Part X

# Across the Land

# 38

# Excursions

EXCURSIONS ARE A PART of a reporter's life. By excursions I mean sallies into another locale - it can be a town or a city - than the base from which the reporter operates. It is not a journey involved with politics, although according to their purest definition "the science of government," politics are inextricably woven into the life of the smallest village.

Nor is an excursion an assignment to cover a convention, meeting or other public gathering. It is a short trip, ostensibly for pleasure, and involves both a sense of expectancy and adventure.

## CULTURE AT FREDONIA

Until comparatively recent times, people on the Eastern Seaboard did not talk about "culture." They spoke of "cultivation"; people were cultivated or they were not.

The culture that the older cities of the East possessed, along with the word, had sunk deep into their environment, and Boston perhaps excepted, flourished or slept beneath the surface of their daily life. This did not mean that such cities necessarily were intellectual or artistic; they simply were entrenched in their way of life and did not evoke its origins unless they were historic, a pedal upon which they stepped heavily.

In recent years, however, a great renaissance of intellectual and artistic activity and appreciation has swept the East, "giving tongue," as they say in hunting circles, to the word culture.

I shall never forget how surprised I was in 1969 to receive an elaborate book from Gov. Raymond P. Shafer of Pennsylvania, entitled "Pennsylvania Culture - The Arts - The Artists - The Audience." In all my youthful years of gallery, museum and concert going in Philadelphia, I do not remember ever having heard the word, except perhaps at Burton Holmes travel lectures or in reading the National Geographic Magazine. Culture was a remote, tribal affair in say, Borneo or South Africa, where no one wore much above the waist. In our education too, the word used was "civilization."

Rare is the suburb or small town in the East today, however, that does not have some literary, musical or artistic thrust and center. The New Guard, a blend of college educated young men and women from East and West, demands and often sponsors and supports it. To them the buried culture is unsatisfactory; they want to see and experience it.

But as you head westward, it has long been different. Culture, frankly vocalized, is a goal earnestly to be sought, the potential equalizer of the cities beyond the East Coast with it. And its manifestations often draw a more intense and active patronage and attendance then the Eastern communities.

I once remarked on this verbalizing of culture and the effort to pursue and promote it to a Roman Catholic priest, aboard a flight between Buffalo and Philadelphia.

"They talk about it, Father," I remarked, "in the East we never did; it was people we spoke of, 'cultivated' or 'uncultivated.'"

The priest, a Scotsman, lifted the whole subject into perspective:

"Cultivated?" he asked. "It's kind of like a berry patch, isn't it?"

Reared in a royal framework with eons of devotion to higher learning and the arts, I suppose he would have differentiated between the "educated" and "uneducated." At any rate, the difference of approach to those who had received more education and developed more appreciation of the so-called civilizing influences, and those who had not, seemed less important after our chat. While it's really a question of semantics, older communities have looked down on newer ones since time began.

America is waking up to the fact that culture is not an Eastern Seaboard exclusive; it is spreading handsomely and elegantly to major cities throughout the United States, and even to lesser ones, some of which give their indigenous flavor to it. One culture may differ from another, but they both represent the upward rise of the mentality and sensibility of their citizenry.

Nobody for example can visit the McNay Art Institute in San Antonio, with its exquisite highly polished mosquite-floored galleries, let alone the great galleries of Buffalo, Cleveland, Chicago and San Francisco, and smile at Western concern with "culture."

The performance of "Don Giovanni" in the $4.1 million Michael C. Rockefeller Art Center of the New York State University at Fredonia in 1970, (the populaton was then 10,000), was to use the overworked word "culture," at its grassroots.

"It is an example that culture is not dependent on big towns," I wrote, "but on occasion, can and must rise on indigenous soil to meet its own esthetic needs. It is part of the outreach of many arts today, across field as well as city.

"Fredonia is a heartening illustration of what a college can do for a village - and a village can do for a state university."

Grand opera is not something that just happens in a village in the shadow of the Allegheny foothills. The people there have to want it to happen.

In 1824, a group of culturally-minded subscribers banded together to build an academy in Fredonia. They each gave what they could - Leverett, $25 in money, $50 in cattle and $25 in leather...Squire White, $10 in money, $50 in cattle and grain...William Sage, $25 in hats and shingles...Orris Crosby, $20 in labor...Samuel Marsh, $40 in grain and 6000 clapboards, etc.

Tuition would be $3 per quarter, and board in private families could be obtained for $1 per week.

The Academy became the Fredonia State Normal School in 1881, and by the time it joined 10 other Colleges of Education within the State University of New York in 1948, had a long reputation for excellence in musical instruction. Today the Fredonia State Chorus frequently appears with the Buffalo Philharmonic Orchestra.

The thrust for musical culture in Fredonia stems back to Jessie Hillman a stately, dark-eyed beauty from Greece, N.Y., (current pop. 16,177), who came to the Normal School in 1884 to teach music. She was one of three instructors. Laying the groundwork for today's Music Department, she taught there for 40 years and gave private instruction for 20 more. The whole town took lessons from her. It was the 110-member Hillman Memorial Association, Inc., established in her memory to provide scholarships for expecially gifted FSTC music students, that sponsored "Don Giovanni."

The college's Opera Theatre was in its 13th season. Both traditional and modern operas had preceded the current performance - from *Die Fledermaus, The Marriage of Figaro* and *Madama Butterfly* to *The Ballad of Baby Doe* by Douglas Moore and John Latouche, and *A Midsummer Night's Dream* by Briton. But this was the first operatic performance in the new center, and the first at which the audience was requested to wear formal dress.

Beyond, just out of town in the night, stretched the great farms and vineyards which have made the Dunkirk-Fredonia area of Western New York one of the largest Concord grape centers in the United States.

In this upstate village "culture" had found a way, not just that of the vine, but culture in the form of one of the most esoteric of its social forms - grand opera - in a setting provided by a munificent benefactor. The opera, however, was not born because of the $4.1 million theater, but rather the theater was a response of the people of

Fredonia, a chosen few perhaps, nor did it evolve because of indebtedness to Jessie Hillman alone.

Culture in Fredonia arose from the spirit of villagers who yearned and were ready to work for some aesthetic interpretation of life, other than the rustic daily round. If one is very literal, it grew out of the desire, cattle, grain, shingles, clapboard and labor of the men who raised that Academy in 1824. Love finds a way; so does aspiration. Mr. Rockefeller was impresario, but Fredonians were the cast.

People who live in cities and ignore or look with disdain upon small-town culture miss a lot; they miss perhaps the salient American fact that it can, has and is rising like yeast over tilled fields of wheat, corn, barley, oats or what have you of the United States.

During the intermission of *Don Giovanni*, Chablis from the vines and winery of gentleman farmer Frederick Johnson's nearby Westfield estate was served. And the dubonnet and white programs held in white-gloved hands bore the names of 521 patrons.

The performance was preceded by dinners, and I went to one. Dr. and Mrs. Dana Wheelock entertained 30 guests at cocktails and a buffet supper in their 120-year-old house where the surgeon's maternal great-grandfather, Willard McKinstry, editor of the late Fredonia Censor, oldest paper in Chatauqua Country, had lived. His portrait looked down from above one of the mantels in the gracious parlors of the Greek Revival house, its antique furnishings reflected in handsome gold mirrors. The atmosphere was sophisticated, but tempered with a lack of pretentiousness not always found in the city.

Mrs. Wheelock, in pale blue satin, served curried chicken from a Georgian silver chafing dish onto heirloom plates in the blue and white dining room.

Then the autos wound around the college's Ring Road, past hundreds of newly-planted Red Maple and Lombardy poplar trees which had been set down on a campus whose enrollment had risen from 750 to 4250 in the past decade, and which today is nearly 5000.

Before them stretched the monumental Michael C. Rockefeller Art Center, named after the Governor's late son, its 120,000-square-feet of reinforced, cast-in-place concrete white against the night. Alighting from their cars, the music lovers of the area, both in and outside the college, trailed across the great outer court and entered the center to attend opera.

Behind the scenes of the 400-seat, superbly equipped theatre - "We say we could give Ben Hur here," said one student, in ultramodern dressing and make-up rooms, one of two alternate casts were rouging, draping mantillas and unfurling capes.

A few minutes before curtain, they assembled in the "Green Room" - it would put many a New York theatre's to shame - and Director Richard Levitt, instructor of voice and director of opera at the college, called them into "a circle of friendship" in which they joined hands and voices in "One for all and all for one," and the whimsical good luck admonition of the theatre - "Break a leg!"

The 38-piece orchestra of young men and women filed into the pit. Dr. Richard Sheil, conductor and musical director, raised his hands for the overture, and with the rise of the curtain, "culture," in full dress, had come to Fredonia.

## SWAMPING

"This is the forest primeval" is true alright about the Bergen Swamp in Genesee County, N.Y., one of the last dying gasps of the glacial Lake Tonawanda, about 20 miles southwest of Rochester.

In 1936, a group of 165 nature lovers, chartered by the State Board of Regents, bought 657 acres of the largely primordial swamp covering less than 5-square-miles. Aim of the Bergen Swamp Preservation Society, as they became known, was to preserve those acres - and the 1243 more they hoped to acquire - as "a natural scene in its full integrity," replete with plant and animal life; to offer access to students and to publish scientific and cultural information on the flora and fauna there.

The Society held an annual pilgrimage for amateur naturalists, and in 1965, I was assigned to it.

Surrounded by the rich reclaimed muck lands of Genesee County, the swamp has remained in virtually primitive condition. More than 2300 species of plant life have been found there. It is obvious that to the biologist, the geologist, the zoologist, the orthologist and the entomologist that the value of preserving Bergen Swamp is unquestioned. But what of the amateur naturalist? The three-hour pilgrimage through the swamp itself answered that question.

"You can get away from everything: people, hot dog stands, gas stations," Dr. W.C. Muensher, professor of botany at Cornell University, the Thoreau of the Bergen area, told the more than 125 pilgrims, composed of both adults and children, at a picnic lunch on the banks of Black Creek, one of the swamp's feeders, before starting off. "You can be by yourself, get out in the woods, see nobody, be near nobody. You can see a red fox or two, a hummock of moss - see almost anything."

I have never been a very outdoorsy person; thickly populated areas were my natural and working environment. The hummocks of moss sounded cozy, but a red fox or two - outside a zoo - was a bit startling.

The pilgrimage party was dressed in every conceivable garb. Rubbers, galoshes and fishing boots. Military puttees over stout shoes. Army khaki dungarees and pedal pushers. Windbreakers, mackinaws and hunting shirts. Hunting caps and bandannas. I wore an old suit and galoshes.

The experienced naturalist had often brought along his kit containing guidebooks, a compass, knife, fly dope, tape measure, gloves and a drinking cup. An 8-x-6-inch magnifying glass to better view small plants and insect life might hang about his neck.

Here is the heart of my report:

Climbing a small hill past a sweeping field of dandelion, we approached the swamp area from the south. Outside the air was fresh and sweet with clover. Once we stepped into the woods, the pungent damp scent of forest took over.

A rim of hardwood, birch, maple and elm towered overhead. It shaded forests of lesser vegatation. The mandrake or May apple, with its parasol-like leaf and its roots which, some say, make good jelly, Canada violets, red columbine, humble catnip.

Heretofore, the trail has been negligible. But now a narrow path begins to appear, bordered with occasional stones. The creamy bunchberry, a dwarf species of dogwood - it only stands about 10 inches high - and feathery foamflowers trace the way.

The woods seem to maze at this point. The air becomes damper and leafier. One is conscious of the contour of the trees, gray stumps uprooted by heavy winds, straight-standing, knarled, leaning and fallen trees.

The wild lily-of-the-valley appears. And the birds break the hush. A warbler offers a serenade.

Denser grows the wood. The roots of the big trees vie with an old corduroy road to form the path. The moss is like carpeting in the lobby of a fine hotel. Small creepers embroider rotting cedar trunks. The air is lush.

We press on to the marls (crumbling earth deposits). The trails now fairly squish with moisture under our feet.

Here, the blue-green and green algae have absorbed the lime for centuries, leaving vast deposits in their wake. Here - owing to the type of soil and climatic conditions - we found the Labrador Tea and the leatherleaf, plants usually thriving in Arctic climates. Here, too, are the Phragmites (tall, thin-stemmed grasses) and arrow grass, more often found by the ocean.

Encircled by a wood of stunted trees and shrubs, including white pine, arborvitae and dwarfed tamaracks - the latter more than 100 years old, but only a few feet high - the pitcher plants raise their spouts from soft hummocks of reindeer moss. Nearby is the sundew. Pitcher plants and sundew are carnivorous plants which arrest and absorb the intruding insect.

A trail of muck, so wet and deep it fairly cries out as the pilgrim plunges in, leads around a bend. Anything may lie beyond. It does. There in a slight opening shines the white lady's slipper, a wild orchid, loveliest and shyest of wood blossoms.

The question of the value of preserving Bergen Swamp for all times seemed answered."

## A DAY IN THE COUNTRY

Sylvia Wilson, 8, of the inner city of Buffalo, had never picked a daisy until one day in June, 1968. She stood in a meadow on the Russell Berryhill farm overlooking the Colden hills and inspected the flower with wonder.

All around Sylvia, 59 other boys and girls from Public School 39 were taking in so much wonder they were fit to burst: blue sky, white clouds, pure, fresh air and grass, grass, grass!

The children were one of the farm tours conducted by the Board of Education under the "Plus Program," an enrichment program for school children in core areas or the inner city, made possible by the Federal Elementary and Secondary Education Act of 1965. Three thousand, five hundred city children would see the country on nearly 50 farms in Erie County under the program that Summer.

Sylvia and her companions were the first of six school groups which were to come to the 112-year-old Berryhill farm.

"Keep it cool!" called Farmer Berryhill as the excited-eyed first and second grade children piled out of the yellow school bus into his barnyard, about 11 o'clock.

Jean, his wife, whose mother was born on the farm, made a little introductory speech about the horses, cows and pigs they would see, and the food raised to feed them.

The children were allowed to run their hands through buckets of wheat and oats and to handle the dried ears of corn.

"It's scratchy," said Karen Williamson, wrist-deep in oats.

They toured the commodious hip roofed barn - how dark and cool...They climbed the pigsty fence.

The calf was led into the barnyard so that more of them could pat him at one time. But even then he wasn't large enough, and admirers stood two rows deep waiting their turns.

Then they clambered into the hay wagons for a trip across the farm. The children on one wagon waved to those on the other, and pretended the tractor-drawn drays were racing.

Up the mud trail, past the orchard with its aged apple trees, over the shallow stone-edged creek, higher and higher than the land beneath them. Hobo and Taffy, the farm dogs, ran on ahead.

Black cattle stood along the way, mooing. The children mooed back.

"They're saying 'Hi!' to us," explained Cary Boyd.

"Old MacDonald had a farm...E-I-E-I-O!" sang the children as the wagons ascended the slope.

The hilltop of 1500 feet was reached.

"All those mountains..." said Dale Harris, awed.

The children bounded from the wagon, and ran like rabbits down the hill to a small pond, coats open, sweaters flying.

After lunch, some played "Here We Go 'Round the Mulberry Bush" on the crest of the hill.

They rode back by way of the wood, abloom with wild hawthorne. Houses drew their share of attention as they neared the farmhouse. And there, in the barnyard, stood the yellow bus.

## THE CREEKS

There comes a time in the life of a reporter when he becomes so sensitized to the scene around him that even his daily enviroment suggests stories. It is like tuning in on a visible music that flows around one, waiting to be recognized and recorded. It need not have anything to do with human behavior, local or national events, the usual generators of news - politics, theft, assault, murder, discorvery of some new scientific bonanza, or even formalized art. It can be gentle thing that is experienced in every-day life, heretofore unnoticed, but now suddenly illumined by the reporter's consciousness of it.  Such stories often involve more intake than output.

I had driven past the creeks - all seven of them - on the way to Niagara Falls, Ont., scores of times.  One October day, I saw them. Photographer Bob Stoddard came out and took pictures, reminiscent of the late great photographer, Wallace Nutting, to illustrate this little story.

I think a very small percentage of the thousands who traveled the ancient willow-shaded Niagara Parkway to the Falls each year, knew anything about the creeks, perhaps even noticed them.  Few people with a fine river view to enjoy stop and read the markers standing by them.  Perhaps my "seeing" them, helped some see them too.

"The placid Canadian creeks which flow into the wide, swift river, along the Niagara Pkwy., murmur an almost inaudible message these days - that peace outlives men and wars.

In Elysian quiet, broken only by the voices of people living on their banks, the putt-putt of a motorboat or the passing motorist, they wind gently, sometimes lethargically, into the great stream that catapults over Niagara Falls.

This autumn, when field and wood from which they flow exult in red and gold, and the purple aster stands sentinal by the gray rocks at their mouth, is a fine time to visit these winding vistas of tranquility.

There is an invigorating freshness in the air, and the fans of sumac vie with berries underfoot in brilliance.

The waters of Frenchman's, Chippewa and Ussher's Creeks once rang with gunshot, flowed with blood and echoed death cries of soldiers in the War of 1812.

On Frenchman's Creek, where the beach plums are ripe and the river breeze whips the willows into flowing veils, Americans made their second attempt to invade Canada along the river.  They were forced back.

At Chippewa and adjoining Ussher's Creek, the British were trounced, but vindicated themselves three weeks later at Lundy's Lane.

Frenchman's Creek commemorates the French who settled on the Frontier before 1759.  Chippewa, of course, is an Indian name.

Ussher's Creek was named after Capt. John Ussher, a retired British naval officer, who settled in Canada at the close of the 18th Century.

Boyer's and Baker's creeks are named after United Empire Loyalists who migrated from the United States after the American Revolution.

Miller's Creek derives from the four Miller brothers, who emigrated to Canada in the 1789s from Pennsylvania.

Black Creek was christened so because its waters are so dark.

A fur trading post, shipyard and portage terminus animated one or another of the creeks.

And the sound of marching feet along the dirt road beat steady accompaniment.

Now all is quiet. Only the rusty soldiers of oak and beech line the road; old willows weep silently into the river.

The creeks flow under gray or brown stone-arched bridges in varying moods; as a looking glass for trees along the banks, or marshy inroads into adjoining fields.

Here and there a weathered boathouse or pier, a moored craft or the water rippling in the wake of a small boat pattern their surface. And always the jubilant confetti of leaves.

Inevitably, like the future, the creeks bend into the unknown, the mysterious.

Both sides claim to have won the War of 1812. Today, it doesn't seem to matter so much. To the creeks belong the victory, as they flow seaward - in peace."

# 39

# Every House Is A Story

THE ARCHITECTURE OF western New York falls into three periods: Post-Colonial, circa 1810-1825, Victorian, 1837-1901, and Contemporary. The American Revolution, in which I had been so sociologically and historically indoctrinated, is, with the exception of forts and outposts, not represented.

Do not be mistaken, however. There were many 17th and 18th Century settlements in the Great Lake region, both in the United States and Canada and further West, as well as those of esteemed Jamestown, Va., (1607), and Plymouth Rock, (1620). The difference is that such settlements were the outreach of explorers, missionaries and fur traders, rather than homesteaders.

An historical map composed under the direction of Col. C.H. Morrow, 28th Infantry, U.S. Army, in 1932-33, from an original in the Historical Institute of Old Fort Niagara at Youngstown, N.Y., where La Salle erected a blockhouse in 1769, shows numerous exploration sites and colonizations before the French and Indian Wars, the North Colonial wars between Great Britain and France from 1689-1763. And lest Virginia and Massachusetts get too cocky, let's not forget that Jacques Cartier, first explorer of the Gulf of St. Lawrence and discoverer of the St. Lawrence River - although he established no settlements - gained the site of both modern Quebec and the present city of Montreal in 1535-1536.

It was my interest and pleasure to visit nearly 50 of these houses for the *Buffalo Evening News*. Houses of pioneers made from the once surrounding forest; log cabins and veritable mansions which had developed from cabins; houses designed by the country's top architects; houses of small town leaders; houses of corporation executives and houses of statesmen. A long enriching historical and architectural pilgrimage.

"The Homestead," the William Perkins Wadsworth house in Geneseo, N.Y., which I have described, stands unmatched. Its mixed aura of pioneer settlement, spawning ground for statesmen, a steadfast family line and evolution as a fashionable hunting center is unsurpassed by any house I visited. The compressed attar of the place and its lively modern activity knows no equal in Western New York. But a wide spectrum beneath its composite height was spread out before me. All sorts of houses.

Behind the door of every house on any street is a drama, sometimes pacific, sometimes amazingly violent; sometimes filled with years of "patient" living, sometimes galvanized by questing restlessness. Each of these houses represented people - a life story involving joy, sometimes tragedy and occasionally mystery.

I have selected three, which I have not chosen solely for their architectural distinction, but for the period they represent, their story and occasionally, legend. With the exception of "Belvidere," which it is suspected was designed by Benjamin Henry Latrobe, who did the Capitol in Washington, they are not the "noted" houses of the area. My travels covered some more elaborate and sophisticated dwellings, done by nationally-known architects and sometimes belonging to more widely-known people, ones by Carrère, or Stanford White - most of which are now available to public inspection. The houses provided required special access a newspaper provided. Houses that reflected the life and architecture of the region over a prolonged period, houses often with a moving story.

Generally, the selectees mirror the indigenous quality and variety of Western New York and Ontario dwellings, and I hope will serve to tell others, in other parts of the country, of the aura and distinction of life in an area that has been sadly unheralded, and about which there is a great ignorance throughout the land. Some of the property has changed hands, and one house at least, has become a museum. But it is unlikely that abodes so innate to a region do not remain preserved, gallantly facing time and change. I have kept their stories current, however, while noting the date upon which I visited each of them.

## THE PINK HOUSE

"The Pink House," in Wellsville, Allegheny County, New York, is as Victorian as a moss rose pressed in a copy of Thomas Moore's *Irish Melodies.*

One of the Italian or "Tuscan" villas which effervesced throughout the East in the wake of increased European travel, it was built in 1869 by Edwin Bradford Hall, grandson of William Bradford, second governor of the Plymouth Colony. (When Back Bay Boston or corresponding Eastern locales glance patronizingly toward the West, it behooves them to remember that *all* the Colony did not remain in New England. The United States is dotted with families who hoisted sail on the Mayflower or its successors, and who eventually found the overpopulation of rocks and people in the

Northern Seaboard States just too many, and moved westward as far as they cared or could afford to go in search of more tillable ground and wider spaces.)

Young Hall, a native of Fairfield, Conn., came to Wellsville in 1852, and established a drugstore. Business flourished. He also is said to have done well selling whiskey during the Civil War, having bought it before the conflict when the excise tax was low.

After the war, Mr. Hall and his wife made the Grand Tour, and upon their return he personally designed his luxurious house. The builder is unknown. No pains nor expense were spared.

When the house was built, Edwin Hall had it painted pink - a lavender pink with a zinc-base formula mixed in his drugstore, which remains a secret to this day. The house never has been any other color, and the paint is still mixed (according to that formula) in Hall's drugstore, which continues in operation in Wellsville today.

A circular driveway leads up to the Pink House which is set in about three acres of lawn, planted with a small arboretum. The property originally was surrounded by a wooden spindle fence, punctuated by several gates.

Two classic, hollow-lead figures, painted white, hold aloft cornucopias (emblems of abundance) at today's entrance, set in a privet hedge. The driveway curves around a plot, in which a round flower bed circles about a cast-iron fountain.

The house stands on a terrace, with stone steps flanked by a large pair of moulded-lead lions leading up to it. Formerly, the lions were yellow, but as they seemed to frighten the horses, they later were painted a bluish-gray.

Built of wood and completely insulated with sawdust, the Pink House is hung with ornamentally-railed balconies and porches, crowned with medallions and a wide fringe of jigsaw work.

It is two stories, with a balconied observatory. Before the great variety of trees on the property grew so high, fires in the town could be easily spotted from its height.

A finial, Turkish in design and topped by a crescent moon, crowns the tower.

One enters the Pink House by a double ash door, topped with a strikingly simple yet beautiful transom. Edwin Hall was a connoisseur of wood, both in the trees he planted and the lumber he used for doors and woodwork in his house. Original building specifications state:

"All doors to be made of best quality clear seasoned chestnut...mouldings to be seasoned black walnut...All stairs to be built of clear seasoned chestnut. The newels to the main stairs to be black walnut and chestnut combined..."

In the front hall, a bronze figure of a cavalier on the main newel post at the foot of the staircase, holds a ruby glass-shaded lamp aloft to the glory of the house.

As a cucumber wood railing sweeps upward in a straight course, it is supported by hand-turned balusters. Carved clusters of grapes and nuts ornament each bracket. The flight becomes serpentine as it mounts to the observatory.

Downstairs ceilings are 11-1/2 feet high, doors 8 feet, 4-1/2 inches. The drawing room, now known as "The Blue Room," but formerly referred to as "The Parlor," fulfills the ornamental promise of the exterior of the house. Double carved wooden arches, between which hangs a graceful globular finial, bisects the ceiling. Pilasters, exquisitely carved by Frederick Gaede and his son, Otto, local German artisans, in an idyllic design, including calla lilies, ivy and birds, topped by medallions, rise from rope molding to flank the arches. The room is embellished with elaborate gold leaf cornices over the double arches and windows, and mirrors and pier glasses at either end are matching gold.

A large white marble mantel in the front section supports 4-foot alabaster vases, which are attached to it, creating a pristine picture. Mr. Hall imported them from Italy. Pierced brass chandeliers form filigree reflections in the pier glasses.

The Victorian furniture and draperies in the "Blue Room" are done in pale blue satin, as they have always been. Little gilt chairs, decorated with colored sprigs of flowers, add an airy note. They were painted by a sister of Mrs. Hall, who also executed an arch of pale pink roses about the front pier glass.

The floricultural motif is further enhanced by a gilt cabinet to the rear, displaying a set of painted flower plates done by Mr. Hall's only child, Mrs. J. Milton Carpenter, who occupied the house for 88 years.

Mrs. Carpenter liked to dine on those plates, each of which features a different flower - i.e., wild rose, damask rose, violet, clover blossom and lilac - at least once a year.

Across the hall is the living room with black marble mantel. It opens into a music room, added between 1875-80, to accommodate the grand piano.

Distinguishing features abovestairs include gold leaf cornices in the four bedrooms, and the enchanting custom of painting each section of the wide, moulded door casings a different pastel color.

The house, built in a day when huge wardrobes were the thing, has bedroom closets.

Like the house, the outside buildings are rare and engaging. In addition to his home, Edwin Hall was deeply interested in collecting fossils, a fad in those days. By train, stage, horse and buggy, and hiking cross-country, he explored a large part of the southern tier of New York and the northern part of Pennsylvania to collect more than 5500 sponges, which 300,000,000 years ago, lived on the floor of the upper Paleozoic seas, at that time covering the greater area of the North American continent. The collection was awarded a first prize at the Pan-American Exposition in Buffalo in 1901. It was presented to the Carnegie Museum by Mrs. Carpenter.

The 30-by-60-foot private museum where Edwin Hall kept these rare sponges still stands on the property.

And it is pleasant to sit in the summer house that Mr. Hall built, like one in New York's Central Park, and muse on days when sunburn was unfashionable and nights when the moon prompted "courting," rather than scientific investigation.

The Pink House has had its share of sorrow, in legend and fact.

The legend: In the mists of the past which veil the house lived the daughter of a rich lumberman, who fell in love with a boy from the "wrong side of the tracks." Her name was Mary Frances. The girl's father had no time for the boy and wanted his daughter to marry a prosperous druggist, who also sold paint and other sundries. He was considerably older than the girl.

Desperate, the father forged Mary Frances' name to a letter sending the youth on his way. The pair became estranged, and a day was set for the girl's marriage to the druggist. By chance, the boy and girl met the day before the wedding, and the truth was out. Next morning, a corpse was found in the millrace running through the lumberman's property. It was the body of Mary Frances.

*Pauline*, a long narrative poem by Hanford Lennox Gordon, a poor boy from the wrong side of the Wellsville tracks, appeared in 1873. It tells the story of a girl and a boy whose romance was cut short by a letter fabricated by the girl's father. The girl drowned herself on the morning of the day set for her wedding to an older man whom she did not love.

A Mary Frances Farnum lived in Wellsville before the Civil War. She died in young womanhood. It was her sister, Antoinette, who became the bride of Edwin Bradford Hall, the town's first druggist.

The fact: A pool around the fountain on the front lawn of the Pink House today is filled with flowers instead of water. A 2-year-old grandchild of Edwin Hall fell in and drowned there as he sat on the porch, paralyzed with fright and unable to come to her aid or call help.

It is for such memories, that the Pink House at Wellsville, N.Y., sheds its jigsaw tears.

July 15, 1963

## BELVIDERE

Elegant and mellow - yet with the eternal freshness of beauty - stands "Belvidere" on the Genesse River, near Angelica, in Allegheny County, N.Y., one of the most imposing houses in the state. The pines on its 200 acres sigh; the river murmurs, and a meaningful silence speaks of a century-and-a-half of American life under its famous roof.

Its 13 hearths roar against the winter wind and sleep is sweet in any one of its ten bedrooms. Wrap us in your cloak of serenity, venerable house; share with us your story!

The 100,000 acres, of which you once were a part, were settled by Capt. Philip Church, U.S. Infantry, Eton-educated son of one John B. Church, an Englishman, who sympathized with the Colonies in the Revolution.

The senior Church was in the Commissary Department of Jean Baptiste de Rochambeau, the French general who fought for America. John Church married Angelica Schuyler, beautiful daughter of Gen. Philip Schuyler of Albany. She was the sister-in-law of Alexander Hamilton.

Philip Church and his father obtained the Genesee Valley tract of 100,000 acres at a foreclosure sale in 1800. Robert Morris, financial backer of the Revolution, had borrowed $880,000 from the senior Church and put up the land for security. The Churches paid $81,679 for the land.

Philip established the village of Angelica, N.Y. - named after his mother - and set aside a fine site, about 150 feet above a bend in the Genesee, on which to build a summer house for his parents.

He was living there in a temporary two-story, white frame house - the first painted house west of Canandaigua - in 1804, when news reached him that Alexander Hamilton had been shot by Aaron Burr.

A year later, Philip married Anna Matilda Stewart, daughter of Gen. Walter Stewart of Philadelphia, who was an aide-de-camp to George Washington. In fact, young Church met his future bride at Washington's funeral.

He brought her and a Quaker cook back to the "White House," as the temporary house at Belvidere was flatteringly called. And here his parents, who had led a highly sophisticated and elegant life in England and France, (for example, Mrs. Church Sr. had known Mme. de Stael in Paris), visited them in summer.

The senior Churches came with an entourage to the wilderness, including a French chef named Godey, father of Louis Antoine Godey, founder of Godey's Lady's Book. Such elegancies, as well as Philip's rising position as a land developer, called for more prestigious housing.

About 1807, the big house was started. Some authorities believe it was designed originally by Benjamin Henry Latrobe, who did the Capitol at Washington.

The *Dictionary of American Biography* says: "Even before going West, Latrobe had furnished designs for houses beyond the mountains, such a 'Belvidere,' the home of John Barker Church and his wife, Angelica Schuyler, in the upper Genesee Valley."

Similarity of the floor plan of Belvidere to that of "Adena," early governor's seat at Chillicothe, Ohio, built by this master architect, also bears out this statement.

The 27-room Federal (or Post-Colonial) mansion is approached by a winding drive through towering maples, elms and pine. Even in the midst of such horticultural splendor, sighting it is a breathtaking experience.

Belvidere faces the river, its four massive yet slender Ionic white wooden columns supporting a handsome matching cornice with lofty classicality.

The house is of mellowed brick - remnants of the kiln have been found on the place - and of stone, probably from a large quarry across the road. Combination of the stones gives fascinating variety. Bricks have grown rosy, stone silvered. Two stone wings flank the main structure where ceilings rise to 13 feet.

White pine felled in the forest, which covered the area when Philip Church arrived, composes joists, beams, trim and the magnificent pillars themselves.

The fan window-topped front door, paned in medallion-patterned leaded glass, was brought by later owners from England. It is at the back of the house in a recessed porch with lower pillars.

Shutters are of fairly dark green, and the many-paned, high downstairs windows, overlooking the river, are constructed in three sections, as at Monticello. An elliptical, leaded glass window in the pediment is unusual in that it is placed vertically, instead of horizontally.

The Church family occupied the house for more than 80 years. It was bought in 1947 by Robert B. Bromeley, publisher of *The Bradford Era*, and his wife, the former Marian Grow.

In addition to installing gas and electricity as well as central heating in Belvidere - for the first time - they have done research on the history of the house in libraries and museums throughout the country.

The Bromeleys have redone the handsome interior in soft Williamsburg colors and reproductions of historic wallpapers. The hallway, from which open the 17-x-22-foot drawing and dining rooms, has Williamsburg blue woodwork. The wallpaper in the red damask-curtained, moss green carpeted drawing room is a replica of one used at Mount Vernon in 1800.

Mr. and Mrs. Bromeley have retrieved as much of the original furnishings as possible to date, exposed original oak floors, revitalized fireplaces with their pleasing Colonial paneled mantels and plaster hearths (a bake oven in the kitchen hearth still works!).

Excavation of a disposal pit on the grounds disclosed fragments of Bell Flower glass and Lowestoft china, the pattern used at Belvidere. Corner cabinets in the gold damask-curtained dining room display pieces of these patterns, as the Bromeleys collect them.

A rare, nine-sided barn and carriage house, built of brick similar to the house by Philip Church, now shelters a few fine hunters on which Robert Bromeley rides to hounds with the Genesee Valley Hunt.

The seven-sided teahouse by the river's edge, which Church also constructed, still stands, and the garden of Belvidere, occupying about an acre, is still planted according to an 1851 plan - fragrantly encircled with lilacs, climbing roses, sweet William, phlox and pinks as the season progresses.

Stories of unidentified footsteps along the great porches of this historic house have wandered down through the years. Old Man Genesee River who "don't say nothin', but must know sumpthin'" probably recognizes them - but won't tell.

August 20, 1963

## BRECKENRIDGE-HAWLEY HOUSE

This is a story of a dying old house and a man who restored it to life.

"Put a match to it!" said several friends of Frank McD. Hawley, when he bought the Georgian-Colonial homestead of the

Breckenridge family at 392 Mississauga St., Niagara-on-the-Lake, Ontario, 10 years ago.

Mr. Hawley, wiry, debonair vice-president of the W.S. Tyler Co. of Canada Ltd., St. Catharines, Ontario, smiled, and in the quiet, determined British way began to restore the house to its former glory.

Today, the Breckenridge-Hawley House, built in 1800, with land deeds dating back to 1796, is one of the few in the country which has been restored as a private dwelling with museum techniques.

"There are two ways to restore," says Frank Hawley, standing before his house with justifiable pride, "to restore it as it was and use it as a museum, or to restore it for contemporary living by an average family.

"I chose a happy medium - to restore this house so it would be a museum piece, yet serve the purpose of a dwelling. And by taking this medium view, the life of the house has been promoted for years to come."

Mr. Hawley feels he had learned from the experience that you have to take the bull by the horns when you undertake the difficult task of recreating the past and stay with it - or lose a pile of money.

"You've got to be dedicated in order to pursue a restoration, to see it through," he explains. "You can't take halfway measures."

"Say you can't find brass doorknobs of the period (I did, at a nationally-known Pennsylvania brass designer); and you compromise and get china ones.

"It doesn't work. You'd never be able to liquidate the property at anything like the price you invested. It wouldn't have truth."

As many people are restoring old houses today, I am giving Mr. Hawley's experience in full, with the hope that they may find some guidelines for their own renovations.

He has been assisted in the long restoration - about six years of actual work - by two, now 70-year-old, master craftsmen, Lloyd Davis, a cabinetmaker, and William Hoare, a stonemason. Mr. Davis did all the carpentry and cabinetwork in the house and coach house, and Mr. Hoare, all stone and brickwork.

"There was no contract," explains Mr. Hawley, "no 'go go' slapdash. A work fund was established, from which the men drew their salaries on a time basis."

Before starting the restoration, Mr. Hawley visited the curator of Williamsburg, Virginia, who instructed him in points which might reveal something of importance about the house, as the work progressed, and gave him considerable literature on the subject.

The house originally had six rooms, including two bedrooms and a wig room, but in 1840, four more bedrooms, and additional kitchen and pantry space were added at the rear.

Clapboard with slot bricks put between the studs is the building material used throughout. The old part stood on a 2-foot-deep dry wall which caused it to sink in wet weather, leaving the hearths higher than the floors. First move was to raise it on hydraulic jacks, dig down two additional feet and build a stone and block wall. The section was then lowered onto its new foundation. Brick steps and paths were restored with bricks from Williamsburg.

The breach in the asphalt tile roof between the old and new sections of the house disclosed that the original roof was of cedar shingles, which were again applied. Here are some subsequent developments in the restoration of the interior of Breckenridge-Hawley House:

FLOORS - Original northern white pine ones were scraped down and hand-sanded; filled in with two applications of half boiled linseed oil and half turpentine, applied with jute rags and finished with two coats of straight beeswax paste.

WALLS - Original plaster of lake sand and lime mixed with eggs generally was still sound and hard. Six to eight coats of paint and as many as 27 layers of wallpaper were removed for new paint and paper. Any patching required was done with an old formula plaster to prevent shrinkage.

WOODS - Two originals are pine and black walnut. All pinewood paneling, doors and trim were stripped of old paint "to recapture old moldings and show delicate details." Six to eight coats of paint, some of its made with buttermilk which adheres like cement, were removed. All damaged, lacking or missing trim was reproduced in the old manner with molding tools, ground to the existing trim.

HARDWARE - Doors were leveled, some would not even shut, and all 18th Century cast-iron fittings, including a carpenter lock about 1800, with the seal of George III, and box and rattail hinges were repaired or replaced by custom-made replicas.

STAIRCASE - The 13 sagging-stepped flight with broken stringer (horizontal timber supporting tred and risers) was entirely reconstructed; the black walnut rail was polished to a glow.

FIREPLACES - Five, including a great 4-x-5-foot country kitchen one with bake oven and fire pit at side, had bricks repointed.

WINDOWS - All original glass left in, but later glass removed and replaced with old, collected by Mr. Hawley from Canada to Virginia.

GUTTERS - Original wooden trough gutters and downspouts reproduced by hand, in copper.

SHUTTERS - The house has 13 windows. Six of the original pairs of shutters were repaired and seven pair made to match them. They were painted the original bottle green.

As a concession to modern living, Frank Hawley turned the old kitchen into a "country one, or study," and installed a modern kitchen in the old pantries. All cabinetwork, however, is a strict reproduction of that in the old kitchen, even to the wooden dowels in cupboards. Pine that Mr. Hawley's grandfather had harbored in a barn about 100 years ago composes the woodwork. (Apparently it's in the blood.)

Inconspicuous perimeter heating emanates from a furnace in the old root cellar, which also houses utilities. Modern copper plumbing and electrical wiring have been installed throughout.

Other liberties taken with the house are a wig room, now converted into a dressing room with cabinetwork of the period; the removal of a partition in a bedroom, which formerly shut off a space known as a nursing room, and the adaptation of a former blanket box into a cedar chest.

In the course of restoration, Breckenridge-Hawley House yielded its surprises. Prize surprises were a set of sterling flat silver and miscellaneous pieces from London and Edinburgh, dating as far back as 1731; a pewter grog mug, circa 1780, an early sterling pepper shaker and sugar tray.

The cache was found between the ceiling of the old kitchen and a bedroom above, carefully wrapped in oiled paper of the type used for meat.

Speculation on why the cache was hidden ranges from pressure of the War of 1812 or the Fenian Raiders, to departure of the house's former master on an extensive trip.

A knothole gave up a salt spoon; the garden, the key to the back door's lock, and the ground, a bladeless handle of one of the six knives in the silver set, for which Mr. Hawley had a blade designed to match the others.

He has kept all woodwork in the house early Colonial off-white, except in the country kitchen, which is left in the original pine finish.

Wallpapers of the period and of a color originally used on the walls of the various rooms and halls are used. The house is furnished with family antiques. Period curtains are custom-made. Chandeliers are Waterford glass and French.

Breckenridge-Hawley House has one possession more precious perhaps than all the rest - a dated signature etched with a diamond ring on a glass pane of the china cabinet in the dining room. The date is 1876.

It is the initials of Edward VII, then Prince of Wales. Records show he lodged there overnight.

Well, princes, as well as George Washington, must sleep.

August 10, 1968

# Part XI

# Ripe Unto Harvest

# 40

## Light And Shade

IT HAD BEEN MY PRIVILEGE, indeed my aim, to cover a variety of assignments. I like the carrousel, the kaleidoscopic color of different phases of life. I have had assignments that embraced deep sentiments of a community, and those as light as beer froth.

So, as my story draws to a close, I have gathered together some featherweight in subject, some profound. Among many, they have stood out, reflective of the life and eulogy around me. The gamut.

### LORD BLEARS AND I

Every once in a while, tongue in cheek, an editor gets tired of assigning the usual people to certain types of stories. Chained to his or her desk, restive and probably regretful of not being able to cover it himself, he decides to break a link in precedent and send a different reporter to the scene.

The assignment of a woman to a story usually covered by a man, or visa versa, is an old ploy which generally slightly flatters the woman, but infuriates the male reporter; I recall the simmering rage of a very able one at having to cover "new Christmas toys." The following story was my turn at the reversed bat:

The sport of wrestling was in full swing in 3000 B.C. and it doesn't need any vitamins today.

Wrestling is an intimate sport. It's a lot cozier than boxing. It's a grand sport for people who like to go into a huddle.

Personally - a rousing wrestling match like the fracas Friday evening between Lord James Blears of Manchester, England, and Hungarian-born Sandor Kovacs in Memorial Auditorium reminds us of a seafood platter, one that's cooked while you wait.

The seafood plate consists of two crabs (at least that's how the wrestlers think of each other). They are lively and full of pep when they start cooking. But gradually they get softer, redder and more unconscious.

By the end of the match (or boil), they're lucky if they can wiggle a feeler. And the people who pay to go to wrestling matches or eat seafood dinners are really sorry if they can wiggle at all.

All the public cares about at that point is the tartar sauce.

Wrestling has some funny rules. We bet they would bewilder Emily Post. For instance, you can't throttle your opponent, pull his hair or kick him with your toe. But outside of that anything else goes. And you can kick harder with a foot than a toe anyhow. So you see, the sport has possibilities.

It is perfectly possible that you can get killed and get put under the daisies. But if you kick hard enough even then, you've still got a fighting chance.

We haven't felt so close to William the Conqueror (1066) for years as when Lord Blears strode through a hissing crowd to the ring Friday night. Incidentally, his 222-pound lordship is the real McCoy. The only son of Lord Blears, he traces his line back to 1170, only 104 years after William made his successful sortie against England.

Lord Blears - the name used to be Bleard - looked pretty medieval himself when he made his entrance. He appeared in a hinterland style black sateen tunic trimmed with silver and somebody's - we presume his own - family's crest on the chest. The tunic had a trim little silver sash. His wavy golden hair cascaded to his neck.

Mr. Kovacs, his opponent, an average mortal with no historic hangover whatsoever, was nattily attired in a turquoise blue bathrobe. But nobody noticed it particularly. He seemed pretty much alone in the ring.

Lord Blears, however, was accompanied by his adviser and manager, Capt. Leslie Holmes, who sat genteelly at the ringside in faultless dinner clothes, listening to the pleasant orchestration of flesh on flesh and flesh on wood throughout the evening.

Before his lordship joined in the round, he handed the captain his monocle which he had worn since entering the arena. He also doffed his tunic disclosing a fine physique and a pair of old-English brick-colored shorts. The audience jealously hissed. Mr. Kovacs modestly doffed his turquoise blue bathrobe, disclosing royal purple shorts.

The wrestlers started off by going into a friendly knot just to get to know each other again. Of course Lord Blears, who had won 17 successive previous matches here, had whipped Mr. Kovacs last week. But you lose track of a fellow in seven days.

It wasn't long before the floorboards began to groan in protest. The wrestlers answered right back with noises reminiscent of steaming kettles. They were a well-groomed, sunburned pair when they started out. But soon they were a brilliant lobster red.

Mr. Kovacs gave the British scion a good whack with his right foot; toes under control, of course. It had all the animation but none of the friendliness of an Hungarian folk dance. The British scion reciprocated with a whaling wallop on Mr. Kovacs' left flank - with the flat of the hand, of course. His lordship's curls were quite disarrayed by now.

The pair soon reached a seething sizzle, scrunching, scratching and slapping each other all over the place. They played hopscotch, leapfrog and the age old game of "let's-see-who-can-kill-each-other-first."

Every once in a while, his lordship would play dead. He'd lie still as Old Dog Tray. But he wasn't dead at all. He was just taking a short nap or something before he lambasted Mr. Kovacs over the ropes. And Mr. Kovacs returned the compliment by heaving his opponent into the lap of the audience.

Ropes don't count for much in a wrestling match, you know. But they are nice to hang on to get your eighth wind.

The object of all this rumpus, of course, was for one of the wrestlers to get the other's shoulders down on the floor for three seconds. It sounds easy. But it isn't.

Mr. Kovacs kicked his lordship in the face. (I don't understand it, do you, Mrs. Post?) But we warned you, the rules are peculiar.

By now the wrestling pair was articulating sounds reminiscent of a novice attempting to open a batch of clamshells. And the audience was roaring like the sea on Maine Coast rocks. Dinner was almost served!

"Don't baby him" yelled an enthusiast.

At this strategic moment, Lord Blears deemed it wise to confer with Capt. Holmes at the ringside. The audience didn't like this. Someone baptized the captain with a cooling spray of beer. The law removed the beer slinger from our midst. After all, this was a wrestling match, not a shot put contest.

The bell rang as Capt. Holmes shook the last drop of nut-brown ale off his vest. It was a draw. Mr. Kovacs' trainer helped him on with the turquoise bathrobe. His lordship was assisted into his tunic. (It zips up the back.)

As the metal slide zimmed into place, a woman in the audience watching the procedure turned to her neighbor: "Say Rose - that's class," she said.

## THE OPEN WINDOW

The bird with an injured wing does not always know it wants to fly. Sometimes, someone has to open a window. But once it leaves enclosure, how wonderful the world is!

It was that way with Barbara L. Miller, who today is running the Home Service Department of Buffalo Goodwill Industries. The department handles employment, social activity and special services for severely handicapped men and women.

"I was homebound for 27 years," says Miss Miller, from a wheelchair in her 153 North Division St. office. "I didn't know I wanted to get out."

"Seven years ago, my brother, Harold, saw a Goodwill exhibit at the Erie County Fair. He told them I crocheted doilies."

Goodwill Industries called on Miss Miller, daughter of Mr. and Mrs. Raymond S. Miller, 281 Hoyt St., and invited her to visit the plant.

"At first, I didn't want to go," she recalls, "then I said I would. But I lost my nerve, and had my mother called to tell them I couldn't."

Goodwill came again. And this time, they were successful in getting Miss Miller to come in for a few hours.

"I cut out a few aprons," she says, "and they asked me to come back. I said I'd think it over - but when I left, I knew I would."

She started to work in the agency two days a week. Goodwill shortly opened a party service to make favors on special order. It was Barbara Miller who designed many of the patterns. Ideas flew like bright butterflies from her mind to her fingers. She also showed marked managerial ability.

Soon, she became secretary of the Home Service Department, which she has run for eight months. It now has 146 severely handicapped men and women on its list. Whenever a new homebound person is referred to the agency, Miss Miller personally calls on him to see how he may be helped.

"We try to get him to come into the agency for evaluation, as I did," she explains, "to see if he can work here. There are a lot of people who think, as I did, that they are bound to their homes, when they're really not. I try to persuade them to see if they can come out."

She personally visits an average of five homebound men and women a week. Alfred Mercer, 87, an agency employee, drives her.

Some of her calls are new contacts, and on others she performs services for people who really cannot leave their homes - shopping, telephoning and writing letters.

If a person cannot come into the shop, she also helps him find a job he can do at home. It may range from stringing tags and knitting to watch repairing or typing.

More than 50 members of the Matinee Club, a social group of severely handicapped, meet under her leadership monthly at the agency. A women's volunteer committee provides transportation.

## MORE THAN "TIME PLANS"

Tucking a sprig of holly in our cap, and winding our muffler around one more time - extra tight - we went out on the town and asked it what Christmas means?

We got wonderful answers!

People say Christmas has become an emphasis on material things. Slippers for father, a new percolator for mother, a doll with a permanent wave, chemistry sets that could blow up a house.

But you'd be surprised.

Most everyone we asked "What is the meaning of Christmas?" gave us an answer that warmed the cockles of our heart.

We got answers from deep down, way below a new refrigerator or even the latest hi-fi, or the "time plans" that pay for them.

Postman George A. Smith of 66 Coburg Avenue looked a bit sheepish when we asked him. Then he forgot all about his heavy bag and said:

"Christmas is a time of joy!" (Right in the middle of Ellicott Square, too.)

Lost in a flurry of white at Adam, Meldrum & Anderson's handkerchief counter, salesgirl Antoinette D. Parente of 158 Davey St. murmured shyly: "Christmas is Christ's birthday."

Slapping the russet polish on our shoes, bootblack Louis A. Menza of 58 Virginia St., thought several minutes.

"Christmas means Christ's birthday...the joy of all the kids...and the reunion of families," he said.

("I didn't know I had it in me," he confessed afterward, looking a bit proud of himself. "It just seemed to rhyme and come out.")

Carpenter Frank H. Blazicko of 58 Newman St., Lackawanna, shivered in the wind despite his sheep-lined jacket. But he took time out to elaborate.

"We celebrate our own birthday," he said. "How much more must we celebrate Christ's birthday - who gave us life."

Have you noticed that so far we haven't heard a word about a new refrigerator?

Stoking the little coal burner of his chestnut barrow, vendor Mohammed Benali of 140 Broadway - a Moslem - was brief:

"Like it means to anybody - it's difficult to explain," he muttered through fragrant aroma.

In the quiet halls of the Lafayette Square Public Library, librarian Shirley B. Stowater of 80 Hill St., Tonawanda, reflected:

"Christmas is the high point of our religious year, for the promise it means in our Christian faith - the central part of it..."

"It's getting the family together," bus driver Roy Avey of 60 Orchard Ave., Blasdell, called over his shoulder, as he hurried to work.

He didn't mention comfortable slippers.

"The first thing I'm interested in is my grandchildren," reported butcher Edward H. Young, Stall 4, Washington Market. "I just pass by grown-ups who are able to care for themselves - but the missions, that's something different."

Bartender Mike Palermo gave his long mahogany counter in the Statler a meditative rub.

"The happiness we have at home getting prepared..." mused Mike, "the shopping my wife did (we wrapped all

our presents in November), and all our cards are written out
- it's the joy we have in doing these things."

"Hark! the herald angels sing, Mike!" we cried.

## WE TOO, NARCISSUS

Narcissus - the pinup-boy of Greek mythology - took a
look at himself in the waters of a fountain and decided he
looked like a million dollars.

After covering the Fall openings of about 50 clothes
designers in New York recently, we looked at ourselves in a
full-length mirror

We looked like two cents.

Action was imperative. We'd always wondered about
the claims of beauty salons to make women over. So - we
called up probably the best known one in the world and
made an appointment.

The place smells like just this side of Paradise. We
thought how easily we could just loll on an Empire sofa and
dream. But at half-past-nine the day was just beginning.

Clad in a French blue bathing suit and paper raffia
slippers, we found ourselves in the gymnasium,
confronting Miss M., our figure analyst. The gym was lined
with mirrors like a ballet practice hall. Mirrors are so frank.

We were glad to learn, however, that our problem was
typical. If we'd started a few years earlier, we could have
accomplished even more. But it was not too late! We were
not much overweight - just a bit plump in the wrong places.

"You can improve at any age, but if you start at 30 you
have a much better chance of retaining an ideal figure
through life," said Miss M.

"Once a woman has lost her figure completely - she can
never bring it back." Here she issued a warning: "Do not
progress in your reducing program any faster than you can
without loss of muscle tone. It's better to be a little stouter
and firm, than featherweight and flabby."

Our goal, we learned, was to have our lower hip
measurements the same as - or a little more than - our bust
measurements; our waist, 10 inches smaller than our bust.
This meant whisking an inch off the hips, and whittling two
inches off the waistline.

Miss M. advised three exercises a half-hour daily. "But it's better to do them five minutes each day than half-an-hour once a week," she cautioned. Here they are:

1. Fine for lower hips and thighs. Sit on floor and place right hand palm down on floor away from body. Roll as far as possible to the right; repeat on left side.

2. Great for upper thighs. Lie on floor and kick legs scissors fashion to and fro. Snip, snip!

3. Swell for upper arms. Clasp hands to form rounded circle over head and press back as far as possible. Move arms rhythmically from side to side.

Indians, it seems have the finest posture in the world. "A woman can be in perfect proportion according to tape measurements," Miss M. explained, "yet she can still not look well because her posture is poor."

Unlike the Mohawks, it seems, we were locking our leg muscles as we walked. We were bid to relax our knees slightly, pull in the base of our spine so that our backbone supported our abdomen, and keep our ears on a line with our shoulders - which in turn, should tally with our hip and ankle bones. Didn't the Delta Rhythm Boys sing a song about something like this?

Now we are ready to walk. In standing, we learned, our weight should be over the outer border and ball of the foot - not over the arch. In walking, our whole foot should touch the floor.

"You want to see a person - not her feet arriving." said Miss M. "Think of the whole body moving. Lead with the chest!"

Proudly - like a chieftain - we advanced.

Miss J. was waiting for us with two reducing remedies. We climbed up onto her massage table for a scientific Swedish workout. Miss J. was not rough - but she was firm.

Miss J. then led us into a pink-tiled tunnel. As we huddled at one end of the aperture, she riddled our frame with twin hoses. Nobody's hips could resist them.

Did you ever have your hair analyzed? It's pretty serious business. Muffled in a white dressing gown, we were escorted to the hairdressing salon. A consultation of four experts was held.

Our hair analysis was "dry ends and too long;" we'd been recuperating from a "poodle," and had been barber shy for months.

The crusade began.  A shampoo with fresh eggs in it. The scalp was scrubbed with a small brush.  Feeling too refreshingly liquid for words, we were finally baptized with a pink cream rinse to soften the hair.

The next step was to find a coiffure to suit.  The hair stylist, Mr. A., attacked the problem with a razor.  He made the hair about 2-1/2 inches long in front and cut the back just to the hairline.  (For Winter, the general minimum length is expected to run about 4 inches from the crown - but it's still Summer.)  A wide, fairly loose permanent was recommended.

Now came the most difficult moment of all.  We must look Miss I. in the face and have her tell us what was wrong with ours.  Miss I. has been looking women in the face for 15 years.  You can't be doublefaced (or chinned) with her.

Miss I. reported this:  Skin dry, chin and neck contours in need of "firming."  Emphasizing that beauty care is not costly if the cosmetics are properly applied (apparently some women use far too generous quantities), she instructed us on how to care for the face at home.

The usual routine takes 12 minutes - when you know how.  The five steps are cleaning your face, toning it up, lifting and firming it, smoothing it down and applying a foundation for your makeup.

Miss I. had some neat tricks.  Cotton pads dipped in ice water were used in applying cleansing cream and skin lotion. She made the mandatory upward and outward application motions into a rhythmic exercise.  She prohibited any patting around the eyes.  She advocated an occasional masque and hormone cream.

When it comes to makeup today - almost anything is possible.  If your nose is a bit long (most reporters' noses are), or your jaw a bit sturdy - you can do something about it.  You can apply a dark foundation to the areas you want to forget - and a light one to those you wish to accentuate.

Incidentally, brows should look natural, the most flattering neat line possible.  Eye shadow should accentuate the color of one's clothing, not the color of the eye.  Are you aware that each eye has about 100 lashes?  Cupid's bow lips are as passe' as horses.  Mouths are being built up at the sides, on both the upper and lower lip.

When it was all over at half-past-five, we stepped out on Fifth Ave.  Whittled of hip, streamlined of head, our 200 odd eyelashes casting a pleasant shadow on our shortened nose and new mouth - we strolled up to the Hotel Plaza's fountain.  We took a good look into its depth.  This time we, too, looked like a million, Narcissus.

## THE TRIUMPH OF WINNIE OHLANSCHLAGER

The institution for the care of the sick and the aged is a part of every general assignment reporter's experience.  From the elaborate nursing home with its real flat silver and private nurses to the long institutional wards of beds, the sights, sounds and antiseptics of which are familiar to us.  Here one finds loneliness, frustration, disablement, pain and senility.  Here are visitors and guides, well-meaning men and women earnestly striving to bring cheer and solace to people whose plight they can see, but do not fully understand.  Here are the chaplains who, in the face of an inexorable wall of confinement, day after day, often year after year, can only offer that freedom so difficult of attainment-freedom of spirit.

But such freedom is a possibility.  Here is one who was achieving it:

There are different kinds of victory in this world.  Victory at war, victory in sports and victory over personal weakness.

There is also victory over circumstance.

Mrs. Winifred Ohlanschlager, 79, a resident at the Erie County Home and Infirmary, is winning out in this field.

Day by day, she is making her life at the home a triumphant experience.

And the whole institution responds to her success:  Her cheerful voice; her courteous manner and her belief in the fundamental goodness of life.

"Winnie," as she is known to most of the residents, has lived among them since 1964, 8 years.  She is a widow with five children, 12 grandchildren and one great-grandchild.

A long trail of both good and bad times brought Winifred Ohlanschlager to the home.

We found her there, seated in her oversized wheelchair, a massive, smiling woman afflicted with arthritis for the past 20 years.

She was serving as receptionist at the entrance where visitors sign in.

"Good morning," she said brightly to men and women as they passed. "Sign here, will you?" indicating the register, "and please don't forget to put the section number in."

Mrs. Ohlanschlager began life in Jamestown, N.Y., as the daughter of an optometrist. She came to Buffalo as a girl, and for two years took nurse's training at Buffalo General Hospital.

In 1924, she was married to Charles Ohlanschlager, a house painter, and the couple had six children. Her husband died seven years later, when she was about to have her sixth child, leaving her with Marvin, age 10 months; James, age 2; Bobby, 3; Bertha, 4; and Charles Jr., 6. The sixth child died in infancy.

"After my husband died I had to go on welfare," Winifred Ohlanschlager recounts," but later I did anything I could - housework, washing and ironing and baby-sitting.

"I tried working nights at Spencer Lens Co. (now American Optical Co.) in the instrument division but I was too tired from the days, and I fell asleep."

But somehow Mrs. Ohlanschlager managed to raise her family. Charles and Bobby became mailmen, and James, an auditor. Bertha took up dressmaking and stenography. Marvin became a maintenance man at a local country club.

One by one, the children married and established homes of their one, except Marvin, who lived at home.

At age 60, she was stricken with arthritis. And it confined her more and more, until finally she was obliged to use a wheelchair.

"I knew I was helpless," she recalls, "that I needed help. All the others, except Marvin, had moved out and had families of their own; they couldn't be with me. And Marvin had to go to work. That's the whole thing in a nutshell. So I came here."

And so the adjustment began.

"I was a discouraged woman when I first came here," says Mrs. Ohlanschlager, shaking her head. "I was a Protestant then. But one day the Catholic chaplain, Father Walter Tomiak, came in to see me.

"He said 'Winnie, something's wrong here. How would you like to become a Catholic?' So I was baptized, and then Bishop Stanislaus J. Brzana - he's at Ogdensburg now - confirmed me.

"Maybe I'm old-fashioned, but I think religion is really beautiful, because it drew me out of despondency - the sadness I had here. This is something, somebody to cling to; it's something positive."

On Jan. 8, 1965 - Mrs. Ohlanschlager remembers the day well - she met James Hogan, 69. Another patient introduced them in the hall. "A most beautiful friendship developed between us," says Winifred. "It was a wonderful companionship."

Mr. Hogan had been a railroad freight man, and along the way had broken his neck. He didn't have much education, but Winifred taught him to read and write. They went to Mass and served on home committees together.

"He turned right to me," she says, "until the day he died."

Each Valentine's Day at the home, a king and queen are chosen.

Winnie and James were selected as king and queen on Valentine's Day, 1969. Mr. Hogan died last Dec. 26. Winnie wears the St. Jude medal he gave her and carries his picture in her pocketbook.

Today, on her own, Winifred Ohlanschlager looks out on her world with chin up.

"Many times, you forget all about her handicaps," says Rev. Robert H. Calvert, Protestant chaplain, who also is her friend. She makes a real social contribution to the home."

Adds Mrs. Magdalen M. Stafford, a social worker, "Mrs. Ohlanschalger's morale is always good."

As a receptionist, Mrs. Ohlanschlager serves three days a week, and receives a small recompense.

She is also a member of the Residents Council, composed of 20 representatives from each section of the home. The council listens to complaints from residents, discusses them and takes them up with the administration.

She attends the Tuesday morning sing-along of inspirational music. And she lends a hand to Mrs. Josephine Milozzi, aide in charge of the Remotivation Room, and tries to cheer up downcast patients.

Of herself, she says" "I have lived here for eight years, and I find the less complaints you make, the more you get done for you and the happier you are.  If you thank God for the blessings you get, you get a lot done for you.

"I can't tell you about the care - the beautiful care I've had.  Good food and good care.

"You don't demand too much of the girls.  You have to try to understand the type of girl you're dealing with. Sometimes she may be overworked and get ornery and tired.

"Yes, sometimes the days are very long.  But I spend a great deal of time praying; that helps more than anything else...

"You've got to realize that you're not the only one.  It's hard, I admit, it's awfully hard.

"I have tried to accustom myself to the situation; not to demand, and to pleasantly say 'Please' and 'Thank you.'"

Mrs. Ohlanschlager sees all her family at least once a month, and Marvin comes to dinner every Wednesday.

"They are good to me, they come when they can," she says.  "But they have their own families.  They help if I need it, but actually, I don't.  I have this job and my personal allowance through Social Security."

A visitor was approaching.  Winifred was all business. "Sign here, will you please?" she said, indicating the register.  "And please don't forget to write down the section, will you?"

## FOREST LAWN

One of the most challenging assignments of my time was that of the 101st anniversary of Forest Lawn Cemetery in Buffalo, which occurred after I had been in the city only a comparatively short time.

Situated near the center of town - the city had not been expected to expand so - it was naturally one of the most venerated sites in the area; it also was one of the most frequently visited.  Two hundred and sixty-seven acres, shaded by a great variety of trees - some of them dating back before the cemetery was founded in 1850 - and laced with fine drives, Forest Lawn seemed alive in the consciousness of Western New Yorkers in a way I never had experienced.  They walked and rode and had an active interest in the great variety of birds there.

Cemeteries to me had been heartbreaking places one visited on holidays, for short periods, to leave flowers or a wreath and say a silent prayer.  Forest Lawn was quite different, too, from the simpler Pennsylvania graveyards with their plain upright stones and

only an occasional mausoleum. Forest Lawn was a repository of
exquisite art.

How to approach a subject so entwined with the deepest feelings
of a community so new to me, so cherished by them?

But we must write:  Forest Lawn is surrounded by a high
wrought iron picket fence.  There are two entrances.  The main
entrance on Main Street has a magnificent  arched stone building
designed by Buffalo architect H. Osgood Holland, enclosing an iron
gateway.  The second entrance, at the opposite side of the grounds,
on Delaware Avenue, the city's finest residential thoroughfare, has a
towering ornamental iron portal set in two great stone pillars,
supporting splendid lamps.

I stood before the Main Street entrance and thought.  On a circle
of lawn between the street and the gate, a huge Japanese yew spread
its dark green branches against the backdrop of the entrance.  Later,
I wrote:

"A giant bush stands before a high, black iron gateway
at 1853 Main St.  Seasons come and go, but it grows there -
equally green in Summer and Winter.

"For the bush is a member of the evergreen family.  A
horticultural symbol of life.

"The bush watches over the eastern entrance to Forest
Lawn Cemetery. "Every morning for 101 years, the sun has
risen before this gate. "Every evening, too, it has sunk
before the cemetery's west gate, at Delaware and Delavan."

"Within the confines of this century of sunrises and
sunsets, within the enclosure of the high iron fence, lies the
story of Buffalo - its joys and victories, its sorrows and
defeats, its hope and its unwavering faith.

"It is a story that deals with men who went off to fight
seven wars.  The story of the development of the Niagara
Frontier.  The story of Buffalo's growth.  The story of its
cultural, industrial and financial progress.  And the story of
the attitudes and customs of a century."

Forest Lawn was started under private ownership with 80 acres,
but in 1850 evolved to the jurisdiction of a mutual company without
stockholders, who increased the land to 203 acres; later it embraced
over 50 more.

At the rededication ceremonies in 1867, it was proposed to set
apart sites there, to erect monuments recording "remarkable events
and memorable services."

Wars have left their memorials near the front gate of the
cemetery, where a guide and I began our tour.

"Eternal vigilance is the price of Liberty - One Country. The penalty of treason is death - No North - No South - The Union Forever," reads the inscription on the Grand Army of the Republic monument.

The Spanish-American War and two World Wars also are commemorated. Row after row of military graves surrounded these memorials, among them, in 1951, fresh ones from the Korean War.

We moved further into the cemetery beneath old stands of oak, elm and maple, and later plantings of such specialities as honey locust, Russian olive, crab-apple, sweet gum and Chinese Tree of Heaven.

One hundred thousand persons were buried in Forest Lawn, about 1200 more were laid to rest there each year in mausoleums, sarcophagi, tombs and under monuments and headstones - silent witnesses to the eras in which they were erected:

The simple boulder marking the grave of Erastus Granger, pioneer jurist and U.S. Indian agent for the Six Nations, the Iroquois Confederacy, who built a house on part of the grounds in 1809.

The historic black iron tomb of the Randall, Callender, Russell, Macy and Osborne families raised in 1855.

The Medina sandstone two-story Letchworth mausoleum, where wreaths of a different flower were carved on each marble tomb within, as it was filled.

In Forest Lawn too, rest: Millard Fillmore, 13th President of the United States; William G. Fargo, co-founder of Wells Fargo Express; Gen. Albert J. Meyer, founder of the U.S. Weather Bureau, and Jacob Schoellkopf, creator of Niagara Falls power development.

Perhaps, in every newcomer's entrance into a city, there is a moment or an experience which illumines the place he has come to, in contrast to the one he has left behind. This moment for me was as I stood before the life-sized marble statue of Tacie Hannah Fargo, a member of the pioneer express family, who died when she was not yet 2. It was domed in glass.

"Why?" I asked the guide.

"It's of Italian marble," he answered, "and we cover them to protect them from the cold."

A piercing moment.

The famous Blocher monument with its life-sized figures of parents standing by the deathbed of their only son also is enclosed in glass. But it is the image of that marble child under her glass cupola as the snow falls that lingers in the memory. In a way, it epitomized the character and courage of the northern city to which I had migrated.

The obelisk, which rose to prominence in the wake of the Washington Monument, towers in varying heights over Forest Lawn, including the grave of Millard Fillmore.

There were of course, thousands of simpler graves.

We walked on. And as we approached the west gate, the figure of the great Sachem Red Jacket loomed among the trees over his monumental tomb. It was proposed at those ceremonies years ago, to fetch his body and those of the distinguished Indian chiefs of neighboring tribes from their obscure graves to a place of honor in Forest Lawn.

The re-internment there, in the Fall of 1884, of the remains of Red Jacket and Seneca chieftains, Little Billy, Destroy Town, Tall Peter, Young King and Capt. Pollard, was one of the most significant and empathic native ceremonies an American community has experienced.

But the inscription on the Red Jacket Memorial adds painful overtones to the site. It reads:

"When I am gone and my warnings are no longer heeded, the craft and avarice of the white man will prevail.

"My heart fails me when I think of my people so soon to be scattered and forgotten."

We had come the length of the cemetery and were at the great ornamental west gate, with "Forest Lawn" carved in the stone lintel above it. I thanked my guide, and returned to the paper.

As I sat finishing the story, I wondered how I could end it. What I had written seemed so inadequate to the subject. How conclude it?

Then the words of Solomon, so often quoted at burial services, came to my aid, and I added:

"According to century-old custom, the gates of Forest Lawn are closed at sunset. The great lanterns by the Delaware Avenue gate are lighted. They burn far into the night - glowing symbols 'until the day break, and the shadows flee away'."

I could think of no better closing. But then another thought occurred to me - were those lamps lit? Did they actually glow in the dark? I telephoned the cemetery's director.

"No," he said, "they do not; they haven't been lit since the war. But, Miss Taussig, we'll see that they are."

Now, years later, if I happen to drive by Forest Lawn at night, I see them shining brightly in the dark.

## WHISTLES IN THE NIGHT

When a lonely train whistle rends the Buffalo air as a Penn Central train heads for New York, Ollie Laffoon and James Evans and a few other retired Pullman Co. chefs stir in their sleep and murmur things like:

"Two squabs coming up" or "Shell those peas."

Then they awake with a jolt, see the unswaying walls around them, and realize they're not aboard the Empire State or the Lakeshore Limited.

These grand old 18-or-19 car trains with their forest green mohair pullman seats, drawing rooms, spit 'n polish brass, fresh flowers, observation cars and even a manicurist are alive only in their memories.

Today, the two chefs work alternate shifts in the Forum Romano Restaurant, 57 Main Place. But both were true to railroading to the last.

Ollie Laffoon, 65, of 1283 Jefferson Ave., made the last run of the Empire State from Buffalo to New York, last Dec. 3, after 44 years on the road.

James Evans, 64, of 15 Debra St., wound up 42 years of Pullman service on the 20th Century Limited, from Chicago to New York, last Dec. 22.

Both men have that ineffable dignity and the air of authority that years of successful service in a chosen field brings. Their caps crown gracious, disciplined faces, molded by a way of life that has just about passed from the American scene.

"I started in the commissary on the North Western Railroad out of Chicago in 1920," recalls Kentucky-born Chef Laffoon. "In 1922, I went with the Baltimore & Ohio, on the Capital Limited between Chicago and Akron as third cook, broiling steaks and chops and ham.

"I went with the Central in 1925 on the Lakeshore Limited between Chicago and New York as second cook, making pies - fruit pies - and cooking chicken and meat.

"In 1928, I was made chef, doing the roasting, making sauces and supervising the waiters' orders. I also made soups. Thick mulligatawny (East Indian) soup was my favorite.

"It has a base of onions, apples and celery, you know, chopped fine. You put this in chicken stock with curry powder, and strain it off; garnish with rice and diced-up chicken."

Mr. Laffoon adds: "Yes, we had menus in those days. Calves' sweetbreads, Virginia ham, prime ribs, filet mignon, finnan haddie, baked squabs, Cornish hens, steaks, lamb chops and breast of guinea hen.

Mr. Evans, a West Virginian, started as a dishwasher in 1922 on a New York-Pittsburgh run.

"A year later, I was made third cook," he recalls, "handling the vegetables - they were all fresh, of course - we shelled our own peas, strung the beans and peeled our own potatoes."

In 1924, as second cook on the Buffalo-Pittsburgh run, he made the salads, dressings and soups. Consumme was his favorite.

"I really enjoyed preparing it. You take beef, chop it up, then mix eggs and eggshells with the meat; add bay leaves, salt and pepper, put on the stove and simmer; strain and cook, then pack in ice and serve jellied or hot."

By 1926, he was chef on the Empire. Finally, he was assigned to the Century.

Between them, Chefs Evans and Laffoon recall some colorful personages and scenery as, year after year, they steamed, then dieseled across the land.

Chef Evans - "Those sunrises leaving Yonkers," he comments, "and you know, I don't think there's anything more beautiful than the Palisades."

Chef Laffoon - "I was running when the cyclone hit St. Louis in 1927. We stopped the train on top of the MacArthur Bridge, across the Mississippi, until it was over."

Mrs. Eleanor Roosevelt - both their faces light up as they speak of her - she often got on the Empire at Poughkeepsie for breakfast. She liked a hearty one, ham and eggs - "always fried," and FDR rode frequently between New York and Albany. He liked his steaks "medium."

Clarence Darrow came to the galley and complimented Chef Laffoon on his "bacon and medium boiled eggs."

The Duke and Duchess of Windsor and theatrical travelers like Mae West and retinue, dined in their drawing rooms.

It was a life as rich as mulligatawny soup and as golden as consumme.

"The train whistles bothered me when I first left the railroad, but they don't now," says Ollie Laffoon. "I felt pretty fit, and I didn't want to sit around and get stale, so I came back to work."

James Evans admits he "gets lonesome, at times." But trains are so different today, he adds philosophically.

Once in a while though, he gets on one (with a diner, of course) and heads for Chicago. Just for the ride you know.

## THE INEVITABLE

A ticket back home. The thin slip of paper rests lightly in your hands, the pass between past and present. Or is it?

Home. You're going home. Tomorrow, the next day or the day after that, you'll be home again - back where you came from. Is it possible?

What a wonderful place it is, home. The streets. You can see them now, lined with your childhood, your youth, filled with all the experiences of living in a place a long time.

They'll all be there. The experiences and the actuality.

The drugstore, the tailor, the grocer's. Old friends. The people you grew up with.

"Grew up with." Ah! There's the difference.

The houses will be there, too.

Old Mrs. Kinnard's with the big brass knocker that always made you think of "Pinafore."

The Louises who always kept their shades down, even in the daytime.

The run-down Van Cortlands, whose manners were not run down at all.

People will come out of the houses, of course, and walk along the streets.

You can see them now, just as they looked a year or five or 20 years ago, when you left.

How you hope they'll think you look young and well. You never doubt for a moment that they will.

So you go home. You board the train and the whistle that tells the world you're coming sounds a bit mournful in the night.

Or you catch a plane and telescope a year or more of living into an hour or two.

You step out on the ground and it seems good and familiar under your feet.

The joy of reunion sweeps all before it. The old house, with its new acquisitions, which you scarcely notice. The familiar beds, the remembered butter dish, and, above all, the pictures.

In a flood of news, gossip and reminiscence, it's a day or two before you're really down to earth.

It is then that the faint uneasiness starts. Main Street is there, but it's not the same street. It's become a thoroughfare lined with "smart" shops.

It's hard to connect the old soda fountain with the coin machine that dispenses packages of ice cream.

The tailor is showing pink shirts in the window, and the grocer delights in frozen desserts. We really connected him with cornstarch and unwashed spinach.

The movie theater has been torn down, and there's a new art center. A motel replaces the old hotel.

Mrs. Kinnard has died, and her hospitable house has become the Rest-a-While Nursing Home.

The undertaker has taken over the Louises' old shaded house, and the Van Cortlands have disappeared from the face of the earth.

And beyond, on land we knew as fields, in colorful conformity stretch the ranch houses.

The people on the street are different, too. Is that handsome matron really the former bucktoothed Saunders girl?

Could that bent, but still stately man walking with a cane possibly be Mr. Louis?

The incorrigible Edison boy has become a distinguished surgeon, and the new librarian - while still unmarried - is one because she wants to be, not just to make a living.

There is a growing sense of being in a place to which you are no longer attached.

As your stay draws to a close, you start to look forward to going back to the place from whence you came home.

A wondering about what's doing in the town where you now live stirs within you. The place you thought you'd never like or even get used to. A place that needs you, and where you have something to give.

It's always a tug to leave relatives. And some old music, a bit sad, crosses the heartstrings as you board the train or the plane to return.

Once again, the home you knew and belonged in seems very real. You look out the window a while and wonder about life...

The thing inside your head that contracted when you came stretches out again like an accordion.

The past is the past and the present, the present. And the future is ahead.

A ticket back home is to a place that doesn't exist anymore.

Because it's not the same place. And you're not the same person.

And you need a ticket to get there.

## ELM-SET

Every clear night, we go out and look at a star shining down through an open patch in our elm tree. Like a diamond in a velvet box, it sparkles there, trillions of miles away, yet somehow more important to us than the great tree towering toward it.

But how much more beautiful the star is when seen through those arching branches! The thick gray column of trunk spreading out, then ascending again. And beneath the trunk, roots that go deep.

They say the roots of a big tree spread great distances underground. And we believe it. Certainly, our own roots go down way beyond the point where we can see them. But when the wind blows and the storm breaks, we know that they are there.

A root, incidentally, is not something we or a tree can grow in a spring or a summer.

A star alone in the sky is an awesome sight. It is so electric and bright, we can see it clearly across all those miles.

But we can't feel it. We can really only feel a star when it's seen through our own frame of reference. Through an elm tree, for instance.

The tree, we muse, is like our life: Its roots, our faith; its trunk, our aspirations, and its branches, our accomplishments. Of course, there is blight; but one never thinks of that on a starlit night.

Myriad leaves, like myriad experiences, flutter in its heights. A few become branches. Like their mother trunk, it is the aim of every branch and leaf to reach the star. Just as it is ours.

We and the tree have a lot in common. But it is wiser than we are. It can look heaven in the face, unabashed.

We wonder too much. Why? How far? How long? And what will we find when we get there?

A tree softens a star's awesomeness; we like our stars elm-set.

# 41

## The Unmelted Melting Pot

IN THE LAST QUARTER of the 20th Century, the descendants of European immigrants to the United States began to inquire into their native origin. Americanized, educated and generally successful, the third and fourth generation of men and women whose forebears had sought fortune and often refuge in the United States were stirred by a desire to look back from whence they had come. Perhaps this urge was prompted by realization that all personal characteristics were not welded together in the American melting pot and the wish to better understand their own deep-seated motivations and inclinations; or again, by familial pride in their progenitors who with such labor and sacrifice had accomplished a merger with the American way of life and in turn, been given such opportunity for advancement. Or possibly it was that deeply-rooted tide of ethnic consciousness, backed by centuries on older and more precedential shores, that inevitably rolled up again.

Whatever, until comparatively recent years, it was not the fashion for ethnic groups to make a conscious effort to look back; in fact, most of the European contingents shied away from it. This was America - the melting pot. But after three or four generations of accomplishment, when Americanization was an indisputable fact, the sense of *original* nationality, and characteristics and tastes arising therein, surfaced.

The ideal of a new and promising country can call and enlist groups from other lands; but it cannot, in a few short generations, remake their mores, any more than their physique, priorities and appetites.

**********

In 1971, the *Buffalo Evening News* wanted a series on ethnic groups in Buffalo. I was assigned to do the history of each of these groups, six in all, and various reporters, preferably of matching background, were to do a contemporary report. Both reports would compose a special section on each group.

The assignment which extended over a three-year period - with some interruptions for others, of course - was the climax and apex of my career as a newspaper staff reporter. Although exposed to people of numerous nationalities down the years, I had never

seriously analyzed them from an ethnic viewpoint. Philadelphia, as
I have mentioned, is a very English place, and my own milieu had
been largely so. From this standpoint, I had viewed the great throng
from many countries objectively; I had observed and recounted what
they said and did, but had hardly realized - aside from the usual
popular conceptions, i.e., the taste of the French; the industry of the
Germans; the temperament of Italians - what they were really like. It
follows that I had no idea of how their individual characteristics
influenced their lives, and indeed the country. This was America -
the melting pot. I had much to learn.

How to approach such a formidable task? To write history go
back to it. I started out at the Buffalo & Erie County Historical
Society, housed in the beautiful white marble building, once the
New York State Building of the Pan-American Exposition. There,
in a modern office, I found Dr. Stephen A. Gredel, senior reseach
historian, who in 1960, had been assigned by the society to study
the area's ethnic mix. He had written two small books - *Eight
People of Our City and County*, and *Pioneers of Buffalo, Its
Growth and Development*. He outlined where I should start.

Most important of all were the census lists of early settlers that
Dr. Gredel had compiled, copies of which he provided. He also
delineated the general characteristics of the various national groups
and how they had manifested locally. The information and
encouragement he gave me was both a sketchy road map and fuel
for my endeavor; but it was a long way from a rounded description
of the activities of the various leaders and history makers.

Armed with a list of pioneers and notations on those among
them who had particularly left their mark on the city, reading the
record came next. With the exception of a history of the Jews in the
area, (*From Ararat to Suburbia* by Dr. Selig Adler, professor of
history, and Dr. Thomas E. Connolly, acting provost and professor
of arts and letters, both at the State University of Buffalo, (Jewish
Publication Society of America, 1960), no book on individual ethnic
groups in Buffalo had been published. But down the years, the
press had produced. I read what was available and dipped into the
standard histories.

Then, again guided by the good Stephen Gredel, I went out into
the community and one by one met with the descendants of those
pioneers, or current leaders within each group. It was here that the
individual trails of history blossomed and became fascinating, fresh
expeditions.

**********

Nobody not born in a city, in my judgement, can fully understand it. They are not privy to that intricate network of lore, recollection, rumor, and deduction that the native is. They do not know the gradations of status in social circles, the characteristics of certain families, the means of accumulation of wealth, the innate attitude of the city toward other cities. They can gain readable knowledge of the city's history. They can observe the current life and listen to the recollection around them. But the emotional reaction of the peoples, covering such a wide expanse of time, and which, except for the literati, generally is unexpressed - is held only by the native through observation of whom the outlander comes nearest to the truth.

However, as often in life, there is another side of the coin. The outlander can be more objective; he is not swayed and influenced by the many personal frustrations and accomplishments of the city around him, as he would be on his home ground. He can *look* at his new environment whole, even if he can only *record* it in part.

Nevertheless, so began the most educational and rewarding assignment of my more than 40 years of newspapering. More than encounters or "a brush" with royalty, as the *News* put it; more than Presidential inauguration or political platforms; more than reportage of Presidents' wives; more than all the ships, shoes and sealing wax that I had encountered over the years, these prolonged articles (each one took three months, a long time for a newspaper), these meetings with leading and average citizens in each ethnic group taught me the pattern of a city's fabric, a pattern duplicated in any other city in the world with a similar ethnic constituency.

There is no question that the United States is honeycombed with groups of various national origin or descent who want to be citizens; who do not want to return to their native or ancestral country except on visits, but whose taste-from food to music - is that of their forebearers' "Old Country." They joyously accept the opportunities and advantages of America, but they still indentify with their original land or that of their progenitors.

What I learned in writing of these six ethnic peoples was their indigenous characteristics, their motivation and their priorities. And once one knows that, one does not confuse them, nor expect the dominant qualities of one group to be predominant in another. Intermarriage is a blender, of course, but even then the characteristics of the components are often apparent. Thus one can in truth, realize that each makes its contribution to that amazing stew kettle called America, fulfilling the axiom that "it takes all kinds of people etc...."

The assignment gave me insight into six great strains and enabled me to better understand them. I was better able too, to understand myself.

Our lives are held together by invisible, tenuous threads that support it throughout, and it was with a sense of assuring continuity and appreciation that I recalled the words of Dr. Henry Pancoast, professor of history at the University of Pennsylvania and instructor of my Springside School days, who wrote in his *An Introduction to English Literature*, a classic textbook of the time, of:

"The reserve and steadfastness" of the English; the "imagination and sentiment" of the Celts, and the "endurance and inventiveness" of the Teutons."

In later years, I was to meet these characteristics, often merged with each other, across the face of the vast sea of men and women I would encounter. If I had really understood Henry Pancoast's words and similar perceptions of other racial and national groups, and the importance of them in human relationships - it would have greatly helped me in my journey around "the whole wide world."

## THE POLES

The worn brown stone steps of Buffalo's nearly century-old St. Stanislaus Polish Roman Catholic Church told me that the Poles are a deeply religious people. Zealously religious.

They brought to America a heritage of political upheaval and persecution; between 1772-95 Poland was partitioned three times, lastly among Russia, Prussia and Austria. The country disappeared as a united nation. The Poles arrived with a background of fear - up to the most recent newcomers.

Devotion to a submerged nationalism and the Church are the two dominate characteristics of the Polish people.

Awaiting them was the post-Civil War boom of shipbuilding and industry - steel blast furnaces and factories manufacturing railroad equipment; construction and clothing industries.

"They had never seen a machine," said the Rt. Rev. Msgr. Peter J. Adamski, spiritual patriarch of the Buffalo Polish community. "They didn't know the language, and they were lost - lost."

Nevertheless, over protests of their predecessors, the Germans, under instigation of their church, the Poles got work; (ironically, it was the Germans who instructed them in the plants).

Poles are thrifty. I learned that from a survey of their estate made 35 years after the start of their arrival in Buffalo in 1875. They had savings bank deposits of $2.5 million; their taxable property assessment was approximately $5.5 million, and their non-taxable holdings (mainly church properties) more than $7 million. Total worth was estimated at more than $15 million.

But they were generally uneducated, indeed unable to comprehend the value of education. They not only did not know the English language - they had little desire to learn it.

It took two generations for the Poles to develop a desire for professionalism. The Polish language had by then become an elective in the public schools. Although second generation mothers went out to work to send their children to school, those third generation children did not learn Polish.

World War I brought the Poles more into the mainstream of American life. Before the war their thought and energies were directed to the "Old Country," but after Poland became free in 1918, there was not a pressing need for such overt fidelity. Innately loyal, they had given their wholehearted support in the war to the U.S. Now, too, there was dispersion from the ghetto-like neighborhoods to the suburbs.

Poles are not pushy; they were cautious about entering the professions. They suffered from an inferiority complex which stemmed from not knowing the language. Their names were difficult for Americans to spell and pronounce. Some Poles changed or abbreviated them.

They were held back in the professions by those early isolated communities, caused to a great extent by the priests of the Polish Roman Catholic Church. With the sociological outlook of the Europe they had left, these religious were interested in preserving their authority, and insisted on retaining Polish customs and language without simultaneously integrating into the American society.

Immigrants from a country run on capitalistic principles, Republicanism was native to the Poles. But again they were cautious; their assumption of public office was slower than some other ethnic groups.

Realizing that in the more complex environment in which they found themselves, they could succeed only en masse, the Poles formed organizations, first church, then fraternal and other secular ones. But they were confined to their native groups. And again, as in the church and their societies, they consolidated their national strength in their businesses. They were Polish businesses.

As the standard of living among Poles in the United States rose, they reached out for cultural aspects of life, once more harking back to their native country. After World War II, this outreach was accelerated and strengthened by a new emigration of Poles to the United States, the intelligentsia, forced out of Europe by political circumstances.

## THE GERMANS

The Germans are a serious people

Early arrivals in the 1820s came almost entirely from Alsace (then under French rule) and Southern Germany, sections of the Fatherland which had been devastated by wars and ruled in despotism. The trauma of 1848 in Europe brought 435,000 Germans to the United States between 1841 and 1850.

Beneath the German consciousness stirs the myth and mysteriousness of a dark and forested country, distressed by centuries of conflict.

The Germans sought security here, and they brought with them their habits of industry, frugality and order to secure it, moving at a stolid, dogged and imperturable pace.

"They were doers," a political leader told me. "They were people who gave the new country a stability so sorely needed during the first trying years," writes Virginia Brainard Kunz in "Germans in America", (1966).

Germans shared two goals: the desire for accomplishment and a need for social entertainment outside the home.

"In the field of drama, German tragedies outnumber comedies by at least five to one," writes Werner P. Friederich, professor of German Comparative Literature at the University of North Carolina. And again: "German authors have constantly sought to evaluate man's relationship to God and nature."

Yet there is a balance, perhaps arising from the need to shake off, at least temporarily, the contemplative life. It was Martin Luther himself who wrote:

> "Who does not love wine, wife and song
> Remains a fool his life long."

The Germans call this social outreach "Gemutlichkeit." Bands, singing societies and annual Octoberfests help them achieve it.

"To the American, the fireside is all and everything," noted a former newspaper editor. "Not so with Germans. However comfortable and cheerful the home may be, it lacks, in his opinion, the spirit of a good-humored crowd."

"Friendship, happy-go-easy," is the way a veteran German-American described it to me.

Accomplishment comes first, however, although it does not have to be achieved alone. The great majority of Germans are a subjective people; they take orders and work in unison for a group.

The board chairman of one of the nation's largest banks, telling of his German forebears who came to the United States four generations ago, said:

"They had a strong work ethic. Germans believed in certain virtues like family discipline, religion and mother. And there is solicitude for the young and the elderly."

Inventiveness and a love of learning are innate German characteristics. Gutenberg's printer's ink runs in their blood, with a deep interest in physical culture to balance it.

Eager to understand and participate in the government of their accepted country, the Germans entered politics early, and in wartime, transferred their inborn sense of nationalistic solidarity to the loyal defense of their new country.

## THE IRISH

The Irish helped build the Erie Canal, which in 1825 connected the Great Lakes with the Hudson River and opened up the West.

Between 1845-55, 1-1/2 million Irish men, women and children emigrated to America. Many were poverty-stricken farm people burnt by the English Penal Laws, which barred education and landownership to the masses, and were ravished by the potato famine. The land had failed them and they sought city life.

Met with resentment, suspicion and hostility upon their arrival, they were not cowed, only strengthened, as they drew together, retaining a fierce pride in the land of their birth. The Irish today, are perhaps the proudest and most tenaciously nationalistic group in America.

*********

Irish character is hard to define. Here is a quality that slips through the fingers (or perhaps over the head) of the Anglo-Saxon and the Teuton.

"Sentiment, according to a great critic," wrote my old professor, Dr. Pancoast, to whom I now listened, "is the distinguishing mark of the Celtic nature. Not only was the Celt emotional, he delighted in his emotions with the delight of the artist and the poet.

"His strong imagination, his deep sense of wonder at all things, brought him very near to the invisible and the unknown. He lived on the borderland of a world of mystery, and his belief in unseen powers in shown in innumerable myths and superstitions."

In the heart of an Irishman there always is a castle to which he aspires - not for its badge of gentry - the Irish like quality but are indifferent to status - but as a symbol of fulfillment of his innate epic dream.

"We like life" a lawyer of Irish descent told me. "Material values are not as important as some other things; you may call it laziness, but they just aren't."

"A fierce loyalty to this country as evinced by the number of casualties of Irish descent in the wars," listed a State Supreme Court Justice, and the "spirit of community" in extending help in times of trouble among old Irish families.

"Their religious faith was very, very deep," said a priest.

"The author Liam O'Flaherty has said the Irish respect the poet, the warrior and the priest," noted a prominent politician. "The poet's sense of beauty, the warrior's courage, and the priest's immorality. I think those are the values which have motivated the generality of the Irish."

"They established Catholicism in America," declared a professor, "and America was fortunate that the dominant Catholics were Irish, whose faith also was coupled with a rude respect for democracy. Irish Catholicism is a harsh Catholicism. If it had been European Catholicism, the more mellow, cultivated type, it would have been more involved with the Crown."

The Irishman brought with him a keen political sense. "They have a talent for politics," commented the professor. "They never evolved political institutions, but they were master maneuverers within the institutions evolved by their conquerors." (In a throwback, he pointed out that in the past the Irish assimilated their conquerors - "The Normans became more Irish than the Irish, and the Norse were assimilated, too.")

Independence as a cause is indigenous to the Irishman. He has an innate sense of authority, and wants to give, not take orders. But the Church has continued to be the final authority, even after secular aspects of living altered his practical way of life.

Irishmen worked on the canal, on the docks and on the railroads (at 50 cents a day and 5 jiggers of whiskey), but not for long. Quick to sense the threat of repression and prejudice in Yankee America, they realized the remedy lay in group strength and political representation, with which they joined the police force and fire and other civil service departments.

"There was a terrific bond that existed between Irish mothers and their sons," said the Supreme Court Justice, "and the former were strict disciplinarians. You might be able to 'get around' Father, but not Mother."

And it has long been the dream of Irish mothers, the particular inculcators of religious principles in the family circle, to have a son in the priesthood or a daughter as a nun.

## THE ITALIANS

The story of the Italians, more than 300,000 of whom poured into the United States in the 1880s, is one of extroversion, of action, of temperament and talent, of hardiness and a strong zeal for life.

Ability to sight a goal and work, save and sacrifice for its was theirs, as well as the faculty to sense and take advantage of opportunity.

"The Italians are more independent than collective, perhaps more so than any other nationality," Dr. Gredel told me.

"You must not be afraid to strive for the things you want," a leading industrialist of Italian descent exorted at a Junior Achievement gathering in the 1960s. "Like your parents and their parents before them, you must strive, drive and struggle for your own private profit. By your so acting, our economic system, and thus society, gains."

A vanguard of fanatical Italian revolutionary activists sought refuge in the United States in the mid-19th Century. They were followed - in the wake of the rise of industry in northern Italy - by skilled tradesmen, small businessmen and artisans such as cabinetmakers, blacksmiths, shoemakers and metal workers; by stonemasons, too, from Tuscany in central Italy.

Overpopulation and underproduction - too little land and too many people, and agricultural competition from other countries, resulting in poverty and illiteracy - brought a mass migration from the south of Italy. They were unskilled men and women accustomed to farm work.

"The great majority of these people were peasants," the dean of the Buffalo Italian spiritual community told me, "many could not even sign their names."

An industrially booming America needed such men and they needed it. The Italian strove. He brought a two-fold dream to America - a love of the earth and of education. To achieve this dream, he possessed a two-sided coin; willingness to work at any trade that offered a livelihood until opportunity came, and ability to save for it.

"We and the people around us made tremendous sacrifices," recalls a monsignor of the church, one of seven sons of a Sicilian laborer. "We had very simple meals - macaroni, homemade bread, pasta."

The Italian love of the earth was typified by the growing plants that flourished on small platforms outside their tenement windows and below, by the pushcart and later, a horse-drawn cart, filled with fruit, vegetables and flowers that they drove toward the attainment of their own prosperity.

In southern Italy, the average man could not enter a profession such as law or medicine. The aspiration to produce one doctor, one lawyer and one priest was the second half of the Italian immigrant's dream. In America, he realized he could achieve that through education.

Noted a County Judge: "The immigrant said, 'I'm going to have a son who is going to have a profession,' and when it happens, it is the cap of his existence. He knows tremendous pride."

"We were raised with education as the mecca," a former school principal recalled. "All my grandsons go to college," an 86-year-old great-great-grandmother who came to America when she was 16, proudly announced.

Domestic life is the core of the Italian's existence. Such thrift and subsequent advancement would have been impossible without family solidarity - a dominant Italian characteristic. The husbands and the fathers are the heads of the family. And there is deep solicitude for the care of the aged. Grandparents particularly are venerated.

From the start as newsboys and bootblacks, there was competition between the Italians and the Irish. After World War I, Italians entered politics and many early arrivers embraced Republicanism. The Irish were staunchly Democratic and the dislike by the Italians for the Irish and the Democrats became almost synonymous. After the turn of the century, however, social and economic changes veered the Italian vote increasingly toward the Democrats.

## THE JEWS

"No term is more familiar to the ear of the Jews than Tachlis, which means purpose, aim, end or goal," writes Werner Sombart in *The Jew & Modern Capitalism*, (1913).

"If you are to do anything, it must have tachlis; life itself, whether as a whole or in its single activities, must have some tachlis, and so must the universe."

Jews from Germany or German-speaking countries such as Austria and Bohemia immigrated to America, and others came from the westerly parts of the Russian Jewish Pale, in Lithuania, Poland and the Ukraine. Of the nearly 6 million Jews living in the United States today, the vast majority arrived after 1880.

The social position of the Jews in Europe had greatly improved during the French Revolution and under Napoleon. But after his defeat, age-old discrimination again set in. Germans resented some Jews who had financed the French and were rankled by their general affluence during the war. In large part, Russian oppression caused the immigration of Polish Jews.

"From the beginning in America there were marked differences between the Polish, or eastern Jews, and those from Germany..." state Drs. Selig Adler and Thomas E. Connolly in *From Ararat to Suburbia*.

The reason? The Polish Jew spoke Yiddish, a hybrid German which German Jews considered uncultivated, and the Poles often occupied jobs that the Germans had outgrown. Social relations between them were uneasy.

**********

Yet five overall factors frame Jewish history in America:

Religious identity - "The Jews belong to various nationalities, but their religious identity surmounts their ethnic origins," Dr. Gredel pointed out.

Age-old respect for learning and resultant intellectual acuteness - "For Jews education was not imposed," a nationally-known rabbi said, "it was in the mores of the people."

Charity - the centuries old precedent that it is a moral responsibility - "A sense of responsibility is almost built into the Jewish pysche," said another Jewish leader.

Speciality, a sense of distinctiveness - "We have managed to survive," a college professor commented, "there must be something about it (the Judaic heritage). No one has been able to destroy it."

Sporadic discrimination by the Christian world - Notes Harry Golden in *Travels Though Jewish America*, (1973): "While there has always been anti-Semitism in America - and there still is - it has never been respectable. In Europe, anti-Semitism is a profession."

**********

The Jews also brought with them the Talmudic maxim that - "The law of the land is the law to be obeyed." They accommodated themselves to American life.

Arriving when the Frontier was edging West, many German Jews became peddlers, rising in rank from those carrying their wares in baskets, packs or by horse and wagon, to little trunks of jewelry. Many progressed through the ranks to a small store in some congenial town. They were the vanguard of today's department stores magnates. Later arrivals, familiar with the needle trades in Europe, entered them here. Labor unionism taught the Jew democratic procedure, unknown to him in Europe.

But someone has said of the American Jew: "He is neither the son of a laborer nor the father of one."

"The great immigration of East European Jews," writes Stephen Birmingham in *Our Crowd* , (1967), a history of New York's great German-Jewish families, "were ragged, dirt-poor, culturally energetic, toughened by years of torment, idealistic and socialistic." The phrase "culturally energetic" is the key.

"They brought with them a habit of learning and respect for knowledge, so typical of Jewish life, that made them eager to learn new ways and practices," state Adler and Connolly. "They consequently, easily transformed their hunger for Jewish learning to hunger for secular knowledge, and were the first group of immigrants to break into American colleges and the professions."

In the wake of the new immigration, American Jewry engaged in settlement work. But not for long; the desire to learn greatly accelerated the Jew's progress, and as he prospered, he moved out of the poor area of cities. After World War I, the concept of social services began to replace that of charity, and Jewish women moved from segregated seats in the synagogue to the boards of these temples.

Zionism, a movement to return Jews to their homeland, crested in World War II, resulting in the establishment of the State of Israel in 1948.

The Holocaust saw the extinction of more than 6 million Jews in Europe. But it reenforced the speciality of the Jew:

"Until the Holocaust, we thought we could be like every other group," another distinguished rabbi told me. "Now we have returned to the mystique of being part of Jewish history, with the requirement for a pattern of living reflecting our own religious ideas and historical experiences...

"With the establishment of the State of Israel," said the rabbi, "the specificity of the Jew was reestablished. Before this, the Jew thought of himself in general terms. Now the reality of a particular land compelled him to reconsider what are the specifics of being Jewish."

## NEGROES

Many immigrants to America came from countries that had been racked by war, but the Negroes of Africa entered the United States as slaves. This fact added an entirely different dimension to their life here. The cloud of slavery has been the backdrop of this ethnic group, and their aspiration and endurance to rise above its stigma colors their composite personality today.

I knew this ethnic group better than any of the rest, but as respected domestics, who sometimes became an esteemed "member of the family." But of their past - other than that slavery and their emancipation - I knew practically nothing. The color lines between neighborhood and social association were firmly drawn in Philadelphia, the juncture of North and South, when I was growing up.

But it was with both personal understanding and affection that I inquired into this group, which now seeks across-the-board equality in the United States.

**********

Toil, journey from bondage and decades of transition has been the road of the Negro in America. Religion braced by patience has been his staff.

A dignified and proud people, deeply spiritual by nature and seeking comfort in their servile state, the Church became a personal bulwark for the Black, a nomenclature preferred by many Negroes today.

The Underground Railroad, the clandestine thruway of escape for slaves from the South, began soon after the War of 1812. Many Northern families, including the Society of Friends (Quakers), gave shelter to fleeing Blacks, nearly 75,000 of whom were helped to freedom in the northern states or Canada before the Civil War.

Antislavery societies were formed and convened in the North in the 1840s. In 1853, the Black poet James Monroe Whitfield in his 238-line verse cried:

> "How long, O gracious God, how long
> "Shall power lord it over right:
> "The feeble trampled by the strong,
> "Remain in slavery's gloomy night?"

The Civil War was his answer:  186,000 Black men served in the Union Army, 93,000 from Confederate states.

In 1863, President Lincoln issued the Emancipation Proclamation, ending slavery in the rebel states.

The ratification of the 13th Amendment, outlawing slavery, (1865); the 14th, guaranteeing "equal protection of the laws" to all citizens, (1866), and the 15th Amendment, prohibiting denial of voting rights on grounds of "race, color or previous condition of servitude," (1870), all reinforced the Negro's cause.

Nevertheless, from the emancipation to today, the course of the Afro-American has been a rugged one.  Even in the North, schools were largely segregated until the 1870s.

To overcome the image of servitude, gain education, hold employment beyond the service fields and win opportunity to participate in the mainstream of American life has been a steep climb.

"The struggle has been eternal and is perennial," commented an associate in education of the disadvantaged in the New York State Education Department.  "All your life, you never give up.  You are constantly figuring new strategies, individually and collectively."

In the 1890s, Negroes, who in the North had been largely working in white households, responded to the need for workers in rising northern industry.

The turn-of-the-century expansion of the railroads also gave wide employment to Blacks, particularly with the Pullman Co.  "Mr. Pullman (George M.) requested colored men on his trains," an instructor of porters for nearly 50 years told me.  "Courtesy and honesty were absolutely necessary."

The Niagara Movement, the first widely organized Negro protest group - harbinger of the organization known today as the National Association for the Advancement of Colored People - was founded in 1905.

It grew out of the philosophy of Dr. William E. B. DuBois, the first Black to be awarded a doctorate at Harvard, which was in opposition to that of Booker T. Washington, a former slave, who emerged as a spokesman for the Negro in 1895. Founder of Tuskegee Institute, Macon County, Alabama, Washington favored the practical and utilitarian aspects of education for Blacks.

Initially in agreement with Washington, DuBois later favored liberal arts education for Blacks. The Niagara Movement, though short-lived, served to arouse liberal Whites in the North against denial of Negro rights, and the *NAACP* was formed.

In 1916, as war in Europe mounted, northern industrialists brought trainloads of Blacks from the south to produce war materiel, creating labor competition. Little race prejudice was shown until then; unions were not hospitable.

The Depression was a period of transition for the Black. He began to realize the force of his voice politically, and it impressed upon him the need to acquire a skill to assure regular employment. An awakening of his racial pride and desire for equality followed. Blacks proved they could withstand economic hardship and were solidified. Their population increased. Housing became a problem.

In 1934, the Federal Housing Authority was created to administer funds for modernizing homes and to lend money for new construction. Its government secured, insured loans increased the purchasing power of many Blacks.

The Social Security Act, which among other things provided unemployment insurance, brought many more Blacks from the South. Those from deep rural areas found adjustment to city life difficult. (Blacks today are the largest ethnic group in four major U.S. cities - Atlanta, Georgia; Gary, Indiana; Newark, New Jersey and Washington, D.C.)

Two pioneer laws also were helpful: The New York State Anti-discrimination Law (1938), declared discrimination unconstitutional, and the Mahoney Law (1941), also of New York, barred bias in housing or employment of workers in war industry, based on race, creed or national origin.

Such a great sweep of legislation and its affect on the Black were, in the words of a New York State Commission Against Discrimination official in 1973, "a part of a mounting transition and growing upheaval and change," which have risen with undreamed of rapidity ever since.

# 42

# Fotsam And Jetsam

FLOTSAM IS THE FLOATING wreckage of a ship or its cargo. Jetsam is whatever may be thrown overboard to lighten a ship.

In the course of releasing a stream of consciousness experienced over a more than 40-year period, bits of experiences are found floating in the mind, as the ship of one's story nears port.

To progress the mainstream of such a journey, one also has thrown memories overboard to figuratively lighten the ship. Some of these memories are only small tributaries, even creeks and brooks, contributing to the mainstream, but they are there, like dragonflies - skimming over the water of the mind - and will not be permanently dismissed. It is for this reason that I now recount a few of them; I shall not make any attempt to tell them in chronological order, but simply write them as the peak in memory, vignettes against the larger portraiture.

## BEHIND THE MASK

I have seen a good many theatrical people in my time, and I am convinced that some of the most bizarre and clownish ones have a deep, abiding philosophy. Liberace is such a one. When interviewed, Liberace gives a reporter his whole attention, sincerely and seriously. He endeavors to understand what the newsman asks and what it really means. He answers directly and modestly. I have no doubt Liberace's philosophy has prompted him to help and probably, at least partically support, scores of persons.

Personally, he is a rather serious, sincere one. His besequined coats are no more than the shell of a man who has found a gimmick and with it made success.

## PSYCHICALLY ARRIVED

Of all the theatrical people I have talked to, Jack Benny was the most natural. I saw him in a restaurant at the top of a revolving tower at Niagara Falls, Ontario, where he had come to play at the neighboring Melody Fair theatre, across the Niagara River. He had on a gray turtleneck sweater and a dark sports coat. His complexion was sallow and his face sort of flattened. He looked as if he spent most of his time indoors. But as he chatted with us, his poise was

*LIBERACE- Sincerity behind the glitz. Robert M. Metz photograph.*

perfect. He did not seek to put himself forward, nor was he overly retiring. For a man who bristled with egotism and defensiveness on stage, he was one of the most charming, urbane yet natural people offstage imaginable. It is very pleasant in this world to see someone who has psychically arrived.

## "MORE WOULD BE VULGAR"

Elizabeth Taylor has the most beautiful violet eyes and perfect white complexion. When I saw her, her eyes were fringed with natural dark black lashes, her complexion, partially calcimined; but you knew that underneath it was perfect - before she started to guild the lily.

She came to Buffalo with her second or third husband, Michael Todd (whom they say she really loved), to attend some event at the University of Buffalo, and Ed Kovalewski, a *Buffalo Evening News* staffer, and I met them at the airport; Mike was Ed's story, Elizabeth, mine.

When they got off the plane, the University of Buffalo had provided a large young heifer - the U.B. sports teams are called Bulls - wearing a horse blanket emblazoned with the university's letters. Publicists and photographers were on hand, anxious to get a picture of Mr. and Mrs. Todd with the heifer

Elizabeth bridled: "You do it, Mike," she said, "you're more of a ham than I am." Mike Todd obliged.

We than went into the airport lounge where the interviews took place. On the fourth finger of her left hand, Miss Taylor wore an aquamarine ring that reached to the knuckle.

"How many carats is that ring?" I asked her.

"It's 29-1/2." she said, "Mike said if it were 30, it would be vulgar."

## AND THE BAND PLAYED ON

My Father used to sing a song - "Daisy, Daisy, give me your answer do, I'm half crazy all for the love of you." It was introduced at the turn of the century by a young singer named Willie Howard. About 50 years later, I heard Willie Howard sing it (or at least a little of it) at the Town Casino, a large nightclub in Buffalo.

Mr. Howard, then in his 80s, appeared on the stage in white tie, tails and topper. With a certain amount of body motions, he sang the first two lines of the song. Then the orchestra came in and drowned out his voice. Two lines were about all he could vocalize, but he brought back memories to scores of people sitting in the club.

More than half of a popular entertainer's success is himself, his appearance, actions and mannerisms. Willie Howard just kept on going, turning the golden memories into platinum piping.

In 1951, the great chanteuse and danseuse Josephine Baker, who delighted Paris wearing a bunch of bananas - and little else - around her waist, came to Buffalo. Despite the city's pride in having been an Underground Railroad center, in those pre-Martin Luther King days the Statler Hotel, the city's largest, declined to give her accommodations.

However, Miss Baker was granted lodging at the Hotel Buffalo, the old Statler, indeed the first in the chain. I was sent there to interview her. When I arrived at the suite assigned to her, the only person there was a goodlooking Black woman, seated in an armchair in the sitting room.

"Are you Miss Baker?" I asked.

"No Honey, I'm not," said the woman, "I'm Susie Smithers (fictitious) of the *Lackawanna Times*." (Lackawanna was a steel-producing city adjoining Buffalo.)

In due course, Miss Baker came in, a magnificent figure of a woman, forward moving and alert. My deadline was approcaching - what could I do with the few minutes left?

I don't know where I got a tape measure, but with Josephine's gracious permission, I measured her bust, waist and hips 43-25-38.

Then I hurried to the telephone. That's what most people wanted to know anyhow.

## HEAD VS. HAND

When the atom bomb fell on August 6, 1945, *Record* City Editor Fred Shapiro sent me to Princeton to try and find Albert Einstein, who in 1939, at the request of a group of scientists, had written to President Roosevelt to stress the urgency of investigating the possible use of atomic energy in bombs.

The great physicist was then living in Princeton, where he had a post at the Instititute for Advanced Study, a research center for advanced study in the physical and social sciences.

My mental image of Einstein's house was that of a dark, somber one, with a slight air of Charles Addams, the New Yorker cartoonist's drawings about it. To the contrary, it was a cheerful, white New England-type dwelling that I approached and rang the doorbell.

A motherly, wholesome-looking housekeeper answered and informed me that Dr. Einstein was not there. Wishing to avoid reporters, he had probably left the moment the news that the bomb had been dropped was out. Nor could or would the good housekeeper tell me where he had gone.

However, deciding to leave no stone unturned, I made my way through the town to the institute - he might just be there... But a tour of the building failed to find him. Fred Shapiro told me to come home.

I called a taxi to take me to Princeton Junction, the Pennsylvania Railroad connection back to Philadelphia. It was a lovely, clear afternoon, and I went out and sat on the broad steps of the institute, waiting for the cab. The building overlooked a great field of wheat, and as I sat there, I noticed that it was "ripe unto harvest."

The taxi came, and on the way to the junction, I asked the driver about it.

"It's this way, lady," he said, "the institute owns that field, but it can't get nobody to cut the wheat."

Learning has its price.

## SCALING THE IVORY TOWER

The press must be practicval in the face of the obscure, no matter how erudite its cloak. The necessity of understanding in order to inform; deadlines and the assumption that a newsman will come back with *the* story makes it so.

My interview with Dr. Laura Crayton Boulton, the noted ethno-musicologist (ethno stands for ethnology, a branch of anthropology that deals with the comparative cultures of various peoples), illustrated this need for clarity.

I talked with her at the house of Chauncey J. Hamlin of Buffalo, a former president of the American Association of Musuems and of the Buffalo Musuem of Science, which he had developed into one of the finest in the country. They were among a party which had just returned from a cultural expedition to the Greek Islands.

Dr. Boulton, a small, alert woman talked for 10 minutes about the journey and its discoveries, when I realized that I understood little of what she had said, and that the general public would understand even less. Her discourse was way up on Mt. Olympus, far, far removed from the corner newstands.

Nearing the avalanche of my deadline, I reached for the grappling hook of Rudolph Franz Flesch, a realistic man who had developed a series of rules for clear writing called "readability," which some wire services and newspapers throughout the country had taken seriously. Mr. Flesch advised us to aim for the reader in the seventh grade.

I explained this as politely as possible to the highly intellectual woman I now faced.

Dr. Boulton was courteous as well as smart, and she came down from the mountain fast. Together we engaged in a writable, readable talk. As I was leaving, I asked for her resume'. She complied at once, leaving the room and returning with four single-spaced sheets. I gave them a quick look, and blushed.

Laura Boulton had traveled around the world listening, recording, writing, filming and lecturing for about 25 years. She had been on expeditions across the globe - from Borneo to Timbuktu - and had directed and edited films on subjects ranging from Haitian voodoo to British Columbian totem poles. She has recorded music ranging from that of the Bushmen and Hottentots of Africa to the Chinese and Hill tribes of Formosa. A lecturer at Harvard, Cambridge and the University of London, such conductors as Walter Damrosch, Leopold Stokowski and Aaron Copland had foreworded her prolific papers.

Seventh Grade, indeed!

In sheer cultural and scientific achievement, the resumé was staggering.

I looked up from it at her: "You must think I'm an ass, Dr. Boulton," I said.

She was very gracious.

Despite it all, when the Man in the Street picked up his paper that night, he knew what both Laura Boulton and I had talked about.

*EVENING EDITION, 1986*

# Before I Write "30" *

THE DEADLINE FOR MY story approaches.

Newspaperwomen are public property in the sense of social association. To the public they represent the great potential of the press - with all it can do for or detract from them - woman, and a unique sharer of their lives.

So I have been privileged to step out of a circumscribed environment to join hundreds of others in the communities in which I have worked, with whom I have shared this singular relationship.

It is a broadening almost fictional experience. An expansion has been built into me that refuses to contract; it follows me down the street, in public and private places - a freedom born of contact with "the whole, wide world."

Nor does one lose the vista and memory of it when one is no longer reporting. For in encountering the world around him, one has gained a kind of unity with it, and become, even in a modest way, a person in his own right.

Newspapering has been an interest that has never forsaken me. It took me far from the place where I was born; it pioneered trails that none of my family had known (Great-Grandfather Knefler, who covered the musical events of the Chicago World's Fair for the *Louisville Courier-Journal*, excepted); it stabilized me in trouble. It made every day a day to look forward to, a day which moved on a river of natural momentum when the whole world seemed just around the bend. I rose to it, slept on it, and never lost the desire to go out on my day off to buy the paper.

It changed me from a groping, ineffectual, circumscribed person - largely oriented to the past - to someone with a commitment, who at least *tried* to listen to and see the passage of current life. *It gave me wings on my heels.*

Although I never went to college, I feel as if I gained at least a master's degree in the newspaper business. Scholastically, my training has not been deep. But at a certain level, and at times a profoundly elemental one, I have learned to cope with life. I have learned how to cut through situations, rank, words and roads to reach a point. I have seen history lived; scientific discovery announced, and human nature - in both inspiring and sad forms - not through the pages of a book, but by face to face confrontation.

For such an encounter, I had religious training; the example of upright, devoted parents, and a general introduction to history and

---

*The newspaper sign for a story's ending.

the classics; much French; Latin and mathematics, the latter you'll recall, tenderly bolstered by English teacher Edith Grace Moses. Inadequate, you say, to meet the demands of an intricate modern society?

Not if you've found your niche.  If once a man or a woman finally has tuned in on his own aptitudes and capabilities - the latter are often incalculable, but the former are precise - the way opens up, the road is clear-if the wind of desire is at his back.  He will acquire what he needs to know en route.  He is his own compass.

Yet perhaps, the journey is not complete until the flight is over. Until the passion is spent, one cannot see the country as it is, until the calm, one realizes that the power to fly came from beyond oneself, and that inevitably, one will return to It.

For now - I still can do no better than this:

"A newspaper will take all the imagination, strength, speed, resourcefulness and stamina you can give it.  In return, it will give you a sense of being a listener to and observer of life.

"At times, you will have the privilege of participating in the creation of some phase of this life.  For this, all is worthwhile - no training is too arduous.  For in those shining moments one glimpses the force of creation itself, at work.

"People say today's news is dead tomorrow.  But the visions glimpsed, the signs seen, the sounds heard and the human encounters of a newspaperman are incorporated within him.  They cannot be taken from him.  They are his own as long as he lives.

"He has earned them in wind, storm, heat, cold and occasionally, through persecution - by registering the life that passed by him in his time. - Ellen Taussig

Reprinted from *Editor & Publisher*.

-30-

*Postscript:* I still carefully turn my clothes right-side-out when I "turn in" for the night.  I must be ready.

Who knows but that the spirit of Walter Lister, Fred Shapiro, Alfred H. Kirchhofer or Nelson Griswold - all gone where all good editors go - will call me to fire, wreck or exploit?